# Reality Macromedia ColdFusion MX

## Intranets and Content Management

# Reality Macromedia ColdFusion MX

## Intranets and Content Management

**Ben Forta**
**David Aden**
**Andi Hindle**
**Stephen Milligan**
**David Schnell-Davis**
**John Stanard**

*With help from:*
**Andrew Hewitt**
**Teo Graca**
**Debbie Eddy**
**Dmitry Krantsberg**
**Seth Morris**

macromedia® PRESS

# Reality Macromedia ColdFusion MX: Intranets and Content Management

Ben Forta, David Aden, Andi Hindle,
Stephen Milligan, David Schnell-Davis,
John Stanard

## Credits

Macromedia Press Editor
Angela C. Kozlowski

Development Editor
Mark L. Kozlowski

Production Coordinator
Connie Jeung-Mills

Copy Editor
Jacqueline Aaron

Indexer
Ron Strauss

Proofreader
Corbin Collins

Technical Editor
Rob Brooks-Bilson

Interior Designer
Randall Goodall

Cover Designer
David Brier

Page Layout
Maureen Forys
Kate Kaminski

Illustrations
Chris Gillespie

## Macromedia Press

1249 Eighth Street
Berkeley, CA 94710
510/524-2178
800/283-9444
510/524-2221 (fax)

Published by Macromedia Press,
in association with Peachpit Press,
a division of Pearson Education.

Find us on the World Wide Web at:
www.macromedia.com
www.peachpit.com

To report errors, please send a note to
errata@peachpit.com

ISBN 0-321-12414-6

9 8 7 6 5 4 3 2 1

Printed and bound in the
United States of America

## Dedications

Dedicated to my wife Marcy, Happy 12th Anniversary!
—Ben Forta

Dedicated to my family: Corwin, Eleanor, and Amber, who make it all worthwhile.
—David Schnell-Davis

Our contribution to this book is dedicated to L. Ron Hubbard whose insights on the subject of education and study helped us get through what we needed to learn about ColdFusion MX and helped point out better ways to write about it.
—David Aden and John Stanard

# Contents at a Glance

# Contents

# I:   The Intranet

The Intranet is a full blown Intranet system. It features an underlying content-management engine, security and access control, as well as interfaces for searching and personalization.

# II: Personal Information Management

Personal Information Management (PIM) provides access to email, directory services, and other corporate back ends.

# III: Human Resources

Human Resources is a forms and workflow application. It features form management and routing, data import and export engines, XML integration, as well as data reporting and analysis.

# IV:  Product Requirements

Product Requirements is a project-planning application. It features systems to create and define projects and associated tasks, manage data, provide feedback, and more.

# V:   User Interaction

User Interaction is a collection of related community applications. Included are a real-time chat engine, instant messaging, and threaded discussions.

# Bios

**Ben Forta** is Macromedia Inc.'s Senior Product Evangelist, and has two decades of experience in the computer industry in product development, support, training, and marketing. Ben is the author of the best-selling *Cold-Fusion Web Application Construction Kit* and its sequel *Advanced Cold-Fusion Application Development*, as well as books on SQL, JavaServer Pages, WAP, Windows development, and more. Over $1/2$ million Ben Forta books have been printed in a dozen languages worldwide. Ben co-authored the official Macromedia ColdFusion training material, as well as the certification tests and Macromedia Press study guides for those tests, and is now working on several new titles in the *Reality ColdFusion* series. He writes regular columns on ColdFusion and Internet development, and now spends a considerable amount of time lecturing and speaking on application development worldwide. Ben welcomes your e-mail at ben@forta.com and invites you to visit his web site at http://www.forta.com/.

**David Aden**—As his mother is fond of recounting, David started his computer experience (this lifetime anyway) with a small plastic and metal toy given to him for Christmas too many decades ago to admit. By placing thin plastic sheaths over strategically placed metal knobs and sliding an armature back and forth, the toy could be "programmed" to mimic basic binary calculations or the "logic" of an elevator. Many years later, after a long, fun and rewarding stint in public affairs and community activism, David went on to work in HP's now-defunct Distributed Computing Environment (DCE) lab in Massachusetts, and then at an MCI development lab in Virginia. In 1997, he arrived at Careerbuilder, Inc. where he hooked up with current *Webworld Studios, Inc.* partner, John Stanard, to work on his first ColdFusion project. Since then, he's worked on a variety of ColdFusion projects for Microsoft, CNET, Cable & Wireless USA, the FAA, NASA,

Goodwill Industries, Datatel and others. As Webworld's Chief Technology Officer, David directed the company's research and development efforts using ColdFusion MX many months before the program's public release. The results were the requirements gathering application in this book, and the Webworld Content Manager™ version 3.0, believed to be the first enterprise level content management system designed completely from the ground up with ColdFusion MX and Flash MX.

In the course of studying for his degree in Japanese, **Andi Hindle** was suckered into building the web site for the Tokyo-based city magazine, Tokyo Journal. After a number of other web development positions, Andi worked for a number of years as a pre-sales technical consultant for Allaire, based in Europe, before moving into his current position as Macromedia's European Server Product Manager. He contributes regularly to development communities across Europe, and worked as a technical editor for Ben's WAP book. This is his first attempt at serious writing, and he recommends not trying to do it at the same time as moving house and launching 2 major product upgrades!

**Spike** has been working with internet technologies since his college days the early 1990s. After college he spent a several years teaching network administration and web development courses, before moving on to full time development and consulting. Since 1998 he has worked primarily with ColdFusion and related technologies such as Spectra and, more recently, Flash. Originally from Ireland, he spent 10 years in London before the dot boom coaxed him to the sunny shores of the South of Spain. After 2 years of Sangria and sun, he decided to return to more temperate climes, and was last spotted leaving an all night internet cafe in Rotterdam.

**David Schnell-Davis** has been programming Cold Fusion full time since 1996 (version 1.5). During the Internet boom, he ran an ISP in Las Vegas which specialized in creating ColdFusion driven sites, where he dealt directly with customers and learned exactly what they wanted from their Web sites. Many of the ideas and techniques he describes in this book come directly from those experiences. David has a BA in Economics from the University of Chicago, as well as a CCNA and MCSE. He and his wife, Amber, are currently starting another Internet business in North Carolina, where they live with their two children, Eleanor and Corwin.

**John Stanard**, the CEO and founder of *Webworld Studios, Inc.*, has over ten years consulting experience in the computer industry, the last six of which have been devoted exclusively to Internet consulting and Web application development. Most of the application development work was done with ColdFusion starting at version 1.5 (although there was a short stint where John fell in with an ASP crowd, but he doesn't like to talk about that now). John's background includes management, public and government affairs and design & print publishing, providing him a unique set of skills with which to approach Web application design and development. Since forming *Webworld Studios, Inc.* with David Aden, clients have included CareerBuilder, Inc., NBC Interactive and all the ones David cited in his bio.

# Acknowledgements

First and foremost, thanks to my coauthors, David Aden, Andi Hindle, Stephen Milligan, David Schnell-Davis, and John Stanard for investing so much time and energy into this project—I don't think any of us realized the scope of this endeavor when we started out on building this new series, I hope they are as pleased with the results of their hard work as I am.

—*Ben Forta*

I have a better understanding now of why authors always seem to want to thank their families and friends after working on a book: the thanks are well deserved. Special thanks to the team that put together the application: Debbie Eddy, Teo Graca, Andrew Hewitt, Dmitry Krantsberg and Seth Morris. All solid developers and great people to work with. I love your enthusiasm for taking on new challenges. To my sons, Jason and Jesse and my wife who continues to both motivate me to keep my nose to the grindstone and helps make the going fun—thank you.

—*David Aden*

In no particular order, and with apologies to the people he knows he will have unwittingly omitted, Andi would like to thank: the creators of CF and the thousands of developers who contribute to the product and to the community every day; Greg for getting me started; Ben for the opportunity; Mike, for general brilliance (and a handy tip); Sue and Clare for letting me; Jan and Peter, for everything; and Anna, without whose constant love and support section 3—and most other things—would never have been.

—*Andi Hindle*

For all the help and encouragement, I thank very much my editor, Angela Kozlowski, and my brilliant (and over-worked) co-author, Ben Forta. I could never have completed this project without their help. Also, for all the support and tolerance, I thank my wife, Amber, who put up with all the long days (and nights) writing this book.

—*David Schnell-Davis*

Many thanks to the team who helped put this book together. My co-authors, the publishing team at Peach Pit, and the ColdFusion MX development team at Macromedia. Special thanks to Angela Kozlowski our publisher for her patience and cat herding skills which would grace any diplomatic corps. Not forgetting the local coffee shop which made those late nights that much more bearable.

—*Stephen Milligan*

I want to thank my partner David for his dedication to getting our chapters of this book done despite all the demands on his time, and the guys on his team who helped us (named in Dave's acknowledgement). He is either a very hard and dedicated worker, or a glutton for punishment. I also want to thank the Macromedia team for some truly breakthrough products, ColdFusion MX (thanks, Libby!) and Flash MX, which have given us developers some new and powerful tools with which to work (and play!) Please keep up the good work! Lastly, I want to thank Ben for having us again, and Angela for putting up with us (mostly Dave).

—*John Stanard*

# Introduction

## The "Reality ColdFusion" Series

There are lots of computer books out there on all sorts of subjects, some of which are actually very good. That's a good thing—readers should indeed have options when learning products and technologies, and should be able to find titles that best suit them and their learning styles.

But this has actually not been happening. While the number of titles on any given subject continues to grow, more often than not these additional titles are simple more of the same. In fact, the significant majority of product based computer books on the market fall into one of two categories—how-to books, and reference books (or a combination thereof).

ColdFusion is no exception—the number of books on ColdFusion has mushroomed over the past few years, a testament to the success and popularity of ColdFusion itself. But most of these books are merely more of the same. And so you have lots of ways to learn ColdFusion, but then what?

With each new version of ColdFusion the product has grown in complexity. Once upon a time (not that long ago, actually) mastering Cold-Fusion was easy—you learned some SQL, mastered basic flow control, picked up HTML, and you were all set. Much ColdFusion development still occurs in just that way, but over the years ColdFusion has matured and can do so much more. Suddenly knowing syntax and tags is not enough—new ColdFusion features require an understanding of how product integration works, how real-world applications are designed and built, and what processes are used to get there.

Existing ColdFusion books—the tutorial and how-to books—cannot cover these topics. ColdFusion has gotten so big and powerful that most tutorial books just cannot do justice to topics like Flash integration, leveraging J2EE, implementing content-management, managing shared and hosted environments, and more. These topics need their own books—not how-to and tutorial books, but books full of real world experience.

And thus was born the *Reality ColdFusion* series—a collection of highly focused and concentrated titles on very specific topics. These books will not teach you syntax, they'll not teach you how to install software, they'll not teach SQL, and will not teach CFML tags and functions. In fact, you'll not find a single step-by-step set of instructions anywhere within these titles.

So what exactly will you find in *Reality ColdFusion* books? Simply put, you'll find real problems addressed with real development culminating in real solutions. *Reality ColdFusion* titles are collections of case-studies—problems and their solutions along with the chronological sequence of events and processes that make up application development in the real world. And when all is said and done, you'll be left with complete applications that you may use, and the knowledge and experience that went into building them.

*Reality ColdFusion* is your invitation to join real development teams—these are real applications (or adaptations of real applications) that solve real problems, and you're invited to come along for the ride.

> Names have been changed to protect the innocent (or the guilty, as the case may be).

## About This Book

*Reality Macromedia ColdFusion—Intranets and Content Management* explores content-centric applications, the most frequently build ColdFusion applications.

ColdFusion has always been the simplest and most efficient way to bind back-end databases to the Web (or other Internet based front-ends). Indeed, to this day (with ColdFusion in its sixth major version and seven years since it was created) the significant majority of all ColdFusion development is still database integration and basic content management.

From basic access control to content storage, from mail and directory services integration to forms and data manipulation, from project tracking to user communities—ColdFusion can do it all. And ColdFusion MX's new technologies and features provide a rich framework on which to build (or rebuild) these key applications.

*Reality Macromedia ColdFusion—Intranets and Content Management* is your invitation to rethink ColdFusion based content management and Intranet applications from the ground up.

# Who Should Read This Book

This is not a beginners book. The *Reality ColdFusion* series assumes a good working knowledge of ColdFusion and prior application development experience. If you are new to Cold-Fusion then this is not (yet) the book for you.

This book will not teach you ColdFusion, nor will it teach you databases, SQL, and related technologies.

If you use ColdFusion for any data manipulation whatsoever then this book is for you. If you are an experienced ColdFusion developer and want to experience structured development the way the experts do it then this book is for you. If you are responsible for the development of your organizations Intranet then this book is for you. And even if you are just starting out and want a glimpse of what the future holds for you then this book is for you too.

**instant message**

▶ If you are new to ColdFusion you'll want to grab a copy of *ColdFusion MX Web Application Construction Kit* (Macromedia Press, ISBN 0-321-12516-9)—the original and best-selling ColdFusion tutorial and guide.

# How to Use This Book

The *Reality ColdFusion* books are not designed to be read from cover to cover, although you are more than welcome to do so. Each title in this series contains a set of sections—each section is a case-study, an application explained, analyzed, designed, built, and deployed. *Reality Macromedia ColdFusion—Intranets and Content Management* contains the following five sections:

- **The Intranet** is a full blown Intranet system. It features an underlying content management engine, security and access control, as well as interfaces for searching and personalization.

- **Personal Information Management** provides access to e-mail, directory services, and other corporate back-ends.

- **Human Resources** is a forms and workflow application. It features form management and routing, data import and export engines, XML integration, as well as data reporting and analysis.

- **Project Requirements** is a project planning application. It features systems to create and define projects and associated tasks, manage data, provide feedback, and more.

- **User Interaction** is a collection of related community applications. Included are a real-time chat engine, instant messaging, and threaded discussions.

Each section is made up of five chapters:

- **Product Requirements** introduces the client and explains the problem to be solved.

- **Initial Thoughts** presents the ideas and brainstorming culminating in a proposed solution.

- **Development** walks through the actual development process, pointing out key technologies and walking through implementations as needed.

- **The Solution** presents the finished solution and ensures that the objectives were met.

- **Delivery** wraps up deployment and delivery, analyzes the successes (and failures), lists what was learned along the way, and suggests plans for future versions of the application.

While the sections and applications are presented in order of complexity, starting with the least complex, there are no cross-dependencies and you are thus free to start at whichever section you wish. However, it is recommend that within each section you do read the chapters in order, starting with the first.

## The Accompanying Web Site

The applications created in the book are real and usable as is (and may be adapted for your own use as needed). The complete applications (including all source code) may be downloaded from the book's Web page at:

`http://www.forta/com/books/0321124146/`

The Web page also contains other relevant information including an errata (if one is needed) and links to other books that may be of interest you.

And with that, turn the page, start reading, and welcome to Reality.

# Part I

## The Intranet

The Intranet is a full blown Intranet system. It features an underlying content-management engine, security and access control, as well as interfaces for searching and personalization.

# Product Requirements

## Client Overview

EduHealth is a nonprofit organization dedicated to promoting the awareness of good health and healthy living. EduHealth provides two distinct but closely related services:

- **Data collection and research.** Providing data to the medical and health industries (for a fee); highly localized and targeted data collection is possible because of the organization's vast affiliate network.

- **Public education.** Publishing content, providing presentations (and occasionally speakers), creating teaching materials—all provided at no cost to the public.

EduHealth has regional offices throughout the United States and Canada, and it's in the process of recruiting affiliates in Europe, Asia, and Africa. Many of these affiliates are not part of the core organization, functioning instead as independent "feet on the street"—gathering information, conducting research and surveys, and distributing published content.

EduHealth is not a technology company; it might even be considered technology averse. Founded almost 30 years ago by a team of dedicated health-care professionals, EduHealth still operates as it did in the beginning and seems to have ignored the technology revolution for the most part. Information is stored on paper in endless rows of filing cabinets; volunteers type up documents that are then printed and saved (or distributed as needed); and content is circulated manually for editing and approval. In fact, aside from email and Internet access, computers seem to be used more as glorified typewriters and phone books than anything else.

Despite having good intentions, EduHealth now spends more time managing its aging content than it does responding to new requests. And with its impending international growth, some big changes need to happen—and fast.

## Project Overview

David Keyes is an EduHealth volunteer in his early 20s. He does not have a formal IT background, but he is pursuing an advanced education in computer science and is very tech savvy. He is generally considered the EduHealth's computer guru (a title he doesn't mind at all).

David sends the following email message to Dr. Jerome Fisher, EduHealth's current director.

**We're dead unless . . .**

**Email**

**Date:** June 8

**To:** Doc Fisher

**From:** Dave Keyes

**Subject:** We're dead unless . . .

Dr. Fisher,

Please forgive the subject line, but, well, we've got real problems.

Do you (or does anyone) know how many articles we have filed away? We can guess, because we number them sequentially, but does anyone know what they all are? For example, can anyone tell me how to find everything we have published on drug recalls in the '90s? Can a writer working on a paper on HIV easily find out if anyone else has done the same (or is working on it)? Does anyone know how many articles are in the queue right now and what the respective priorities are?

I hate to sound this negative, but we have lots of volunteers wasting their time digging through mountains of paper and acting as mail-room boys. And with the translators planning to start work soon, this is going to get much worse.

I don't know what the right answer is, but other organizations must have had to deal with an issue like this. We need advice and we need it fast.

I chatted with a friend at school who is interning at a local development firm called XR Solutions. He said that this is the type of problem the firm has dealt with before. I'd like to have them come in and talk to us.

What do you think?

Dave

David's email elicits a quick response:

**Re: We're dead unless . . .**

**Email**

**Date:** June 8

**To:** David Keyes

**From:** Jerome Fisher, M.D.

**Subject:** Re: We're dead unless . . .

Dear David,

Thank you for your message. Your timing is impeccable. The department heads in Europe have been voicing similar concerns, and we know we need a solution.

What you might not be aware of, however, is we actually budgeted for a project like this a couple of years ago. We even had vendors come in and present solutions. Of course, as you so clearly articulated, we are still doing things the old-fashioned way. Why? Well, actually, we did not know how to start.

So yes, if you know someone who may be able to help us, by all means, invite him in. I will be in town all next week, and although I suspect I'll be out of my depth in this meeting, I'll make myself available.

Thank you.

Jerry

At the meeting with XR Solutions, which takes place the very next week, Dave keeps informal minutes:

## MEETING NOTES

**Date:** June 15
**Present:** Jerome Fisher, M.D., director, EduHealth
Lorraine Michaels, research coordinator, EduHealth
Claudette Bouvier, EU director, EduHealth
David Keyes, volunteer, EduHealth
J.P. Levine, CEO, XR Solutions
Maria Chavez, sales, XRS
Al Sharpe, Intern, XRS (Dave's buddy)

### Good first step.

Doc Fisher explained EduHealth's mission, as well as its current difficulties.

J.P. introduced XRS and listed some current customer success stories. (Note to self: Ask for references in health field.)

Maria explained that the problem we are facing is a common one, and the solution is referred to as "content management."

Doc asked what a solution would cost and how long it would take to implement. J.P. said that it was too early to answer that one.

Maria talked about "buy" versus "build." Buying an existing solution would allow for faster deployment, but it would not be tailored to the way we work. Building our own would take longer, but we would have exactly what we need. Buying could be cheaper, but not necessarily.

Maria would not recommend whether we buy or build; such discussion is premature. XRS will return and interview personnel to better understand the way we operate and the processes we use (yeah, processes, right!), and will make a recommendation only then.

### Action items:

- Dave and Lorraine to compile list of "requirements" for Maria. (Important: List problems and what is needed, not technology. "We'll find technology that works for you; don't adapt to fit a specific technology"—J.P. quote).
- Claudette to discuss with her team and the translators what they need.
- Doc to feed us when we have long meetings like this (hint, hint).

Over the next two weeks Dave and Lorraine compile the following list of requirements (some high-level, some rather specific):

### Content

- Space to store lots of content; we can't run out of room.

- Ability to handle free-form content; not all articles and bulletins have the same design.

- Grouping by categories (no idea how many categories; need option to add them ourselves).

- Search function.

- Easy usability; most contributors are not techies.

- Multilingual feature, allowing different language versions of each item.

### Workflow

- Way for managers to know what needs approval, and for them to approve or disapprove content as needed.

- Ability to install software and (and do other kinds of work) via the Internet; too hard to install software on so many computers at so many locations.

- Ability to enter and use content from different locations.

### Tracking

- Way to record who created the content and when it was created.

- Way to track any changes.

- Way to know what changed, who changed it, and when it changed.

## Publishing

- Ability to give different users access to different content.

- Ability to specify a language preference (can we use English instead of localized version if not present?).

- Would be nice to be able to publish content to the Web site (right now there is only some content there saved from Word as a Web page).

## Security

- Ability to make some content free for everyone.

- Ability to make some content password protected.

- Password protection for any management content and any content creation or approval screens.

Dave sends the list to Maria at XRS via email. She replies that it's enough to start with and that the teams should meet again ASAP.

MEETING NOTES

**Date:** July 1

**Present:** Jerome Fisher, M.D., director, EduHealth

Lorraine Michaels, research coordinator, EduHealth

Wendy Lu, writer, EduHealth

Susan Hoss, writer, EduHealth

Baining Feng, writer, EduHealth

David Keyes, volunteer, EduHealth

Maria Chavez, sales, XRS

Al Sharpe, Intern, XRS

Maria reviewed the requirements and asked questions. Recommendation is to build our own application. Commercial solutions would likely be overkill (too many features and processes that would hinder us) and would not be customizable enough for us.

- Application would be entirely Web based.
- System would be a Web site and an intranet rolled into one.
- Content would be typed right onto the Web page (need to discuss how this will work; most Web forms are not very friendly).
- Content would be stored in databases.
- Content would be retrieved as needed and displayed based on log-in (if there is one) and affiliation (group membership).
- Multilanguage support is no problem; there will be a report of which content is in which language and which is not.
- Approval can be done, but need to know if it is more than just a yes/no proposition (how many steps are involved).
- Tracking can be done easily; called an "audit trail."
- It will be easy to use. I think Maria is getting sick of us reminding her of that. :-)
- It can be done well within budget (Doc seemed to like that idea).

Lorraine asked about all our existing material—how it could be put into the system. Maria suggests starting from scratch, not be limited by existing content, and that we'd find a way to import it later once system is up and running.

**Action items:**

- XRS to return with detailed proposal.
- Dave to research how much of existing data is in .doc files (may be able to import those).
- Al to look into OCR (Optical Character Recognition—scanning the pages) as a way to import stuff.
- Doc to talk to board about project and get their buy-in.

The next day Dave receives this email message:

---

**Congratulations**

**Email**

**Date:** July 2

**To:** David Keyes

**From:** Jerome Fisher, M.D.

**Subject:** Congratulations

Dear David,

I'd like for you to be our point person for the XRS team. If you are so willing, I'd like to make this your project—you now own the project and will report to me directly.

You could call this a promotion if you'd like, but as a volunteer, you won't be seeing a salary increase (or any salary at all, for that matter). On the plus side, this would look wonderful on your resume (not that I want you job seeking any time soon).

I know your school schedule is lighter over the summer, and I'm hoping that you'll be able to continue to drive this effort.

Thanks for your continued support and enthusiasm.

Jerry

# Initial Thoughts

The folks at XR Solutions make a point of evaluating clients and applications individually, resisting the urge to try to solve every problem with the same solutions. As J.P. Levine, the CEO, too often reminds his team, "If all you have is a hammer, every screw looks like a nail."

J.P. assigns the EduHealth content-management project to Mark Foster, a senior development manager who is just wrapping a project for a local government agency. Team members are assigned to projects by the development manager on a project-by-project basis. XRS finds that by mixing the team makeup, individuals are exposed to a greater variety of skills and talents, and can thus be more creative in problem solving.

Mark emails J.P.

---

**EduHealth team**

**Email**

**Date:** July 3

**To:** J.P.

**From:** Mark Foster

**Subject:** EduHealth team

JP,

Wanted to get this to you before you took off for the 4th. Here are my team preferences:

Teri Martin

Vijay Singh

Sam Carlson

Al Sharpe (I am assuming he'll be with us the whole summer, right?)

I'll meet with them when we get back after the break.

Mark

---

The next day, while most of his coworkers are enjoying beer and barbecues, Mark reads up on the notes and requirements obtained by Maria Chavez in sales. He scribbles and doodles all over the printouts, and prepares for the first team meeting.

With J.P.'s approval (and verification that Al is staying until the start of the next semester) the team meets the next day.

MEETING NOTES

**Present:** Mark Foster, team lead

Sam Carlson, developer

Teri Martin, developer

Vijay Singh, database administrator

Al Sharpe, intern

Mark reviews Maria's notes and then launches a buy-versus-build discussion. All are in agreement that any bought solution would be overkill, since this is a simple app and doesn't need all the features and overhead of a commercial content-management systems. Plus, any commercial system would place additional burden on users, and it would be too hard to create a simple interface that provided only the needed functionality.

Sam hands out copies of the kind of content (articles) that's typical of what EduHealth creates. Most of the content consists of text, and there's no standard structure for the most part.

Teri says that based on her experience, the folks at EduHealth probably have no idea what they really want—and won't until they see a finished product and figure out what they don't like. Mark agrees, and says that's why whatever we create needs to be flexible and structured properly.

Al asks for an example, and Mark draws something like this on the whiteboard (see Figure I-2.1):

Figure I-2.1

The screen scribbles show different ways to present the same information. If the screens are designed properly, using data in different screens is just a matter of presentation, and underlying data is not affected. Mark has an email message he wrote for a previous project on separating presentation from content, and he will circulate it.

Vijay says that database design is most of the work. (He always says that.)

Sam mentions that he wants a rules engine. It's not part of the specs, but it will allow for additional features later on, when they are needed. Those features could include the following:

- Show content on certain days
- Show different content by time of day
- Hide or show specific articles based on source of request

Mark thinks a rules engine may be unnecessary; Sam will investigate what would be involved.

**Action Items:**

- Mark to send out copy of e-mail
- Sam to look into rules thing
- Vijay to research database schemas used in other projects

Meeting adjourned.

With the unanimous decision to build a custom application, Mark meets with Maria and J.P. to bring them up-to-date. Maria says she'll talk to David (Dave) Keyes at EduHealth and asks if she can schedule a meeting for next week to present a formal proposal to the EduHealth people. Mark agrees but asks Maria to articulate that at this point the team will concentrate on functionality and not on a pretty interface. Maria nods.

## Separation of Presentation and Content

Mark sends out an excerpt from e-mail he saved in his *Really Good Stuff Worth Keeping* folder. The gist of it is this:

The biggest problem facing most developers (both static-page designers and application developers) in the Web space is that they routinely mix presentation and content. Consider the following:

- Web pages contain content and HTML formatting in one page. This makes reusing that content with different formatting very difficult, essentially requiring all formatting to be manually removed and then reapplied.

- Application pages—written in ASP, Perl, PHP, Macromedia ColdFusion, and so on—usually contain database calls, conditional processing, output formatting, form validation, and more. So a change in database design, for example, necessitates all sorts of code changes.

- Whoever creates a Web-based application design needs to know SQL and database layout. Similarly, whoever works on basic business logic needs to know about data presentation. And so on. This is not scalable at all, and this kind of cross dependency does not allow development teams to grow and work on more complex projects—developers should be able to concentrate on what they do best, not spend time brushing up on stuff they don't need to know.

The content tier is also referred to as the data tier.

Structured development requires breaking applications into tiers or levels. At a minimum, the content and presentation tiers must be separate: Content must never be tied to presentation, and presentation must never be tied to content.

For example, if the content in a database was going to be displayed in an HTML Web page, a Macromedia Flash movie, or a wireless application protocol (WAP) device, and rendered in PDF format, the content should always be the same. Only the presentation should differ.

Similarly, the presentation code that generates HTML output should be able to do so for all sorts of data; it needs to be reusable too.

Developers refer to this issue as *separating presentation from content*. There are lots of different technologies and buzzwords used to accomplish this, but all seek to do the same thing.

Al instant messages Mark:

```
Al:  Sounds like an added level of complexity.
Mark: Not really. If done properly, it's actually
less work and less code.
Al: Where can I see examples of this?
```

Mark: Look at the CFC files in the project we just finished. Try user.cfc and catalog.cfc; both are good examples of encapsulating data and supporting code into black boxes so that presentation code can concentrate on presentation and not have to know how users and products are stored in databases.

Al: Thanks, will grab those right now.

Mark: Enjoy. Oh, and FYI, CFCs are a great (and simple) way to make all this work. You might want to play with those.

Al: Will do.

Al opens the user.cfc file and scans the code. He has never used Cold-Fusion or CFML before but the syntax is easily read and the code well commented—he has no problem getting the core concepts. He makes some notes for future reference:

All database calls live inside an object.
The object exposes methods like "Get" or "List" or "Add."
Methods take arguments.
Methods return data.
All processing lives inside the method.
Methods can be called by presentation code without having to know about how things work internally.

Al looks at some of the presentation code and notices that the Get user method is used all over the place in all sorts of user interface (UI) code, and none of the code knows that the data is being pulled from a LDAP directory. Suddenly it all clicks. He fires off another instant message:

Al: I get it! I'm a believer!

Mark: Glad to hear it. There's hope for you yet. :-)

### The Basics of Content Management

Al drops by Sam's office. Teri is next door, hears them chatting, and wanders in. Sam tells her to grab a chair and says, "So, who wants to talk content management?"

Sam draws a sketch on the whiteboard (see Figure I-2.2). Teri says his drawing looks like Mark's and accuses him of plagiarism.

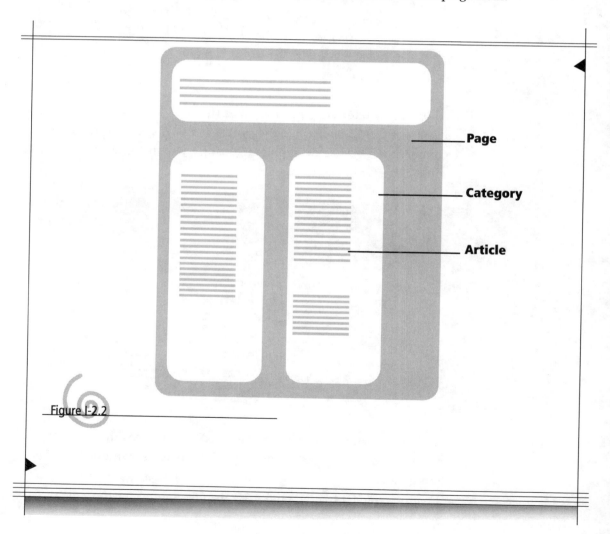

Figure I-2.2

Sam explains his drawing. At the center of any content management system is the actual content, articles. Content can be rendered in all sorts of ways and so presentation is never tied to content. Al is thankful that he took the time to browse that cfc file.

Sam continues, "Articles are just records in a database, that's the easy part. Where it gets tricky is designing underlying data structures so that they are flexible enough to allow data to be used as needed."

Al asks "So why not just store each article in a database table, and then have a screen that allows people to pick from a menu selecting which articles they want displayed on a page, and then render the page dynamically?"

"That won't scale," Teri objects. "If you have hundreds or thousands or even tens of thousands of articles you'd never want to select them individually. You need to group them and allow a group to me selected, if group A is used in a page then articles in group A are displayed."

"Correct," says Sam. "But there is a more important reason to group data. Content management almost always involves some form of access control – restricting or allowing access to data based on security clearance, job, department, membership, or whatever. You'd never want to assign access on a per article basis – you'd do it by group and then put articles in groups."

He walks back to the whiteboard and writes this list:

- **Article.** Actual content

- **Category.** Logical grouping of articles; articles go into categories

- **Page.** A page as seen by the user, made up of one or more categories and laid out as needed

Al asks if an article can be in multiple categories. Teri shakes her head vehemently, and Sam agrees: "It's much too hard to explain that to users. They'll never understand why content is displayed when they remove it from a category, not realizing it is in another. Plus it makes access control an absolute nightmare."

Al suggests, "I guess they could always create additional categories as needed."

As has been discussed, users request pages that are rendered on the fly. Pages contain articles from one or more categories, and exactly what the page will look like will thus depend on the categories included, the articles within a category at the time of the request, and any access control associated with categories.

The discussion moves to articles—what they actually are and how they are stored. Teri explains that there are two basic approaches to data storage:

- **Highly structured.** Define fields for all types of data, store headers body, images, and so on in their own fields.

- **Free form.** Save the whole article as a block of text.

As Teri explains, there are varying degrees between these two extremes, but the basic question to ask is this: Will all content be so consistent in layout that a tight structure can be used, or will content vary so dramatically that a tight structure will get in the way? The group looks through the samples that Maria gave Sam and unanimously agree that content will have to be free form. Sam notes the following:

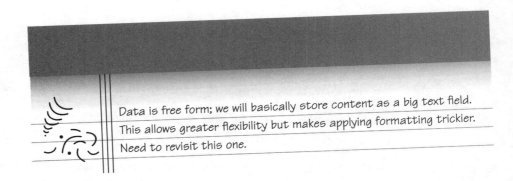

Data is free form; we will basically store content as a big text field. This allows greater flexibility but makes applying formatting trickier. Need to revisit this one.

Al asks about user preferences and how they are stored and used. The group has differing opinions in this area. Teri says that the only way to truly integrate users with a content-management system is to make users and user management part of the core content-management code. This way users can select desired categories, save preferences, and be tightly integrated with the content itself. Sam disagrees, and walks to the whiteboard again (see Figure I-2.3).

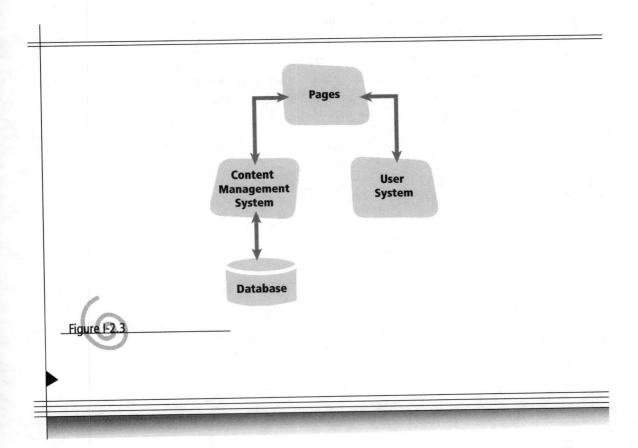

Figure I-2.3

Sam's diagram suggests that the user system and the content-management system are separate entities that are completely independent from each other. In fact, the underlying data store for users may be an LDAP server, while content may be in a database; there is no requirement that they have anything in common.

Teri disagrees: "They are not as separate as you imply, Sam. If a user sets a preference that says he or she wants Category No. 123, that information needs to be stored somewhere, either with the user or with the content."

They argue back and forth for a while until Sam gives in, kind of. Sam does not want user information stored in the content-management system itself, but user preferences pertaining to content do indeed belong there. So, User No. 10 will have preferences stored along with the content so that when he or she requests specific content, those preferences are taken into account. However, the content-management system will have no idea what a user actually is or who User No. 10 is; that kind of information wouldn't matter at that level. All the content-management system would need to know is that it is User No. 10 who is making the request so it can, for example, filter results appropriately.

Sam updates his whiteboard drawing (see Figure I-2.4).

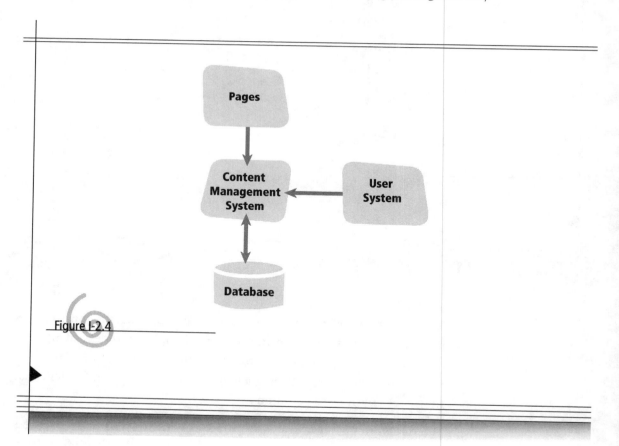

Figure I-2.4

Sam's phone rings, and the tone of his voice tells Teri and Al that they'd better be off on the other side of his office door. They gesture and leave, and Sam fires off an email to Vijay while on the phone.

## The Rules Engine

Sam emails the group:

**Rules**

**Email**

**Date:** July 6

**To:** Mike Foster, Al Sharpe, Teri Martin, Vijay Singh

**From:** Sam Carlson

**Subject:** Rules

OK, so I know you all think this is unnecessary, but, well, you're wrong. In every project I have worked on, the client has invariably wanted something tweaked or changed the day we deliver. So, I want to build the flexibility to do intelligent processing without needing to recode right into this app.

Here's what I mean:

Right now all articles are displayed all the time, but what if users want some displayed based on the time of day? Or what if they want some articles excluded based on the geographical location of the user? Or what if . . . well, you get the idea.

A rules engine is simply a way to let rules be applied at page-generation time. When the content management system generates content, it can check to see if any rules are associated with a category, and if so, execute the rule and include content-based on the value returned by the rule.

We might not even use this thing now, but it won't be a lot of work to plug it in, and the first time the client asks for a "tweak" (BTW, I hate that word), we'll be able to provide it quickly and easily.

## Rules

### Email (continued)

The tricky part is the rules engine itself. There are a few ways to create one:

- Have a defined set of rules. When content is created, there will be a form to fill in values for specific rules (for example, a user might pick "day of week" and enter 3 so the content shows up only on Tuesdays). The database stores these values, and when data is selected, the SQL statement used will filter out the rows that fail the rule. This type of interface is easy to create and use, but adding rules is a pain.

- The opposite extreme is to let users enter rules themselves; they write a little script that gets evaluated. For example, they'd enter Dow(Now()) IS 3 for Tuesday, or something like that. The expression entered by the user is stored and evaluated when data is retrieved. This approach is really powerful—it allows for anything—but users have to know scripting and function usage (and worse, we'd have to create a way to clean up their sloppy coding and mistakes).

- A middle ground is to have a quasi-finite set of rules; we have to write them ourselves and they are stored in a file (some sort of include file, maybe). What gets stored in the database is the name of the rule and the value to match against. So maybe the rule is named Day of Week, and the value associated with it is 3. We know somehow that Day of Week maps to a function we already wrote named dow(), and we evaluate that function and match it to the value. Users can't add their own rules easily (we have to do that for them), but it's easy to do, and we could keep adding rules without needing to make database changes. (Vijay will kill me if I design another app that requires him to write database migration scripts.)

---

**Rules**

---

**Email (continued)**

The first option is the most usable, the second the most powerful, and the third somewhere in between (and my preference).

Thoughts?

Sam

---

Sam articulates the problem and solutions very well. Still, Mark is not convinced and responds to Sam's email:

---

**Re: Rules**

---

**Email**

**Date:** July 6

**To:** Sam

**From:** Mark Foster

**cc:** Vijay, Teri, Al

**Subject:** Re: Rules

I like the idea. But I really don't think storing the names of external functions in a database is a good idea. What will you do if function names change or if code breaks? I'm not saying no, but I want to see how this will work.

Mark

---

Sam takes Mark's email as a challenge, and experiments with ways to accomplish what he wants.

## The Database Layer

While Sam, Teri, and Al have been brainstorming application design, Vijay has been creating preliminary plans for a database layout (see Figure I-2.5). He hasn't actually created any databases yet, as that would be premature at this point (after all, no final design exists). But he knows that visuals will help the team think through the design when they meet later this week.

Vijay breaks content into two tables—one for the definition of the content (what it is, what category it's in, when to display it) and another for the content itself. He notes that the original design calls for supporting multilingual sites, and by allowing multiple content body records per content item, he can support as many languages as needed.

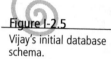

**Figure I-2.5**
Vijay's initial database schema.

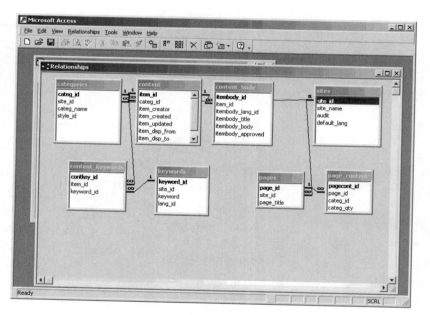

Categories are stored in their own table.

Pages are stored in two tables. The first is the page definition, the second is a related table listing the categories to be included in the page.

Vijay also creates two tables for keywords. The ability to search for content is part of the specification, and this requires allowing either free-form searches or keyword searches. Vijay thinks that they need to support both, since keyword searches (using predefined keywords) is fast and accurate, but limited to the specified keywords. Free-form searching allows for any and all searches but is generally less accurate, and slower too. He creates one table to contain keywords and a second to store keyword-to-content relationships.

He prints copies of his database schema.

### The User Interface (UI)

While Sam plays with creating a rules engine, Teri plays with UI ideas. There are actually two very different interfaces needed: the one seen by the end user and the one used to create content. The end-user UI is not an issue at this point, given the separation of presentation and content and all that. But to better understand how content would be entered into the system, Teri makes some initial notes:

Need a log-in screen.
When logged in, user sees menu like this [Figure 1-2.6].
Need a categories screen to add and create categories.
Need a way to enter content, HTML form.
Pages are simply collections of categories. Need a way to select them and put them in order.

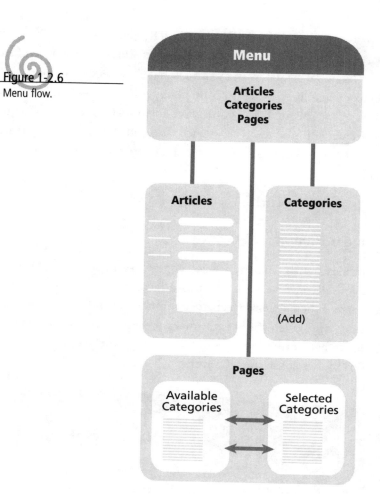

Figure 1-2.6
Menu flow.

Teri's UI thoughts are clearly influenced by her chat with Sam and Al earlier that day. She knows that there is probably a lot more needed and decides that she can't do much more without seeing the final application flow and the details of the underlying content management system.

## Putting It All Together

On Friday the team meets. This time Teri is volunteered to keep minutes:

MEETING NOTES

**Present:** Mark Foster, team lead

Sam Carlson, developer

Teri Martin, developer

Vijay Singh, database administrator

Al Sharpe, intern

Al explained the content-management system. Here are the key points:

- We will build it ourselves.
- We'll use a ColdFusion component (CFC) to encapsulate all content-management functionality. The component methods would expose still more methods for creating and managing categories, creating and managing articles, creating and managing pages, and supporting methods.
- User information would be stored in whatever system EduHealth currently uses, while user preferences for the content-management system would be stored in the content-management system itself.
- Al and Teri will build a prototype together.

Mark asked if all were in agreement to use ColdFusion for this project. There were no objections, and no one could think of any reason not to use ColdFusion. So, CF it is.

Sam presented his findings on the rules engine. Mark is still cynical but allows Sam to go off and create it. Mark wants regular feedback.

Teri presented her UI scribbles. Sam says she should stick to coding. Teri could call him a name that will not go into these meeting notes.

Teri asked what would be used to enter content? HTML forms can be used, but an editor of sorts might be needed. Need to research.

Vijay explained his database ideas.

Mark has enough information to meet client with sales rep.

**Action Items:**

- Al and Teri work on content-management prototype
- Teri to look at editor options
- Sam to keep playing with rules
- Vijay to build databases and host for team

Meeting adjourned.

### The Proposal

The following Monday, Mark and Maria meet with Dave at EduHealth's offices. Maria makes the introductions and Mark walks through the plan and design.

Dave asks lots of questions and is satisfied that Mark and team understand EduHealth's needs. He's also pleased that his pal Al will be on the team and realizes that they'll be seeing way too much of each other over the next couple of months.

Maria hands Dave a written proposal for a signature. Dave promises to take it to Doctor Levine, immediately.

# Development

Over the next week the team meets regularly—both informally and at regularly scheduled meetings. Ideas are bounced around, code snippets are shared and analyzed, and the projects details start to fall in place.

The XR team learned long ago that the term *content management* is ambiguous and confusing at best, and is used differently in different situations. Content management always refers to an application that is used to create, store, and render content—but exactly how that works, the extent to which content may be customized, the complexity of the interface, and the number of actual pages (as opposed to dynamic pages rendered using those pages) varies considerably.

EduHealth's content-management application is typical of most in that it actually has very few *pages*—there is a front page (home page), a news page, search screens, and not much more. All of these pages are dynamic and so appear to be different pages all the time—but in fact, they are not at all.

This is important—some content-management systems require that users be able to create complete pages, whereas others require that they add content to existing pages. The former is a far more complex application involving creating and edit files, manipulating directory structures, and creating and maintaining links between files. And while most content-management systems (particularly commercial ones) do all this and more, more often than not this is not needed at all.

This realization has an important impact on development—users will rarely create new pages on the site. However, they'll regularly be adding content to be rendered in existing pages.

# The Plan

The team decides to create a single ColdFusion component (CFC) as the entire content-management system, essentially encapsulating all the functionality and exposing it to user interfaces (UI) via published methods.

The application has two different interfaces (both created using the same CFC):

- The administration screens are used to create and manage content.

- The application itself creates pages rendering them using the saved content.

The application is thus divided into several tiers:

- **Database.** The underlying database stores all data, and is only ever accessed via the content-management CFC (never directly).

- **Content-Management System.** The content-management system itself contains all application logic and database access, it renders no content at all, and returns data to the presentation tier (in various formats, often as queries). This is created as a CFC named `cm.cfc`.

- **Administration.** The administration screen requires a user log-in and then allows for the creation and management of content (using content-management system methods). The administration application is written in ColdFusion.

- **Application.** The end-user application, also written in ColdFusion.

The team members develop portions of the application concurrently. As the various sub-systems are often highly interdependent, they stub code so as to develop in isolation as much as possible. They also write test code to test each of the systems independently.

# The Database

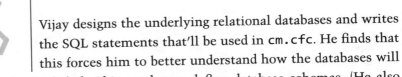

Vijay designs the underlying relational databases and writes the SQL statements that'll be used in `cm.cfc`. He finds that this forces him to better understand how the databases will be used, which helps him to better define database schemas. (He also thinks that his SQL is better than what the others would write).

He fires off the following e-mail to the team:

**Database schema**

**Email**

**Date:** July 12

**To:** Mark Foster, Al Sharpe, Teri Martin, Sam Carlson

**From:** Vijay Singh

**Subject:** Database schema

Here is the current EduHealth database schema based on the discussions thus far:

- The sites table contains the names of the sites managed by the system. I know that there'll just be the one initially, but we need to store defaults and language settings and other options, and so this table will do the job.

- The languages table is a list of supported languages, all the languages supported by all sites. languages stores a language id (en for English, de for German, etc.) and a name (for display purposes).

- The pages table stores pages (not finished pages, but the list of categories stored in each page). pages stores the unique page id, the site id (from the sites table), as well as a descriptive name.

## Database schema

### Email (continued)

- The categories table defines categories used to group related content. Categories are placed into pages (one or more per page) as defined in the page_content table.

- The page_content table maps categories to pages, and a page is made up one or more categories. Each category listed includes a quantity—the number of articles in that category to include.

- The content table defines content including the category association, display dates, as well as created and updated flags.

- The content_body table stores actual content, the title, body, display date range (if needed), and more. content_body is separated from content so as to support multiple languages. A single content_body record is defined for each article, and the actual body text is stored in a separate table (one-to-many relationship)—one record per language.

I have no idea how to handle Sam's rules thingy yet. Sam, when you work out what you want let me know.

Oh, all ID's are UUID. We can have the database generate it or your code, your choice. I have no idea if they plan on using clustering or not, but if they do this will be a must (and if not there is no downside).

We need to brainstorm about storage of presentation stuff. For example, will HTML be stored? How will multiple presentation layers be supported? Etc?

This should cover everything I have seen thus far, if you need additional changes let me know ASAP.

VJ

P.S. Attached is an Access MDB file with this schema for you to start using.

Vijay, Al, Teri, and Sam get together later that day. Vijay keeps notes:

MEETING NOTES

**Date:** July 12
**Present:** Sam Carlson, developer
Teri Marin, developer
Vijay Singh, database administrator
Al Sharpe, intern

Vijay asks about presentation storage.
Al suggests storing finished content (complete with HTML or other formatting).
Teri suggests that if storing presentation to store embedded codes that will be used in rendering content. **[tag]** format is used by many sites and applications.
Sam says the best way to handle styles is not to - not store styles in the database at all. Create a "cargo" field. Just allow a style id to be stored with categories and content. Just store it and return it. If a style id is present for specific content return that, otherwise return the style id stored for the category it is in, otherwise return no style. Let the UI folks work out what to do with the style — they can store CSS style ids, or whatever.
Teri says that this will only work for general formatting, and not to highlight specific words or create specific links.
Sam agrees, but says it is worth it anyway. Adding support for Teri's suggestion later is possible on top of a general style identifier, so not to go to the bother unless really needed.
Meeting adjourned.

Vijay likes the recommendation (and is rather relieved too) and adds style columns to both the categories and content tables.

# The Content-Management Component

Sam and Teri (with help from Al) work on the core content-management system—essentially a single CFC. Each time the component is used a set of steps must be performed—the site record must be read, available languages must be determined, and more. Sam suggests that an `Init()` method be defined that must be invoked before any other method. To make this work there needs to be a way to determine that `Init()` has been invoked from within other methods, and so Teri creates simple constructor code as follows:

```
<!--- Constructor --->
<CFSET THIS.initialized="no">
<CFSET THIS.dsn="cms">
```

A constructor is a block of code that is executed automatically whenever a component is instantiated. In CFCs any code that is not within a method is constructor code, and so she places the above code after the `<CFCOMPONENT>` tag but before the first `<CFMETHOD>`.

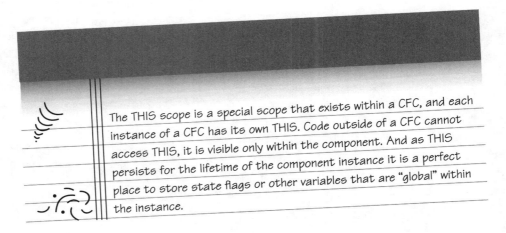

The THIS scope is a special scope that exists within a CFC, and each instance of a CFC has its own THIS. Code outside of a CFC cannot access THIS, it is visible only within the component. And as THIS persists for the lifetime of the component instance it is a perfect place to store state flags or other variables that are "global" within the instance.

Teri's constructor defines two variables within THIS; the first is a flag indicating whether or not the system has been initialized, and the value is set to FALSE (no) initially. The second variable is the data source used within the CFC (so as to not have to hard code it).

She then writes the `Init()` method itself:

```
<!--- Initialize method --->
<CFFUNCTION NAME="init"
OUTPUT="no"
            RETURNTYPE="boolean"
            HINT="Initialize content management system">
            <!--- Site name is required --->
  <CFARGUMENT NAME="site"
            REQUIRED="yes"
            TYPE="string"
            HINT="Name of site to initialize">

  <!--- Only if not initialized --->
  <CFIF NOT THIS.initialized>

    <!--- Get site record --->
    <CFQUERY DATASOURCE="#THIS.dsn#" NAME="THIS.site">
    SELECT site_id, site_name, default_lang, audit
    FROM sites
    WHERE site_name = '#site#'
    </CFQUERY>

    <!--- Check if got site --->
    <CFIF THIS.site.RecordCount IS 1>
```

```
    <!--- Load categories --->
    <CFSET LoadCategories()>

    <!--- Load language list --->
    <CFSET LoadLanguages()>

    <!--- If loaded set initiailzied flag --->
    <CFSET THIS.initialized="Yes">
  </CFIF>
 </CFIF>

 <CFRETURN THIS.initialized>

</CFFUNCTION>
```

Init() takes a single parameter—the name of the site to be initialized (the name must be defined in Vijay's sites table). Init() then reads the site record using a <CFQUERY> tag. The query itself is stored in THIS (so that it will persist for subsequent method invocations).

Teri creates a method named CheckInit() and tells all that they need to invoke it from within any other method to check that initialization had occurred.

If the <CFQUERY> was successful (and returned a single row as determined by checking THIS.site.RecordCount) then two methods are invoked to load language and category options. These are cached in THIS to improve performance, and within the invoked methods the calls are locked with named exclusive locks. Teri explains why she is doing this in an email to the group:

## To <CFLOCK> Or not to <CFLOCK>

### Email

**Date:** July 12

**To:** Mark Foster, Al Sharpe, Sam Carlson, Vijay Singh

**From:** Teri Martin

**Subject:** To **<CFLOCK>** Or not to **<CFLOCK>**

All,

I've been experimenting with ColdFusion MX and it looks like everything we know about locking and the use of <CFLOCK> changes (for the better). I've been exchanging dozens of emails on this one, but here's the punch line as I understand it . . .

<CFLOCK> in ColdFusion 4 and ColdFusion 5 was primarily used to prevent memory corruption that could occur when data in shared scopes was accessed during a write operation (for example, request 2 tries to read a SESSION variable while request 1 is updating it, or both request 1 and request 2 try to write APPLICATION variables at the same moment). ColdFusion MX works very differently, and shared scopes will not become corrupt even if concurrent write access occurs.

So, no more <CFLOCK>, right? Well, not exactly. Consider this scenario - request 1 is reading a block of data into APPLICATION. While this is happening request 2 reads that data. Request 2 gets incomplete information (as request 1 is still processing it). Or consider this slightly different scenario—request 1 updates (rewrites) that block of data in APPLICATION, and so request 2 gets old data or new data or a mixture of old and new data and will never know exactly what was obtained.

## To <CFLOCK> Or not to <CFLOCK>

### Email (continued)

The only way to prevent these scenarios is to still lock requests, and so in situations like this <CFLOCK> is still needed.

The irony of this is that I doubt any of us even thought about these scenarios, and we had to lock anyway and so this was ever a problem. But now that the potential for memory corruption has been eliminated this is now an issue. Or could be one.

Teri

The two Load methods simply read data into the THIS scope:

```
<!--- Load languages --->
<CFFUNCTION NAME="LoadLanguages"
            OUTPUT="no"
            RETURNTYPE="string"
            ACCESS="private"
            HINT="Reload language list">
 <CFLOCK NAME="CMSLanguage" TYPE="exclusive"
TIMEOUT="30">
        <!--- Read from DB --->
        <CFQUERY DATASOURCE="#THIS.dsn#" NAME=
        "THIS.language">
        SELECT lang_id, lang_name
        FROM languages
        ORDER BY lang_name
   </CFQUERY>
 </CFLOCK>
</CFFUNCTION>
```

Al creates a series of methods to expose data in THIS so that the data is accessible from outside of the component if needed:

```
<!--- Get language list --->
<CFFUNCTION NAME="GetLanguageList"
```

```
                OUTPUT="no"
                RETURNTYPE="query"
HINT="Get complete language list">
 <!--- Check initialized --->
 <CFSET CheckInit()>

 <CFRETURN THIS.language>

</CFFUNCTION>
```

GetLanguageList() simply returns the saved query, but first it calls CheckInit() so that processing will not continue if initialization has not occurred (the data will not be THIS if this is the case).

Al creates additional methods to expose specific data (both for use internally, within the component itself, as well as externally). By making all access to this information go through a single method it will be easier to make changes or perform other needed processing later on.

```
<!--- Get site name --->
<CFFUNCTION NAME="GetSiteName"
            OUTPUT="no"
            RETURNTYPE="string"
            HINT="Get current site name">
 <!--- Check initialized --->
 <CFSET CheckInit()>

 <CFRETURN THIS.site.site_name>
</CFFUNCTION>

<!--- Get site id --->
<CFFUNCTION NAME="GetSiteID"
            OUTPUT="no"
            RETURNTYPE="string"
            HINT="Get ID of current site">
 <!--- Check initialized --->
 <CFSET CheckInit()>
```

```
<CFRETURN THIS.site.site_id>
</CFFUNCTION>

<!--- Get default language --->
<CFFUNCTION NAME="GetSiteDefaultLanguage"
OUTPUT="no"
              RETURNTYPE="string"
              HINT="Get sites default language">
<!--- Check initialized --->
<CFSET CheckInit()>

<CFRETURN THIS.site.default_lang>
</CFFUNCTION>
```

Al sets OUTPUT="no" on all of his methods, taking the lead from Teri's code. He asks Teri why she did this:

Al: Teri, why do you set OUTPUT="no" on your methods?

Teri: I am away from my desk and will respond when I return. This is an automated message.

Teri: Just kidding :)

Al: Very funny

Teri: OUTPUT="no" suppresses all output, the CFC writes nothing to the screen so output is never needed

Al: I know that, but why bother specifying OUTPUT, just don't write anything?

Teri: Two reasons . . .

Teri: One, prevents lots of white space

Teri: Two, if someone does accidentally (or not so accidentally) write something it'll be ignored and won't break the app

Teri: Default in CFCs is "yes", but I always set to "no"—CFCs doing content manipulation should never we writing stuff anyway

Al: Ah, thanks, guess I'll do the same then

Al also writes a set of utility methods—private methods that may be used by the rest of the group. Instead of everyone having to write code to verify if a specified language is valid, for example, they could use this method:

```
<!--- Check if a language exists --->
<CFFUNCTION NAME="LanguageExists"
            OUTPUT="no"
            RETURNTYPE="boolean"
            HINT="Check if a language exists">
            <CFARGUMENT NAME="lang_id"
            REQUIRED="yes"
            TYPE="string"
            HINT="Language name">

  <!--- Check initialized --->
  <CFSET CheckInit()>

  <!--- Init return --->
  <CFSET result="no">

  <!--- Find language --->
  <CFLOCK NAME="CMSLanguage" TYPE="readonly" TIMEOUT="30">
          <CFQUERY DBTYPE="query" NAME="language">
          SELECT lang_id
          FROM THIS.language
          WHERE lang_id = '#lang_id#'
    </CFQUERY>
  </CFLOCK>

  <!--- Check if got it --->
  <CFIF language.RecordCount IS 1>
   <CFSET result="yes">
  </CFIF>

  <CFRETURN result>
</CFFUNCTION>
```

This method simply performs a query against the query in the THIS scope. The actual <CFQUERY> is locked with a read-only lock to prevent the search from being performed while the language list is being read.

## Starting the System

Methods with **ACCESS="private"** are only accessible to other methods within the same component.

The CFM is designed to be instantiated (which calls the constructor code), initialized (using the Init() method), and then accessed. This design requires that the component be instantiated as an object so that it persists. Teri adds the following code to her test pages:

```
<!--- Load component --->
<CFOBJECT COMPONENT="EduHealth.cm"
          NAME="cm">
<!--- Init it --->
<CFINVOKE COMPONENT="#cm#"
          METHOD="init"
          SITE="EduHealth"
          RETURNVARIABLE="initRet">
```

She then realizes that she is re-creating the object on each page, and reinitializing it in every page too. She changes the code and moves it to an Application.cfm:

```
<!--- Load component --->
<CFOBJECT COMPONENT="EduHealth.cm"
          NAME="APPLICATION.cm">
<!--- Init it --->
<CFINVOKE COMPONENT="#APPLICATION.cm#"
          METHOD="init"
          SITE="EduHealth"
          RETURNVARIABLE="initRet">
```

instant message

► Components may be created in **SERVER**, **APPLICATION**, **SESSION**, **REQUEST**, and **VARIABLES** scopes. **VARIABLES** is the default.

The <CFOBJECT> creates an object an instance of the content management CFC. The <CFINVOKE> then invokes the Init() method specifying the previously created object as the COMPONENT. Any subsequent method calls would be invoked the same way.

She then wraps the `<CFOBJECT>` and `<CFINVOKE>` calls into a `<CFIF>` statement that checks to see if `APPLICATION.cm` exists. If it does there is no need to reload it.

### Working with Categories

All content has an associated category. Content is never placed directly in a rendered page. Rather, a category is placed there, and whatever content happens to be present at that time in that category is displayed on the rendered page. As such, before creating content, categories must be defined.

The terms "content" and "articles" are often used interchangeably.

Categories are used to group information both for display purposes as well as to implement access control. Granting or denying access to specific articles would not scale, but granting or denying access to categories is highly manageable. Teri realizes that she was right—even though security and user information is not part of the content-management system, basic awareness of users and roles will be required.

Teri sends the following email to Sam and Vijay:

**Access control**

**Email**

**Date:** July 12

**To:** Sam Carlson, Vijay Singh

**CC:** Mark Foster, Al Sharpe

**From:** Teri Martin

**Subject:** Access control

Sam,
I am not going to say "told you so", well, actually, I just did . . .
The specification requires access control and that needs to happen at the category level. I know Sam is opposed to having any user level code or logic in the content-management system, but I don't think we can ignore it altogether.

**Access control**

**Email (continued)**

At some level content will need to be filtered out based on a user having (or not having) access to a specific category. And I don't want to put that onus on whoever is building pages. That belongs in the core content-management system.

So, what I propose is that we store optional roles along with categories. If no role is associated with a category then it will be visible to all users. But if one or more roles exist, then only users who are members of those roles will see the content.

We'll not actually store user information, don't panic Sam. We'll not even store users and the roles they are in. All we store is roles as they relate to categories. This way when a page is required an optional list of roles may be passed which will be used as needed.

Vijay, this will require an additional table that will store roles for categories.

Teri

The group agrees with Teri, and Vijay creates the new table and sends out a revised database.

Creating a category requires only that a name be provided. The CategoryAdd() method takes a category name as a required parameter. It also takes an option style_id parameter which can be used to store formatting identifiers as decided earlier.

```
<!--- Add a category --->
<CFFUNCTION NAME="CategoryAdd"
            OUTPUT="no"
            RETURNTYPE="boolean"
            HINT="Add a new category">
 <CFARGUMENT NAME="name"
```

```
                    REQUIRED="yes"
                    TYPE="string"
                    HINT="New category name">
  <CFARGUMENT NAME="style_id"
                    REQUIRED="no"
                    TYPE="string"
                    DEFAULT=""
                    HINT="New category style name">

  <!--- Check initialized --->
  <CFSET CheckInit()>

  <!--- Init return --->
  <CFSET result="no">

  <!--- Lock while adding --->
  <CFLOCK NAME="CMSCategory" TYPE="exclusive"
  TIMEOUT="30">

    <!--- Check if exists --->
    <CFIF NOT CategoryExists(name)>
      <!--- Get ID --->
      <CFSET categ_id=CreateUUID()>

      <!--- Write new categ --->
      <CFQUERY DATASOURCE="#THIS.dsn#">
      INSERT INTO categories(site_id,
                              categ_id,
                              categ_name,
                              style_id)
      VALUES('#GetSiteID()#',
             '#categ_id#',
             '#name#',
             '#style_id#')
      </CFQUERY>
```

```
    </CFIF>

    <CFSET result="yes">

    <!--- And reload category list --->
    <CFIF result>
     <CFSET LoadCategories()>
    </CFIF>

   </CFLOCK>

  <CFRETURN result>
 </CFFUNCTION>
```

CategoryAdd() first checks that the system has been initialized. It then defines an exclusive lock so that the category list in the THIS scope may be updated safely. As Vijay requested, all id's are UUID's and so the CFML CreateUUID() function is used to return a unique id for the new category. A <CFQUERY> does the actual record insertion (creating the category for a specific site) if it does not already exist. And then finally, the category list in THIS is reloaded.

Adding a category is then as simple as creating an HTML form that prompts for a name, and then invoking the CategoryAdd() method like this:

```
<!--- Add category --->
<CFINVOKE COMPONENT="#APPLICATION.cm#"
          METHOD="CategoryAdd"
          NAME="#FORM.categ_name#"
          RETURNVARIABLE="result">
<CFIF result>
 Success
<CFELSE>
 Failed
</CFIF>
```

Returning flags and status codes is simple enough. Boolean, string, and numeric data types work well for those. But returning sets of data is more complex. A short email thread circulates among the group with various opinions (as per the norm, Sam looking for the coolest solution and Teri for the simplest). Mark makes a suggestion:

**Re: Returning complex results**

**Email**

**Date:** July 13

**To:** Al Sharpe, Teri Martin, Sam Carlson, Vijay Singh

**From:** Mark Foster

**Subject:** Re: Returning complex results

Sorry Sam, returning everything as XML just does not make sense. Yes, it is portable, and yes, XML is a standard. But not everything need be XML, it would be overkill here—and it would also make creating and extracting information overly arduous.

Teri, making everything a structure makes for really clean access, but if all you want to do is populate a select box with results it's too much work.

I say use queries wherever possible. This requires a little more work inside of your component—you need to use the query function to create and populate the query. But once created any code accessing the data can treat it like any other query. With all the CFML functions and tags that support queries this is the best way to go.

Mark

At Mark's suggestion, Al created a `GetCategoryList()` method which returns a list of categories as a standard ColdFusion query. It can then be used for display purposes, for populating form controls, and more.

## Adding Content

With categories in place, content can be added to the system. Teri creates
a method named ContentAdd( ) which, as its name suggests, adds content:

```
<!--- Create new content --->
<CFFUNCTION NAME="ContentAdd"
            RETURNTYPE="string"
            OUTPUT="no"
            HINT="Create (save) new content">
 <CFARGUMENT NAME="categ_id"
             REQUIRED="yes"
             TYPE="string"
             HINT="Content category (id)">
 <CFARGUMENT NAME="creator"
             REQUIRED="yes"
             TYPE="string"
             HINT="Creator name">
 <CFARGUMENT NAME="disp_from"
             REQUIRED="no"
             TYPE="date"
             HINT="Display from date">
 <CFARGUMENT NAME="disp_to"
             REQUIRED="no"
             TYPE="date"
             HINT="Display to date">
 <CFARGUMENT NAME="style_id"
             REQUIRED="no"
             TYPE="string"
             DEFAULT=""
             HINT="Content style name (uses category
             style by default)">
 <CFARGUMENT NAME="language"
             REQUIRED="no"
             TYPE="string"
             DEFAULT="#GetSiteDefaultLanguage()#"
```

```
                    HINT="Page language">
<CFARGUMENT NAME="title"
                REQUIRED="yes"
                TYPE="string"
                HINT="Content title">
<CFARGUMENT NAME="body"
                REQUIRED="yes"
                TYPE="string"
                HINT="Content body">


<!--- Check initialized --->
<CFSET CheckInit()>


<!--- Generate UUID for new content --->
<CFSET item_id=CreateUUID()>


<!--- Start transaction --->
<CFTRANSACTION>


<!--- Insert item --->
<CFQUERY DATASOURCE="#THIS.dsn#">
INSERT INTO content(item_id,
                    categ_id,
                    item_creator,
                    item_created,
                    item_style)
VALUES('#item_id#',
       '#categ_id#',
       '#creator#',
       #CreateODBCDate(Now())#,
       '#style_id#')
</CFQUERY>


<!--- Does this have a start date? --->
<CFIF IsDefined("FORM.disp_from")>
```

```
   <CFQUERY DATASOURCE="#THIS.dsn#">
   UPDATE content
   SET item_disp_from=#CreateODBCDate(FORM.disp_from)#
   WHERE item_id='#item_id#'
   </CFQUERY>
  </CFIF>


  <!--- Does this have an end date? --->
  <CFIF IsDefined("FORM.disp_to")>
   <CFQUERY DATASOURCE="#THIS.dsn#">
   UPDATE content
   SET item_disp_to=#CreateODBCDate(FORM.disp_to)#
   WHERE item_id='#item_id#'
   </CFQUERY>
  </CFIF>


  <!--- And insert content body --->
  <CFQUERY DATASOURCE="#THIS.dsn#">
  INSERT INTO content_body(itembody_id,
                           item_id,
                           itembody_lang_id,
                           itembody_title,
                           itembody_body)
  VALUES('#CreateUUID()#',
         '#item_id#',
         '#language#',
         '#title#',
         '#body#')
  </CFQUERY>

  <!--- End transaction --->
  </CFTRANSACTION>

  <CFRETURN item_id>
</CFFUNCTION>
```

The required parameters are the category id (retrieved using the `GetCategoryList()` method), the `title`, `body`, and `id` of whoever created the content.

Other parameters are optional. These include the language (the default is the site default as returned by the `GetSiteDefaultLanguage()` method), style (the default is the category style), and display dates (if none is provided then the content will always be displayed).

## Approval

**instant message**

▶ As decided previously, user information (log-ins, names, etc.) would not be part of the content-management system. The user id stored here is whatever is passed to it from the calling code.

One of EduHealth's requirements was an approval process. Content added must be reviewed before it can made publicly available. The development team wanted to build a complete workflow-based system for content approval but decided against it. EduHealth has no tiered org chart, and approval of content is not assigned to managers or individuals but to subject experts. To support a more ad hoc approval process, a far simpler solution was implemented.

All content has an approved flag (a column in the database). When content is added with `ContentAdd()` that flag is set to `FALSE` so that it is ignored by any content retrieval. The only way to access content that has not been approved is with a method designed for just this task. `GetApprovalList()` returns a query with the list of content waiting to be approved.

To approve content the `ContentApprove()` method is invoked, passing the content id and the name of who approved its use. This is stored in the database making the content available for subsequent retrieval.

Teri wonders whether there'd ever be a need to un-approve content. She makes a note of this for future reference:

JOURNAL

Need **ContentDisapprove()** method? Would be easy to implement (just turn flag off). Have Mark check with EduHealth.

### Creating Pages

With content created and assigned to categories, the next task is to create pages. A page is simple a collection of categories. A page is *not* a finished rendered page—rather, it is a collection of all the content needed to render a page.

Teri's PageAdd() method adds a new (empty) page:

```
<!--- Create a new page --->
<CFFUNCTION NAME="PageAdd"
            OUTPUT="no"
            RETURNTYPE="string"
            HINT="Create a new page">
            <CFARGUMENT NAME="title"
            REQUIRED="yes"
            TYPE="string"
            HINT="Page title">

<!--- Check initialized --->
<CFSET CheckInit()>

<!--- Create ID --->
<CFSET page_id=CreateUUID()>

<!--- Insert --->
<CFQUERY DATASOURCE="#THIS.dsn#">
INSERT INTO pages(page_id, site_id, page_title)
VALUES('#page_id#', '#GetSiteID()#', '#title#')
</CFQUERY>

<CFRETURN page_id>
</CFFUNCTION>
```

PageAdd( ) is rather simple. It generates a UUID and adds a new page to the pages table. PageAdd( ) returns the new page id as that will be needed to add page content using the PageContentAdd( ) method:

```
<!--- Add content to page --->
<CFFUNCTION NAME="PageContentAdd"
            OUTPUT="no"
            RETURNTYPE="string"
            HINT="Create a new page">
 <CFARGUMENT NAME="page_id"
             REQUIRED="yes"
             TYPE="string"
             HINT="Page ID">
 <CFARGUMENT NAME="categ_id"
             REQUIRED="yes"
             TYPE="string"
             HINT="Category ID">
 <CFARGUMENT NAME="categ_qty"
             REQUIRED="no"
             TYPE="numeric"
             DEFAULT="1"
HINT="Quantity of category to show">

 <!--- Check initialized --->
 <CFSET CheckInit()>

 <!--- Create ID --->
 <CFSET pagecont_id=CreateUUID()>

 <!--- Insert --->
 <CFQUERY DATASOURCE="#THIS.dsn#">
 INSERT INTO page_content(pagecont_id,
                          page_id,
                          categ_id,
                          categ_qty)
```

```
        VALUES('#pagecont_id#',
               '#page_id#',
               '#categ_id#',
               #categ_qty#)
    </CFQUERY>

    <CFRETURN page_id>
</CFFUNCTION>
```

A page contains one or more sections, or blocks of content. The sections are each added using `PageContentAdd()` which requires that the page id and category to add be specified. By default only the most recent article in each category is displayed. To display more (the three most recent, for example) the desired quantity should be passed to the `categ_qty` parameter.

So, to create a new page and add two sections (the first displaying the three most recent entries and the second showing only the most recent) the following code snippet could be used:

```
<!--- Create page --->
<CFINVOKE COMPONENT="#APPLICATION.cm#"
          METHOD="PageAdd"
          TITLE="What's New"
          RETURNVARIABLE="pageid">
          <!--- Add first section --->
<CFINVOKE COMPONENT="#APPLICATION.cm#"
          METHOD="PageContentAdd"
          PAGE_ID="#pageid#"
          CATEG_ID="8D208F7B-CA63-F141-9032C839B98D93C7"
          CATEG_QTY="3">
          <!--- Add second section --->
<CFINVOKE COMPONENT="#APPLICATION.cm#"
          METHOD="PageContentAdd"
          PAGE_ID="#pageid#"
          CATEG_ID="8DB09D82-D443-15B5-94C7165F9E332132"
          CATEG_QTY="3">
```

Of course, the values in Teri's test snippet are hard coded. In a real application they would be dynamic based on user input and selections.

Teri creates additional methods to update and delete content and pages.

### Retrieving Content

Now that content can be added and approved, and pages can be created, the next step is to retrieve it. To retrieve a page an application need simply call a method and display the returned query. All that need be passed is the desired page id; everything else happens inside of the CFC itself.

```
<!--- Get page categories --->
<CFFUNCTION NAME="GetPageContent"
            OUTPUT="no"
            RETURNTYPE="query"
            HINT="Get page content">
  <CFARGUMENT NAME="page_id"
            REQUIRED="yes"
            TYPE="string"
            HINT="Page ID">

  <!--- Check initialized --->
  <CFSET CheckInit()>

  <!--- Get page content --->
  <CFQUERY DATASOURCE="#THIS.dsn#" NAME="content">
  SELECT pagecont_id, page_content.categ_id, categ_name,
categ_qty
  FROM page_content, categories
  WHERE page_content.categ_id=categories.categ_id
  AND page_id='#page_id#'
  </CFQUERY>

  <CFRETURN content>
</CFFUNCTION>
```

The GetPageContent() method returns a list of sections (categories) to be included in a page (but not the content itself). This method is useful in determining what a page contains, and is also used by the GetPage() method so that it knows what to get:

```
<!--- Get a page --->
<CFFUNCTION NAME="GetPage"
            OUTPUT="no"
            RETURNTYPE="query"
            HINT="Get a populated page">
  <CFARGUMENT NAME="page_id"
             TYPE="string"
             REQUIRED="yes"
             HINT="Page ID">

  <!--- Check initialized --->
  <CFSET CheckInit()>

  <!--- First get page makeup (categories) --->
  <CFSET pagecontent=GetPageContent(page_id)>

  <!--- Create results query --->
  <CFSET q=QueryNew("category, title, body")>

  <!--- Loop through page content --->
  <CFLOOP FROM="1" TO="#pagecontent.RecordCount#"
INDEX="i1">
    <!--- Get items that match this request --->
    <CFQUERY DATASOURCE="#THIS.dsn#"
NAME="items"
MAXROWS="#pagecontent.categ_qty[i1]#">
    SELECT itembody_title, itembody_body
```

**instant message**
► Methods may invoke
other methods in
the same component
as functions and do
not need to use
**<CFINVOKE>** format.

```
    FROM content, content_body
    WHERE content.item_id=content_body.item_id
    AND content.categ_id='#pagecontent.categ_id[i1]#'
    AND content_body.itembody_approved=1
    AND (item_disp_from = NULL
OR item_disp_from < #CreateODBCDate(Now())#)
    AND (item_disp_to = NULL
OR item_disp_to > #CreateODBCDate(Now())#)
    ORDER BY item_created DESC
    </CFQUERY>
    <CFLOOP FROM="1" TO="#items.RecordCount#" INDEX="i2">
     <CFSET QueryAddRow(q)>
     <CFSET QuerySetCell(q, "category",
pagecontent.categ_name[i1])>
      <CFSET QuerySetCell(q, "title",
items.itembody_title[i2])>
      <CFSET QuerySetCell(q, "body",
items.itembody_body[i2])>
     </CFLOOP>
    </CFLOOP>

    <CFRETURN q>
</CFFUNCTION>
```

GetPage() is what actually returns page contents for a specified page id.
GetPage() first invokes GetPageContent() to obtain a list of what the
page contains. Then a <CFLOOP> is used to loop through the returned category list, and a query is executed for each. The results are inserted into
a query constructed on the fly, and the results are then returned as a query
for rendering.

## Using Keywords

Although keyword searches are not part of the specification, Mark feels
that this is an important feature to add:

---

**Keyword searches**

---

**Email**

**Date:** July 14

**To:** Al Sharpe, Teri Martin, Sam Carlson, Vijay Singh

**From:** Mark Foster

**Subject:** Keyword searches

This app is going to need searching capabilities, and free-form text search won't work for a few reasons:

1. Lots of strange spelling and abbreviations in these documents.

2. With multiple languages supported who knows what will get matched?

3. Can anyone actually spell this stuff?

4. Lots of words and names for same thing (English, Latin, and more).

So, I think we need a keyword search interface using a set of defined keywords (per language). Users would create keywords and when creating content assign match keyword to them (we'd have to give them a nice menu or something). Then to perform a keyword search we'd get back a list of matching ids which could then be displayed.

Vijay, could you add database tables for this? Al, can you take a stab at the code for this one?

Thanks.

Mark

Mark's suggestion makes lots of sense. Vijay create two new tables:

- keywords is a list of keywords—keyword id, the keyword itself, the site it belongs to, and the language it belongs to.

- content_keywords maps keyword ids to content ids.

Al first creates methods for managing keywords. GetKeywordList() returns a list of available keywords:

```
<!--- Get all keywords --->
<CFFUNCTION NAME="GetKeywordList"
            RETURNTYPE="query"
            HINT="Get complete keyword list">
  <CFARGUMENT NAME="language"
            REQUIRED="no"
            TYPE="string"
            DEFAULT="#GetSiteDefaultLanguage()#"
            HINT="Keyword language">

  <!--- Check initialized --->
  <CFSET CheckInit()>

  <!--- Get keywords --->
  <CFQUERY DATASOURCE="#THIS.dsn#" NAME="keywords">
  SELECT keyword, keyword_id
  FROM keywords
  WHERE site_id = '#GetSiteID()#'
  AND lang_id = '#language#'
  ORDER BY keyword
  </CFQUERY>

  <CFRETURN keywords>
</CFFUNCTION>
```

GetKeywordList() accepts a language id (and defaults to the default language) and returns a query of available keywords (regardless of if they are being used or not). Keywords are added using KeywordAdd():

```
<!--- Add a keyword --->
<CFFUNCTION NAME="KeywordAdd"
            RETURNTYPE="boolean"
            HINT="Add a new keyword to the master keyword
            list">
            <CFARGUMENT NAME="keyword"
            TYPE="string"
            REQUIRED="yes"
            HINT="New keyword">
  <CFARGUMENT NAME="language"
            REQUIRED="no"
            TYPE="string"
            DEFAULT="#GetSiteDefaultLanguage()#"
            HINT="Keyword language">

  <!--- Check initialized --->
  <CFSET CheckInit()>

  <!--- Add keyword --->
  <CFQUERY DATASOURCE="#THIS.dsn#">
  INSERT INTO keywords(site_id,
                       lang_id,
                       keyword_id,
                       keyword)
  VALUES('#GetSiteID()#',
         '#language#',
         '#CreateUUID()#',
         '#keyword#')
  </CFQUERY>

  <CFRETURN "yes">
</CFFUNCTION>
```

`KeywordAdd()` simply takes a new keyword and inserts it into the keywords table.

To actually assign keywords to content, the `ContentKeywordAdd()` method is used. It takes the `content` item id and the `keyword` id, and stores them in the `content_keywords` table:

```
<!--- Add a keyword to content --->
<CFFUNCTION NAME="ContentKeywordAdd"
            OUTPUT="no"
            RETURNTYPE="boolean"
            HINT="Add a keyword to a content item">
  <CFARGUMENT NAME="item_id"
              REQUIRED="yes"
              TYPE="string"
              HINT="Content item ID">
  <CFARGUMENT NAME="keyword_id"
              REQUIRED="yes"
              TYPE="string"
              HINT="Keyword ID">

  <!--- Check initialized --->
  <CFSET CheckInit()>

  <!--- Add keyword --->
  <CFQUERY DATASOURCE="#THIS.dsn#">
  INSERT INTO content_keywords(contkey_id,
                                item_id,
                                keyword_id)
  VALUES('#CreateUUID()#',
         '#item_id#',
         '#keyword_id#')
  </CFQUERY>

  <CFRETURN "yes">
</CFFUNCTION>
```

Al also creates a method to delete keywords from content (although not deleting the keywords themselves). `ContentKeywordDelete()` takes the `content item` id and an `optional keyword` id—if the keyword id is provided then just that keyword is removed; if it is left blank, then all keyword associations are removed:

```
<!--- Delete a keyword from content --->
<CFFUNCTION NAME="ContentKeywordDelete"
            OUTPUT="no"
            RETURNTYPE="boolean"
            HINT="Delete a keyword from a content item">
  <CFARGUMENT NAME="item_id"
            REQUIRED="yes"
            TYPE="string"
            HINT="Content item ID">
  <CFARGUMENT NAME="keyword_id"
            REQUIRED="no"
            DEFAULT=""
            TYPE="string"
            HINT="Keyword ID, if not specified all
            keywords will be deleted">

  <!--- Check initialized --->
  <CFSET CheckInit()>

  <!--- Delete keyword --->
  <CFQUERY DATASOURCE="#THIS.dsn#">
  DELETE FROM content_keywords
  WHERE item_id='#item_id#'
  <CFIF NOT keyword_id IS "">
  AND keyword_id='#keyword_id#'
  </CFIF>
  </CFQUERY>

  <CFRETURN "yes">
</CFFUNCTION>
```

With keywords assigned, a search can be performed using the Key-wordSearch() method which returns a query containing matching articles.

## Rules Processing

Sam is still adamant that a hook for rules processing must be included in the application so as to support additional content-management control simply and easily at a later date. He sends out this email:

---

**Re: Rules**

**Email**

**Date:** July 15

**To:** Mike Foster, Al Sharpe, Teri Martin, Vijay Singh

**From:** Sam Carlson

**Subject:** Re: Rules

Once you have read this email you should feel free to congratulate me in any way you see fit.

I have a working rules engine, it is clean and simple and oh so extendable.

I tried to write rules as stored procedures (thanks for the help, Vijay) so that a sp could be selected and used as a rule and it would be executed upon retrieval. Turns out that won't work too well, there is too much that the database server would not know (IP address, client browser, etc.) and passing that info to the SQL Server does not make sense.

I also tried to store CFML code in the database. This cannot be done with straight expressions, but functions can be treated as variables so-well, it did not work as I'd have liked.

## Re: Rules

### Email (continued)

So, I resorted to the brute force (and actually incredible quick) method. There is a file named rules.cfm that is included into cm.cfc. It contains user defined functions, as many or as few as needed. I also created a new table (sorry Vijay, I don't need you anymore <eg>) that contains a rule id, a rule name (what the user selects) and a function name. When users add content they may select an optional rule, and if they do it will be evaluated when page content is returned. If a rule is present then that article will only be returned if the rule (function) returns true.

Here are two test rules I have been using for now:

```
<CFFUNCTION NAME="IsWorkDay" RETURNTYPE="boolean">
 <CFSET VAR result="false">
 <CFSET VAR dow=DayOfWeek(Now())>
 <CFIF dow GTE 2 AND dow LTE 6>
  <CFSET result="true">
 </CFIF>
 <CFRETURN result>
</CFFUNCTION>
<CFFUNCTION NAME="IsWeekend" RETURNTYPE="boolean">
 <CFRETURN NOT IsWorkDay()>
</CFFUNCTION>
```

Nice thing about this design is that rules may be written in CFML or <CFSCRIPT> and may do just about anything. In addition, the article itself is passed as a parameter when the rule is called so the code within the UDF can evaluate it or do whatever it needs.

Sweet, eh?

Oh, Teri, you'll need to modify some of your code to account for this.

Sam C. (aka The CF Dude)

Sam's idea is so simple that it could actually work, and if not used has no overhead whatsoever. Mark agrees to let him plug it in but decides not to tell the client about its extensibility–he does not want non-programmers writing rules and possibly breaking things in the process. Still, the ability to add a function to a CFM file and thereby add functionality to the app (if, or when, it is needed) is compelling.

A <CFINCLUDE> is added to cm.cfc to include rules.cfm. And Teri (reluctantly) updates her GetPage() method:

```
<!--- Get a page --->
<CFFUNCTION NAME="GetPage"
            OUTPUT="no"
            RETURNTYPE="query"
            HINT="Get a populated page">
  <CFARGUMENT NAME="page_id"
              TYPE="string"
              REQUIRED="yes"
              HINT="Page ID">

  <!--- Check initialized --->
  <CFSET CheckInit()>

  <!--- First get page makeup (categories) --->
  <CFSET pagecontent=GetPageContent(page_id)>

  <!--- Create results query --->
  <CFSET q=QueryNew("category, title, body")>

  <!--- Loop through page content --->
  <CFLOOP FROM="1" TO="#pagecontent.RecordCount#"
INDEX="i1">
    <!--- Get items that match this request --->
    <CFQUERY DATASOURCE="#THIS.dsn#"
NAME="items"
```

```
        MAXROWS="#pagecontent.categ_qty[i1]#">
          SELECT itembody_title, itembody_body, rule_id
          FROM content, content_body
          WHERE content.item_id=content_body.item_id
          AND content.categ_id='#pagecontent.categ_id[i1]#'
          AND content_body.itembody_approved=1
          AND (item_disp_from = NULL
    OR item_disp_from < #CreateODBCDate(Now())#)
          AND (item_disp_to = NULL
    OR item_disp_to > #CreateODBCDate(Now())#)
          ORDER BY item_created DESC
          </CFQUERY>
          <CFLOOP FROM="1" TO="#items.RecordCount#" INDEX="i2">
           <!--- Validate rule(s) if present --->
           <CFIF ((Trim(pagecontent.rule_id[i1]) IS "")
    OR (Evaluate(GetRuleUDF(pagecontent.rule_id[i1]))))
           AND ((Trim(items.rule_id[i2]) IS "")
    OR (Evaluate(GetRuleUDF(items.rule_id[i2]))))>
            <CFSET QueryAddRow(q)>
            <CFSET QuerySetCell(q, "category",
    pagecontent.categ_name[i1])>
            <CFSET QuerySetCell(q, "title",
    items.itembody_title[i2])>
            <CFSET QuerySetCell(q, "body",
    items.itembody_body[i2])>
           </CFIF>
          </CFLOOP>
         </CFLOOP>

         <CFRETURN q>
        </CFFUNCTION>
```

Teri includes the rules table into her query. She modifies the `GetPage-Content()` method so that it returns the rule id (if there is one), and this way she has both rule ids (the category rule and the specific content rule) if they exist.

She creates a new method named `LoadRules()` to cache the rules in the `Init()`, and another method named `GetRuleUDF()` which returns the function to be executed for a specific rule id.

```
<!--- Get a rules UDF --->
<CFFUNCTION NAME="GetRuleUDF"
            OUTPUT="no"
            ACCESS="private"
            RETURNTYPE="string"
            HINT="Get the UDF associated with a rule">
  <CFARGUMENT NAME="rule_id"
            TYPE="string"
            REQUIRED="yes"
            HINT="Rule ID">

  <!--- Check initialized --->
  <CFSET CheckInit()>

  <!--- Query the cached list --->
  <CFLOCK NAME="CMSRules" TYPE="readonly" TIMEOUT="30">
   <CFQUERY DBTYPE="query" NAME="rule">
   SELECT rule_udf
   FROM THIS.rules
   WHERE rule_id='#rule_id#'
   </CFQUERY>
  </CFLOCK>

  <CFRETURN rule.rule_udf>
</CFFUNCTION>
```

Finally, she modifies the app so that before rows are added to the returned query a test is performs to check whether or not a rule exists and evaluate it if it does.

# The Administration Program

The Administration program is used by EduHealth personal to create and manage content and perform related maintenance.

Administration requires a user log-in, and so to encapsulate all user log-in and log-out activity Teri creates a new component named **user.cfc**. She creates methods named **Login()** and **Logout()** as well as many supporting methods. Initially she hard codes the values in these (not even needing an actual user list), but as all logic is within this component it could be moved to a live security system very easily.

Teri creates the administration pages allowing users to log in and manage the content. When a user is logged in, an instance of the user object is created in the SESSION scope like this:

```
<!--- Otherwise, create user session object --->
<CFOBJECT COMPONENT="EduHealth.user"
    NAME="SESSION.user">


<!--- Try login --->
<CFIF SESSION.user.login(FORM.login_id,
FORM.login_password)>
 <CFLOCATION URL="../">
<CFELSE>
 <CFLOCATION URL="index.cfm">
</CFIF>
```

<CFOBJECT> creates the user object in the SESSION scope, and the Login() method attempts the log-in. Login() returns TRUE if the log-in was successful and FALSE if not. The following code allows Teri to simply check that a user is logged in:

```
<!--- Check if logged in --->
<CFIF (NOT IsDefined("SESSION.user"))
 OR (NOT SESSION.user.IsLoggedIn())>
 <!--- Send to login page --->
 <CFLOCATION URL="login">
</CFIF>
```

The actual administration program uses all the methods described previously.

# The Solution

Maria and Mark meet with the EduHealth people the next week. Maria explains that what they are about to see is a working prototype—it is functional, but does not look pretty, and parts are stubbed for simplicity's sake.

And with that she turns it over to Mark.

# The Demo

Mark explains the two sides of the application—the public facing application and the administrative application—and explains their relationship. He then opens a browser and proceeds to demo the Administration application. He starts at the log-in screen seen in Figure I-4.1.

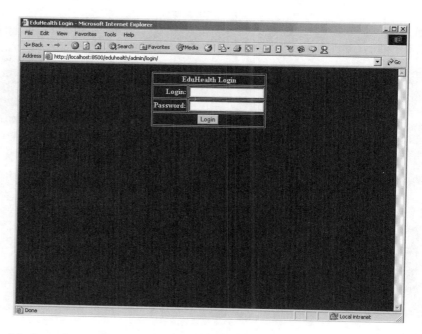

**Figure I-4.1**
The Administration screen is password protected.

Mark explains that the application is password protected and says that he'll make the log-in work with whatever security system or network EduHealth currently uses. Dave Keyes offers to get that information for him.

Mark then continues the demo, starting with the opening menu seen in Figure I-4.2. Options here are used to create and edit content, define categories and pages, manage keywords, and approve content.

Doc asks if the options presented can vary based on login id. Mark explains that access control has not been implemented but that it could be quite easily.

**Figure I-4.2**

The opening page
contains a menu with the
administrative options.

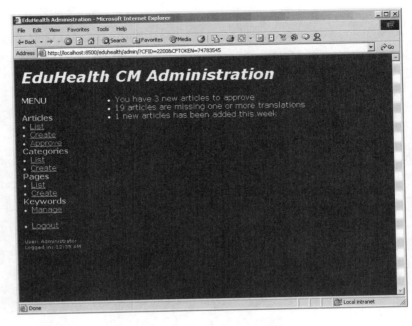

Mark then walks through the process of creating content (see Figure I-4.3),
defining categories (see Figure I-4.4), and creating pages (see Figure I-4.5),
explaining how each of these features work.

**Figure I-4.3**

The content-
creation screen.

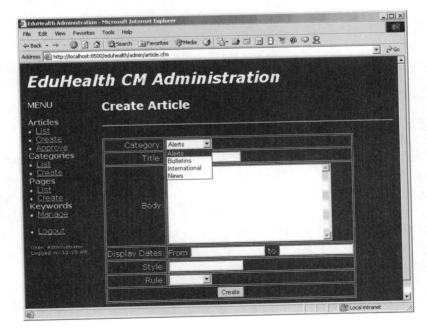

The content-creation screen (see Figure I-4.3) prompts for category, title, body, and other optional information. Content maybe typed into this screen directly, or copied and pasted from other applications (Microsoft Word, for example).

Figure I-4.4
The category-
creation screen.

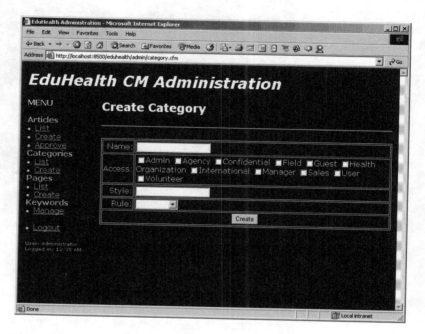

The category-creation screen (see Figure I-4.4) prompts for a category name, as well as for the roles that will have access to this category. If no roles are checked, then all users will have access to any content within this category.

The page-creation screen (see Figure I-4.5) prompts for the page name and for the categories of which it is comprised.

Dave does not like the editor, and Mark explains that an editor is not part of the spec. The truth is, there is no editor in the application—it is a simple HTML form and nothing more. He adds, "there are third-party products that create add-in editors, and they could be used with the system." Mark makes a note for himself:

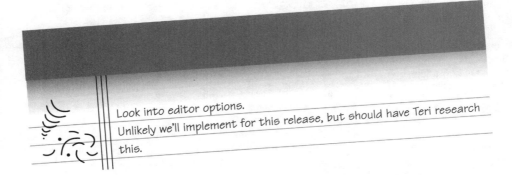

Look into editor options.
Unlikely we'll implement for this release, but should have Teri research this.

**Figure I-4.5**
The page-creation screen.

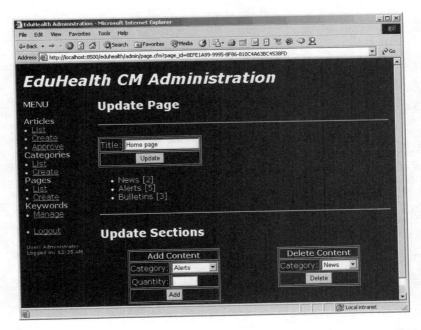

He then opens anther browser window and shows the results of the changes as he makes them. He first loads the page without logging in (see Figure I-4.6) and then logs in as a user with additional access and refreshes the page so that additional content is displayed (see Figure I-4.7).

Figure I-4.6
Guests (anonymous
users) can view a subset
of available content.

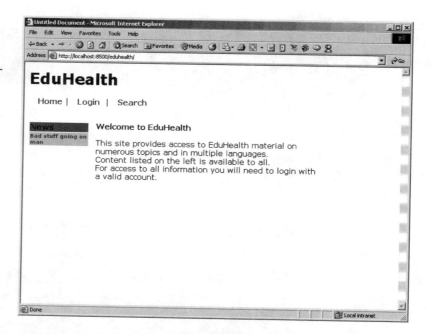

Figure I-4.7
Access control varies the
content seen based on
user log-in.

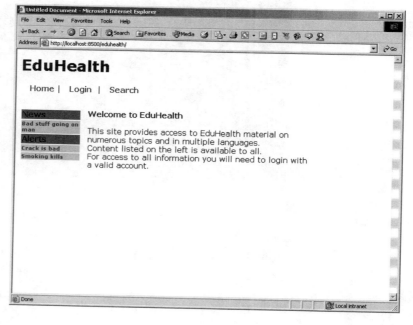

Dave asks how searches will work, and Mark is glad that he had thought of that ahead of time. He explains the pros and cons of full-text searching versus keyword-based searching and recommends the latter. "This will solve most of what you need now, and we can always add full-text search capabilities later if needed" he says.

He shows them how keywords are defined (see Figure I-4.8) and how they are associated with content. Dave thinks the process may be too tedious and that there may be too many keywords. Mark asks him to try it as is and provide feedback. He also acknowledges that eventually both full-text searching and keyword-based searching may be needed, or even a hybrid of sorts.

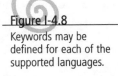

**Figure I-4.8**

Keywords may be defined for each of the supported languages.

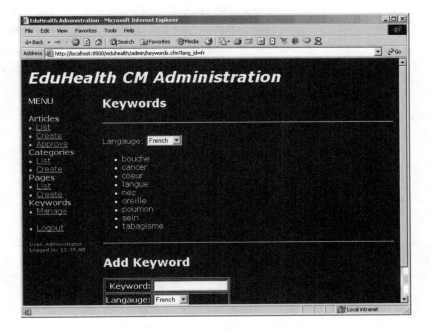

Doc asks, "How can I tell who changed what and when?" Mark asks him to explain exactly what it is he'd like to track. Doc says that he'd like to know who added content, who changed content, who approved content, everything. He'd also like to be able to see reports of what changed.

"Do you want to be able to undo changes, too, or do you just want to know what changed?" asks Mark.

"Can I have both?"

Mark explains that an audit-trail is a log of what changed, by whom, and when. Rollback is the ability to undo changes, restoring content to a prior state. The former could be implemented quickly and without really impacting cost or schedule. The latter, however, is extremely complicated and required complex storage (so as to store the before and after state of every operation) and sophisticated interfaces (so as to be able to select what to rollback and what not).

Mark suggests that rollback features would be overkill. "As long as all of your databases are backed up every day, the worst-case scenario is you roll back to last nights backup," he says. He suggests that he'll discuss the options with his time, but it is clear that he does not want to implement a complete rollback system.

Dave asks about importing existing content. Mark explains that the underlying databases are very clean and easy to access, and that an import mechanism could be created as long as the content was in a known file format. "I can't help you with printed copy," he says. Dave and Doc exchange glances, and Mark knows that they'll ask him to help with that one at some point, anyway.

Mark wraps up, "I'll look into the audit-trail and rollback options, and will also have someone make suggestions about editors." He asks if there is anything else that may have been forgotten.

Dave asks if they can keep the application to play with. Mark says that he'll send someone over later that day to install ColdFusion and the application for them to start using. He cautions them not to use it for live data yet, stating, "while I want you to use the app and need your feedback, we could still end up making changes internally that would require us to recreate the databases, and if that happens you'll lose any content you entered."

Maria and Mark exchange pleasantries with the EduHealth folk, and then head out.

## Final Changes

Back at the office Mark sends out a brief email.

---

**EduHealth**

**Email**

**Date:** July 17

**To:** Al Sharpe, Teri Martin, Sam Carlson, Vijay Singh

**From:** Mark Foster

**Subject:** EduHealth

Meeting in my office in 10 minutes.

Mark

---

Sam is the first one to arrive. "That bad, eh?" he asks.

"Nah," replies Mark, "I just needed to find a way to get your attention after 5:00 PM." "The demo went well, but there are some last minute changes," he says.

Vijay grimaces—last-minute changes almost always involve database changes of some kind.

"Sam", Mark says, "how would you implement complete content roll-back?" he asks.

"You're kidding," Teri responds.

Mark explains Doc's request and the team gets into a long and healthy debate on how to implement rollback. The consensus is that this will be a very significant effort, and hard to cost justify.

Teri offers a partial solution. "If all they want is a log of exactly what changed, maybe even before and after states, but without rollback, that could work. They'd need to rollback manually if needed, but if what they really want is accountability that might be enough."

Mark agrees, "I basically told them that an audit-trial is all they should need. I'll chat with them again, but for now assume that that's the plan."

Mark asks Teri to look into editor options. She says she knows of two off hand and says she'll email him the names and URLs. Sam offers to write a better one (without ever having seen the product Teri is referring to). Mark tells him that it is time to go home.

The group chats for a few more minutes and then disbands.

## The Audit Trail

Vijay gets to work on the audit-trail feature immediately and emails the group several hours later.

Sam creates a new method in `cm.cfc` named `audit()`. It takes the item id (which will obviously be of no use if the operation was a delete), an action, and a name.

**RE: Database schema**

**Email**

**Date:** July 17

**To:** Mark Foster, Al Sharpe, Teri Martin, Sam Carlson

**From:** Vijay Singh

**Subject:** RE: Database schema

Hey folks, the database has changed a bit:

- The audit_actions table contains a list if possible actions to be audited. Actions include page creation and modification, content and category manipulation, and even keyword management.

- The audit_trail table is the actual audit trail; it stores the action, date and time, and who made the change.

I am not storing the actual changes, the amount of data that will need to be stored is ridiculous. If you change an article a dozen times, you'll have more than 25 copies of it. Unless this is absolutely necessary I'd drop it. They'll know who made the change, if someone deletes something they were not supposed to, someone can go yell (or worse), no?

Revised database is attached.

I am going home now. No more changes!

VJ

He also creates a `audit_report()` method which retrieves audit trail information. `audit_report()` takes an optional item id (in which case it will only retrieve activity for that item), and an optional user name (to find all operations performed by a specific user). `audit_report()` returns a standard ColdFusion query.

## An Editor

Teri browses through old email threads and prior project notes and emails Mark:

**Editor options**

**Email**

**Date:** July 17

**To:** Mark Foster

**CC:** Al Sharpe, Sam Carlson, Vijay Singh

**From:** Teri Martin

**Subject:** Editor options

Mark,

Here are two editor options. I've played with both of them and both will do the trick. These might be Windows only solutions, but I don't think that that should be a problem. I have no idea what pricing is, I am sure it is on those sites—and both can be integrated with ColdFusion very easily. Maybe have Dave at EduHealth download demos or look at screenshots online to see what they prefer.

> ActiveEdit—http://www.cfdev.com/
> eWebEditPro—http://www.ektron.com/

Hope this is what you wanted.

Teri

Mark forwards the email to Dave Keyes, and then writes a detailed message to Doc Fisher explaining that his team feels that the audit trail is the better option.

# All Done

Over the next two weeks the team tightens code, tests the app as many ways as possible enlisting the help of in-house QA folks as well as volunteers on the EduHealth side. Experience has taught them that clients seldom use apps as developers would expect them to, and so including the client in any and all testing is imperative.

Mark enlists a tech writer named Julie Powell to document the application for EduHealth. For many organizations, documentation is an after thought, but Mark has found that having an outsider (someone not intimately involved with the application development) write docs often brings issues to light. Doc writers have to put themselves in end users' shoes and are thus an invaluable testing ground for usability. They also tend to find typos, as programmers often can't spell. Julie spends two days getting comfortable with the application, and then pesters Sam, Teri, and Al to get the answers she needs to document the creation. She also makes UI suggestions, which Teri is all too happy to implement.

As the project draws to a close, Mark sends daily updates to Dave Keyes and receives continuous feedback that he shares with the team. Ongoing communication is key, not just within the team, but also with the client. The project has been a relatively smooth one for all, a testament to both parties and their ability to work together.

**instant message**

Documentation should always be considered to be a project deliverable, and should be accounted for (from cost, time, and resource perspectives) as such.

## Delivery

On August 1, a mere month after their initial meeting, XRS delivers the content-management system to EduHealth. The project comes in slightly ahead of schedule, and just under budget too.

# Installation

Sam and Al install the application on the client's server (first removing all traces of prior versions). They test the application one last time while Maria goes over paperwork and shows Doc and Dave the finished documentation.

Doc asks about training, and Maria replies, "We have two trainers on staff; I'll check with Mark to see how much time he thinks we should allow for training and will get back to you." Training can be a great source of supplemental revenue.

It's a good thing they tested the application. The database drivers used on the server are several versions old and do not support the new database being used. Sam debates updating the drivers (and possibly breaking some other application in the process) versus switching to an older version of the database. Neither option is risk free, so after verifying that a good backup exists, Sam updates the drivers. Dave tests the other application, and it seems to run—he tells Sam "hey, if anything breaks I have your cell phone number." Sam promptly turns off his cell phone.

Al and Dave enter several articles together to have initial data so that the application appears usable. First impressions count, and users should be able to see the live (working) application when they first try it out.

Maria puts the signed paperwork in her briefcase and shakes hands with Doc and crew. She'll make another sale to this client in no time.

# Summary

With the experience fresh in his mind, and armed with email threads and stacks of sticky notes, Mark summarizes the application. These notes will be filed away with all project details for future reference:

**Client:** EduHealth, **Rep:** Maria Chavez

**Engagement date:** July 2nd, **Delivery date:** August 1st

**Project lead:** Mark Foster

**Developers:** Sam Carlson, Teri Marin, Vijay Singh, Al Sharpe

EduHealth needed basic content-management—the ability to create and display content in a structured and accessible manner.

XRS built a content-management application using ColdFusion MX. The application is structured in three tiers; a database tier, a content tier, and two presentation tiers (one for the end-user application and one for the administrative interface).

The database tier is Microsoft Access for now, will migrate to SQL Server as soon as EduHealth has budget to buy a license. (Recommended against using a shared file based database on production servers).

Content-management system itself is a single CFC. It exposes several important data types:

- **Site.** A site is an entire application, right now only one site is present but the system can support an unlimited number of sites (which would operate independently from each other)
- **Page.** A page is a definition of what content is to be displayed in any given page (it is not a finished page with formatting), pages contain one or more sections (categories)
- **Category.** A logical (and very open-ended) grouping of content, content is placed into categories so that they may appear in the correct pages, as well as for access control and formatting (a formatting style may be applied to a category)
- **Content.** Actual article made up of a header and a body

The system is multi-lingual, it will not translate text automatically, but it will return localized content if possible. A default language is defined for each site, and if no localized content is available then the default version will be presented.

Keyword searching is supported in all languages. Keywords are defined per language per site and then are associated with content (relative to the language used). No full-text searching at this time. Maybe use integrated Verity K2 for this if needed at a later date.

Content is returned for pages based on category and date ranges. For greater control (essentially to eliminate specific items from retrieval) rules may be specified. Rules are ColdFusion user-defined functions and must be registered in the database. Once registered they may be assigned to categories or articles. If assigned to both, articles rule takes precedence.

Audit trail logs all activity. Rollback is not supported.

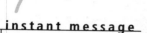

**instant message**

▶ Web Services, such as Alta Vista's Babel Fish, can indeed translate text in real-time, and can be integrated into ColdFusion MX applications very easily.

## Postmortem

Next day the team meets for a postmortem wrap-up. They have a meeting like this after every product delivery, and usually as soon after delivery as possible. J.P. drops in and congratulates the team on a job well done and tells them to relax for a day or two. "I have several new projects lined up for you already."

Mark shuts the door, and the meeting begins.

MEETING NOTES

**Date:** August 2nd

**Present:** Mark Foster, Project Lead

Sam Carlson, Developer

Teri Marin, Developer

Vijay Singh, Database Administrator

Al Sharpe, Intern

Mark is pleased that three back-to-back ColdFusion MX projects have gone so smoothly.

Mark summarizes the application (reading from the notes which he circulates). The others chiming in with details as needed, and Mark scribbles updates on his copy.

Mark then lists some of his concerns:

- Design work is not professional enough, great coding, poor UI, need to involve design people early on
- Need to find a way to better educate clients up front so as to not have to make last-minute changes

Anyone else?

Sam points out that ColdFusion MX is Java based and provides access to Java-based applications. Suggests looking into Java-based add-ons for future projects.

Teri would like to be able to sit with the client and mock-up usable interfaces without having to code back ends. Will look into whether Dreamweaver MX and its support for server behaviors can help with this.

Al is concerned about Sam's rules engine, thinks it is too likely to break. Sam calls Al a name that is better off not listed in these minutes. Mark agrees (with Al, not with Sam's name calling), likes the idea, thinks the implementation needs to be more robust. What if a validation rule has an error in it? What if rules.cfm file is deleted accidentally? Sam says he can make more robust.

Teri points out that the administration application is essentially a bunch of forms and menus. Maybe a candidate for rewriting in Flash? She has tinkered with Flash MX and Flash Remoting and says the integration would be clean and quite easy. Flash MX has included form controls that can be used in forms. Mark asks her to experiment with Flash forms and to report back to the entire development organization.

Al thinks there should be a report that lists all content and which languages are present (or which are not). Also wants a "translation page" which shows content and has space for translation. Mark says should have been in there right now as a feature.

Al won't be around after next week, back to school. Mark tells him to
stay in touch and to email him when he gives up on academia in
search of real work.
Mark asks the group to email him with suggestions of what they'd
like to change in version 2 if given the chance.
Meeting adjourned.

## Where to Go From Here

Mark compiles the emails he receives from the group.

- Replace data entry forms with real editors. Consider using ActiveEdit or eWebEditPro, or maybe write something in Flash.

- Need an integrated spell checker. There are a couple that support ColdFusion.

- Redo all forms in Flash MX.

- Modify audit trail so that it does indeed keep all data (before and after state). One simple way to do this is to add a third table named audit_ details and create a one-to-many relationship back to audit_trail. For add or delete operations a single record is added to audit_details, for updates two records are added (a before and an after state).

- Allow for embedding of formatting codes in the format [I]text[/I] and [A=url]text[/A]. The GetPage() method would need to trap these and replace them with their respective HTML commands. A single CFML ReplaceList() function could do this.

- The rule-processing engine is a great start, but when databases entries are dependent on external files, and runtime execution is dependent on both, things can go wrong. Try/catch handling will make this much safer.

■ All output is now HTML, but with the tiering of presentation and content it would be quite easy to create alternative presentation layers. Might want to create a Flash front end, as well as a front end for devices (perhaps WAP).

■ Look into third-part products that could render content into PDF format for printing.

■ Right now content exists forever. As databases become larger it may be beneficial to move older content into archive table. These tables can have the same format as the content tables, and content could be moved to them based on age (how long since creation date). There would need to be a way to search or list archive data, as well as methods to explicitly archive (or unarchive) items.

■ Users should be able to save formatting preferences; this should be saved to disk and then used when content is rendered.

Mark sends copies of the documents to his team and to J.P. He also sends this last document to Dave Keyes at EduHealth—he'd like to see Dave try to implement some of these features himself.

The following week J.P. hands the team members token bonuses, and expresses his thanks and yet another job well done.

## To the Reader

The content-management system created for EduHealth is based on a real application that solves the needs defined back in Chapter 1. About 1000 lines of CFML code accomplishes a significant portion of what many packaged content-management systems do (packages costing many thousands of dollars). And as the code is all commented CFML (essentially a single CFC) you'll be able to customize it as you see fit.

For simplicity's sake, the UIs (both the administrative and end-user interfaces) are simple HTML only. This will allow you to create your own front-ends to this system, modeled on what was created here. The core content-management system, however, is both powerful and robust, and you are encouraged to create whatever interfaces suit you best.

# Part II

# Personal Information Management

Personal Information Management (PIM) provides access to email, directory services, and other corporate back ends.

# Product Requirements

## Client Overview

FarSight Ltd., based in England, is a company struggling to survive in an increasingly competitive market. FarSight provides software development, consulting, and training services for a range of financial software from companies such as Sage, Epicor, Microsoft, and SoftLine. FarSight has 32 employees in London, 10 in Birmingham, and 8 in Leeds. The London office is the center of operations, with the Birmingham and Leeds offices providing bases for training and consulting services. The company is divided into six departments: consulting, software development, training, IT administration, sales, and marketing.

The majority of the company revenue comes from on-site consulting on the installation and use of financial software. The company uses these on-site visits as opportunities to sell further consulting as well as training and software-development services.

As the economy weakened in mid- to late 2001, FarSight was forced to increase the number of small projects in its portfolio in order to stay profitable. During the first half of 2002, it undertook a program of cross-training staff to enable them to work in at least two of the company's departments.

## Project Overview

Philip Green, the managing director, founded FarSight in 1992, after completing a degree in economics and business at the University of Reading. He is strong-willed and committed to providing the highest possible level of customer service. In recent months he has felt a growing unease with the quality of service his company has been offering. On several occasions employees were scheduled to be simultaneously providing on-site consulting with one client, while developing custom software extensions for another. As a result, one of the clients is disappointed. Philip suspects that a major cause of this dip in quality is FarSight's strategy of cross-training, as it has increased employees' difficulty in communicating internally what each person should be doing on a given day. The company uses Microsoft Exchange Server 5.5 for email and scheduling; unfortunately, the scheduling information is not available outside the London office. The idea of cross-training the staff has been a contentious one with the staff, so Philip needs a solution that appeals to them as much as it benefits the balance sheet. He is unsure about the best way to tackle this problem and calls a board meeting to discuss it.

MEETING NOTES

**Present:** Philip Green, managing director
John White, marketing director
Brian Jones, IT director
Richard Smith, sales director
Sue Miller, finance director

**Purpose of meeting:** To determine the cause of and possible solutions to the problem of communication and scheduling.

**PG:** Outlines several occasions where clients have had consulting, training, or software delivery postponed at short notice. Believes this is caused in part by the cross-training program. Emphasizes that it is important to find a solution that the workforce is happy with.

**BJ:** Confirms the difficulty in coordinating operations between the offices, and mentions the lack of a system to communicate with consultants who are on-site for several days or weeks at a time.

**PG:** Asks how this communication is currently done.

**BJ:** Says that it is a combination of email and telephone, but often one of these is not available to on-site employees. Also, consultants who want to add something to their schedule have to call the office and ask a colleague to log in and change it on their behalf. This is not a good situation from a security or reliability point of view.

**RS:** Mentions that the sales department has no simple way to make sure that a consultant or trainer really is available based on the Exchange server calendar.

**PG:** Asks if this is a problem of enforcing the use of the system, or if the system itself is at fault.

**BJ:** Suggests that it is probably a combination of both. Consultants can't use the system when they are outside the London office, so they are not in the habit of using it when they're in the office. Also notes that some have complained about having to reconfigure their laptops for email depending on whether they are inside or outside the main office. This is much more of a problem for the Birmingham and Leeds offices, which do not have direct access to the calendar and have to rely on having the information emailed to them.

**PG:** Suggests that the real problem is the inability to access the Exchange Server calendar information outside the office.

**SM:** Mentions that the process of collating all the information for billing purposes is very labor intensive and prone to errors, as the Exchange Server calendar doesn't necessarily reflect the work that has actually been done.

**BJ:** Confirms that work is done without being entered into the Exchange server calendar.

**PG:** Asks BJ for clarification on why this is the case.

**BJ:** Says that consultants are regularly out of the London office for more than two weeks at a time. During this time, schedules may change several times as sales are closed. Often salespeople will call consultants directly to confirm their availability, and the consultants will keep a personal diary of where they are supposed to be because they can't access the internal system. In addition to this, the consultants who are on-site don't have a way to book training or software-development resources until they're back in the office. Adds that Birmingham and Leeds are "a law unto themselves," having no way to directly interact with the London server.

**PG:** Requests confirmation from RS.

**RS:** Affirms what BJ said.

**PG:** Asks BJ if it is possible make the Exchange Server information available externally.

**BJ:** Says that while it is possible to do that, it probably won't solve some of the problems such as those mentioned by SM for collating information, and that there is no simple way to manage projects through Exchange Server.

**PG:** Asks what the possible alternatives may be.

**BJ:** Says that he is not sufficiently well informed to recommend alternatives.

**PG:** Suggests that BJ investigate possible solutions and that other board members poll their departments for more feedback and suggestions on the problem. Arranges a meeting for same time next week and names the project "Information Management."

During the week Brian speaks to the trainers, consultants, and software engineers for their input. The consensus is that commercial project-management and scheduling systems are either too expensive or not flexible enough to serve their needs.

## Initial Requirements

At the follow-up board meeting, Brian communicates this to the rest of the board members. They each add their departmental feedback, which reinforces the opinions of the technical staff, and the decision is made to commission a custom system to suit the company needs. An initial list of requirements is drawn up.

- Everyone must be able to send and receive email from a Web browser.

- All scheduling information should be visible to all employees.

- Scheduling information can be edited by the employee or by a manager.

- Employee names can be added and removed as needed.

- Employees can be assigned rights and permissions.

- Simple project information can be added or edited.

- Schedule items should be attached to a project.

- Exchange Server tasks should be automatically added to the schedule.

- All parts of the system must be available through a Web browser.

Everyone agrees it would be best to have this system built in such a way that it can be extended and further developed internally. Experience from their own software development has taught FarSight that the requirements for software are not normally understood completely until the system is in place and in daily use. Brian will investigate the cost and delivery time for the system.

Brian calls a meeting of the managers in the IT department to discuss the requirements and who should be responsible for the project.

MEETING NOTES

**Present:** Brian Jackson, IT director

Alison Grimes, consulting manager

Jim Forsyth, software development manager

Bob Wiles, training manager

**Purpose of meeting:** To determine the requirements and development process for the Information Management project.

**BJ:** Introduces the Information Management project. Provides a slightly more detailed list of requirements he has created from the initial list:

- Must be accessible to staff in Birmingham and Leeds offices and to staff who are working at client sites.
- Must provide project-management facility.
- Must allow staff to modify each other's schedules.
- Must allow for reading and sending email.
- Must allow for scheduled activities to be assigned to a particular project.
- Must allow for scheduled activities to be assigned to a particular location. This may be extended in the future to allow for travel requirements and expenses to be calculated.
- Must integrate with the current Exchange Server calendar system so that existing London office practices can be maintained where necessary.
- Must provide a system to determine who is permitted to add projects, locations, users, and schedule entries for others.
- Must provide a mechanism to email staff members when their schedule has been updated, and to allow them to accept or reject the schedule request.
- Must force the user to accept or reject any pending schedule requests before performing any other action.
- Should be extendable by software-engineering department.

**JF:** There's a lot of latitude for interpretation in those requirements.

**BJ:** Thanks, Jim—I'm hoping that this meeting will cast some of them in stone. Where do you see ambiguity?

**JF:** Well, I suppose we should start with the first point. What do you mean by "accessible"? Are you thinking of opening up our firewall, or installing the Microsoft Outlook Web interface?

**BJ:** Neither, actually. I was thinking of having a Web site built.

**JF:** Built internally or externally?

**BJ:** I was thinking externally, unless you think we have the resources in-house.

**JF:** I'm not sure if we have the internal resources to build something like that. I'm also unsure about the last bullet point. What sort of technology were you planning to use?

**BJ:** No decisions on that just yet, Jim. I was hoping you could suggest a good technology. Personally, I feel that if we have something that we can maintain internally, it's going to work out cheaper in the long run.

**JF:** OK, well, a couple of the guys have played around with some Web-development stuff, but I don't think they've put much time into it. I'll ask them what they think.

**AG:** Should this system be accessible only to staff, or should clients be able to access it to request services?

**BJ:** Good question. I'd say we should probably consider adding that ourselves at a later stage unless it's a real pressing need right now.

**AG:** Yes, that makes sense.

**BJ:** Do we have any ideas on what might be a good way to build this, or do we need to wait until Jim comes back with feedback from the software engineers?

**JF:** Well, based on what I know about the technologies currently in use, I'd say that we're probably best using a fairly simple scripting language like PHP, ASP, or Macromedia ColdFusion.

> **BJ:** OK, this is Tuesday; shall we reconvene at the same time next week? Jim, does that give you enough time to get the information you need?
>
> **JF:** Yes, that should be fine.
>
> **BJ:** I think it's best that you look after this project, Jim, since software development is your area.
>
> **JF:** Sounds sensible to me.
>
> **Action point:**
>
> JF to research appropriate technologies for system.

Jim spends several hours over the next few days discussing the project with FarSight's software developers and comes to the conclusion that they don't have enough experience to develop the system in-house. Based on the feedback he gets from Phil Potts, however, he decides to go with ColdFusion because Phil has been playing around with it for the last couple of years and insists that anyone could learn it. Jim is skeptical, but in the absence of more informed advice, it seems as good a choice as any other. Phil has a friend named Ben Richards who works for Q42, a Web development company. He passes his contact information to Jim.

Ben replies to Jim the same day, saying he has been building Web sites with ColdFusion for the past four years and could easily handle the job. They set up a meeting for the next day at 1:30 p.m., at FarSight's offices. Jim invites Phil along to the meeting, as he will be the developer responsible for extending the delivered application.

The meeting is generally successful, but Ben is unsure if it would be possible to get calendar information from Exchange Server into the Cold-Fusion server.

A follow-up meeting is scheduled for next Thursday, to discuss work so far on the project and a delivery schedule.

---

**Seeking Web development services**

**Email**

---

**Date:** May 30

**To:** Ben Richards

**From:** Jim Forsyth

**Subject:** Seeking Web development services

Ben,

I work with your friend Phil Potts at FarSight Ltd., and would like to talk to you about Web site development work using ColdFusion. Phil tells me your company has some experience with ColdFusion. If that's true, we could use your help.

In a nutshell, we need a system that allows us to manage day-to-day information in the company through a Web browser. We do a lot of on-site consulting and need our consultants to be able to update their schedules, collect email, and so on, when they are at home or on-site with a client.

If this sounds like something your company would be interested in, I'd like to schedule a time to meet with you next week.

Jim

Below are Ben Richards's notes from the meeting.

## MEETING NOTES

**Present:** Brian Jackson, IT director; Alison Grimes, consulting manager; Jim Forsyth, software development manager; Bob Wiles, training manager

**Purpose of meeting:** To fine-tune application requirements

### Accessibility

- Must be accessible from Birmingham and Leeds offices.
- Must be accessible from client sites and from home so that employees who have been on site during the day can get access
- All areas of application must be available from all locations.

### Projects

- A project consists of client, owner, description, due date, downloadable documents, emails, task schedule, and notes.
- It should be possible to add new projects to the system.
- It should be possible to edit project details such as due date and project name.
- It should be possible to add notes to a project to keep track of information gathered from telephone conversations, meetings, and client visits.
- It should be possible to upload documents that are related to a project. These documents should be downloadable by project members.
- It should be possible to mark emails as belonging to a project.

### Scheduled Tasks

- All users can edit their own schedule.
- Some users can edit anyone's schedule.
- Users cannot remove schedule items added by managers.
- Users must give a reason if they reject a task.
- Pending tasks must be accepted or rejected before the designated user can perform any other action in the system.

- Accept or reject notifications must be emailed to the user who added them.
- Tasks must be marked as completed or postponed when the due date has passed.
- Users must give a reason when they postpone a task.
- Postponed task information must be emailed in the same way as accept and reject notifications.
- Tasks must be assigned to a location and a project.
- Tasks must have a due date.

**Email**
- Attachments must be sent and received through a Web browser.
- A copy of all sent messages should be kept in the system for future reference.
- It should be possible to completely delete messages from the system.

**Rights and Permissions**
- Must be able to assign users to groups.
- Must be able to assign permissions to groups.
- Not sure what the groups should be, but three or four should be sufficient.

**Locations**
- Location consists of address, name, and telephone number.
- Location information will be extended in the future to simplify determination of expenses and travel requirements.

**Exchange Server**
- Need as much integration as possible with current server.
- Each employee should be able to access their own calendaring and task information from the Exchange server. Maybe use LDAP for user authentication.
- The email addresses, names, and other details for employees should be retrieved from the Exchange server rather than being entered to the database manually through a Web form.

**Future Extensions**
- Code must be clearly commented and as modular as possible.
- Might need support contract for code maintenance.

When Ben reviews the requirements for the application, the majority of them do not appear to present many difficulties. He is a little concerned about the level of integration that FarSight would like to have with their Exchange Server. He tells them that he cannot guarantee that it will be possible to get task and calendar information for individuals, but that he will make sure that Q42 make every effort to deliver what has been asked. He leaves the FarSight offices with a positive feeling about the new project and the ability of Q42 to deliver it.

# Initial Thoughts

When Ben Richards returns to the Q42 office after his meeting with Far-Sight, he sits down with Tom Green and Dave Phipps to discuss the project and come up with a strategy for producing the application which they have decided to call the Personal Information Management application, or PIM.

Tom is the embodiment of the absentminded professor. Without a doubt he is the creative genius at Q42, but this creativity comes at a price. His ability to interact with the world is, in modest terms, lacking in finesse. He regularly works 24 hours without a break and has some idiosyncrasies that are best left to the imagination. His knowledge is treated with tremendous respect by the other employees, but he tends to be kept away from client situations.

Dave is the organizational force at Q42. He is methodical in his approach to everything. Without Dave, the company would quickly degenerate from its current state of controlled chaos to the business equivalent of Brownian motion. His main strength is in his structured approach to design and coding practices, but he has been known to lament, "Enforcing a coding standard on Tom is a bit like trying to nail jelly to the wall: Before you know what happened. he's gone around it."

Fortunately, Dave has a calm and patient nature that allows him to remain rational in the midst of the chaos that inevitably accompanies Tom.

Ben acts as the Q42 sales team. Although his manner sometimes borders on the abrupt or even rude, he prides himself on the fact that he has never lost a client, no matter what the adversity. He has a sharp eye for the sort of details in a product that appeal to potential clients and, in addition to his sales skills, he is a reliable Macromedia ColdFusion developer who thinks nothing of spending half a day getting the alignment of all the elements on a page just right.

# Task List

After looking over the initial requirements, Dave suggests that they draw up a list of tasks for the project so they can see more clearly how long it will take to build the application. After a brief diversion from Tom about the potential problem of trying to get individual task list information from Microsoft Exchange Server across a network, they come up with the following task list.

1. Project requirements

2. Project diagrams (on paper)

3. Log-in mechanism

4. Email retrieval and storage

5. Task and calendar retrieval and storage

6. ColdFusion MX architecture diagram

7. Database schema

8. User-interface (UI) diagrams

9. Fireworks representation of UI

10. HTML representation of UI

11. Initial ColdFusion UI

12. Application logic

13. Initial deployment and testing

14. Final deployment and commissioning

## Project Requirements

Tom and Dave decide that the project requirements that Ben typed up on his laptop at the meeting with FarSight provide sufficient information at this stage. They will use them as a reference point to answer questions as they move forward with the project diagrams. Questions that are not addressed by the initial requirements will be relayed to Jim Forsyth, the software development manager at FarSight, by email.

## Project Diagrams

The reason for sketching diagrams on paper is that Q42—or Dave Phipps, to be precise—finds that it is much easier to turn thoughts into pictures that way. It tends to be much more efficient than drawing from a typical graphics package. On paper you don't get bogged down with thoughts such as "should I move that icon a bit farther to the left," or "should this piece of text be above or below the line." And once something is on paper, there is little you can do to affect the way it looks. Sketching on paper also tends to keep the focus on the problem at hand. As Dave knows from experience, this is important when you have colleagues whose brains resemble a popcorn machine in full flow.

The initial diagrams are used as a graphical representation of the project requirements. The diagrams aren't used as templates for building the application; rather, they are snapshots of initial thoughts that will be expanded on and changed as the project progresses. Often created in minutes, the sketches may raise questions that aren't adequately answered in the written specifications. The diagrams don't have a fixed structure, but they normally consist of several UI diagrams, a database schema, a ColdFusion MX architecture diagram, and a number of project-specific diagrams that illustrate unclear, complex, or important parts of the requirements.

The sketch diagrams that follow are the results of the first meeting, attended by Dave, Tom, and Ben. Each diagram is accompanied by an explanation of some of the thoughts that went into producing them.

## Log-in Mechanism

The main discussion about the log-in mechanism centers around which system should be used to perform the authentication. Most applications Q42 has built use a relational database with user names and passwords in a table. In this application, however, the user name and password already exist in the Microsoft Exchange Server, and other parts of the application will need them to retrieve email. Therefore, it appears to make sense to use Lightweight Directory Access Protocol (LDAP) to perform authentication directly on the Exchange Server itself (see Figure II-2.1).

The main reason for authenticating directly against the Exchange Server is that the user name and password for the application would have to correspond to the ones for the email account on the server so that email could be retrieved. Although it would be possible to copy the user name and password to a relational database and authenticate against the copied values, they would have to be updated somehow if they were ever changed on the Exchange Server. The only way for that update mechanism to be absolutely fail-safe would be if failed database logins were also tested against the Exchange Server at the time when they failed. Since it would be necessary to build a system that authenticated against the Exchange Server for failed logins, it made sense to skip the relational database login completely.

The downside of this approach is that if FarSight decides to create a secured area for its clients in the future, it will have to create either new accounts on the Exchange Server for the clients or a separate log-in mechanism. Also, there will probably be a requirement to store information about employees that will not exist in the Exchange Server. For now, everyone decides that authentication will be performed against the Exchange Server and that, when necessary, extra information about the user will be stored in a relational database.

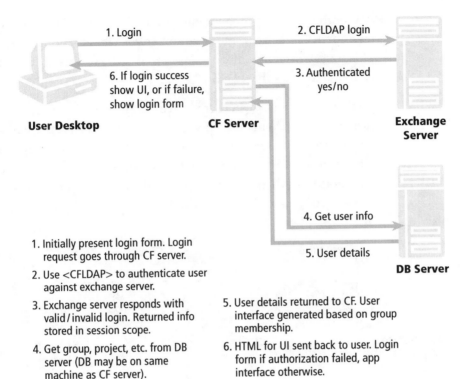

1. Login

2. CFLDAP login

6. If login success
show UI, or if failure,
show login form

3. Authenticated
yes/no

**User Desktop**

**CF Server**

**Exchange Server**

4. Get user info

5. User details

**DB Server**

1. Initially present login form. Login request goes through CF server.

2. Use <CFLDAP> to authenticate user against exchange server.

3. Exchange server responds with valid/invalid login. Returned info stored in session scope.

4. Get group, project, etc. from DB server (DB may be on same machine as CF server).

5. User details returned to CF. User interface generated based on group membership.

6. HTML for UI sent back to user. Login form if authorization failed, app interface otherwise.

**Figure II-2.1**
The initial sketch diagram for the login system.

The possibility of using HTTP-basic authentication is considered briefly. Basic authentication is the mechanism whereby a user name and password dialog box pops-up when a user first visits a site. This dialog box is automatically generated by the Web browser if the user has not already been authenticated. In this scheme, authentication is handled by the Web server. Because of the proliferation of automated scripts for attacking this type of system and the public accessibility of the site, the idea was rejected.

## Email Retrieval and Storage

The email requirements for the application are fairly simple. Email retrieval, sending, and deletion using Macromedia's <CFPOP> and <CFMAIL>

are requirements for many applications that Q42 have built. Handling attachments is a little more complicated when sending messages, as uploading an attachment can cause problems, but this problem has been encountered and solved before.

The main question is whether to save a copy of each message in the database, or to leave them on the Exchange Server. Because there is a requirement to assign messages to projects, and the project information would probably be stored in the relational database, everyone agrees that all message information will be saved in the database server, with the attachments stored in a folder on the ColdFusion Server (see Figure II-2.2).

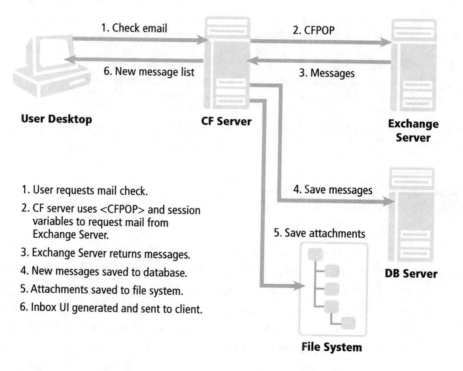

**Figure II-2.2**
The initial sketch diagram for the email retrieval system.

## Task and Calendar Retrieval and Storage

In many respects, this task is the most challenging aspect of the project requirements. Exchange Server, like much software from Microsoft, uses their Component Object Model (COM). COM is a framework which allows different applications to communicate with each other. Each COM application consists of objects and methods, or functions, which can be called for those objects. ColdFusion applications running on Windows can use <CFOBJECT> to create instances of, and communicate with, COM applications. Although COM is only available to ColdFusion applications running on Windows, FarSight had already indicated that all of their servers were running Windows.

In a previous project, Q42 had connected to an Exchange Server by creating an instance of Microsoft Outlook on the ColdFusion server and using the functions the Outlook instance exposed to query information from the Exchange Server. Unfortunately, using that approach, the Outlook instance connects to the Exchange Server using the same user account that the ColdFusion Server uses to log on to the system. Because the Outlook instance is connecting to the Exchange Server using a particular user account, the task and calendar information returned to it from the Exchange Server will be the ones for that account. This effectively means that task and calendar information can be retrieved for only one user, not for each employee.

Some brief research on connecting to the Exchange Server yields the suggestion of using Collaboration Data Objects, but many sources indicate that it isn't terribly reliable, even using it with Visual Basic, and there doesn't appear to be any information on using it with ColdFusion.

In addition, although the team has been developing Web applications for several years, they have no C++ or Java experience, so creating a CFX_Exchange custom tag doesn't look like a simple solution either.

There are also several requirements, such as assigning a location and project to a scheduled task, which would mean having to store task information in the relational database. The more they look at the problem from both usability and programming points of view, the more it seems that the system would best be built with the task information being only read from the Exchange Server rather than being written to it as well (see Figure II-2.3).

## ColdFusion Architecture

Dave has some pretty strong opinions on the ColdFusion architecture. Having spent the last few years watching the company's development methods mature, he decides it's time to push for some more rigidity and modularity in the code they produce.

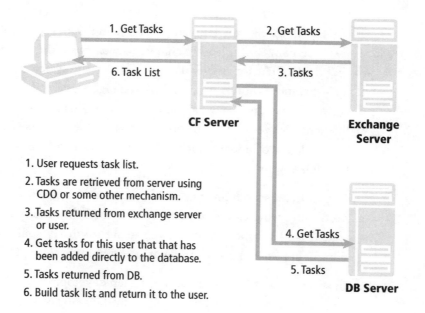

1. Get Tasks
2. Get Tasks
6. Task List
3. Tasks
4. Get Tasks
5. Tasks

**CF Server**

**Exchange Server**

**DB Server**

1. User requests task list.
2. Tasks are retrieved from server using CDO or some other mechanism.
3. Tasks returned from exchange server or user.
4. Get tasks for this user that that has been added directly to the database.
5. Tasks returned from DB.
6. Build task list and return it to the user.

**Figure II-2.3**

Initial sketch diagram for retrieval of tasks from both the Exchange Server and the database.

Dave's idea is to create a set of ColdFusion Components (CFCs) that provide a set of base functions that can be extended and modified as time goes on. Looking back over the last few years, there have been a great variety of user interfaces, but often the database tables have been very similar or identical from project to project.

Two components come to mind immediately: User.cfc and Email.cfc. These components would contain generic functions such as `getMail()`, `addUser()`, and `changePassword()`. The idea is that what happens in the user interface is separate from how the requests from the user interface are handled in the ColdFusion code. In an ideal world this would mean that the CFCs could be reused in many projects with little or no modification, and that the user interface for the manager could stay the same regardless of whether the user component is interoperating with an LDAP server, a relational database, or any other system such as a Web Service. So long as the input and output for the functions stay the same, either the user interface that calls them or the CFC that defines them could be changed independently of each other. Dave thinks of these components as resource services, so User.cfc would be seen as the user resource service.

This is not new as a programming concept, but it would be a big step for Q42. Although each developer has his or her own library of useful custom tags and code snippets, far too often they are rewritten almost from scratch to meet the requirements of a particular project.

Tom suggests that in order to make the functions in these components available to the user interface, they should be loaded in Application.cfm using the `createObject()` function. That way, someone looking at the application could immediately see what services were available by looking in just one file, rather than combing through line after line of code. He also suggests that for each action that can be performed in the user interface, there should be a corresponding "include" file to hold all the logic required to perform that action. The Compose button in the email area would cause a value of Compose to be passed in a URL variable called action to the Index.cfm in that area. This Index.cfm would check if there was a file called Compose.cfm in the current directory and, if so, include it using cfinclude (see Figure II-2.4).

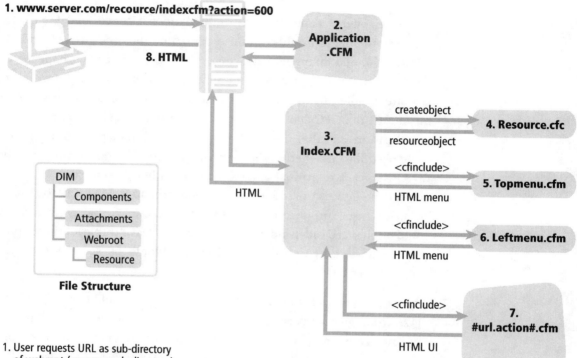

1. www.server.com/recource/indexcfm?action=600

8. HTML

DIM
— Components
— Attachments
— Webroot
  └── Resource

**File Structure**

2.
**Application**
**.CFM**

createobject
resourceobject

3.
**Index.CFM**

HTML

<cfinclude>
HTML menu

<cfinclude>
HTML menu

<cfinclude>

HTML UI

**4. Resource.cfc**

**5. Topmenu.cfm**

**6. Leftmenu.cfm**

7.
**#url.action#.cfm**

1. User requests URL as sub-directory of webroot (resource sub-directory). Action for resource as URL variable(s).

2. Application.CFM sets up application and session scopes. Performs login check. Initiates application variables in request scope.

3. Index.cfm is called in resource directory.

4. CFC for this resource is created as an object. This makes calling functions of the component much cleaner.

5. Topmenu.cfm generates menu based on group membership of current user.

6. Leftmenu.cfm builds menu for this resource for this user based on group membership.

7. Dynamic include for the '.cfm' file corresponding to the action on the URL.

Figure II-2.4
Initial sketch diagram for the ColdFusion architecture.

The parts of the UI that would be repeated many times in the application, such as the menus, could be implemented as either custom tags or globally available include files. Each resource or service would have its own directory inside the webroot. This should improve the modularity of the UI elements for each of the components. Again, ideally it should be possible to copy the complete directory to a new application and have it working quickly.

This approach offers flexibility and extendability. If new functionality is required in the future, a menu item can be added, a new include file created, and the necessary functions added to the existing resource components (or a new resource component created).

## Database Schema

Again, it's Dave who creates most of the database schema. Starting from the Schedule table, which appears to be the core of the application, he adds other tables to allow the schedule to work according to the project requirements (see Figure II-2.5). In this application, projects are closely related to the schedule, as each scheduled task is associated with a project. Projects are also tightly linked to the email system, such that email can be assigned to a project. Tom feels that the close interrelationships between the email, projects, and schedule areas of the system could cause complexity when it comes to implementation, but everyone agrees this can be handled when the time comes to write the code.

As the process of designing this database continues, it becomes apparent to Tom that the project management and scheduling aspects of the application could be useful as a PIM tool for Q42. As a result, they decide to invest a little time adding some information to the database to make it easier to use the application for their own projects.

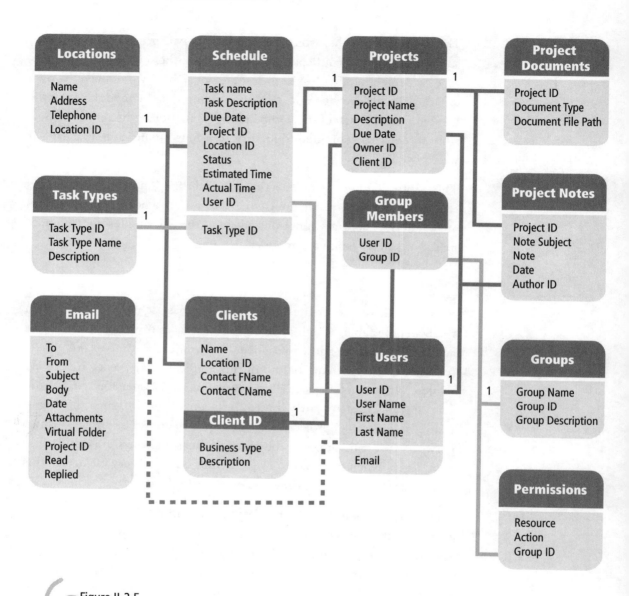

**Locations**

Name
Address
Telephone
Location ID

**Task Types**

Task Type ID
Task Type Name
Description

**Email**

To
From
Subject
Body
Date
Attachments
Virtual Folder
Project ID
Read
Replied

**Schedule**

Task name
Task Description
Due Date
Project ID
Location ID
Status
Estimated Time
Actual Time
User ID

Task Type ID

**Clients**

Name
Location ID
Contact FName
Contact CName

**Client ID**

Business Type
Description

**Projects**

Project ID
Project Name
Description
Due Date
Owner ID
Client ID

**Group Members**

User ID
Group ID

**Users**

User ID
User Name
First Name
Last Name

Email

**Project Documents**

Project ID
Document Type
Document File Path

**Project Notes**

Project ID
Note Subject
Note
Date
Author ID

**Groups**

Group Name
Group ID
Group Description

**Permissions**

Resource
Action
Group ID

Figure II-2.5
Initial sketch diagram of the database schema.

In order to produce estimates of development times for an entire project, the team wants to include the ability to add an estimated time for each task when it is created, and an actual time once it is completed. This would allow Q42 to see how accurate their estimations have been in the past and help them to be more accurate in the future. It would also let them calculate the total number of hours required to complete a given project, and the amount of time each person spent on each project. This information is currently requested by email at the end of each week, which results in notoriously unreliable estimates. The new approach would also allow Q42 to assign a list of tasks to each employee, something that several people requested so they could approach each day with a little more purpose.

Dave, Tom, and Ben also feel that in addition to the project documents required by FarSight, it would be useful for both companies to have a feature that lets any project member add notes to a project. In conjunction with the project documents and the assignment of email and tasks to projects, this should allow for the creation of a unified repository of all project information.

Q42 has a fairly well-established method for creating a security model. Each user is assigned to a group, and each group is given permission to access a resource. Permissions are additive: If a user is a member of two groups, only one of those groups needs to have permission to perform an action. This is implemented as four tables in the database:

- Users

- Groups

- GroupMembers

- Permissions

As a result of the ColdFusion architecture that Q42 has designed, each row in the Permissions table will have an entry in the Action column that corresponds to an include file in the resource directory. A serious benefit of this architecture is that there is a fairly high degree of security, as the

Index.cfm file in each resource directory can dynamically check that the current user is permitted to call a given action prior to including the action template itself. The mechanism for hiding the links and buttons in the UI is slightly more labor intensive, but this may be made easier by creating a security component that exposes a `checkPermissions()` function. The structure of the Email table has also been used in previous projects. The filenames of the attachments for an email are stored in the database, and the files themselves are stored in a directory on the ColdFusion server. The Virtual Folders column is just a text entry that allows for the simple creation of predefined folders (or free text folder names, depending on the UI requirements).

The Task Types table performs the same function as the Virtual Folders column in the Email table. The difference is that the former provides a description for each of the possible task types that can be added to the system.

The Clients table is added to the diagram to address a requirement that FarSight might want to add at some stage later in the project.

## UI Diagrams

The initial thoughts for the layout are to keep it simple. The main navigation at the top of the page would reflect the main resource components or sections for the application. On the left side would be a dynamically generated navigation menu that wouldn't display any actions that the current user couldn't perform in that section. Below this left-hand navigation would be any further contextual navigation, typically consisting of lists such as projects or email folders (see Figure II-2.6). The main UI content would be generated by the include file for the action that is requested.

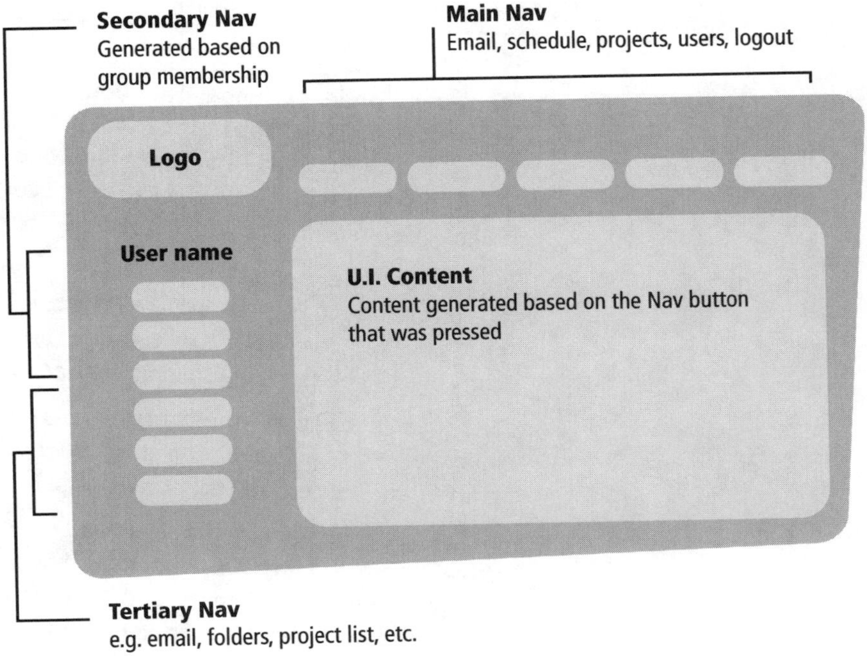

**Figure II-2.6**
Initial sketch diagram for
the layout of the user
interface.

On Monday, June 3, Ben sends the following email to Jim Forsyth at
FarSight in the U.K.:

**A few questions**

**Email**

**Date:** June 3

**To:** Jim Forsyth

**From:** Ben Richards

**Subject:** A few questions

Hi Jim,

I've gone over the project requirements with some
colleagues at the office, and we've come up with a
few questions.

We definitely need to use a database for this
system, and if you already have one, it would make
sense to try to use it.

1. Do you have a relational database system in
place already? If so, what system do you use?

## A few questions

### Email continued)

2. We were wondering how far you want to go with the security of the application. We can pretty easily keep a log of failed log-ins, and since this will be a publicly available site, we thought it might be useful to do that. What do you think?

3. Again on the security front, do you want us to put something in place that will stop a particular computer or user from logging in if they get their log-in incorrect too many times?

4. This is really a question for the UI. Do you want to put a limit on the number of attachments that can be added to a message?

5. We're planning to store email messages in the database so that we can tie them in with the project system. There are several options for what happens to the email on the Exchange Server after we have retrieved them:

   a. They get deleted as soon as they are put in the database.

   b. They get deleted when they are deleted from the database.

   c. The Web system never deletes mail from the Exchange Server.

   Which of these options is best for you?

6. How important is it that tasks and calendar information be synchronized from the Exchange Server? We've done some quick research, and one of the guys here who has done some work with this sort of thing says that it is extremely tricky to get reliable communication for the reading and adding of task and calendar information to and from Exchange. The best option we've seen so far is to use third-party software to read the information from the Exchange Server on a regular basis. Unfortunately, it doesn't allow us to write anything back there.

**A few questions**

**Email continued)**

7. We noticed that client information wasn't mentioned in the requirements and thought that it would probably come up in conversations further down the line. Do you want to store any information about your clients?

Ben Richards
Project Manager
Q42

That afternoon Ben receives a reply from Jim:

**RE: A few questions**

**Email**

**Date:** 3 June

**To:** Ben Richards

**From:** Jim Forsyth

**Subject:** RE: A few questions

Hi Ben,

Thanks for the prompt follow-up to our meeting.

Answers inline below...

—Original Message—

**Date:** 3 June

**To:** Jim Forsyth

**From:** Ben Richards

**Subject:** A few questions

Hi Jim,

I've gone over the project requirements with some colleagues at the office, and we've come up with a few questions. We definitely need to use a database for this system, and if you already have one, it would make sense to try to use it.

1. Do you have a relational database system in place already? If so, what system do you use?

## RE: A few questions

### Email (continued)

**Answer:** We currently work with both Microsoft Access and Microsoft SQL Server. Either is fine for us, but I would prefer to use SQL Server for something like this.

2. We were wondering how far you want to go with the security of the application. We can pretty easily keep a log of failed log-ins, and since this will be a publicly available site, we thought it might be useful to do that. What do you think?

**Answer:** That sounds like a good idea. Could you also provide a warning on the log-in page to that effect? Ideally, it would deter unauthorized users without worrying our employees.

3. Again, on the security front, do you want us to put something in place that will stop a particular computer or user from logging in if they get their log-in incorrect too many times?

**Answer:** I don't think that will be necessary. The last thing we want is to have people onsite who can't log into the system because they slipped up a few times.

4. This is really a question for the UI. Do you want to put a limit on the number of attachments that can be added to a message?

**Answer:** I'm not sure about that. In general messages tend not to have more than three or four attachments, and it's very rare that there would be more than six. Having said that, it's probably more important that the attachments can be sent than that the interface is pretty, so no limit is probably the best way to go.

---
**RE: A few questions**

---
**Email (continued)**

---

5. We're planning to store email messages in the database so that we can tie them in with the project system. There are several options for what happens to the email on the Exchange Server after we have retrieved them:

    a. They get deleted as soon as they are put in the database.

    b. They get deleted when they are deleted from the database.

    c. The Web system never deletes mail from the Exchange Server.

    Which of these options is best for you?

    **Answer:** I think it's best if you just leave them on the Exchange Server. People may well want to keep a copy of them on their machines in the office or at home, and they are sometimes onsite for a few weeks at a time.

6. How important is it that tasks and calendar information be synchronized from the Exchange Server? We've done some quick research, and one of the guys here who has done some work with this sort of thing before says that it is extremely tricky to get reliable communication for the reading and adding of task and calendar information to and from Exchange. The best option we've seen so far is to use third-party software to read the information from the Exchange Server on a regular basis. Unfortunately, it doesn't allow us to write anything back there.

    **Answer:** We'd really like to be able to have two-way communication with the Exchange Server if possible. A lot of the staff in the office are accustomed to using Microsoft Outlook for their email and scheduling, and we'd like to let them continue to do that for productivity reasons.

## RE: A few questions

### Email (continued)

7. We noticed that client information wasn't mentioned in the requirements and thought that it would probably come up in conversations further down the line. Do you want to store any information about your clients?

   **Answer:**  At the moment we store all this information in the Exchange Server contacts. It might be useful to get that into the Web interface too, but we don't really need to tie it into anything like projects or scheduling right at the minute.

Ben Richards
Sales Consultant
Q42

After reading the reply from Jim, Ben speaks to David and Tom, and they decide they have enough information to proceed to the next stage of the project.

# Development

Once the application team members feel they have enough information to proceed, they need to decide on the initial tasks for the project. Their usual approach to projects is to create a representation of the user interface (UI) in a graphics program prior to writing any Macromedia ColdFusion code. Once the client agrees to the interface, ColdFusion development begins in earnest. The team decides that since Ben has the strongest skills in creating graphics for a UI, he will be the one to do it.

In the meantime, Tom will research possibilities for interacting with the Microsoft Exchange Server for task and calendar information. Also, since Jim mentioned in his email that FarSight uses the Exchange Server global address book for all client information, Tom will also look into possibilities for retrieving that information. Dave will work on the ColdFusion architecture. This involves deciding on the ColdFusion components (CFCS), custom tags, and detailed file structure for the application. He will also make an initial list of the functions that will be contained in each component. The team agrees to spend the week working on each of these tasks, and to reconvene to evaluate the progress on Friday morning.

# Exchange Server Research

Although Q42 used COM to communicate with Exchange Server in previous projects, Tom wasn't involved in those projects, and the developer who did the bulk of the COM work has since left the company. Tom begins his research by looking into the problem of retrieving task and calendar information for each user from the Exchange Server. He knows that in previous projects the information retrieved from the Exchange Server always corresponded to the user account that the ColdFusion application server service used to log on to the machine. The first question to answer is whether or not it's possible to get around this somehow, and have the Microsoft Outlook instance on the ColdFusion server log on to the Exchange Server using credentials passed to it via ColdFusion code.

MSDN can be accessed at http://msdn.microsoft.com/

Tom's initial searches on the Internet turn up some useful information in the Microsoft Developer Network (MSDN) on the Microsoft Outlook object model. This consists of an Application object that contains an object called `NameSpace`. This `NameSpace` object has, among others, a method called `Logon()`.

The syntax for using the `Logon()` method is as follows:

```
Logon(Profile, Password, ShowDialog, NewSession)
```

Unfortunately, the `Logon()` method accepts a parameter called `profileName` instead of a user name parameter. Some further research reveals that the `profileName` parameter corresponds to a Microsoft mail profile on the machine from which the request is being made.

Still further research reveals that it should be possible to manually create a series of mail profiles on the ColdFusion server, so Tom decides to create a test page that creates an instance of Outlook. This is called the `Logon()` method, and it displays the name corresponding to the profile specified in the `profileName` parameter. From looking at the code that was used on a previous project, he determines that the class name of the object should be `Outlook.Application`. The MSDN Web site provides the rest of the information Tom needs to create the following template:

```
<cfscript>
  // Create the outlook object
  objOutlook = createObject('com','Outlook.Application');
  // Get the namespace property for the Outlook object
 objNamespace = objOutlook.getNameSpace("MAPI");

  // Logon to the namespace using a profile name on this
server
  objNamespace.Logon("Test Profile", "killer", False,
False);

  // Get the session property name for the outlook Object
  objSession = objOutlook.session;

  // Get the username property for the current session
  writeOutput(objSession.currentuser.name);
</cfscript>
```

Regardless of the value passed to the `profileName` parameter of the `Logon()` method, the name displayed on the page always corresponds to the name of the user whose account is being used by the ColdFusion service. Some more searching on the MSDN Web site reveals that it is using the value set in the registry entry:

```
HKEY_CURRENT_USER\Software\Microsoft\Windows NT\
CurrentVersion\Windows Messaging Subsystem\
Profiles\DefaultProfile
```

This registry entry would normally be created when a user logged on to the machine, but in the case of a service like ColdFusion, it would be created when the service was started.

Now that Tom has more clearly established the reason an Outlook instance would always use the account the ColdFusion server uses to log on, he decides that trying to change this behavior is probably not a sensible solution. At best, it would involve using the `<CFREGISTRY>` tag to rewrite the value of the `DefaultProfile` registry key each time a user wanted to do anything with her tasks and calendar information. Even if this call to the registry is carefully locked, there's no guarantee that it would actually work—and certainly no guarantee that it would not cause instability in both the application and the ColdFusion server itself.

Once Tom knows he can't use Outlook to retrieve the information he wants, he decides to look into the options for connecting to the Exchange Server directly from the ColdFusion server. When he briefly looked into the possibility of using Collaboration Data Objects (CDO) at the initial meeting with Ben and Dave on May 31, his initial impression from the pages he read was that it should be possible to access it from ColdFusion. So he decides to look into that option next.

Starting from the same part of the MSDN Web site where he found the Outlook object model, Tom quickly locates the equivalent object model for CDO. Unfortunately, it's not nearly so complete as the Outlook one, but some further browsing soon brings him to the CDO Library reference, where he notices that CDO has a session object with a `Logon()` method. This method accepts a few more parameters than the equivalent method for Outlook:

```
Logon( [profileName] [, profilePassword] [, showDialog]
[, newSession] [, parentWindow] [, NoMail] [,
ProfileInfo] )
```

Although this method also has a `profileName` parameter, the `ProfileInfo` parameter can be used instead, to explicitly pass the server name and mailbox to which the connection should be made. When the `ProfileInfo` parameter is used, a temporary mail profile is created for the lifetime of the session. This looks like an ideal option, so Tom decides to create another ColdFusion template to see if it would work.

From looking at some of the example code on the MSDN Web site, he discovers that the name of the object class to create should be `MAPI.Session`. The documentation for the session object gives him a lot of information on what to create, but he notices that the format of the `ProfileInfo` parameter should be the following:

```
<server name> & vbLf & <mailbox name>
```

The problem is that he really doesn't have a clue what's supposed to go between the server name and the mailbox name. It looks like an abbreviation for Visual Basic line feed, but that's a guess. He decides to try using the line-feed character chr(10) to see what happens. The following code is what he produces:

```
<cfscript>
    profileInfo = 'mail.q42.co.uk' & chr(10) & 'Tom
Green';
    cdoSession = createObject('com','MAPI.Session');
    cdoSession.Logon( 'tgreen', 'killer',false, true , -
1, false, ProfileInfo);
</cfscript>
```

This results in a very obscure COM error:

```
[Collaboration Data Objects--[UNKNOWN_ERROR(80010106)]]
```

He finds a TechNote on the Macromedia Web site (http://www.macro-media.com/v1/handlers/index.cfm?ID=22922&Method=Full&Page-Call=/support/index.cfm) that explains how to create pre-generated Java stubs for COM objects. It mentions that in some cases Microsoft applications cannot be handled without using pre-generated Java stubs. He follows the instructions in the TechNote but gets exactly the same error as before. After carefully following the instructions several times and still getting the same error, he decides that this is probably not going to provide the solution.

After a fruitless search on the Microsoft Web site, Tom finds that several people have encountered the same error, but none of them seem to have discovered the cause or a solution. He does find out that the error message changes to a failed log-on message if he removes the ProfileInfo parameter, so he investigates further exactly what should go between the server name and the mailbox name.

Unfortunately, everything he reads in an extensive search indicates that vbLf is identical to ASCII character 10, which is exactly what he had tried. In addition, he discovers that using CDO remotely can result in some rather unpleasant problems. Several pages referring to using ASP to connect remotely note that if any of the MAPI sessions fail to log out correctly, the Web server has to be restarted before anyone else can log on to the Exchange Server. This is certainly not a desirable scenario, so he decides to abandon the idea of using CDO.

Tom decides to send an email to Dave and Ben to update them on his progress this far.

---

**wrkfsrt!!!! Exchange Server**

**Email**

**Date:** June 3

**To:** Ben Richards; Dave Phipps

**From:** Tom Green

**Subject:** wrkfsrt!!!! Exchange Server

Hi guys,

I've spent 3 days looking at this Exchange Server stuff, and I'm running into brick walls everywhere I turn.

I can't find any way at all to connect to Exchange using CDO. It just keeps firing back a typically uninformative error message. I've looked all over the Web for solutions, but it seems that everyone else with the same problem hasn't found a solution either - well, I only found 2 references to the error I'm getting in Google, so everyone else is really a pretty small group.

Using Outlook isn't really going too much better either. Outlook always uses one of the profiles stored in the Registry when it connects to Exchange, and I can't figure out a way to make it use anything other than the default profile when connecting to it with COM.

I'm going to have a think about it tonight and see if I can come up with anything better, but it's not looking promising.

Tom

His next step is to see if there are any third-party tools that would let him read and write data from the Exchange Server. After a fairly extensive search, he finds a product from a Swedish company called Competent Software. The product, called Exchange DB, allows the extraction of calendar and task information for all Exchange Server users to a Microsoft Access or Microsoft SQL Server database. Although it does not allow for the addition of information to the Exchange Server, it does provide at least some level of communication, so he downloads an evaluation version of the software from the Web site.

The installation is very simple, and the administrative interface is clear. Unfortunately, every attempt to connect to the Exchange Server results in a dialog box stating, "Could not log on to the Exchange Server." A search of the Competent Software Web site does not produce any helpful information on what the problem might be, and neither does a fairly extensive session with Google.

Tom begins to wonder if it's possible to retrieve any of the required information from the Exchange Server. So far nothing he has tried has yielded any results, and he can't find any useful third-party tools that would let him read, let alone write, task and calendar information.

Since it's already late on Thursday, he decides that it would be best to discuss it with Dave and Ben at the meeting on Friday.

# ColdFusion Architecture

Dave begins by looking over the sketch diagram the team created the previous Friday. He decides to start with the structure of the file system followed by the structure of `Application.cfm`. Once this is done, he will start defining the Cold-Fusion components (CFCs) and custom tags.

## File Structure

Much of the file system structure follows the same principles that have been used in many Q42 projects. Figure II-3.1 shows the structure of the application root directory.

**Figure II-3.1**

The structure of the
root directory for the
application.

```
attachments
components
draft_attachments
includes
project_documents
tags
webroot
Application.cfm
OnRequestEnd.cfm
```

**Application.cfm** and **OnRequestEnd.cfm** are deliberately placed outside
the webroot directory. The main reason for this is that it provides increased
security for the application in the event of any Web server exploits that allow
someone to bypass the application server and download ColdFusion templates with the ColdFusion code still in them. Since the ColdFusion server
will always search up the directory tree looking for an **Application.cfm**
file, putting it outside the webroot doesn't cause any problems for the
application. Once the ColdFusion server finds an Application.cfm, it will
check in the same directory for an **OnRequestEnd.cfm**.

The attachments and draft_attachments directories will be used to store
the attachment files for received and saved draft emails, respectively. The
includes directory is for all the application include files. The reason for
keeping all includes files outside the webroot is the same as for the
**Application.cfm**. It also makes it relatively simple to apply application
security, as permission checks need only go in the **Index.cfm** file in each
section directory rather than at the top of each file. Figure II-3.2 shows the
structure of the includes directory.

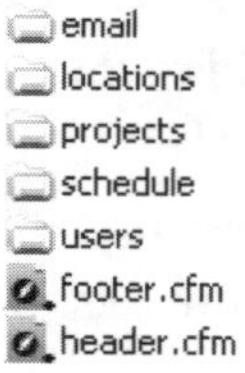

**Figure II-3.2**

The structure of the
includes directory for the
application.

```
email
locations
projects
schedule
users
footer.cfm
header.cfm
```

Inside the includes directory, there's a subdirectory corresponding to each
of the main navigation elements, or sections, and two global include files:
**Header.cfm** and **Footer.cfm**. **Header.cfm** will contain the code to

generate the main navigation, and `Footer.cfm` will contain any code necessary to complete the HTML for the page.

The webroot directory shown in Figure II-3.3 contains a directory for each of the main navigation elements. Since the application will use include files for all application logic, it may have been simpler from a programming perspective to use a single `Index.cfm` in the webroot directory. The main navigation section could be passed as a URL variable to this `Index.cfm`, and the relevant files included. There are two main reasons that Dave decides not to take this approach:

- Many people, especially computer-savvy users, like to type the name of the directory they want to go to directly, rather than having to click on a menu item after they log in.

- When a new developer looks at the application at some time in the future, some inference can be made about the structure of the application just by looking at the directory structure.

**Figure II-3.3**
The structure of the webroot directory for the application.

In addition to the directories for each section, there is a style sheet file and an Index.cfm to display the default page for the application. The style sheet will contain as much as possible of the formatting for the application so that changes can easily be implemented as development proceeds.

## JavaScript

The js directory inside the webroot contains two sub-directories: qForms and DatePicker.

The qForms sub-directory contains files for the qForms JavaScript API. This API, developed by Dan Switzer, exposes a series of JavaScript functions for working with HTML form elements. When using the API, it is first necessary to add the following script between the <HEAD></HEAD> tags of the page that is being called:

```
<!--// load the qForm JavaScript API //-->
<SCRIPT SRC="/pim/js/qForms/lib/qforms.js"></SCRIPT>
<!--// you do not need the code below if you plan on just
        using the core qForm API methods. //-->
<!--// [start] initialize all default extension libraries
//-->
<SCRIPT LANGUAGE="JavaScript">
<!--//
// specify the path where the "/qforms/" subfolder is
located
qFormAPI.setLibraryPath("/pim/js/qForms/lib/");
// loads all default libraries
qFormAPI.include("*");
//-->
</SCRIPT>
<!--// [ end ] initialize all default extension libraries
//-->
```

Once the library has been initialized in the head of the document it can be used as follows in a form:

```
<!--// a simple form //-->
<FORM ACTION="" METHOD="POST" NAME="frmExample">
<P>Enter some sample text:<BR>
<INPUT TYPE="Text" NAME="SampleText"></P>
<INPUT TYPE="Button" NAME="Test" VALUE="Hello World!"
 onClick="objForm.SampleText.setValue('Hello
World!');"></P>
```

```
</FORM>

<!--// this code must execute after the end </FORM> tag
//-->
<SCRIPT LANGUAGE="JavaScript">
<!--//
// replace "frmExample" with value of the <FORM> tag's
NAME
// attribute. you can also substitute "objForm" with any
// variable name that makes sense for you
objForm = new qForm("frmExample");
//-->
</SCRIPT>
```

Q42 has used it in many projects and includes it in the js directory under the webroot as part of their standard file structure.

The DatePicker directory contains the code for a JavaScript pop-up date picker called the Tigra Calendar. Q42 have also used this in a number of projects. The pop-up allows quite a few options such as year scrolling and time entry in addition to a month calendar. The Tigra Calendar is also free of charge for all types of applications. It works on a similar principle to qForms. The following code must be placed between the <HEAD></HEAD> tags of the page that is being called:

```
<!-- European format dd-mm-yyyy -->
<script language="JavaScript"
src="#request.webroot#/js/calendar1.js"></script>
<!-- American format mm/dd/yyyy -->
<script language="JavaScript"
src="#request.webroot#/js/calendar2.js"></script>
```

Once this library has been initialized, the date picker can be used as follows:

```
<form name="tstest">
  <input type="Text" name="input1" value="">
  <a href="javascript:cal1.popup();">
```

```
    <img src="/pim/js/DatePicker/img/cal.gif" width="16"
height="16" border="0">
  </a>
</form>

<script>
<!--
/* create calendar object(s) just after form tag closed
specify form element as the only parameter
(document.forms['formname'].elements['inputname']);
note: you can have as many calendar objects as you need
for your application */

var cal1 = new
calendar1(document.forms['tstest'].elements['input1']);
cal1.year_scroll = true;
cal1.time_comp = true;
</script>
```

Clicking on the hyperlink after the form tag will launch the JavaScript pop-up. Once the date and time have been chosen, the value in the form input box will be updated. More information can be found about the Tigra Calendar at www.softcomplex.com/products/tigra_calendar/.

## Custom Tags

Dave decided at the first meeting that the majority of the application logic would be contained in the CFCs rather than in custom tags. He also decides that custom tags will be used to create user-interface elements that will repeat several times in the application. The following four tags are a good start, but more will probably be added as the project progresses.

- **Login.cfm**—This tag will handle authentication. A call to the tag will be placed in Application.cfm, and the tag will retrieve user details and roles from the database for returning authenticated users, perform authentication against the Exchange Server for log-in attempts, and display the log-in form for non-authenticated users.

- **Datum.cfm**—This is a tag that Q42 has used in several projects for generating a date-selection form control consisting of three drop-down menus for day, month, and year. It provides an alternative to the pop-up JavaScript date picker, where they do not require a specific time associated with the date and do not want to use a pop-up.

- **Containerselects.cfm**—This tag has also been used in several previous projects. It was created from one of the example files from the qForms documentation, and generated a pair of related multiselect form controls to allow for the simple creation of interfaces such as adding and removing users from a group.

- **Menu.cfm**—This tag will be created specifically for the project. It will generate the menu items for each of the navigation areas and will also highlight the menu item corresponding to the current page.

## CFCs

As mentioned earlier, Dave is keen to create CFCs that could be re-used in the future. For this reason he decides to think carefully about how each component will work, and what functions it will contain. Initially he comes up with a list of five components that he feels would be easy to use again with minimal modification. For each of these components he creates a .cfc file in the components directory. His initial components are: email.cfc, exchange.cfc, location.cfc, project.cfc, schedule.cfc, and users.cfc.

In each of the component files he creates an initial set of <CFFUNCTION> tag calls with a brief comment above each one describing what the function should do. At this stage Dave does not create the logic for the functions themselves, just the empty <CFFUNCTION> tags.

## Database Schema

Dave is pleasantly surprised to find that he has managed to get through the bulk of this work by the end of Wednesday. Since he also has the strongest database skills, he decides to create a preliminary database in Access, as that's the most portable format for transferring between members of the team. The database for the final application will be built in SQL Server, but for prototyping and initial development, Access suffices.

Working from the sketch diagram, he produces the database schema diagram shown in Figure II- 3.4.

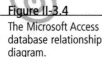

**Figure II-3.4**
The Microsoft Access database relationship diagram.

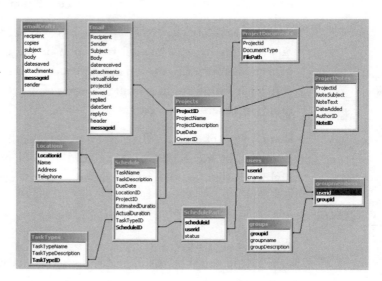

As is usually the case when creating a database from such a sketch diagram, Dave discovered several problems, omissions, and redundancies in the original sketch. As he was adding each of the fields for the tables, he made sure to add a brief description for future reference. Some of the changes he made to the tables are as follows:

- Removed the Permissions table, which seemed superfluous given that the application would use only three or four groups with reasonably well-defined permissions. For the simplicity of the application, permissions would be implemented using the `isUserInRole()` ColdFusion function.

- Added the EmailDrafts table, which will be required for saving draft messages.

- Removed the Clients table, as Jim Forsyth said that FarSight was using the Exchange Server global address book to hold its client information.

- Decided that the Users table would require only a userid column and a column to hold the unique identifier for the user from the Exchange Server. Dave expects that more columns will be added at a later stage if the Exchange Server does not provide all the information about each user required for the application.

Once Dave has added all the tables, he creates a relationships diagram for the database. He has always found that by creating one of these diagrams and looking at which tables have the most connections, he could get a feel for where the core functionality of the application would be. In this case it appears that Projects, Schedule, and Users are the key elements in the application. This validates his initial list of CFCs.

# Graphical Design

Ben decides he should break the design work into a number of simple tasks. Working from the UI sketch diagram, he decides to start by creating the main, secondary, and tertiary navigation elements. He decides to stop short of creating the interface for each of the possible screens in the sections for the application but does create a sample screen for the log-in page and for the email section, to show how a typical page would look with all the navigation elements and some content.

## Navigation

Ben decides to stick with the navigation layout from the initial sketch diagram. All three types of navigation elements should have the same structure: each element will have black text with a white background and a thin black border. The main navigation at the top of the screen will be center-aligned, while the secondary and tertiary elements will be left-aligned. The background color of the navigation elements will change from white to a grayish blue to indicate the navigation element that was clicked to get to the current page.

## Logo

Ben decides to create a simple logo that conveys the purpose of the application, and has the right proportions to fit in the top left corner of the page. Figure II-3.5 shows the logo he created.

**Figure II-3.5**
The logo for the PIM application.

*P.I.M.*

## Log-in Screen

Next, Ben creates the log-in form for the application (see Figure II-3.6). The main reason for creating this form is to set the look and feel of the system, and to ensure that the logo Ben created works in that context. This form will be centered both vertically and horizontally on the screen.

**Figure II-3.6**
The initial login screen Ben created in Macromedia Fireworks.

*P.I.M.*  FarSight Intranet Login.
Authorized access only.

Username: [          ]
Password: [          ]

[ Login ]

## Email Screen

Finally, Ben creates a sample email screen for the application (see Figure II-3.7). All the navigation elements are present, with the main navigation for email highlighted to indicate the page context to the user. The data table for displaying the list of email messages has been added to show the style for the data tables in all sections of the application.

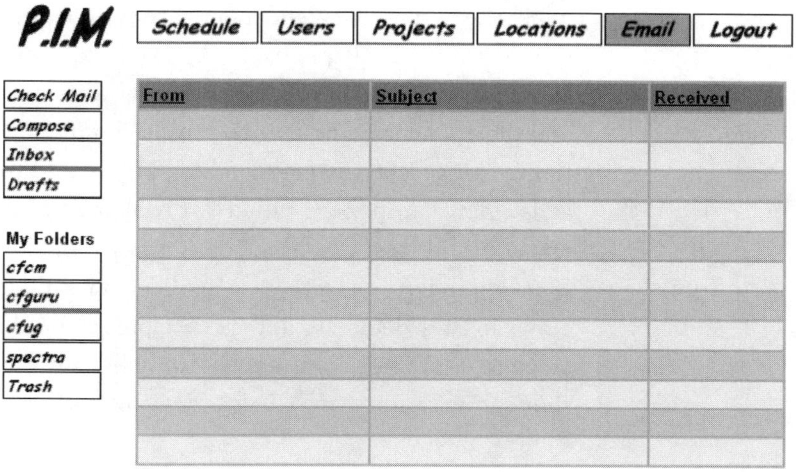

**P.I.M.** | Schedule | Users | Projects | Locations | Email | Logout

| Check Mail |
| Compose |
| Inbox |
| Drafts |

**My Folders**
| cfcm |
| cfguru |
| cfug |
| spectra |
| Trash |

| From | Subject | Received |
| --- | --- | --- |
|  |  |  |

Figure II-3.7

The example email screen Ben created in Fireworks.

# Progress Meeting

At the meeting on Friday morning, Ben presents the graphics that he produced during the week. The others agree with his ideas for the user interface, though it will be up to the client to make the final decision. There's a consensus among them that the graphics are probably close to what they will look like in the final system.

Once Tom relates his less than successful attempts to connect to the Exchange Server, they all agree that getting task and calendar information for each user from there isn't a realistic possibility in the time frame for the project. Ben has arranged a meeting with FarSight for the following Monday, to discuss the UI design for the application. He will raise the topic of the Exchange Server communication at that time. They decide to do as much as they can using COM and a local instance of Outlook on the ColdFusion server. In order for this to work, Outlook needs to be installed on the ColdFusion server. A user from the company needs to configure the default profile in Outlook to log on to the Exchange Server, and the ColdFusion server needs to use that user's account to log on as a service. This should allow them to retrieve information such as the global address book, the corporate calendar, and other items in the public folders that are shared among multiple users. As Dave explains the file structure for the application, he realizes that there's no directory for project documents, and there's no specific component for connecting to the Exchange Server to get things like the global address book and the corporate calendar. He adds a new component called `Outlook.cfc` to the Components directory and adds a corresponding subdirectory for the functions. Tom also notices that looping over a large COM collection in CFMX seems to be relatively slow, so they decide to add more tables to hold this information. At this stage they are not completely sure what information will be stored, but that can wait until after Ben's meeting with FarSight on Monday.

# Client Meeting

As arranged, Ben meets Jim Forsyth and Phil Potts at the Far-Sight offices in Pimlico the following Monday morning. They are very happy with the UI design, as it is simple and unclut-tered. Their mood gives Ben a good opportunity to introduce the problems with the Exchange Server. He explains that although they've used Exchange in the past, they've always accessed information in the public folders. The reason for this is that the Outlook object on the client machine always connects to the Exchange Serer using the default profile for the user that the ColdFusion server is using to log on. The net result is that it's no prob-lem at all to get full information from the Exchange server, but because of the restriction in the mechanism that Outlook uses to log on to the server, that information is only ever for a single user.

The other option that Ben mentioned at the first meeting was to use CDO. When Jim asks about this, he relates several examples that he saw where sites written with ASP had problems maintaining a stable con-nection to the Exchange Server. Since ASP is also a Microsoft technology, he says, it's fairly safe to assume that if it can't be used reliably with CDO, he can't recommend it as a solution. He proposes that Q42 create a system that would connect to the Exchange Server and retrieve infor-mation that would be stored in the public folders. Combining this with email notification should allow for a good deal of the information that's currently being stored on the Exchange Server to be used in the application.

Although Jim and Phil are not entirely happy with this situation, they can see the logic of what's being said and accept that for now the application isn't completely integrated with the Exchange Server.

Ben also finalizes the administrative groups for the application as Project Admin, User Admin, Location Admin, Exchange Admin, and Location Admin.

After returning from the meeting, Ben speaks to both Tom and Dave. They decide that since Tom has done the research on the Exchange Server, he should be the one to create the Email and Outlook CFCs. Dave will begin with the Projects and Users components, and Ben will work on the Cold-Fusion implementation of the user interface he designed.

# Development

Since Dave already created a number of function calls for the components, he has a pretty clear idea of what he wants to achieve in each of them. In order to test the functions as they are developed, he also needs to create the include file for the user interface. For each of the functions, the development process is driven by the need to test what is being created.

Typically the initial need is to have a form to create a new entry in the database. This is followed by the creation of the function to add the data to the database.

Once these are complete, the edit form is created. This normally uses the same form as the one used for creating a new entry. If so, the HTML for the form is moved to a separate file and included as required for editing or creation. Figure II-3.7 shows how the logic would work for a typical edit page. The logic for most of the application is very similar. Each http request would be made to `Index.cfm` in one of the directories under the webroot. This `Index.cfm` has a `<CFPARAM>` tag to set a default value for `url.action`. It then checks if a file corresponding to that action exists in the includes directory. If not, an error message is displayed. If so, the file is included. This include file normally performs further checks for the existence of variables sand for security before making a call to one of the component functions.

## Sample Logic

## Example for Project.cfc

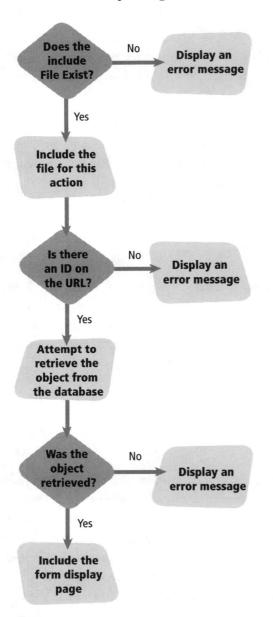

Figure II-3.8
This diagram shows an example of the logic used for a page request in the application.

## UI Implementation

Once Dave settles on this method for building the system, he talks it through with Tom and manages to convince him to follow the same structure. In order to minimize the amount of work required to integrate the work that Ben is doing, they work through the exact navigation elements that will be required for each part of the interface and create a set of cascading style sheets (CSS) class names that will be used for the HTML tags in each part of the interface.

The complete list of navigation elements is as follows (see Table II-3.1):

| Table II-3.1 | Navigation Elements |
|---|---|
| Item | List |
| Schedule | Task List |
| | Add Task |
| | Old Tasks |
| Email | Check Mail |
| | Compose |
| | Inbox |
| | Drafts |
| Users | User List |
| | Add User |
| Projects | Project List |
| | Add Project |
| | Active/Inactive Projects |
| Locations | Location List |
| | Add Location |
| Public Folders | Contacts |
| | Calendar |
| | Logout |

Once these are confirmed, Ben sets about creating the final templates that will be deployed with the finished application.

After reviewing the options for the `Menu.cfm` custom tag, he decides that the most flexible way to build it would be to use style sheet classes to render the menu items from hyperlinks in a table cell rather than creating a set of images for each menu item. The main reason for this choice is that he wants to ensure a consistent look and feel between the tertiary navigation elements that will be dynamically generated from the database and the fixed primary and secondary navigation elements. It will also be much easier to make additions and changes to the primary or secondary navigation elements.

In order to make sure that the user is presented with an interface quickly, he creates a table at the top of the page to contain the primary navigation elements, and adds a `CFFLUSH` tag immediately after it before the opening tag for the table that will contain the secondary navigation and main page contents.

He also creates a data-table custom tag to consistently render the lists of data for each of the sections in the application.

## Component Development

As Dave and Tom proceed with the development of the components, they each take a slightly different approach. Dave sets out all of the functions that will be required by each component prior to writing any code so that he will have minimum duplication of code and maximum efficiency of development time. Tom looks at each component, finds the most interesting function, and starts working on it. Once he has all the code for the function working, including permission checking, display, and validation, he splits up the code into the separate files that will be used in the final system.

For components such as `Project.cfc` and `Schedule.cfc`, which do not communicate with any external systems other than the database, development is simpler. The majority of the time is taken up with tasks such as creating a good interface to display all the information for a single project, or finding a good way to show how urgent a particular task or project deadline is.

As with most systems, the more difficult components are the ones that need to work with protocols or technologies outside of ColdFusion.

### Users Component

The Users component needs to use ColdFusion Lightweight Directory Access Protocol (LDAP) to communicate with the Exchange Server for user authentication. In order to do this, something has to be known about how the information is organized on the Exchange Server at FarSight. Unfortunately, it's not possible to get remote access to the system, so Dave has to rely on getting the information from FarSight and assuming that it will be correct. For development purposes Dave uses the Q42 Exchange Server settings and makes sure that they will be easy to change at a later date. Dave created the template, shown in Listing II-3.1, for testing the LDAP connection to the Exchange Server:

Listing II-3.1

```
<!--- check if the form was submitted --->
<cfif isDefined('form.username')>
  <!--- Wrap the call to cfldap in a cftry block --->
  <cftry>
    <!--- Query the Exchange server using the values
submitted
    in the form --->
    <cfldap  action="QUERY"
             start="cn=#form.cn#,ou=#form.ou#,o=#form.o#"
             name="q"
             server="#form.servername#"
             username="cn=#form.username#"
             password="#form.password#"
             scope="subtree"
             attributes="givenname,sn">
    <!--- Any sort of problem with the query will result
    in an exception. If we get to here the username and
    password are ok so we can set the isAuthenticated
    variable to true --->
    <cfset isAuthenticated="true">
```

```
      <!--- catch any errors and output the error message -
--->
    <cfcatch type="ANY">
      <!--- an error occurred, so we set the
isAuthenticated
      variable to false --->
      <cfset isAuthenticated="false">

      <!--- output the error message --->
      <cfoutput>Error: #cfcatch.message#<br></cfoutput>

    </cfcatch>

  </cftry>
  <!--- Give the user some feedback for the
authentication status --->
  <cfoutput>Authenticated: #isAuthenticated#</cfoutput>

  <!--- Dump the query returned by the CFLDAP call if it
  was successful --->
  <cfif isAuthenticated>
    <cfdump var="#q#">
  </cfif>

</cfif>

<!--- initialize the form values so that after the form
is
submitted, the submitted values are displayed for easy
testing --->

<!--- The username for the user to authenticate --->
<cfparam name="form.username" default="">

<!--- The name or IP address of the server to connect to
--->
<cfparam name="form.servername" default="">
```

```
<!--- The organization part of the Exchange directory
structure.
This will often be the company name, or something similar
to it.
--->
<cfparam name="form.o" default="">


<!--- The organizational unit part of the Exchange
directory structure.
For smaller companies this will often be the same as the
organization,
For larger ones, it will often be a department, or
regional division.
--->
<cfparam name="form.ou" default="">


<!--- The container that you want to query on the
Exchange Server.
The recipients container is set as the default as it is
almost always
Available for querying.
--->
<cfparam name="form.cn" default="recipients">


<cfoutput>
<form action="#cgi.script_name#" method="post">
  <table>
    <tr>
      <td>username</td>
      <td><input type="text" name="username"
value="#form.username#"></td>
    </tr>
    <tr>
      <td>password</td>
      <td><input type="password" name="password"
value=""></td>
```

```
      </tr>
      <tr>
        <td>Server Name</td>
        <td><input type="text" name="servername"
  value="#form.servername#"></td>
      </tr>
      <tr>
        <td>Organization</td>
        <td><input type="text" name="o"
  value="#form.o#"></td>
      </tr>
      <tr>
        <td>Organizational Unit</td>
        <td><input type="text" name="ou"
  value="#form.ou#"></td>
      </tr>
      <tr>
        <td>Container</td>
        <td><input type="text" name="cn"
  value="#form.cn#"></td>
      </tr>
      <tr>
        <td colspan="2"><input type="submit"
  value="test"></td>
      </tr>
    </table>
  </form>
</cfoutput>
```

### Outlook Component

The Outlook component causes the most problems. On previous projects
in which Q42 developers used COM with ColdFusion, they often used the
following syntax to loop over a collection of COM objects:

```
<cfloop collection="#object#" item="i">
```

Unfortunately, trying to do this with the collections being returned from the Outlook instance results in an error. Although the MSDN Web site indicates that it should be possible to use the Index() function on most objects to retrieve a numbered index in a collection, trying this method also produces errors. Eventually, Tom discovers that the number passed to the Index() function works when the number is passed in single quotes. Even this syntax doesn't always work, despite all indications to the contrary in the documentation. With a little further investigation Tom discovers that most Outlook collections have getFirst() and getNext() methods. With the combination of these, he is able to successfully loop over the collections that are being returned from Outlook. Listing II-3.2 demonstrates this a little more clearly:

Listing II-3.2

```
<CFSCRIPT>
  // Create the outlook object
  objOutlook = createObject('com','Outlook.Application');

  /* Get the object name space - currently MAPI is the
only option */
  objNameSpace = objOutlook.getNameSpace("MAPI");

  /* If you're on Windows NT or 2000, use the next line
*/
  objNameSpace.Logon("", "", False, False);

  /* We want to set the folder to get the contacts in -
'10' or the 'Contacts' folder */
  objFolder = objNameSpace.getDefaultFolder(10);

  /* Return the 'Items' collection */
  objAllContacts = objFolder.Items;

  /* This should work, but doesn't seem to
  count = 0;
  for (i in objAllContacts) {
    thisItem = objAllContacts,Item('#i#');
  }
```

```
*/

/* This works on some collections
for (i=0;i LT objAllContacts.count;i=i+1) {
  thisitem = objAllContacts.Item('#i#');
}
*/

/* This works on most collections that support the
getFirst() and getNext() methods
  for (i=0;i LT objAllContacts.count;i=i+1) {
    if (i eq 1) {
      thisitem = objAllContacts.getFirst();
    }
    else {
      thisitem = objAllContacts.getNext();
    }
  }
  */
</cfscript>
```

In addition to the problem of looping over collections, it turns out that the looping is a slow process—particularly noticeable when looping over large collections. To get around this, Tom creates a set of structures in the application scope to hold the collection data. For each collection he creates a time-out value that can be configured as a variable in the **Application.cfm**. When a request is made to a function in the Outlook component, it first checks if the data exists in the application scope, and if the time-out value has expired.

### Email Component

When using the **checkMail()** function to retrieve a large number of email messages, Tom finds that the page often hangs without ever returning an error message. The ColdFusion MX process does not appear to be consuming much processor time, so he's a little mystified about what the cause might be. With Dave's help, he tracks it down to some sort of locking problem when trying to delete the attachments for messages that already exist in the database. He is looping over the list of attachments for each message, deleting each one for messages that are already in the database. Although he has a named exclusive lock around the call to the CFFILE tag inside the loop, the system still seems to get stuck trying to delete the attachments. He tries several options, including creating a wait function to force the loop to run more slowly, but nothing seems to make a difference.

Finally, Tom finds the solution: use an initial CFPOP tag call to retrieve only the message headers, check which are already in the database, and then use a second CFPOP call to retrieve only the new messages. Since the attachments are retrieved only for new messages, there's no need for the code to delete the duplicates. This solution has the advantage of speeding up the retrieval of email when there's a large number of messages with attachments. Listing II-3.3 shows the final code for the checkmail() function.

Listing II-3.3

```
<cffunction name="checkmail">
  <!--- Mail server is required --->
  <cfargument name="mailserver" required="yes"
type="string">
  <!--- The path to any attachment files --->
  <cfargument name="attachmentpath" required="yes"
type="string">
  <!--- The pop username for the user whose email we are
retrieving --->
  <cfargument name="username" required="yes"
type="string">
  <!--- The pop password for the user whose email we are
retrieving --->
  <cfargument name="password" required="yes"
type="string">
  <!--- The email address for the user whose email we are
retrieving --->
  <cfargument name="emailaddress" required="Yes"
type="string">
  <!--- The datasource name where the retrieved messages
will be stored --->
  <cfargument name="datasource" required="yes"
type="string">
```

```
<!--- initialize a structure to hold the returned
information --->
<cfset var stReturn = structNew()>


<!--- This structure key is used to indicate if the
operation completed
Successfully --->
<cfset stReturn.bSuccess = true>

<!--- This structure key is used to pass messages back
to the caller of the
function. It should be used for passing developer
messages to assist debugging --->
<cfset stReturn.message = "">

<!--- This structure key is used to hold any data which
the function returns --->
<cfset stReturn.data = "">

<!--- Wrap the initial CFPOP tag in a cftry/cfcatch
block --->
<cftry>
  <!--- Create an empty variable to hold the list of
messages to
  retrieve once the headers have been checked against
the contents
  of the database. --->
  <cfset lMessageNumbers = "">

  <!--- Attempt to get the messages for this user --->
  <cfpop
    action="GETHEADERONLY"
    server="#arguments.mailserver#"
    attachmentpath="#arguments.attachmentpath#"
    username="#arguments.username#"
    password="#arguments.password#"
```

```
        generateuniquefilenames="Yes"
        name="qHeaders">


    <!--- Loop over the returned headers checking each
    one to see if it exists in the database --->
    <cfloop query="qHeaders">


      <!--- Check if the message is already in the
database --->
      <cfquery datasource="#arguments.datasource#"
name="qCheckMessage">
        SELECT dateSent
        FROM email
        WHERE sender =
'#left(urlencodedformat(qHeaders.from),500)#'
        AND dateSent =
'#left(urlencodedformat(qHeaders.date),500)#'
        AND recipient = '#arguments.emailaddress#'
      </cfquery>


      <!--- If this message is not found, add the message
      number to the lMessageNumbers variable --->
      <cfif not qCheckMessage.recordCount>
        <cfset lMessageNumbers =
listAppend(lMessageNumbers,qHeaders.messagenumber)>
      </cfif>



    </cfloop>


    <!--- Get any messages that are not currently in the
database --->
    <cfpop
      action="GETALL"
      server="#arguments.mailserver#"
      attachmentpath="#arguments.attachmentpath#"
      username="#arguments.username#"
```

```
                    password="#arguments.password#"
                    generateuniquefilenames="Yes"
                    messagenumber="#lMessageNumbers#"
                    name="qMessages">


    <!--- Catch any errors --->
    <cfcatch>
        <!--- Set the bSuccess key in the return structure
to false --->
        <cfset stReturn.bSuccess = false>
        <!--- Add the message and detail keys from the
cfcatch
        structure to the message key in the return
structure --->
        <cfset stReturn.message = "#cfcatch.message#
<BR><BR> #cfcatch.detail#">
        <!--- Exit the funtion --->
        <cfreturn stReturn>
        <!--- Make extra sure the function exits --->
        <cfexit method="EXITTEMPLATE">

    </cfcatch>

  </cftry>

  <!--- Loop over the new messages retrieved by the
second CFPOP call
  inserting them one at a time into the database --->
  <cfloop query="qMessages">


    <cftry>

      <cfquery datasource="#arguments.datasource#"
name="qInsertEmail">
          INSERT INTO email
```

```
(recipient,sender,replyto,subject,body,datereceived,dates
ent,attachments,header,messageid)
        VALUES

('#arguments.emailaddress#','#left(urlencodedformat(qMess
ages.from),500)#','#left(urlencodedformat(qMessages.reply
to),500)#','#left(urlencodedformat(qMessages.subject),100
0)#','#urlencodedformat(qMessages.body)#',#Now()#,'#left(
urlencodedformat(qMessages.date),500)#','#qMessages.attac
hments#','#left(urlencodedformat(qMessages.header),4000)#
','#createuuid()#')
        </cfquery>


        <!--- Catch any errors and set the values for the
        keys in the stReturn structure accordingly --->
        <cfcatch>

            <cfset stReturn.bSuccess = false>
            <cfset stReturn.message = cfcatch.message &
"<br><br>" & cfcatch.detail>
            <cfset stReturn.stError = cfcatch>
            <cfset stReturn.data = "">
            <cfoutput>Error:
#cfcatch.message#<BR><BR>#cfcatch.detail#<BR></cfoutput>

        </cfcatch>



    </cftry>



    </cfloop>

    <!--- Retrieve all messages in the inbox --->
```

```
<cfquery datasource="#arguments.datasource#"
name="qInbox">
    SELECT *
    FROM email
    WHERE recipient = '#arguments.emailaddress#'
    AND virtualfolder = 'Inbox'
    ORDER BY datereceived DESC
</cfquery>


<!--- Put the query containing the inbox messages
in the data key of the stReturn structure --->
<cfset stReturn.data = qInbox>


<!--- return the stReturn structure to the caller --->
<cfreturn stReturn>


</cffunction>
```

Another interesting problem is creating valid email addresses that can be displayed in an HTML form field when replying to emails. Many modern email systems format an email message as follows:

```
"John Doe" <jdoe@company.com>
```

This is very useful for the purposes of reading email in an email client, as there is a friendly name to go along with the email address. It is not so useful when the email address appears in an HTML text input tag. The double quotes cause the input to prematurely close the value field of the tag, and the opening and closing angle brackets cause the end of the input tag to be incorrectly rendered in most browsers.

After a little playing around with regular expressions, Tom comes up with the following pair of expressions that seem to take care of all the addresses he tests:

```
<cfset recipient =
reReplace(recipient,'^([^<])*(<)([^>]*)(>?)','\3','all')>
```

## Testing

Once Dave and Tom complete the components, and Ben tidies up the interface so it has a consistent look, they're ready to start testing the application.

The first step in this process is to migrate the database from Access to SQL Server and to remove all the data to simulate the state of the system after it's installed at the client site. As usual, after doing this, they encounter a number of problems in the user interface: an error is produced because a query did not return any records or because there were no users in the system with a particular administrative role. Once these are fixed, the team asks some of the other employees to try to use it for several days to check their email, to add scheduled tasks, to add and edit projects, and so on. The employees are told that they will most likely be moving to the system some time over the coming month, and that they should report anything that doesn't work, or any area the system is lacking in functionality. This test performs two useful functions:

1. Since the employees believe that they will be using the system to manage their daily lives in the near future, they are much more inclined to test the system thoroughly than if they were just asked to test the system prior to its deployment to the client.

2. The results of the test will give the team a good indication not only of the usability of the application, but also of its suitability for use within Q42.

The results of these tests are encouraging, and several changes are made to the code where the interface is unclear, or where errors occurred because of lack of knowledge of the system.

Once this testing is completed, and the changes are made, the team is ready for the initial deployment of the application at FarSight.

# The Solution

## Initial Deployment

Once the initial testing phase at the Q42 offices is completed, the team spends a few days working through the code and making changes to the system. After this is complete, Ben sends an email to Jim Forsyth at FarSight.

## Ready for beta

### Email

**Date:** June 24

**To:** Jim Forsyth

**From:** Ben Richards

**Subject:** Ready for beta

Hi Jim,

We've spent the last few days testing the PIM application in our office, and everything seems to perform well. We'd like to get it deployed down at the FarSight offices for a beta test sometime in the next few days, if possible, so we can iron out any issues there may be with getting it to work with your systems before it goes live.

If we could have it running alongside your current system for a week or so, I think we'd probably see any major problems.

I'd also like to have a chat about training for Phil on how the PIM application was developed and how to extend it in the future.

Let me know what date and time are good for you.

Regards,

Ben

Ben Richards
Project Manager
Q42

Ben spends the rest of the day putting together a handbook for the system in Microsoft Word format. The guide works through each of the sections of the application using series of screen shots to explain how the system should be used. He found from previous projects that this sort of handbook makes a big difference in how well the PIM application is perceived. Many of the reported problems with previous applications came down to a lack of understanding of what the system was supposed to do rather than to a bug. The next morning he receives the following reply from Jim:

---

**RE: A few questions**

**Email**

**Date:** June 25

**To:** Ben Richards

**From:** Jim Forsyth

**Subject:** RE: A few questions

Hi Ben,

That's great news!

If you could make it here sometime on Wednesday or Thursday morning, that would be good. That would give us a chance to get the system up and running and test it in the tech department for a couple of days this week before letting the rest of the company test it next week.

Jim

---

Ben speaks to David, and they agree to make the trip to FarSight's office in Pimlico on Thursday, June 27. That gives Ben enough time to finish the handbook and David time to do a final check for inconsistencies in variable naming and code structure.

This code review is important going forward with the PIM application, as it's quite likely that the company will want Q42 to build extra functionality above and beyond what Phil will be able to achieve on his own. Once Phil starts adding changes to the code, it will be hard enough to keep track of those changes without the added complication of having things done several different ways in the original code.

### Installation

At the FarSight office in Pimlico on Thursday, Ben and Dave decide that it would be best if Ben handled the business and meeting items with Jim while Dave installed the PIM application on the FarSight servers.

Dave takes careful notes detailing each step of the installation so that if there are any problems in the future, he can easily reproduce the system and FarSight has a record of how to deploy the PIM application for its development server:

### File Migration

1. Create a SQL script for all the tables from the SQL server database running on the laptop.

2. Save the script as createAll_27_June.sql to the root directory of the PIM application.

3. Remove all data from the tables in the Microsoft Access database in the root directory of the PIM application.

4. Use the Compact and Repair option in Microsfot Access to minimize the size of the database file and ensure that all of the tables are error free. This should ensure that there won't be any problems with it if it is used for development in the future.

5. Create a Zip file called pim.zip from all the files and directories in the root directory of the PIM application.

6. Copy the Zip file from the laptop to the FarSight Macromedia Cold-Fusion MX server.

## Database Creation

1. Copy the SQL script file to the SQL server.

2. Open SQL server Enterprise Manager.

3. Create a database called pim on the SQL server.

4. Choose Tools > Query Analyzer.

5. Open the SQL file that was created in step 2 under "File Migration."

6. Ensure that the active database in the Query Analyzer drop-down box is the pim database.

7. Run the SQL script to create the database tables.

8. Open the database in Enterprise Manager to ensure that the database tables exist in the pim database.

## ColdFusion Server Configuration

1. On the ColdFusion server, create a datasource called pim that points to the database on the SQL server.

2. Create a ColdFusion mapping called pim that points to d:\pim.

3. Create a virtual directory on the Web server that points to the d:\pim\webroot directory.

4. Ensure that the ColdFusion MX Application Server service is set to "log on" using a user account that has an account on the Microsoft Exchange server.

## Exchange Configuration

1. Open Microsoft Outlook on the ColdFusion server.

2. Ensure that it is logged on to the Exchange server and that the public folders are available.

3. Right-click on the Contacts folder in the public folders.

**instant message**

▶ If you use a
datasource name
other than pim,
the value of
**request.dsn** will
have to be changed
in the **_config.cfm**
file in the root
directory of the
PIM application.

4. Choose Properties.

5. Choose the Summary tab.

6. Check if there is an entry in the Folder Contacts list that looks like a Lightweight Directory Access Protocol (LDAP) entry (something like /O=FARSIGHT/OU=FARSIGHT/CN=RECIPIENTS).

7. Copy the files `testExchange.cfm` and `testOutlook.cfm` to a Web-browsable folder on the ColdFusion server. Make sure this file is outside the webroot of the pim application, as it will be used to determine the settings for the Exchange server, and the pim application requires a log-in for all areas.

8. Browse `testExchange.cfm` in a Web browser.

9. Use the information you retrieved in step 6 to test the configuration details for the Exchange server with a user name and password for a valid email account.

10. If you get a message telling you the user was authenticated, you can copy these settings to the `_config.cfm` file in the D:\pim\.

11. Browse to http://localhost/pim/index.cfm with your Web browser.

12. Attempt to log in with the same user name and password you used in step 9.

13. Open `testOutlook.cfm` in a text editor.

14. Check the names of the folder hierarchy to the public contacts and calendar folders in Outlook.

**instant message**

▶ If you use a
ColdFusion mapping
name other than
pim, it will have
to be entered in
the **request.mapping**
variable in
**_config.cfm**
accordingly.

15. After the comment that starts: "You will need to change the names of the folders," change the names of the folders in the code, as instructed by the comment, to match the names of the folders in your hierarchy to the public contacts folder.

16. Browse `testOutlook.cfm` to see if you get a list of the first 20 contacts from the public contacts folder. Once you've managed to get this list, you can edit D:\pim\includes\outlook\_config.cfm to reflect the folder names on your system.

Once he's happy that the PIM application is configured correctly, Dave quickly walks Phil through the structure of the PIM application. He explains how the ColdFusion components (CFCs) are loaded into the request scope in `Application.cfm` and used as required by the various parts of the PIM application.

By the time he finishes showing Phil the file structure and order of execution and calling of the various files, Ben has returned from his meeting with Jim.

During the meeting they decided that FarSight would test the PIM application up until the end of the following week. During this time, Phil would attempt to add several more of the folders from the Exchange server to the interface. Doing this should allow FarSight to see how much training and assistance they will require from Q42 in the future.

### Application walkthrough

Now that both Jim and Phil are both together, Dave decides that it would be a good opportunity to demonstrate the working application so they can see how it is supposed to work. His walkthrough is as follows:

Browse to the application in a Web browser. The log-in screen appears. When an invalid log-in is used, a message appears above the log-in form telling you that you have entered an invalid user name or password. Below the form is a warning telling you that your IP address has been logged. Failed log-ins are recorded in login.log in the cfusionmx\logs directory.

### Schedule

Once logged in with a valid user name and password, you are presented with a list of the tasks that are currently assigned to you. They are ordered by start time, beginning with the first task for today. If you want to see older tasks you will need to click on the schedule button in the top menu bar and then click on the old tasks button in the left hand menu bar.

Since there are no tasks in the system at the moment, we should add one by clicking on the Add task link on the left menu. Once you enter the task details, you should be able to see the task in the task list. If you are a

**instant message**

▶ If you use a Web directory name other than pim, you will have to change the value of the `request.webroot` variable in `_config.cfm` accordingly.

**instant message**

▶ If you place the pim directory anywhere other than in the root of the D: drive, the `request.fsroot` variable in `_config.cfm` will have to be changed accordingly.

member of the schedule administrators group, you will be able to choose the employee to whom the task should be assigned. If not, you can only add tasks for yourself.

## Email

In the email section, you are able to view your emails. The default view is the inbox, but you can choose a folder to view from the folders in the left menu. Clicking on the subject of a message allows you to view the message. When viewing a message, you can move the message to a different folder, assign it to a project, and reply to the message.

On the left menu the Compose button allows you to create a new message, and the drafts button allows you to view previously saved messages that have not yet been sent.

## Projects

Clicking on the Projects button on the top menu will display a list of all the active projects of which you are a participant. The background color for the due date indicates how urgent the project is. Projects that have a due date more than 60 days in the future have a grey background, projects that have a due date today, or in the past have a red background. Projects with a due date less than 60 days in the future have a background color between grey and red, the redder the background, the sooner the due date.

Clicking on the name of a project shows the details for the project, including the overview, project members, project notes, project emails, project notes, project documents. For each project member you can see the total hours that person has spent on the project. This number is calculated from the start and end times for the project tasks, so it is important to make sure that these are correct when the task is marked as done. On the left menu you have buttons to allow you to add notes and documents to the current project.

Moving back to the project list, project administrators can add new projects, deactivate projects, and edit projects. The owner of a project can edit the project details, activate, and deactivate the project. All project members can add notes and documents to a project.

### Users

Clicking on the Users button in the top menu will display a list of all the users in the system. Clicking on a user's name will show the details for that user including the email address and other contact information such as telephone number. Members of the user administrator group can edit the group memberships of other users.

### Locations

Clicking on the Locations button in the top menu displays a list of the locations in the system. The list shows the name and summary address information for each location. Clicking on the location name displays all the information for that location. For each location there is the possibility to enter the telephone number, the address, and a description. Members of the location administrators group can add new locations and edit existing locations.

### Exchange

Clicking on the Exchange button in the top menu displays a list of the contacts in the Exchange Server public contacts folder. Clicking on a contact name will show the full details for that contact from the Exchange Server. Clicking on the calendar button on the left menu will display a list of the events currently in the public calendar on the Exchange Server. This list will show the events that are happening in the future.

### Log-out

Clicking on the log-out button in the top menu will log you out of the system and show the log-in form. If you are using the application at a client site, or on a shared computer, you should use this log-out button before browsing to any other sites.

## Testing Results

By the end of the following week, Dave receives several bemused phone calls from Phil about how to read and understand the Outlook Object Model from the MSDN Web site. During the course of these calls, Dave ascertains that the PIM application is working pretty well. There have been some problems such as people assigning email to projects and not having a way to unassign them, but otherwise the system seems to be running as expected.

Ben calls Jim to arrange a meeting for Monday, July 8, to discuss the results of the test and see what work needs to be done in the future.

At the meeting Jim comes up with the following problems and enhancement requests:

- **Project email.** Can assign email to a project but need way to unassign email from a project.

- **Schedule.** Can't assign a task to only a project. Would be good if we could assign a task to no one in particular.

- **Email folders.** No way to filter email messages as they arrive. Do they have to be manually added to a folder?

- **Schedule.** Once a task has been accepted, there is no way to reverse that. If someone can't perform a task for some reason, it would be useful if they could unaccept a task.

- **Log-in.** Would it be possible to take the password out of the log file that is generated for invalid log-ins?

- **Projects.** Would it be possible to get a sum of the hours per person on a project, and a sum for the project as a whole? Also, need a way to sent email to all project members.

- **Email.** The received date seems to be the same for a lot of email. Presumably this is the date they were added to the database. Would it be possible to use the date each email was sent?

- **Public folders.** Would it be possible to view all the public folders?

Ben and David both feel that most of the items on the list are enhancement requests rather than bug fixes or problems with the PIM application design. Two exceptions are the reassignment of project email, which they agree should be a two-way process, and the date for email messages, both of which could be considered bugs as they directly affect the usefulness of the system.

Most of the other requests are minor and can easily be accommodated in the budget for the project. Two are considered outside the scope of what the project was budgeted for:

- **Filtering emails as they arrive.** There are entire applications written to perform this task. It would be no simple matter to write a system to do any sort of filtering. At the very least, it would require the creation of several more pages in the PIM application.

- **Viewing all public folders.** This could easily turn into a major headache. Although Tom solved many of the problems with looping over and interacting with COM objects, there are just too many unknown aspects to be sure of being able to deliver a solution in a reasonable amount of time.

Ben suggests that Q42 should fix the problems and add the enhancements (except the two that don't fit the budget) during the rest of the week. The two exceptions will have to be negotiated as a separate contract, as they would require quite a lot of work and are beyond the scope of what Q42 promised FarSight.

Although Jim is not entirely happy with the inability to retrieve all information from the public folders, he eventually concedes that even at the very first meeting Ben mentioned how difficult it could be to connect to the Exchange Server and retrieve information.

This leads to the suggestion that once he becomes more familiar with ColdFusion and COM, Phil might be able to implement that functionality. Phil is quick to point out that he got precisely nowhere with the problem during the week, and certainly does not want the burden of expectation thrust upon him.

It is suggested that it may be better if Phil tries to add a simple email filtering system that filters email based only on all or part of the email address from which the email is sent. Since many of the messages come from corporate clients, this should be adequate to handle the bulk of them.

In order to assist with this, a support contract is agreed on. FarSight can use this contract to request telephone, email, or on-site support at 50 percent of the normal fee that Q42 would charge. For the first month after installation, this support will be provided at no extra charge above the cost of the PIM application development. Thereafter, FarSight can purchase further support at a monthly rate.

Once these terms are established, Ben and Dave return to the Q42 office to begin implementing the changes.

II-5
II-5
II-5
II-5
II-5 ▶

Delivery

# Finalizing the Application

While Dave and Ben are on-site with FarSight, Tom is busy playing around with the Q42 Exchange server. After a little puzzling over the details, he manages to discover that the Exchange server administrator has access to all the mailboxes on the server. He reasons that if he uses the Exchange server's administrator account as the log-in account for the Macromedia ColdFusion MX application server service, he should be able to use Microsoft Outlook and COM to get full information about the calendar and tasks for all the Exchange server users. After some experimentation, he finds that he can indeed get full access to the mailboxes from ColdFusion MX. Unfortunately, he doesn't see an easy way to automate this, as the names of the mailboxes and their exact structure can't be easily determined. He also finds that working with the Outlook object is particularly slow if he has to loop over all the folders and mailboxes to find the specific one he wants to work with.

Once Dave and Ben return, Tom shares his discovery with them. Although it gives them a huge increase in the amount of data they can access, and could ultimately allow them to meet all the original requirements for the project, they decide that it's not tested well enough to add to the application at such a late stage. They do, however, decide to tell FarSight once they investigate a little further.

After they implement the changes and fixes in the application, Ben sends the following email to Jim:

**Ready for prime time**

**Email**

**Date:** July 2

**To:** Jim Forsyth

**From:** Ben Richards

**Subject:** Ready for prime time

Hi Jim,

Just a quick note to let you know that we have completed the fixes and modifications to the application. If you let us know a suitable date and time, Dave will pop over and add the modified files.

We've also had some success with getting more information from the Exchange server, but we're still in the process of figuring out the best way to make it reliable.

I trust that the app is running smoothly apart from the issues we discussed last week.

Ben

First thing the next morning, Ben receives a reply:

---

**RE: Ready for prime time**

**Email**

**Date:** July 3

**To:** Ben Richards

**From:** Jim Forsyth

**Subject:** RE: Ready for prime time

That's great, Ben.

We should be able to accommodate Dave if he comes around either Thursday or Friday of this week. Phil is on holiday next week, and I'd really prefer him to be here when the application is being modified so he has a clear picture of what's changed.

Apart from a few minor things that Phil is looking into, we haven't had any more problems with the app. We've had a few teething problems, as the staff doesn't always understand where to go to perform a particular task, but that's to be expected in any new software.

We've noticed that there are a lot of requests coming in from the staff for things they would like to see added to the system—things like a search engine for email and contacts, a way to easily find the best time for a meeting based on availability, and a few others. The Exchange server stuff sounds very encouraging. Maybe we should have another meeting in a few weeks to discuss adding the various bits and pieces to the application. I think Phil is going to be a bit overwhelmed if we hand it all to him.

Regards,

Jim Forsyth

This is more than Ben was hoping for as far as a second phase for the project is concerned. He writes himself a note to call Jim one week after the final application has been deployed. This will allow him to check that the application is running smoothly, and to schedule a meeting to plan the next phase.

The following day Dave visits FarSight to deploy the updated application. He has already spoken with Phil, who wants to add his simple email filter to the system at the same time.

The filter simply lets users specify the folder to which new email would be assigned based on the domain name from which they are sent. Phil added another button on the left menu, in the email section of the application, to give users access to the filter configuration page. He also added another table to the database called Emailfilters. This table has three columns: userid, domain, and folder. When the messages are retrieved from the server, the domain from which it is sent is checked to see if it matches any of the entries in the Emailfilters table for that user. If so, it is assigned to the relevant folder instead of the in-box.

With a little modification from Dave to improve the performance of the filter system, it works as expected, so it's added to the live server along with the updated code that Dave brought with him.

After adding all the new code to the server and testing the various sections, Dave is happy that the application can now be considered complete. He gives a copy of the code to Phil to use on his development server and returns to the Q42 office.

## Postmortem

As was mentioned earlier, Dave has a very structured approach to almost everything he does. Once he returns to the Q42 office, he takes some time to reflect on the project.

Reflecting on the project as a whole, Dave can't help thinking that with their current level of knowledge of communication with Exchange Server it would probably make a lot of sense if as much information as possible was kept there rather than in the relational database. This would allow much tighter integration with the Exchange server. Since Exchange Server already exposes a wide range of options for collaboration, messaging, calendaring and it would have been nice to leverage these features rather than rewriting large portions of them as ColdFusion components (CFCs). Taking advantage of the features of Exchange Server may well also have allowed them to add more features to the application, such as making a distinction between tasks and calendar events.

### Exchange Server

Although the Q42 developers were unable to meet all of the requirements for communicating with the Exchange server, they're now well on their way to getting the tasks and calendar entries for individual users. They will be able to deliver that as a future upgrade. In addition, they learned a lot about the possibilities for communicating with Exchange, and—in theory at least—should be able to reproduce the same level of functionality as in the standard Microsoft Outlook Web interface.

The email system could have been more fully featured, but it is certainly adequate for normal email needs. In addition to the current features, Dave decides that the virtual folders would probably be more useful if they were structured as a hierarchy rather than a single level. Some email filtering rules would also be a good addition, so that messages could be automatically moved or copied to a folder when they arrived. Another useful addition would be a search engine that allowed for the searching of words in the subject line and message body. Despite these possible enhancements, the system performs well for basic email handling.

### Task Scheduling

This part of the system would really have benefited from communicating directly with the Exchange server tasks for each user. Even without this capability, it allows for a reasonable level of task scheduling. Some possible additions would be a graphical view of utilization to supplement the task list. Also, it would be useful to be able to see the availability of employees when scheduling meetings.

### Projects

David is fairly happy with the level of functionality in the projects system, but he feels that it would also be good to provide a mechanism to allow clients to view some of the information and for them to add notes and documents. If anything, the projects system could benefit from being more tightly integrated with the schedule system. If it's possible to specify the dependencies between tasks, it should be possible to create a simple project time line. This would help in management of project costs and deadlines, and would provide a graphical way to see the amount of work a project takes.

### Architecture

Using the CFC architecture provides new ideas for future systems. Dave finds that components can be seen in a number of ways:

- As a collection of user-defined functions, or a function library.

- As objects that have properties and functions that operate on those properties.

- As services for data management that provide functions to manipulate, store, and retrieve data.

- As an alternative to custom tags.

Each of these ways of looking at components appears to be perfectly valid.

Using a component as a function library would not really yield any of the benefits provided by inheritance, nor would it take advantage of the metadata that can be stored in the `cfproperty` tags.

Using components as an alternative to custom tags is really only applicable for tags that don't have an end tag, but apart from that there isn't really any reason not to use them in that way. Dave did set a rule that the components would not output any data, to make them more flexible if they are later used with Macromedia Flash or another interface, or as Web Services.

Since CFCs are compiled to Java-class files, using them as objects with properties can be seen as the most correct thing to do. However, as a long-time ColdFusion programmer, Dave feels that using components as objects is a little more complex than he really needed in the application. Just deciding on what the objects in the system should be is difficult enough without having to decide on exactly what the data type should be for each of the object's properties. Should the attachment for an email message be a separate object type with methods of attach, remove, and download? Or should it just be a property of the email component that contains the same methods? Although considering such factors would undoubtedly result in a well-designed system once all the objects and properties were defined, Dave feels that this particular application really did not require this level of detail.

Using components as services seems to make the most sense in this application. The data returned by the component is often a query coming directly from the database. There isn't a large amount of business logic to perform on the data after it's retrieved, so normally the query can be returned directly to the calling page without further processing after being retrieved from the database.

The system for creating the functions as include files for the components works well from the viewpoint of quickly seeing what is happening. But because the functions were often called by an include file of the same name, editing them became a little confusing at times, as often the include file would be opened instead of the function file, or vice versa. Dave decides to change the way the system works in the next project: All function include files will be prefixed with "fn_" so the editor will more easily recognize them.

The modularity of the system is also something Dave tried hard to achieve, and with a little modification it should be possible to use the individual components with their include files in other projects.

## Phase 2

Looking to the possibilities for the second phase of the application, Dave notes that several features have already been requested by FarSight, either as part of the original application requirements, or since the initial deployment. They are as follows:

- Task and calendar information in the Exchange server for each user should be made available in the PIM application.

- Task and calendar information added to the PIM application should also be added to the Exchange server so that managers at the main FarSight office can see the information in their Outlook interface as well as in the PIM interface.

- It should be possible to create custom email filters to filter emails into folders when they arrive. This could also include more complex filter rules such as always forwarding messages from a particular person to another person, or group of people.

- All Exchange Server public folder information should be available from within the PIM application interface.

- A search interface for each of the sections of the PIM application.

As well as these, David would like to make the following changes and additions:

- All tasks should be stored in the Exchange server. The current schedule table in the database would just be used for the purpose of calculating the amount of time each employee has spent on a particular project.

- The current JavaScript date picker to be replaced with a Flash MX component as that could be embedded directly in the page rather than working as a pop-up window.

- A new interface would be created for displaying tasks in a graphical calendar format rather than as a list. This interface would include the buttons to add new tasks and make it impossible to schedule multiple tasks at the same time for an individual.

- As a more ambitious goal, Dave would also like to do some research into re-creating the same functionality as the Microsoft Outlook Web interface using Flash MX for the interface, and CFCs as the link between the interface and the Exchange server.

Once Dave has finished this review, he is happy to say that the project has gone pretty well in general. The client is happy with the application that was delivered, and they have already begun to ask for future enhancements and improvements, which is always a good sign that they were reasonably happy with what was delivered to them. Q42 have also gained a Personal Information Management application which they can easily modify for their own use. Now if he could just get Tom Green to put comments in his code, he'd be a happy man.

# Part III

# Human Resources

Human Resources is a forms and workflow application. It features form management and routing, data import and export engines, XML integration, as well as data reporting and analysis.

Product Requirements

## An Interesting Problem at Linley Engineering

Linley Engineering is a medium-size engineering company headquartered in the United Kingdom, with offices in France, Italy, and Japan. Since three years ago, after very poor results that prompted the departure of its then-CEO, they're now well underway with a major restructuring program led by a new CEO, Stephen James, who was parachuted in as a Mr. Fix-It by Linley's board of directors.

Stephen quickly realized that one of the company's main problems was its longstanding underinvestment in IT infrastructure. All of Linley's competitors had taken advantage of Internet technologies to streamline their operations. They were also handling more work than Linley, taking less time per project, and making more profit on each project just by having more efficient internal processes.

Over the last two years, many of Linley's internal processes have been updated. Traditional paper-based systems have gone, replaced with Internet solutions. The IT department approached the human resources (HR) department 12 months ago with plans to modernize its functions as well, but HR was insistent on retaining its paper-based systems. That's all about to change.

## 21st-century job loss

### Email

**Date:** April 1

**To:** Laura (HR Director)

**From:** Stephen (CEO)

**Subject:** 21st-century job loss

Laura, I'm very concerned about HR's refusal to join the 21st century. During the all-hands meeting this week, I discovered that our employees are still filling in paper-based forms for all sorts of tasks: travel requests, purchase orders, and so on.

I'm tired of having my hard-working staff whine about simple day-to-day stuff. More importantly, the board is pretty concerned in general about our commitment to modernizing the organization. Everyone else is on board and making great progress, so your team is looking pretty bad.

I know HR isn't sometimes seen as a core part of our business, but it is critical to how we perform; and right now, it's costing us too much money and taking up too much time.

So, Laura, you have a month to get your team into shape. Or I'll be happy to find someone else who can.

Stephen

---

**HR wasters need our help**

---

**Email**

---

**Date:** April 1

**To:** Toshi

**From:** Jane

**Subject:** HR wasters need our help

Hi Toshi,

Sorry to bother you with this, but HR is imploding and needs our help to build its intranet. I just had Laura on the phone, and apparently Stephen is finally twisting the screw and getting the department to join the rest of company in our drive to get systems updated. I know they bounced us over a year ago when we proposed this, but I guess we should try to help even so. Are you free on Monday to discuss with the HR director? She's still stuck in the dark ages—she doesn't really understand why Stephen's being so "unfair"—so bring a stress ball!

Oh, and they need this stuff done within the month. Will that be OK?

Jane

---

**Oh dear.<eom/>**

---

**Email**

---

**Date:** April 2

**To:** Jane

**From:** Toshi

**Subject:** Oh dear.

## Core Requirements

Human resources needs an application that provides a wide range of forms, four of which are key to the daily running of the organization: time sheets, travel requests, expense claims, and purchase (or procurement) requests. In addition, HR staff need the application to offer a library facility that will let employees locate forms easily. Before the IT team has its meeting with HR, Toshi takes a quick look at the existing paper-based solutions.

> We need to have a drop-down menu for the activities choice!

> Keep the core work time flexible!

### Time Sheets

At Linley, employees must complete time sheets on a daily basis. The time sheet records which activities employees spend their time on during the day, and allows managers and HR to establish staff utilization levels. An example of the current time sheet is included in the project folder for reference (see Figure III-1.1).

Once completed, the paper form is passed to a line manager, who reviews the time sheet, logs any data needed for departmental reports, and then passes the approved form to HR for archiving. Clearly, this process is inefficient; in fact, while managers do approve staff time sheets, they rarely have time to do any reporting. In the end, staff and managers are wasting time on a process that produces no results.

### General requirements:

- Form to collect time spent on activity
- Approval cycle
- Reporting functions

### Travel Requests

The travel request process is a little more productive. Staff members fill out a travel request form, indicating the date, mode of travel, and destination for the trip. The line manager is responsible for approving the trip request, leaving the employee free to book travel. Currently there's no single travel agency for the company; employees are free to make their own arrangements. However, I've heard that we may be signing up a global agency to handle all our travel; we should make sure the new app can integrate if that ever happens.

### General requirements:

- Form for date, mode of travel (drop-down menu), and country
- Approval cycle
- Notification mechanism to employee
- Need to ensure architecture is modular enough to allow remote access by new travel agent!

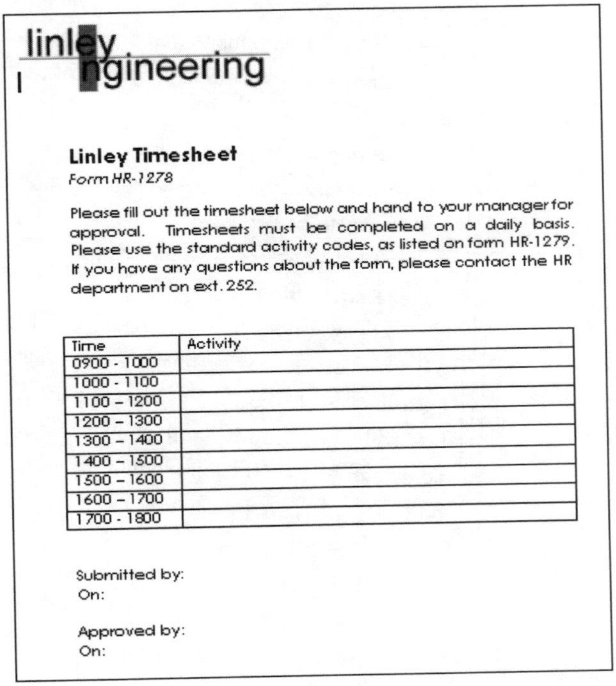

**Figure III-1.1**
Linley's paper-based timesheet is simple, but inflexible and inefficient.

# linley ngineering

### Linley Timesheet
*Form HR-1278*

Please fill out the timesheet below and hand to your manager for approval. Timesheets must be completed on a daily basis. Please use the standard activity codes, as listed on form HR-1279. If you have any questions about the form, please contact the HR department on ext. 252.

| Time | Activity |
|------|----------|
| 0900 - 1000 | |
| 1000 - 1100 | |
| 1100 - 1200 | |
| 1200 - 1300 | |
| 1300 - 1400 | |
| 1400 - 1500 | |
| 1500 - 1600 | |
| 1600 - 1700 | |
| 1700 - 1800 | |

Submitted by:
On:

Approved by:
On:

### Expense Claims

Expense claim forms are currently distributed as an Excel spreadsheet that staff members fill out and submit on a weekly basis to managers. Managers approve claims and then forward them to the accounts department for payment to the employee. Employees need to see when a claim has been approved. We need to allow for multiple currencies and for a range of standard expenses types.

**General requirements:**

- Form for date of expense, submission date, currency, amount, and purpose
- Approval cycle (again!)
- Reporting/view function for employees

### Purchase Orders

This one should be easy, but we have a messy business process (due to cost-saving issues). Any employees who need to make a capital purchase must fill out a request for purchase indicating the item, the value, the supplier (if known), and the purchase date. This must be approved by their line managers, and then by accounts, before going to the procurement manager for action. The workflow is a little messy; anyone in accounts can sign off, so this has to go to multiple individuals.

**General requirements:**

- Form to support item, supplier, value
- More complex workflow
- Email notifications at each stage

### Other Requirements

It seems like we might need some kind of forms library, but I think just a simple list of existing forms, maybe linking to Portable Document Format files (PDFs), will be OK for this. We also need to think about how to handle security and authentication, and we need to remember to design for the future. Modularity will be key to getting this done on time!

## Not as bad as I thought

### Email

**Date:** April 5

**To:** Jane

**From:** Toshi

**Subject:** Not as bad as I thought

Hi Jane. I've done some basic analysis of the requirements. Actually, I don't think this will be too bad. There's not too much complexity, and I think we can modularize really nicely to save ourselves time both in the initial phase and for any future extensibility. We should be able to lock down requirements pretty solidly during our meeting on Monday (I booked a room, BTW), and then I should be able to get the blueprint system design in place by the end of that week. A couple of weeks to build, a week to test, and we should have the system live for around May 8. Do you think that will work for Linley's month deadline?

Have a great weekend. I'll see you Monday.

Toshi

III-2
III-2
III-2
III-2
III-2 ▶

Initial Thoughts

**Planning**

**Email**

**Date:** April 8

**To:** Toshi

**From:** Jane

**Subject:** Planning

Hi Toshi,

Seemed like a pretty good meeting with HR earlier. Laura's requirements don't seem too hard. I agree with the rough schedule you proposed in your mail late Friday night.

Do you have some time later today? I'd like to throw around some ideas about architecture. Seems to me that we have a couple of high-level issues to consider: reuse and extensibility. I think there should be a good solution to both of those by using a component-based architecture, but I'd like to talk it through. See you in the boardroom around 15:00? It has a nice whiteboard.... ;-)

Jane

# General Architecture

The application that needs to be built for Laura and the human resources (HR) department doesn't look too tricky on the face of it. As the team starts to plan the application, they need to consider four key sections: time sheets, travel requests, expense claims, and procurement—plus a simple forms library and some kind of security or authentication mechanism. The team also needs to be aware, however, that client requirements have a tendency to change—particularly where the client isn't highly technical—so the application needs to be built in such a way that it can easily evolve. In addition, in doing some early requirements gathering with the end-users of the application (Toshi's coworkers), Toshi has become aware of some additional features that he'd like to add to the application, even though Laura hasn't actually requested them.

In thinking about the general architecture for the application, then, the team needs to bear in mind the following:

- **Data persistence.** How the data generated by the application will be stored, and how the application's architecture will interact with the storage mechanism. The team is concerned not with the persistence of session data—this is a relatively simple matter and handled in the usual way using either session or client variables—but rather with how best to have their application code interact with the data storage layer. In order to easily be able to add additional functionality later, the team needs to avoid using queries straight in the page, but rather needs to find a way to reuse code that interacts with the database. This then is the 'persistence layer' the team needs to develop.

- **Code reuse and extensibility.** How the application can maximize code reuse, while at the same time be optimized to allow for the rapid addition of new features. This applies not only to the underlying application logic, but also, where possible, to the style and the layout of the user interface (UI).

- **Application structure and layout.** From the user's perspective, how the application will be laid out—including sections and pages, the general look and feel, and navigation.

Now that Toshi has had a chance to consider the general architecture, he starts to figure out how best to deal with key elements of the application, always bearing in mind that last-minute changes to the requirements are almost guaranteed.

SUBJECT: PLANNING FOR CHANGES

I'm not sure Laura has a good sense of what requirements are for, so we need to assume that our deliverables will change during the build. I also think we might need to add some features the HR team hasn't thought of yet.

I'd rather start with a full set of signed-off specs, but I don't think we'll be able to do that this time. So we need to make sure that we plan an architecture that allows for last-minute changes. ColdFusion MX components (CFCs) should help with this. If I wrap most of the logic inside a few components, it will be much easier to alter or enhance the application later. We just need to be careful not to let this add too much extra time to the development cycle (I don't think it will, and the savings will be worth a little extra effort later on).

## Persistence

Central to Toshi's early thinking about the application is the question of how to store data, and how to handle interactions with the database. First, though, he needs to make some decisions about how tightly to integrate this new system into their current application's infrastructure.

SUBJECT: WHERE TO STORE DATA

We have some interesting choices here. We could integrate this system with the other internal systems we've done. That would mean tying the authentication system into the LDAP back end. We'd also have to think about how to alter our existing tables in SQL Server to allow for this new data. Hmm, with the deadlines we have, perhaps it would be better, for now at least, to make this a stand-alone system with an MS Access database back end. I can always migrate the data later if I need to, and it'll be much quicker to prototype the system this way. I don't want to run on Access for too long, though—all sorts of scalability issues here—so we'll make sure to plan migration to SQL Server as part of phase two. See the project file for a rough of the database architecture.

Toshi's schematic of the database architecture is shown in Figure III-2.1.

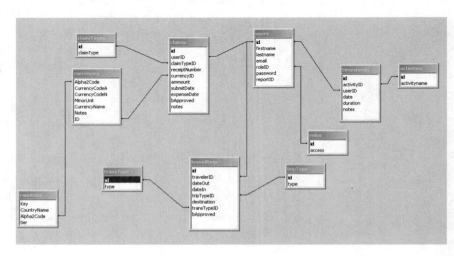

**Figure III-2.1**

This is an early schematic of the database architecture Toshi is planning to use.

### Persistence Architecture

The development team needs to make some decisions about how to store the data and how the application should interact with the storage mechanism. Most of the forms will generate some data that needs to be stored, or "persisted." In most cases this data is structured, so the logical place to store the data is a database. The team needs to consider how to structure the database, but it's likely that a standard structure will be the best option.

A more complex issue is deciding how to have the application interact with the database. There are three options for this:

- Place query statements at various points within the code, whenever required. This makes for very quick coding in the first instance, but if anything changes later during the build, or if there's a second phase of construction, the team would need to make many changes throughout the code.

- Build custom tags containing the query statements. This is a better option: It allows for database operations to be held separately from the presentation code. It also allows it to be more centralized, thus reducing the impact of any future application changes. However, Macromedia ColdFusion MX presents a third interesting alternative.

- Build CFCs for each type of data that will be generated. This is the most flexible of the three options. Components essentially allow the team to model the various data structures within the application code. Component code can contain the logic to access the database and provide a modular way to build and develop the application.

### Code Reuse

There are two major issues to contend with when it comes to code reuse: form handlers, and style and layout reuse.

## Form Handlers

### A revelation

### Email

**Date:** April 8

**To:** Jane

**From:** Toshi

**Subject:** A revelation

Hey Jane! Following our meeting earlier today, I had a great vision for the architecture we need to use. Here's the trick: Any content generated by a given forms process is actually a CFC. The component itself includes the code for content persistence as well as other utility code written to handle that particular content (such as reporting). In addition, we'll make a user component, which should make authentication a little simpler.

Once we've taken that step, forms and handlers get really easy! The form self-posts; we can then invoke a component of the correct type and simply run the relevant method (update, store, delete, whatever).

Now for the really clever part. I can have a top-level component called something like persistedData that contains any generic persistence methods—delete(), for instance. Now, every time I need to delete a given item, I know that I have a method to do it. Neat, huh? I attached a simple diagram to show conceptually how this works.

I'm going to try to build a prototype overnight. I'm really excited about this!

See you tomorrow.

T.

Toshi's diagram is shown in Figure III-2.2. The architecture Toshi is proposing solves a number of problems. First, it means that the code for handling the content is separate from the form. That's a huge bonus when it comes to updating either the back-end business logic or the front-end design and presentation logic. It also makes it much easier for other developers to understand how the application works—particularly useful if new developers come to the application in a few months (or years)

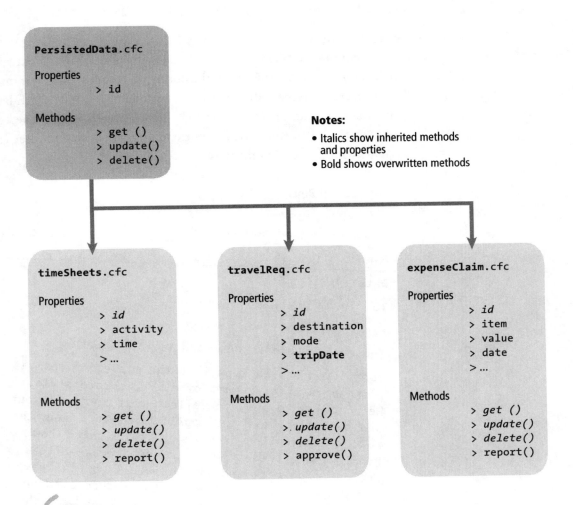

**Figure III-2.2**
A conceptual model shows how Toshi can use components and component inheritance to build reusable form handlers.

time. The handler code can be found very quickly, and CFCs self-document, so it's easy to learn the application's structure.

Second, it means that Toshi will easily be able to extend the application to other systems both inside and outside the company. CFCs can quickly be exposed through the Simple Object Access Protocol (SOAP) as a SOAP-based Web service, meaning that any SOAP-enabled application can call methods on Toshi's components. Likewise, Toshi can make use of other (external or internal) Web Services within his CFCs.

Third, it means that the application's UI can evolve over time from that of a straightforward HTML-based interface to that of a rich Internet application using Macromedia Flash on the front-end. Toshi can plan this migration to occur incrementally over time, introducing simple Flash-based components within HTML pages first. Later, if appropriate, the team could use the entire application front end built in Flash—another great possibility for a second build phase.

### Style and Layout Reuse

**Design issues (and working late)**

**Email**

Date: April 9

To: Toshi

From: Jane

Subject: Design issues (and working late)

Toshi, you should know that the marketing team is planning a major revamp of our corporate style. We're going to need to reflect that in the layout and design for all our applications—including the new HR application. You should think about how to handle that. I don't want to spend weeks after we deploy going back and fixing page layout. I have our graphics agency lined up to produce all the relevant bits and pieces as soon as we have the new guidelines from marketing. We'll probably need to get all these changes live in June.

---

**Design issues (and working late)**

---

**Email (continued)**

---

Also, I know you're very excited about being able to use CFMX and CFCs for this new project, but please be careful working too late in the office. Stephen was in late last night as well, and was on to me this morning about taking care of my staff... Two a.m. is probably pushing it.

Thanks.

Jane

---

**RE: Design issues (and working late)**

---

**Email**

---

**Date:** April 9

**To:** Jane

**From:** Toshi

**Subject:** RE: Design issues (and working late)

Sorry about last night. I was really psyched about what we can do with this new component architecture. It's going to save us a lot of time. We should plan on revising some of our old applications as well.

As for the design changes, no problem. We'll build a wrapper tag to put around each page. That wrapper tag will provide the layout and we'll use cascading style sheets (CSS) for the style. We should have only a few files to update, then, when they make these changes.

T.

So, although CFCs provide a neat way to encapsulate and reuse logic, there are still plenty of places where traditional custom tags make a lot of sense. In deciding to build a custom tag that contains the generic layout for every page, the team ensures that every page in the application has a consistent look and feel. It also means that if the design needs to change at any point, there's only the one file to update.

## SUBJECT: DISPLAY OPTIONS: COMPONENTS OR CUSTOM TAGS

- Using a custom tag to handle the layout and the look and feel is a nice easy way to solve the display reuse problem. Worth noting for other projects, though, is that you could put display handling into a CFC. There's an argument about whether it's 'right' or 'wrong' to put display elements into components. The benefit is that you can inherit the display logic, which promotes reuse. The downside is that you end up with presentation tags (HTML and so on) locked into your code, which makes it harder to designers to change.
- The team will need to figure out whether to put all the display logic into a single CFC and inherit it, or whether to put display functions into each component. Both are valid options—it would really depend on the nature of the application itself.

The team will also be using cascading style sheets for the design elements of the application. This is a good solution for this application, since Jane and Toshi have control of the end-user browser. For other external applications, CSSs still have benefits, but it can be hard to ensure that a given style sheet will give consistent results across multiple browsers and platforms.

### Application Structure and Layout

With regard to usage scenarios, there are really only two kinds of users in this system: managers and non-managers. The view each type of user has of the application will differ: Specifically, they will allow managers to view everything—reports, requests, and so on, for every employee. Given their new open-management ethos, they don't need to lock this down by department for now, but they should leave this option open for later.

Each user, then, will do the following:

1. Log in.
2. Select a section.

3. View the current status in that section. Non-managers will see the current status of any of their own items in that section; managers will, in addition, see an overview of general activity.

4. Select an action. This could be to create a new item, to edit or delete a current item, or, for mangers, to built a report. For some sections they will also need an option to approve an item, though that could be wrapped into an edit.

5. Once an action is complete, the user returns to the main page. The project file contains a sample workflow for the travel request process (see Figure III-2.3).

Now that the team has a good sense of how the application will be used, they can start to think about the general structure of the application in terms of what pages will be needed and how the pages will be linked together. The draft plan they'll use to start the build is shown in Figure II-2.4.

The simple structure allows for easy expansion. Because of Toshi's use of a custom "wrapper" tag in each page to handle look and feel, the developers don't need to worry about the design until later in the build. They can make sure all the logic works first and, as long as they've included the custom tag in each page, they can instantly apply the design later just by updating that single custom tag.

The only exception to this will be if a particular section needs a custom layout. At this point in the planning, the team is assuming that all sections will have the same layout. Normally this is a reasonable assumption, since most users like to have a consistent look and feel through an application to avoid any confusion. However, the team has also considered the possibility that a given section will need a custom look and feel.

**instant message**

The custom look-and-feel tag `<CF_WRAP>` will need a "section" attribute to allow breakout from the app's standard look and feel, if required.

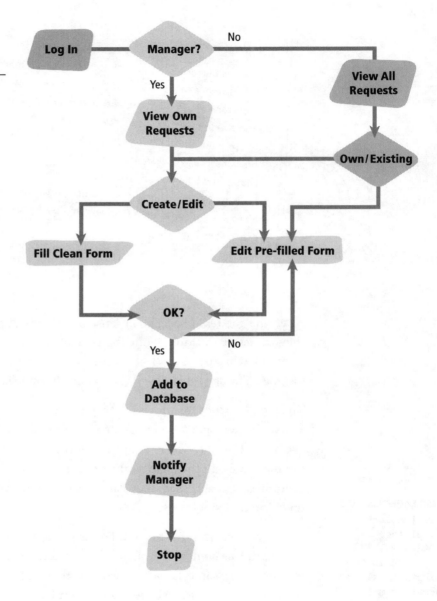

**Figure III-2.3**
A simple workflow diagram shows a travel request progress from creation to approval.

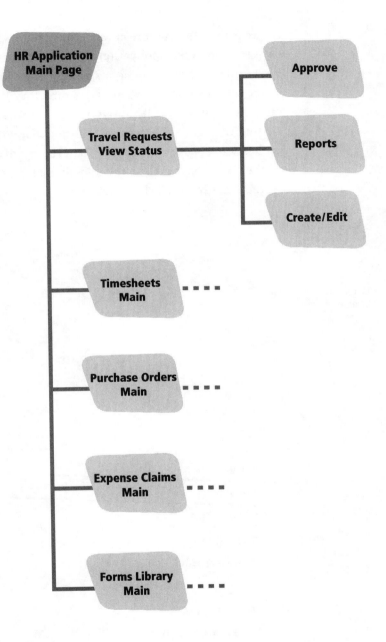

**Figure III-2.4**
Here is the plan showing
the general structure
of the application.

As far as the file structure is concerned, there will be a single directory for each section of the application. Any assets (images and so on) specific to a section will live in an assets subdirectory of that section's directory. There will also be a general assets directory located off the application directory root; this will contain images, database resources, style sheets, custom tags, and other general utilities that will be used throughout the application. Finally, the team will build a system directory that will contain all the CFCs that make up the underlying forms-handling and persistence system. Figure III-2.5 shows the initial directory structure.

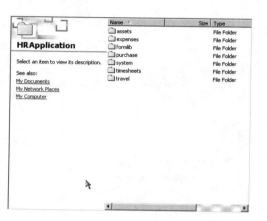

**Figure III-2.5**

Here is the initial directory structure for the application.

**Off we go**

**Email**

Date: April 10

To: Jane

From: Toshi

Subject: Off we go

Hi Jane,

I think we have enough now to start building a prototype. I'll string some code together over the next few days. How about we get together to review progress early next week?

> **Off we go**
>
> **Email (continued)**
>
> For design, I'll leave things simple—maybe just a menu bar at the top of each page with the corporate logo and a plain background? I don't think we need anything too clever for now. We can add in whatever the design folks come up with when they're ready. I've attached a sample image for you. BTW, can you let me know when you expect to get the creative so I can plan some time to turn the design into something approaching reality? ;-)
>
> Later,
>
> T.

Toshi's image appears in Figure III-2.6.

Figure III-2.6
Toshi will use a prototype design for the application until the design team provide the final creative.

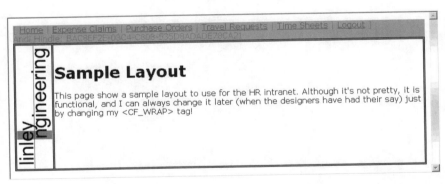

# Development

Toward the end of the second week of the project, Toshi starts to write some test code for a prototype of the human resources (HR) application. Given the tight development schedule, Toshi is planning to turn this sample code into the final code for the application. This organic development process isn't Toshi's preferred way to build an application, but it's a pragmatic solution for this particular project. Also, Toshi knows that the application is only for internal use and will be evolving rapidly over time, so he can afford to follow a somewhat less rigorous process.

Toshi thinks about each application problem like a lock that is missing a key. He needs to find the right key to solve each problem. As we saw in Chapter 2, Toshi's key to unlocking the HR application lies in a single concept: Every form process ultimately generates a document—or data that must be stored.

# First Attempts

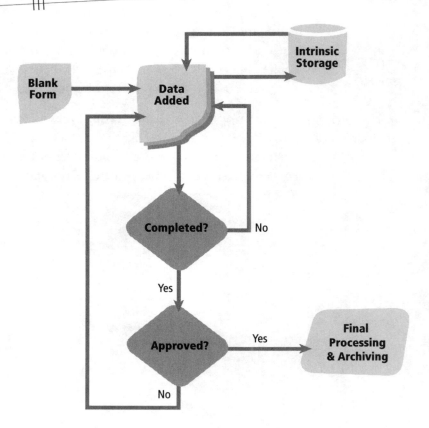

TOSHI'S PROJECT NOTEBOOK

**The Fundamentals**

Let's think about this as a physical process first. That way we should be able to derive the application structure.

Looking at how people currently handle forms, we know that every HR process generates data. That data needs to be stored, and it may be altered or updated during the process. Some of the data also needs to be approved during the process before it can be stored.

Check out the illustration below (see Figure III-3.1).

**Figure III-3.1**
Every HR process generates data that is stored.

Blank Form → Data Added → Intrinsic Storage

Completed? No → Data Added

Completed? Yes ↓

Approved? Yes → Final Processing & Archiving

Approved? No

Notice that the process includes storage of data. This is intrinsic in a paper-based process: Data is naturally stored as it gets written down. For the new Web-based system, though, Toshi needs to take this factor into account in the design.

So, how should I translate this to a Web-based system?

The key is exactly this: Every form generates data for storage. If I represent each document type (or artifact) as a component, then I should have an elegant mechanism for handling data within the application. Here's the logic:

- Every form generates a document (=artifact/data).
- Every document is represented by a ColdFusion component (CFC).
- Each CFC is tied to a structure in the database.
- Any CFC which persists extends **persistedData**.

Aha! Here's the really clever part. Because CFCs give me inheritance, I should be able to code the relevant database calls into **persistedData**. If I can do this, then I can put my SQL statements in a single place. Any other data that needs to be stored lives in its own component which extends the code system component. This should save a lot of time.

Plus, later, if I decide to change how I interact with the database (once I move to SQL server, I should probably used stored procedures), I only need to change a few lines of code.

I need to test this as a concept. Hmm. I'm going to need some users in the database, so let's start with that.

## Core Requirements

Toshi's plan is the essence of simplicity. ColdFusion MX introduces a component architecture that allows for inheritance. Toshi has made a link between data and components. If he represents his real data as logical components, he can handle his data easily within the logic of the application. Further, many data elements have a shared requirement: They need to be stored during and after an HR process. Shared requirements like this lend themselves well to inheritance.

As always, using new technology and techniques means that ideas have to be tested before being deployed wholesale into an application build. In this case Toshi begins by figuring out how to apply his conceptual model to a real-use case. His system needs a way to store user data—names, passwords, and so on. It also needs a simple process for adding new users—a form, in other words. This will make a good, contained test case.

## TOSHI'S PROJECT NOTEBOOK

### User Properties

Users have the following properties:

- **id.** unique ID number for this user
- **firstName.** user's first name; they'll use this as their user name to log in. Note that I might need to change this later in case I need to have unique user names; in any event, the user name/password combination will have to be unique, so I must remember to test for that
- **lastName.** user's last name
- **eMail.** user's email address
- **roleID.** an ID number representing the user's role. We'll use this for security later.
- **password.** user's password. We'll use this for security later.
- **reportID.** the unique ID number of the user to whom this user reports directly

### User Methods

I need to be able to do the following things with users:

- **list.** Lists out all users. Inherited from **persistedData**?
- **get.** gets specific user details. Inherited from **persistedData**?
- **create.** creates (and updates) a new user. Inherited from **persistedData**?
- **update.** updates existing user details. Inherited from **persistedData**?
- **check user.** authenticates a given user name:password combination. Not inherited.
- **delete.** deletes an existing user. Inherited from **persistedData**?

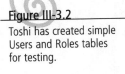

**User Design**

Now that I have a good idea of what I need my user component to do, I need to build a database table to store the data in. I'm actually going to build two tables: one for the users, and one for the various roles. Later, I can build an interface to allow for new roles to be created, updated, and so on. For now, though, I'll just add in three simple roles to get going.

I'll also need a simple form to handle users. I'll put all utilities like this under the system folder, along with the core system components like **persistedData.cfc** and **user.cfc**.

Time to build code!

## First Build

Toshi now has to build out two components and one form to test that his conceptual model makes sense in a real application. First, though, he builds the database tables he needs to store the data. Figure III-3.2 shows the initial tables; Toshi has prepopulated the Roles table for testing purposes.

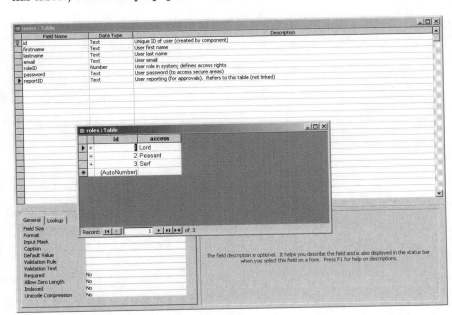

**Figure III-3.2**

Toshi has created simple Users and Roles tables for testing.

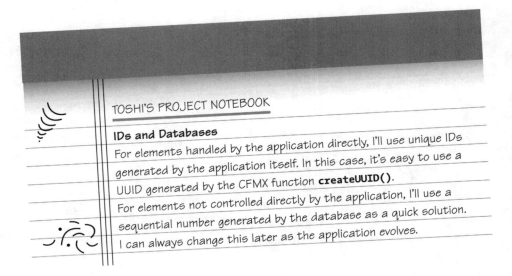

TOSHI'S PROJECT NOTEBOOK

**IDs and Databases**

For elements handled by the application directly, I'll use unique IDs generated by the application itself. In this case, it's easy to use a UUID generated by the CFMX function **createUUID()**.

For elements not controlled directly by the application, I'll use a sequential number generated by the database as a quick solution. I can always change this later as the application evolves.

First, Toshi builds his persisted data component: **persistedData.cfc**. This is the parent component for all the data Toshi needs his application to store in the database—in essence, the product of any form process. The component builder in Dreamweaver MX—shown in Figure III-3.3—makes this a quick process, as long as Toshi has planned his component carefully up front.

**Figure III-3.3**

Using the component building in Dreamweaver MX to build functions for **persistedData.cfc**.

Once Toshi has defined the various functions and parameters in the component builder, Dreamweaver MX generates the code skeleton for the component. It's now fairly simple to build out the logic for each function within the component.

## TOSHI'S PROJECT NOTEBOOK

### Application-Level Variables

Using the application scope presents all sorts of challenges in terms of locking. Instead, I'll use the request scope to store vars I need through the application:

```
<!--- set up generic vars and object instances --->
<CFSCRIPT>
    stApp = structNew();
    request.stApp.date = now();
    request.stApp.odbcDate =
createODBCDate(request.stApp.date);
    request.stApp.shortDate =
dateFormat(request.stApp.date,"dd - mmmm - yy");
    request.stApp.longDate =
dateFormat(request.stApp.date,"dddd dd mmmm yyyy");
    request.stApp.owner = "Toshi Matsumoto";
    request.stApp.dir =
getDirectoryFromPath(getBaseTemplatePath());
    request.stApp.dsn = "forms";
    request.stApp.longCache = createTimeSpan(1,0,0,0);
    request.stApp.shortCache = createTimeSpan(0,0,0,5);
    request.bAuthenticated = "no";
</CFSCRIPT>
```

This can all live in **Application.cfm**. Remember to use an initial cap for this filename in case you need to move to a Unix-based system later.

**instant message**

▶ Query Caching

Create your cache time-spans in **Application.cfm** as request-scope vars. That way, it's easy to tweak them for performance tuning, and it's very easy to clear the cache during testing (just set **timeSpan** to 0,0,0,0 and hit the page you need to test).

First, Toshi needs to deal with storing data. In the normal run of things this would be a simple SQL statement, but in this case, Toshi needs to build some code that can handle storing data for any component. This is a harder problem: How to write generic SQL that can store data in any table or set of fields? That's impossible, of course, but it is possible to build the entire SQL statement dynamically, as long as Toshi figures out the structure of the component he's dealing with. Luckily, there's a new CFML function that will allow him to do this: getMetaData(). As long as Toshi builds well-architected components that declare all their properties, and as long as each of those properties has an equivalently named field in the database, then building the SQL statement dynamically becomes a simple matter of looping through some arrays.

## TOSHI'S PROJECT NOTEBOOK

Introspecting Functions

Tried out **getMetaData()**—neat! Check this out:

```
<CFSCRIPT>
thisObj=createObject("component","user");
</CFSCRIPT>
<CFDUMP var="#getMetaData(thisObj)#">
```

The resulting dump is shown below (Figure III-3.4) (and I love the new layout CFMX has for the output from **<CFDUMP>**).

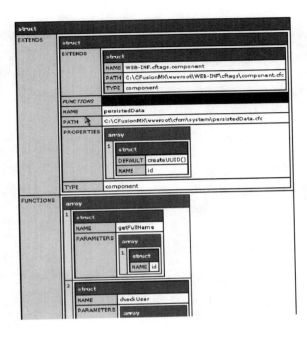

**Figure III-3.4**

cfdump can be used to display any ColdFusion variable; here, Toshi uses the tag to show component metadataNote.

## Introspecting Components

As Toshi has discovered, the getMetaData() function will return a structure containing the description of a given component. Toshi will need to be careful to pass in an instance of a component, not just the component name. So this, for example, won't work:

```
getMetaData(myComponent)
```

But this will:

```
myObj=createObject("component","myComponent");
metaData=getMetaData(myObj);
```

A quick-and-dirty introspection only for testing purposes can be achieved this way:

```
<CFDUMP var="#getMetaData(createObject
("component","myCFC"))#">
```

But nobody in their right mind should do this in anything other than a development or testing environment!

TOSHI'S PROJECT NOTEBOOK

**Progress**

So, now that we have a way to get the metadata from the component, I can easily build SQL to handle inserts. Here's how it should work:

1. In the **create()** function, I'll call a separate function to expose the metadata for this particular component (**getMetaData(this)**). Let's call this function **getProps**.

2. **getProps()** will expose the field names for this particular component. Note to self: Remember you have to do a **<cfproperty.../>** statement for each field you want to have in the database.

3. **getProps** returns a list of properties that I can loop through to build my SQL statement

Easy!

Hmm, except—where do I get the table name? I could hard-code it, but that seems inelegant. The other solution would be to expose the table name as a property in each child component. As long as that property always has the same name, it's easy for me to skip it in **getProps()**.

Let's look at the code Toshi writes for the **getProps()** function (see Listing III-3.1) and then for the **create()** function (see Listing III-3.2).

In **getProps()**, first Toshi sets up some local variables to hold the component metadata (**st_MD**) and to hold a list of properties (**lProps**). Then a couple of loops build out a list of all the properties for this particular component. Note the use of the *this* keyword. This will return all the metadata for this particular instance of a component. In this case, Toshi will have access not only to the properties of the `persistedData` component instance itself, but also more important, to the properties in any child component (such as the user component Toshi has yet to build).

The `getProps()` function, showing the use of `getMetaData(this)`.

```
<!--- this function returns the properties for a given
component --->
<CFFUNCTION name="getProps">
  <CFSCRIPT>
    // set up local vars to hold values;
    st_MD = structNew();
    st_MD = getMetaData(this);
    lProps = "";

    // loop through parent and current objects and append
    property names to lProps
    for(i=1; i LT arrayLen(st_MD.extends.properties)+1;
i=i+1) {
      lProps = listAppend(lProps,
structFind(st_MD.extends.properties[i], 'name'));
     }
      for(i=1; i LT arrayLen(st_MD.properties)+1; i=i+1) {
      lProps = listAppend(lProps,
structFind(st_MD.properties[i], 'name'));
     }
  </CFSCRIPT>
  <CFRETURN "#lProps#">
<CFFUNCTION>
```

In the `create()` function, then, Toshi is able to call `getProps()` to get a list of relevant properties. Based on that, he can loop through to build the relevant SQL statement for this particular insert. Note also the use of another custom function inside the component: `getTableName()`. This function simply returns the name of the storage table—which, you'll remember, must be exposed in each component—so that it can be removed from the list of values to insert in the SQL statement.

Listing III-3.2    The create() function, showing the use of getProps() and getTableName() to get the data from which to build the dynamic SQL statement.

```
<!--- 'create' function creates a new instance and
persists it --->
<CFFUNCTION name="create">

 <CFSCRIPT>
 // declare vars
  lProps = getProps();
  lFields = "";
  lVals = "";
  thisTable = getTableName();
  arguments.ID = createUUID();
  stStatus.bOK=true;
  stStatus.id = "";

 // strip the table name from the properties list
  lProps = listDeleteAt(lProps,listFind
(lProps,'persistIn'));

 // build the Values list for the SQL statement
  for(thisKey in arguments) {
   lFields=listAppend(lFields,thisKey);
   thisVal = chr(39) & arguments[thisKey] & chr(39);
   lVals=listAppend(lVals, thisVal);
  }

 // now make sure we have the right number of values for
properties
  if(listLen(lFields) NEQ listLen(lProps)) {
   stStatus.bOK=false;
  }
 </CFSCRIPT>
 <!--- insert the data --->
```

```
<CFIF stStatus.bOK>
  <CFQUERY name="q_Create"
datasource="#request.stApp.dsn#">
    INSERT INTO #thisTable# (#lFields#)
    VALUES (#preserveSingleQuotes(lVals)#)
  </CFQUERY>
  <CFSET stStatus.id = arguments.id>
 </CFIF>
 <!--- return the status struct --->
 <CFRETURN "#stStatus#">
</CFFUNCTION>
```

Now Toshi can build a simple self-posting form to handle the data input. Self-posting forms are an efficient way to handle forms posting, since all the form handling logic is in the same place. Note, though—and this is the real power of components—that the data-handling logic, or business logic, resides in the component itself, not in the form.

## TOSHI'S PROJECT NOTEBOOK

### Handling Forms

I'll use self-posting forms for all my forms entries. Much simpler this way. For reference, here's the basic template I'll use for all my forms (see Listing III-3.3).

Note the use of the CGI variables to build the post URL. This means I can reuse the same template for every form. Nifty!

To handle the form post, all I need to do is build an instance of the relevant component, populate it with data from the form fields, then call the relevant method. So the code should look something like this (see Listing III-3.4):

Then I can wrap error handling around the status code I'm returning.

**Listing III-3.3**    The template Toshi builds for his self-posting forms.

```
<!--- self-posting form --->
<CFSWITCH expression="#isDefined('form.btnSubmit')#">

  <!--- handle the form --->
  <CFCASE value="true">
  <!--- handling logic goes here --->
  </CFCASE>

  <!--- the form --->
  <CFCASE value="false">
    <CFFORM method="post"
action="#cgi.path_info#?#cgi.query_String#">
      <!--- form elements go here --->
    </CFFORM>
  </CFCASE>
</CFSWITCH>
```

**Listing III-3.4**    Toshi uses a script block to pass form data into a component.

```
<CFSCRIPT>
    // set up the args struct and populate
    stParams = structNew();
    stParams.firstname = form.firstname;
    stParams.lastname = form.lastname;
    stParams.email = form.email;
    stParams.roleID = form.roleID;

    stParams.password = form.password;
    stParams.reportID = form.reportID;
    // invoke the create object
    thisUser = createObject("component", "user");

r_stStatus=thisUser.Create(argumentCollection=stParams);
</CFSCRIPT>
```

## Another way to call functions

### Email

**Date:** April 12

**To:** Toshi

**From:** Jane

**Subject:** Another way to call functions

Hi Toshi,

Glad to hear the project's going well. Hey, I just got mail from an old friend of mine—ColdFusion expert by the name of James—who said there's a cleaner way to call functions on components. Check this out:

```
<cfscript>
    // Create a component instance to play with
thisObj = createObject("component", "myCFC");
    // Populate the properties for this instance
thisObj.firstName="Jack";
thisObj.lastName="Daniels";
    // Now call the update method on this instance
thisObj.update();
</cfscript>
```

James indicates that the update function will now execute using the values for this instance of the component. What do you think?

## Re: Another way to call functions

### Email

**Date:** April 12

**To:** Jane

**From:** Toshi

**Subject:** Re: Another way to call functions

Hi Jane,
Thanks! That's _much_ cleaner code. Kudos to your friend!

T.

Now Toshi is in a position to test his code for creating new users. He has a simple self-posting form that collects the data. The data is posted to logic that will create an instance of the component, populate the properties of that instance with the data from the form, and then call a function (`create()`) on that instance. Using James's shorthand code, Toshi doesn't even need to pass in any arguments; the function will act using the data that already exists in memory for a given instance of a component.

This methodology forms the basis for the rest of the application. Although it's taken a couple of days for Toshi to work through this, building out the rest of the application following this pattern is practically a matter of cut and paste.

### Deleting, Listing, and Other Core Functions

There are some other core functions that Toshi will need for his data handling. Most of these are easily dealt with. Recall that Toshi is generating a unique ID number (using the ColdFusion function `createUUID()` for each "document" he creates in the database) and that he is using this unique ID as the primary key. Where an operation applies to an entire record—such as a delete operation—Toshi can simply pass in this ID to a function. The following code, again taken from the `persistedData` component, shows a delete operation (see Listing III-3.5):

Listing III-3.5    The `delete()` function deletes data from the database.

```
<!--- 'delete' function deletes a persisted instance --->
<CFFUNCTION name="delete">
  <CFARGUMENT name="id" required="yes">
  <CFSET thisTable = getTableName()>
  <CFQUERY name="qDelete"
datasource="#request.stApp.dsn#">
    DELETE '#arguments.id#'
    FROM #thisTable#
  </CFQUERY>
</CFFUNCTION>
```

Toshi will also build a `list()` function, shown in Listing III-3.6, which will list out all the component instances stored in the database.

**Listing III-3.6** The list() function from the persistedData component is used to retrieve all data instances for a component from the database.

```
<CFFUNCTION name="list" access="remote"
returntype="query">
 <!--- get the table name --->
 <CFSET thisTable = getTableName()>

 <CFQUERY name="q_Data" datasource="#request.stApp.dsn#">
 SELECT *
 FROM #thisTable#
 </CFQUERY>

 <CFRETURN "#q_Data#">
</CFFUNCTION>
```

These functions, and any additional functions Toshi may create in the core persistedData component, will be available to any other component that extends persistedData. Toshi now has a very flexible and powerful model for his application, and new capabilities can be added to all his components in one core location.

## Building Out

**Progress**

**Email**

Date: April 12
To: Jane
From: Toshi
Subject: Progress

Hi Jane,

Just wanted to let you know that I tried out the architecture concept, and everything seems to work fine. This should significantly reduce development time: Much of the fundamental logic is now built, so I can reuse it for the other pieces of the application. I'm hoping to have a first draft by the middle of next week. I'll keep you posted.

T.

Now the real power of CFCs, and of Toshi's application architecture, really comes into its own. As Toshi rolls out the new sections—time sheets, travel requests, purchase orders, and expense claims—all he needs to do is build the relevant database tables, create a component for that particular form type, and ensure that the component extends his core `persistedData` component. He also has a form template he can reuse, so building the fundamentals of the application—getting data from the user, validating it, and storing it—should go very fast.

There's one remaining core requirement that Toshi hasn't addressed yet: forms routing. Without a routing mechanism, Toshi has no way to build workflow. In addition, each individual section has its own specific requirements that are outside the core capabilities provided by the `persistedData` component. These requirements need to be added to each individual component during development.

### Forms Routing

TOSHI'S PROJECT NOTEBOOK

**How to Handle Workflow**

Most of the forms have a workflow process associated with them. I need to figure out an easy way to handle this.

One option would be to build a routing component. I'd need to store the route for each form in a table, and I'd need another table to store each individual flow in progress. Although this would be a very flexible solution—the workflow could be changed via a form interface, for example—in practice we don't need that flexibility right now.

So I'll keep that idea in reserve for another time. For now, I can build a "chase" function for the components that need flow. This function can be called by an administrator, and could also be triggered as a scheduled task on a weekly basis.

Only two of the sections will really need this function: expense claims and purchase orders. For travel requests and time sheets, we only need instant notification, which can be built into the travel request and time sheet creation process.

For purchase orders, a couple of people need to approve each request. In order to keep track of the process—so that a purchaser can see what the status of a request is, for instance—I'll add some Boolean fields to the database, one for each approval cycle. Then it's just a matter of setting the flag appropriately at each approval stage. I'll also add a function **sendMessage** to the user component I just built. I can then call that function when required, passing in a message and a list of user IDs as arguments.

Let's take a look at the code that Toshi ends up writing for the expense-claim component. Listing III-3.7 shows a new function, `chase()`, which Toshi adds to his expense-claim component, `claim.cfc`. Notice that this function is secured so that only a certain level of user can call it—in this case, managers. We'll look at the security model Toshi has implemented a little later in this chapter.

First, Toshi builds a list of the users that have claims outstanding. Notice that Toshi builds this list by creating it as a string, not a list, since Macromedia now recommends that you avoid `listAppend()` and `listPrepend()` if possible. Then, Toshi simply creates a user component and calls two functions on that component: `getManager()`, which returns the userID of a given user's manager, and `sendMessage()`, which sends a given message to a list of users.

**Listing III-3.7**   The `chase()` function in `claim.cfc` builds a list of users with oustanding claims and then prompts—or 'chases'—managers to approve those claims.

```
<CFFUNCTION NAME="chase" ROLES="lord">


<!--- first, find out which users have unapproved claims --->
<CFQUERY NAME="qData" DATASOURCE="#request.stApp.dsn#">
```

**Listing III-3.7** (continued)

```
  SELECT DISTINCT userID FROM claims
  WHERE bApproved = false
</CFQUERY>

<CFSCRIPT>
 // build a list of outstanding users
 lUsers = "";
 for(i=0;i LT qData.recordCount; i=i+1) {
  lUsers = lUsers & qData.userID[i+1] & ",";
 }
 lUsers=removeChars(lUsers,len(lUsers),1);
 // create a user object to play with
 thisUser=createObject("component","cfcm.system.user");
 // get the ids for each users manager
 qMgrs = thisUser.getManager(lUserIDs="#lUsers#");
 // create a message for notification
 thisMessage="You have expenses to approve.  Please check the
system!";
 // and now notify the managers
 // first build a list of managers
 lMgrs="";
 for(i=0;i LT qMgrs.recordCount; i=i+1) {
  lMgrs = lMgrs & qMgrs.reportID[i+1] & ",";
 }
 lMgrs=removeChars(lMgrs,len(lMgrs),1);

thisUser.sendMessage(lRecipients="#lMgrs#",strMessage="#thisM
essage#");
</CFSCRIPT>

</CFFUNCTION>
```

I can just call **sendMessage()** whenever I need to send a message to a user or a group of users.

So that seems to deal with the routing requirement. It's worth noting that Toshi's solution is very pragmatic. He's identified that a more complex process—perhaps involving some kind of workflow component with associated data storage—would be a more flexible solution in the long term, and the team may well decide to implement such a solution in the second phase of development. However, for now Toshi's primary goal is to get the functionality the HR team needs built by the required deadline. This time factor forces Toshi to avoid any "feature creep" during the development cycle. Hopefully, any significant functionality changes will occur only at the behest of the client, and Toshi's core architecture should make it fairly easy to accommodate any such requests.

## An Interesting Problem

Toshi has all the pieces in place to start really building out the application. He has a design for the database, he knows how to store data in an easy and extensible way, and he knows how he will handle forms. Now he'll start building the time sheets section—probably the easiest section in terms of the requirements he has.

Based on his organic development approach, Toshi doesn't worry too much about the use-case flow of the application at this stage; it's easy enough to change that later by calling different component functions. To start, he just needs to get the basics in place: create and amend time sheet entries, and submit them to a manager for approval.

At this point Toshi runs into an interesting issue with the SQL insert and update statement he has built in his `persistedData` component:

## TOSHI'S PROJECT NOTEBOOK

### Problem With Typing

I knew it was too good to be true. The SQL I need to update time sheets looks like this:

```
<CFQUERY NAME="qUpdate"
DATASOURCE="#request.stApp.dsn#">
    INSERT INTO timesheets
    VALUES (
        '#this.id#',
        '#this.activityID#',
        '#getAuthUser()#',
        #createODBCdate(now())#,
        #this.duration#,
        '#this.notes#'
    )
</CFQUERY>
```

Here's the problem. Although I can build a similar statement in **persistedData.update()**, figuring out which fields are string (and therefore need quote marks) and which aren't is a real pain.

I could store the database structure somewhere and refer to it, but I think the overhead of doing that—or of querying the database itself—would be too high, not to mention the admin overhead.

Another option would be to make sure I type all the properties **<CFPROPERTY NAME="duration" TYPE="integer">**. I can then get at that using **getMetaData()** and handle building the SQL appropriately. This second option is probably the best, though it requires highly rigorous coding. On balance, given the time frames I'm working with, I think I'll just overwrite the core functions when and where I need to in a specific component.

Overwriting functions essentially means writing a function in a child component that has the same name as a function in the parent component. In such a case, the function in the child component will be used. This concept becomes clear if you look at the HTML documentation generated by the `persistedData` component (see Figure III-3.5) and the timeSheet component (see Figure III-3.6). The `persistedData` component shows a number of functions, including an `update()` function. The time sheet component extends `persistedData`, but shows the `update()` function listed as a method, not as an inherited method. Toshi will use this capability for a number of other functions throughout the application.

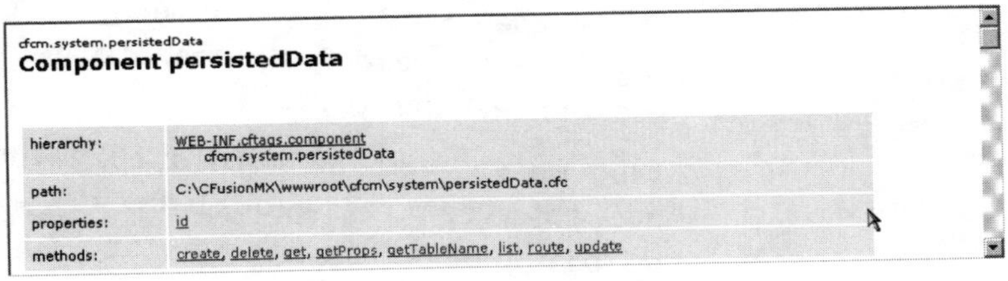

Figure III-3.5
The self-documentation for `persistedData.cfc`, the parent component, shows the core `update()` function.

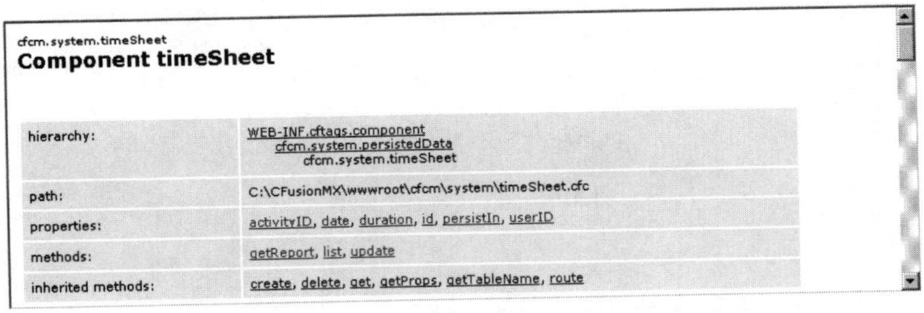

Figure III-3.6
The self-documentation for `timeSheet.cfc`, the child component, shows the overloaded `update()` function.

**re: Progress**

**Email**

**Date:** April 15

**To:** Toshi

**From:** Jane

**Subject:** re: Progress

Hi Toshi,

Glad to know things are going well.... Er, you should know that Laura was on to me last week to make sure you knew about the need to output hardcopy of time sheets. Some government requirement, apparently. I hope that won't be too much of a problem at this stage? Laura said they need to get the data in an Excel spreadsheet....

Also, we've just been told that there's a plan to move to a central global travel agent. It won the pitch based on its ability to take bookings electronically; apparently it offers some kind of XML-based service that we can write to. So we need to make sure we can handle that.

Let me know if any of this causes problems!

Cheers,

Jane

### Dealing with the Unexpected

Just as things are getting going, the team is hit with two major requirements: outputting hard copy of some documents, and integrating with a travel service outside the immediate organization.

instant message

▶ http://msdn.
microsoft.com/
library/default.
asp?url=/library/
en-us/dnexcl2k2/
html/odc_xlflatnr.asp
has more details
about XML and
XSL in relation
to Excel 2002.

**New reqs.**

**Email**

**Date:** April 15

**To:** Jane

**From:** Toshi

**Subject:** New reqs.

Hi Jane,

Typical.

Luckily, we should be OK with these. Thank goodness we went with the component-based architecture: I should be able to just add some extra functions to the relevant components to handle this. Plus, we can now deal with XML and Web services, so handling multiple formats and systems integration should be OK. I'll keep you posted.

T.

## Output for Print

The requirement from HR is to be able to output hard copy. Their current procecure is to read the data into Microsoft Excel, so that functionality must exist in Toshi's application. Fortunately, Excel 2002 features a very simple XML interface, so as long as Toshi can build a valid and well-formed XML document, this requirement shouldn't be too hard.

ColdFusion MX offers a number of new tags and functions that allow Toshi to build what he needs. Toshi decides to try out some of the new capabilities in a scratch file before building the final version of this requirement into the component itself.

## TOSHI'S PROJECT NOTEBOOK

### Handling XML

Well, it turns out that this is a lot easier that I thought it was going to be. First, let's look at the typical format of an XML file for import into Excel:

```xml
<?xml version="1.0" encoding="UTF-8"?>
<dataroot xmlns:od="urn:schemas-microsoft-com:officedata">
  <Q3Sales>
      <productID>1779-8</productID>
      <productName>Flanged grommet</productName>
<productPrice>26.75</productPrice>
      <customerName>Nancy</customerName>
<orderDate>25 Feb 2002</orderDate>
      <quantity>5</quantity>
      <totalValue>133.75</totalValue>

      ...

  </Q3Sales>

  ...

</dataroot>
```

The key element here is the `<dataroot...>` element. As long as that's in, the rest of the file can be defined the way I like. Later, I can also provide a style sheet for the formatting so that the doc looks pretty when it opens. For now, though, this will do.

So, to build this from the app, I need to get the data, then build a new XML document. I'll get the data by calling the list function on the component:

```
<CFSCRIPT>
  myTS =
createObject("component","cfcm.system.timesheet");
  qList=myTS.list();
</CFSCRIPT>
```

`<CFDUMP VAR="#qList#">` will show me the query that results (see Figure III-3.7):

Then I'll build a new XML document:

```
<CFXML VARIABLE="thisTimeSheet">
    <dataroot xmlns:od="urn:schemas-microsoft-
com:officedata">
        <timeSheet>
            <cfoutput query="qList">
            <entry>
                <date>#qList.date#</date>
                <activity>#qList.activityName#</activity>
        <duration>#qList.duration#</duration>
        <notes>#qList.notes#</notes>
            </entry>
            </cfoutput>
        </timeSheet>
    </dataroot>
</CFXML>
```

This time I can use `<CFDUMP VAR="#thisTimeSheet#">` to view the XML document on screen (see Figure III-3.8):

Finally, I can dump this to a file using the **toString()** function:

```
<CFFILE ACTION="write"
FILE="C:\CFusionMX\wwwroot\cfcm\fileDump\output.xml"
OUTPUT=#toString(myDoc)#>
```

When I build the final version, I'll create a dynamic filename based on the user name and the current time. I could also use **sendMessage()** to notify HR that a new timesheet is ready for them to view. Note that if I need to build PDF later on, I can just add more functions where required and use a custom tag like query2pdf from the Macromedia Exchange at **http://devex.macromedia.com/**.

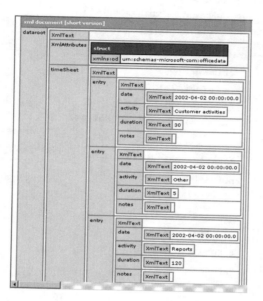

| | ACTIVITYNAME | DATE | DURATION | NOTES |
|---|---|---|---|---|
| 1 | Customer activities | 2002-04-02 00:00:00.0 | 30 | [empty string] |
| 2 | Other | 2002-04-02 00:00:00.0 | 5 | [empty string] |
| 3 | Reports | 2002-04-02 00:00:00.0 | 120 | [empty string] |
| 4 | Phone calls | 2002-04-02 00:00:00.0 | 15 | Call-outs to customers |
| 5 | Customer activities | 2002-04-02 00:00:00.0 | 5 | Shot all my customers |
| 6 | Other | 2002-04-24 00:00:00.0 | 25 | Test entry for today |

**Figure III-3.7**

A data dump shows the time sheet listing.

**Figure III-3.8**

A data dump shows an XML document created from a query.

The same concepts can be used for the integration with the travel-request system, but the fundamentals can be extended. As well as building XML documents in a format that the external system can consume, Toshi can also expose some of his system's functionality as a SOAP-based Web service that the external system can consume. Until Toshi gets to talk to the travel agency and find out what it needs, exact requirements will be unclear, so most of this development will fall into a second phase. Fortunately, the team always knew that this would happen, so it has developed the application in a way that lends itself to ongoing development and new requirements.

For now, Toshi will expose a simple Web service that will expose any outstanding requests to the external system:

```
<cffunction name="listUnbooked" access="remote"
hint="Lists all requests not yet booked by the agency."
returntype="query">
        <cfset qList=this.List()>

        <cfquery name="qUnbooked" dbtype="query">
        SELECT * FROM qList
        WHERE bBooked = 0
        </cfquery>

        <cfreturn qUnbooked>
    </cffunction>
```

Once the team has the final requirements from the travel agency, it can easily add functionality.

## Security

As Toshi has been building out the application, he's kept everything insecure to avoid logging in and out repeatedly. However, a number of functions, such as approval and reporting, need to be restricted to certain managers. Toshi can lock down component functions to be accessed only by certain roles; the chase() function on the expense claim component we saw earlier shows the syntax he needs to use:

```
<CFFUNCTION NAME="chase" ROLES="lord">
```

However, in order to get the role data, Toshi needs the user to log in so that he can get the relevant user data. Once he has that, it can easily be reused elsewhere in the application.

Listing III-3.8 shows the simple log-in code that Toshi adds to Application.cfm, following the examples given in the ColdFusion documentation and using new tags such as <CFLOGIN...> and <CFLOGINUSER...>. Notice also that Toshi has added a new function checkUser() to his user component.

**Listing III-3.8**    The security mechanism in Application.cfm shows the use of Toshi's new `checkUser()` function.

```
<!--- require login --->
<CFLOGIN>
  <CFIF NOT isDefined('form.j_username') AND NOT
isDefined('form.j_password')>
    <CFINCLUDE template="assets/loginTemplate.cfm">
    <CFABORT>
  </CFIF>


  <!--- if we get this far the form is submitted --->
  <CFSCRIPT>
    // create a user instance to test the validity of
this user
    // note that we can use this user instance in other
pages now it's created

thisUser=createObject("component","cfcm.system.user");
    stAuth=thisUser.checkUser(form.j_username,form.j_
password);
    </CFSCRIPT>


  <!--- bounce if not valid user --->
  <CFIF NOT stAuth.bAuthenticated>
    <CFINCLUDE template="assets/loginTemplate.cfm">
    <CFABORT>
  </CFIF>


  <!--- if we get this far, user is OK--->
  <!--- log in the user --->
    <CFLOGINUSER NAME="#stAuth.id#" ROLES="#stAuth.role#"
password="foo">
</CFLOGIN>
```

## Show Time

**Progess?**

**Email**

**Date:** April 18

**To:** Jane, Toshi

**From:** Laura

**Subject:** Progess?

Hi,

I haven't heard much from you about my application, and I'm getting a little concerned. The end of the month is very close and I'll be very disappointed if you let me down.

Please can we have a walkthrough of the application on Monday?

Thanks,

Laura

As ever, the client is pushing hard to make sure everything is set, while ready to blame the team if anything goes wrong. Fortunately, Toshi is nearly at a point where the application can be shown.

Unfortunately, when Toshi gets into the office on Friday, he learns that the external design agency is still behind and won't be able to deliver the new corporate layouts in time for the Monday meeting.

## Monday meeting

### Email

**Date:** April 19

**To:** Laura

**From:** Jane

**Subject:** Monday meeting

Hi Laura,

As confirmed yesterday, Toshi and I are looking forward to walking you and the rest of the HR team through the work that we've been doing.

Unfortunately, the design agency still hasn't produced the materials we need for the final layout and design of the application. For now, Toshi will use an interim design, but I wanted to let you know in advance so that during our walkthrough we can all focus on how the application works rather than on how it looks.

See you on Monday, and have a great weekend.

Jane

# The Solution

Toshi and Jane's meeting with the human resources (HR) department takes place on Monday, April 22, with just over a week to go before the final deadline. The HR application is broadly complete in content and functionality, though the final design hasn't yet arrived. Toshi and Jane have decided that Toshi will present a full walkthrough of the application to give the HR team a good overview of how the new system will work.

## Introduction

Before I get started, I just wanted to remind everyone that what they were seeing was a prototype of the application. All the functionality that you requested for phase one is there, but the design isn't finalized, and some things may not work quite the way you expect. We still have a week to make any final changes, so we would appreciate your feedback.

The application is split into four main sections, all accessible from a main screen (see Figure III-4.1). Please note that in order to use the application, employees have to log in to the system. This lets us keep employee data secure and provides secure access to management and administration functions.

**instant message**

► Recording presentations you make to the client (as Toshi and Jane have done here) is useful for review after a project.

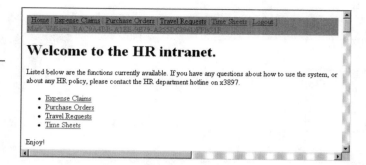

**Figure III-4.1**

The main menu screen provides access to the four sections of the human resources application.

First let's look at the application from an employee user perspective. Then we'll look at the additional tools and administrative functions we've given managers.

# Users

Right now I'm using a set of fictitious users. When the system goes live, we'll make sure all our current user details are in here. I'm going to log in as a user named Mark, who is a lead engineer in our concept structures group.

Once Mark has logged in, his user details are listed at the top of the page. There's also a simple menu that helps Mark navigate to various sections of the site. This menu will change depending on the permission Mark has (later we'll see that additional menu items are listed for managers and administrators). Note that there's also a log-out function for when Mark wants to leave the application (see Figure III-4.2).

**Figure III-4.2**

After log-in, the navigation menu shows the user's log-in status and is customized according to the user's role.

## Time Sheets

First, we'll have Mark fill out a time sheet entry. When he navigates to the Time Sheets section, he sees a list of his most recent time sheet entries. The system shows Mark basic information about each entry, including an Approved column, where Mark can see whether a particular entry has been approved by a manager (see Figure III-4.3). In case you forget that the cross is 'not yet approved' and the tick means 'approved', notice that if you hover your mouse pointer over the tick or cross, there's a hint that pops up to remind you.

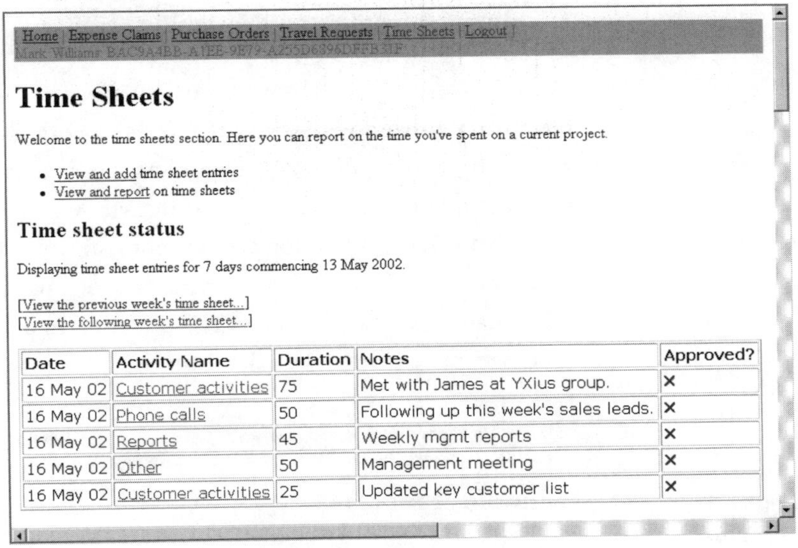

**Figure III-4.3**
In the main Time Sheets screen, the user gets a report on time sheet status and can navigate to the main areas via a simple menu at the top.

From this point, Mark can change an entry or create a new one; either way, he ends up using the same form. This makes it easy to learn how to use the application, since the user experience is consistent. If Mark chooses to edit an existing entry, the form will be prepopulated with data; in this case, Mark is about to create a new entry using a blank form (see Figure III-4.4).

Once Mark has filled in the data, the form is submitted, and then the entry is added to the list on the main page and to the database.

**Figure III-4.4**

In a time sheet entry form, the user interface is consistent even when prepopulated for editing purposes.

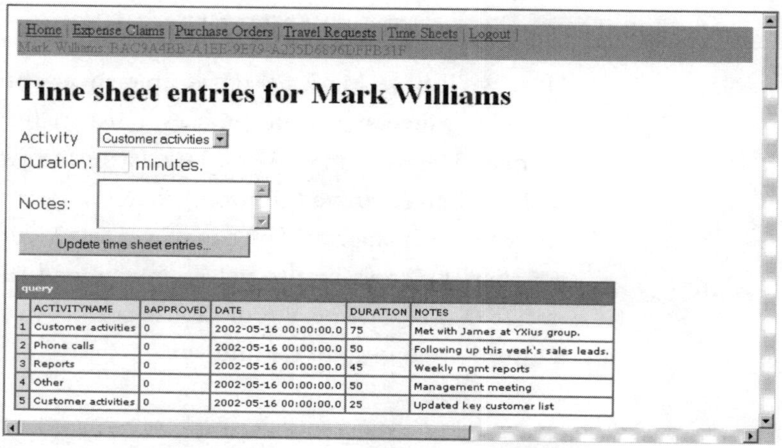

Mark can also get reports on how he has been using his time by navigating from the main Time Sheets page to the reports area. The reports area lists a range of reports Mark can access. As we'll see later, managers have some additional reporting options, while Mark can view only his own time sheet data. Here, we'll look at a report on the number of hours Mark has spent on a particular task over the course of a week (see Figure III-4.5). Once Mark has this chart, he can drill down to look at specific days or hours spent on an activity, by clicking on the relevant pie segment in the graph.

**Figure III-4.5**

A pie chart shows the breakdown of hours during a week spent on particular tasks.

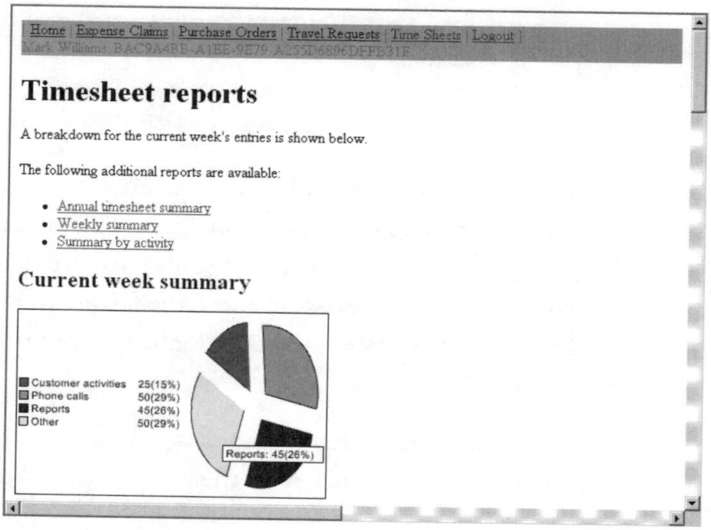

## Travel Requests

Once Mark has completed his time sheet, he needs to book a trip to the U.S. office, so he'll navigate to the Travel Requests section using the menu at the top of the page. The Travel Requests section follows the same pattern as the other sections. On the first page, recent requests are shown, along with their current status. Mark selects the link to make a new travel request and fills out a simple form (see Figure III-4.6). Once he submits the form, Mark is returned to the main page, and an email notification is automatically sent to his manager, who can then approve the request. Since request approval is a management function, that section is not visible to Mark.

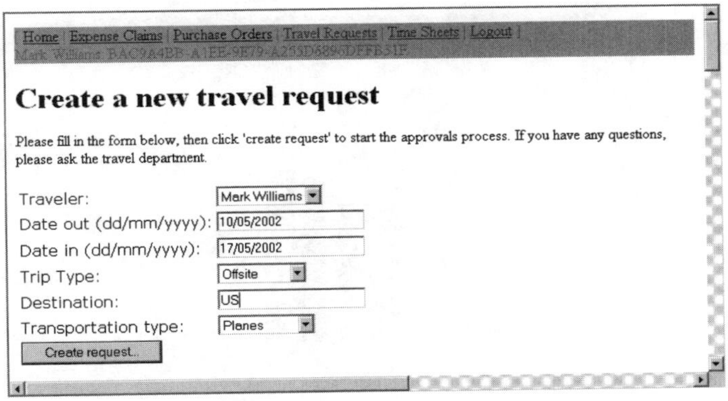

**Figure III-4.6**
Mark fills out a travel request form.

## Expense Claims

Once Mark has made his U.S. trip, he needs to file some expenses. The Expense Claims section is very easy to use because it follows the same logic as the other sections. Entering the Expense Claims section, Mark can see the status of any previous claims he has made. He now enters each individual claim using a simple form. He can select the currency from a drop-down list and indicate the purpose of an expense in the Notes field (see Figure III-4.7).

The system itself automatically ties together expenses for a given week into a single claim, so later Mark's manager can approve the entire week's expenses in a single action. The details for each claim are left as individual entries for reporting purposes.

Mark can view his own expenses breakdown, so he can quickly see where the company's money is going (see Figure III-4.8). Again, managers have a range of additional reporting capabilities.

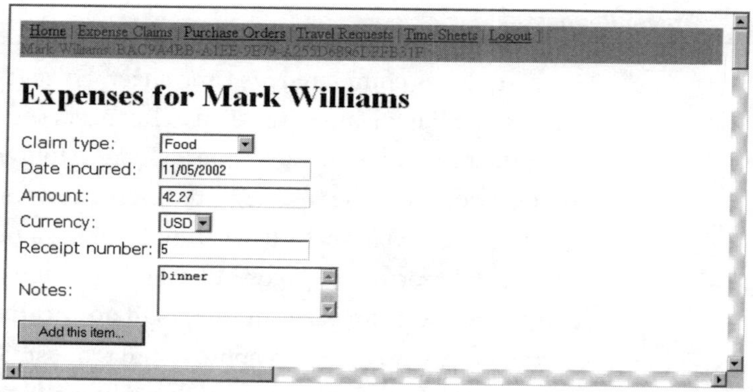

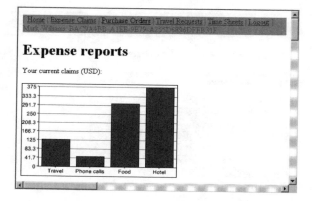

**Figure III-4.7**
Mark enters expense
claim data using a
simple form.

**Figure III-4.8**
Mark pulls a report on
his own expense data.

## Purchase Orders

Finally, as a result of his U.S. trip, Mark needs to place a purchase order for some new equipment. The Purchase Orders section of the site has the same user design as elsewhere. The first thing Mark sees in this section is a list of options, plus a status report on any current purchase orders.

Mark can now enter details for a new purchase order request. Once he submits this information, his request appears in the status list on the main page. In the background, the system automatically assigns a purchase order number to the request and passes on the request to his manager for approval. Assuming the request gets approved at this stage, the system then notifies the purchasing team, which gives final approval and, if appropriate, places the order. Mark can track status at any stage by looking in the status report on the main page.

# Manager Functions

In addition to the standard user functions already discussed, managers have some additional reporting and approval tools. To do this, we'll log in as Jane, who is Mark's manager, and we'll start by looking at the reporting features in the Time Sheets section.

### Reporting

Navigating to the reports area of the Time Sheets section, you'll see that Jane can call up some additional reports; for instance, she can look at reports for all of her employees to see workday trends (see Figure III-4.9).

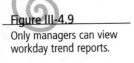

**Figure III-4.9**
Only managers can view workday trend reports.

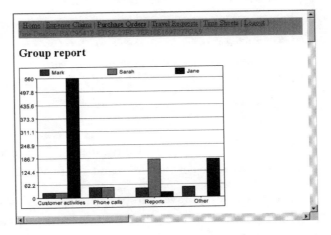

Similarly, in the Expense Claims section, Jane can view reports with a range of criteria, including total spend, spend by category, spend per employee, and so on. All of these reports can be filtered by date.

### Approvals

Jane can also approve items or requests that Mark submits. As a reminder, when Mark submitted his series of expense claims, Jane received an email alerting her that she needed to check and approve those claims. On Jane's main Expense Claims screen, in addition to her own recent claims, there's a section containing claims to be approved (see Figure III-4.10). The system takes care of collating each individual claim item for a given calendar week into a single claim, and Jane can simply click on the tick to approve the entire claim. If she needs additional detail on the claim, Jane can drill down to see the individual items that make up that particular claim by clicking on the claim owner's name.

**Figure III-4.10**
Managers can see expense claims that need approval as well as their own claim status.

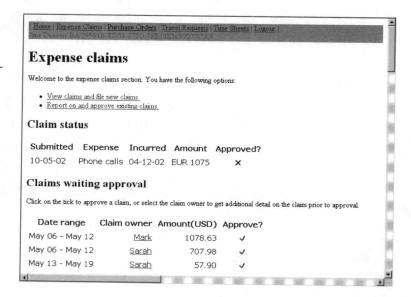

Assuming Jane is happy with the claim, she can go ahead and approve it. If not, she can reject the claim and notify Mark of the reason via email.

Jane can also approve purchase orders. In this case, the workflow is slightly more complex, but the mechanism is broadly similar. As Jane enters the Purchase Orders section, she can see a list of P.O.s pending her approval. She can drill down to get details on the purchase orders, and can then approve or reject each one. This is all very similar to the expense claims process. However, once a purchase order is approved, the system notifies the folks in the purchasing department, who will then perform the purchase.

## External Integration

Sometimes it's helpful to be able to pull data from the system and into another package such as Microsoft Excel for further analysis and hard copy printing. In the case of time sheets, the law requires this option; for expense claims, it's a useful extra for managers.

In both cases, once a report has been generated via the reporting screen, that data can then be exported in a file format that Excel understands and then downloaded to the local machine. Only managers have this ability. The data is actually delivered in an XML-based format and can simply be imported into Excel. At that point, the user can perform any of the normal actions in Excel. We may extend the range of output formats in the future.

I should also point out that we are starting to build integration with external systems such as the travel-booking system in use at our new travel agency. We're still waiting for final details from the agency about its requirements, but for now we've made it possible for its system to connect to ours to get details of any pending bookings.

## One Final Challenge

**A final request**

**Email**

**Date:** April 24

**To:** Toshi; Jane

**From:** Laura

**Subject:** A final request

Hi. Thanks again for your presentation on Monday. I think the whole team was astonished not only at what you've been able to achieve, but also at the way this new system will help streamline our processes. I'm converted! ;-)

## A final request

### Email (continued)

I do have one final request, though, if you can do it in time. We sometimes need to create simple forms—internal surveys and questionnaires, that sort of thing—and it would be great if we could build those ourselves, rather than having to come to you to build them for us.

Is this something you could build into the system?

Oh, and I just spoke with Stephen. He's out on business for much of next week, so he'd like to see this in its final form on Monday, April 29, if that's possible. I'm sure it won't be a problem for you.

Laura

## Laura's request

### Email

**Date:** April 24

**To:** Jane

**From:** Toshi

**Subject:** Laura's request

Hi Jane,

I knew there'd be something! Fortunately, I think this will be easy to do, since they only need a simple forms builder.

I already have a way to store data in the database, so all I need to do is to create a new component for each new form—based on a template—that extends persistedData and inherits all its properties. I'll need to store data about each form so that new forms can be added to some kind of library; otherwise no one will be able to find them or use them!

---

**Laura's request**

---

**Email (continued)**

---

I think I'll use frames for this. I don't like frames much, but in this case they probably make sense. On the right, we'll have a series of options for choosing and naming a new field; on the left, as new fields are submitted, a preview of the form. Once the creation process is over, the form will be automatically added to the forms library for use. How does that sound?

See you tomorrow....

Toshi

And so Toshi's application design proves its worth again. Because of the generic persistence layer, all the functions for storing and retrieving data in the database are already there. Just by building a new component extending `persistedData`, Toshi benefits from all his work by reusing his code and should be able to get this final functionality built by the revised deadline. Figure III-4.11 shows a prototype of the forms builder that Toshi will deploy.

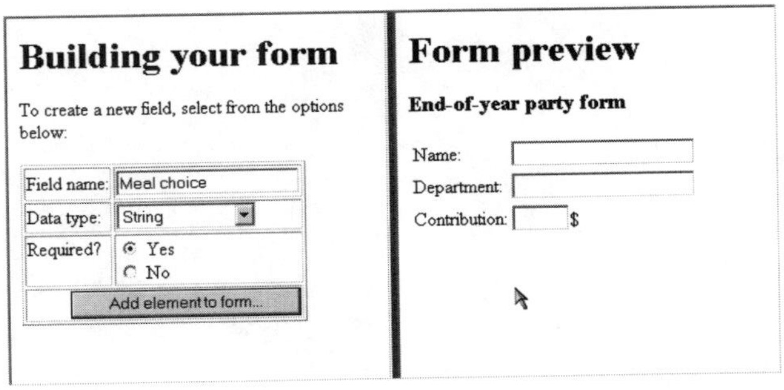

**Figure III-4.11**

A prototype of the new forms builder displays the form creator on the left and a preview of the form on the right.

**Building your form**

To create a new field, select from the options below:

| Field name: | Meal choice |
| Data type: | String |
| Required? | ⦿ Yes<br>○ No |

Add element to form...

**Form preview**

**End-of-year party form**

Name: [        ]
Department: [        ]
Contribution: [    ] $

Delivery

Following Toshi and Jane's successful meeting with the human resources (HR) department on April 22, the development team has a week to complete the application. Fortunately, even the last-minute request from HR (for a simple forms builder) can be accommodated.

The final application is deployed as a Macromedia ColdFusion archive on Monday, April 29, one day ahead of the deadline imposed by Linley Engineering's CEO, Stephen James.

## The Final Application

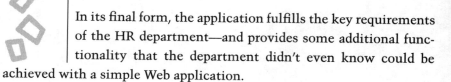

In its final form, the application fulfills the key requirements of the HR department—and provides some additional functionality that the department didn't even know could be achieved with a simple Web application.

Employees can now submit, edit, and manage the following on their own:

- Time sheets

- Travel requests

- Purchase orders

- Expense claims

Managers have additional capabilities, such as these:

- Approval

- Reporting

- Output to other desktop packages for offline processing

Finally, the team added a simple forms builder that lets employees produce their own forms for internal data gathering. Currently, the HR department builds these forms themselves, but Toshi has been able to reduce their workload even further by allowing all employees build simple forms. These forms reside in a library, helping users to quickly find and use the forms they need.

## Postmortem

Well-managed development projects typically have at least five phases: requirements, development, testing, deployment, and postmortem. Many of these phases will repeat; for instance, some developers prefer to test application functionality as they develop. But having a clearly defined, phased plan before work starts in earnest typically saves time (and money) through the life cycle of the project.

For their postmortem meeting, Toshi and Jane look at each of the phases of this HR intranet project.

## Requirements Phase

In many ways, the requirements phase of this project was the hardest for the team to deal with. The client was initially unsupportive of the project and had little understanding of how Web technologies could improve their business processes. In order to get a better understanding of what was really required, Toshi went directly to the end users of the systems: his fellow employees.

### POSTMORTEM ON REQUIREMENTS PHASE

Jane and I both feel that this was the toughest part of the whole project. HR's processes are in and of themselves inefficient and poorly understood. Add to that the fact that no one in the HR department is really championing the project, and it becomes impossible to get a real picture of what's required. Fortunately, these are for the most part systems that everyone uses, so I was able to get some real user data from others in the company. Gathering requirements this way is far from ideal; had this been an external project, I'd have been tempted to bounce it after this phase. For an internal "quick-win" project, though, it's just about OK. We did get enough data to kick the project off.

As expected, a number of last-minute requests came up. Three spring to mind: integration with the external travel system, data export to Microsoft Excel, and the forms builder.

Fortunately, we were pretty sure that unpredicted requirements would come up. Accordingly, we explicitly designed the application architecture to be rapidly extended. The component-based methodology coupled with the simple persistence layer allowed us to address these additional requirements quickly, even during the build; they also provide a great platform for future development.

Because of the problems gathering requirements, it was inevitable that something would be missed. In this case, the major missing requirement turned out to be the forms builder, though there were others.

Overall, given the circumstances, the requirements phase went as well as could be expected, and the architecture the team adopted helped them handle last-minute functionality requests with minimal disruption to the tight schedule.

## Development Phase

The development phase started out with a learning exercise. It was clear to the team that the right way to build this application would be to use the new component architecture offered in ColdFusion MX. However, since ColdFusion components (CFCs) were new to Toshi, he had to spend a little time learning the best way to work with them. Although the learning curve was pretty steep, some techniques that Toshi learned didn't make it into this iteration of the application.

### POSTMORTEM ON DEVELOPMENT PHASE

CFCs were pretty easy to learn. The basics of them really are just that—basic. The most useful part for me, in this application, is the ability to introspect a component: The **getMetaData()** function returns a struct containing data about a given component. It's this feature that really gave me a way to build the data storage layer I needed for this app. Unfortunately, I didn't realize until too late in the development stage that by explicitly providing a type for each component's properties (using the type argument to **<CFPROPERTY...>**), I could then use this function to get the property type and thereby build a more intelligent SQL statement that would handle any of my components.

Ultimately, this doesn't affect the performance of the application, but it does make the code slightly more laborious that it might otherwise be.

The shorthand approach to invoking methods in a `<CFSCRIPT>` block did save me some time, though. It avoids passing lengthy argument structures and makes the code much simpler to read and maintain. The rest of the application didn't cause any significant complications. I did use some of the other new features—in particular, the new XML handling functions—but otherwise this was a fairly typical ColdFusion application.

Other challenges for the team were mostly organizational—the non-delivery of the new corporate graphics and layout was a frustration, as were the additional requirements that came up during the development phase. But these issues were relatively easy to handle, and Toshi managed to avoid too much "feature-creep"—always a risk when requirements are not precisely defined and approved before development starts.

## Testing Phase

POSTMORTEM ON TESTING PHASE

This phase was by no means ideal. The tight time frame meant that we couldn't perform proper load-testing on the application. Fortunately, since this is a fairly low-traffic app, I'm not too concerned that we couldn't hammer the application before deployment. However, we will need to schedule load testing—and address any code revisions—as a matter of priority.

> The closest we got to user testing was the walkthrough we carried out last week. That was a useful exercise in getting approval from the HR department, but for the most part, it's not they who will use the application. I'd therefore also suggest that we do some user surveys over the next few weeks to establish what we need to improve in the next release.

Here we see the real value of the postmortem. Jane and Toshi can identify that some significant parts of their normal development cycle were omitted. Although this was the right decision at the time, given the nature of the application, performance testing was less critical than it might otherwise have been. They've now ensured that serious action will be taken to uncover any hidden issues that might otherwise surface later.

### Deployment Phase

This application never really went through a true deployment phase. As is typical of tactical applications, where performance testing is curtailed or sacrificed to make a deadline, deployment engineering isn't a major component of the cycle. However, Toshi's memo points out an important consideration for future revisions.

> POSTMORTEM ON DEPLOYMENT PHASE
>
> We had no real deployment phase, predictably, but we do need to make sure we have the right tools in place to manage future releases. Let's get the application up on the testing server ASAP, and then start building CAR files so we can handle releases properly with future revisions.

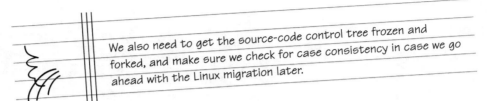

We also need to get the source-code control tree frozen and forked, and make sure we check for case consistency in case we go ahead with the Linux migration later.

Toshi also needs to consider documentation—both technical and end-user—and training. The review of the application with the HR team should help that team use the application, but Toshi should also consider providing training for the company at large to make sure they understand how to use the application correctly.

# Future Enhancements

Having discussed the various phases of the project, the team is now free to consider—and document—any enhancements to the application that should be included in the second phase of development.

There are already some known user requirements—for example, the integration with the new, outsourced travel booking system. However, there are also enhancements that the team members themselves have derived from the development phase.

FUTURE ENHANCEMENTS

As we go on to the next phase of development, let's make sure we consider the following enhancements along with any functional requirements the HR department identifies for us.

- User interface: The current UI, while functional, isn't as effective as it might be and certainly isn't visually appealing. Given the nature of the application, it would make a lot of sense to use the new features of

Macromedia Flash MX to build a rich Internet front end. Since we already have a component-based architecture, it should also be pretty easy to reuse our functions via Flash Remoting. Take, for example, the **list()** function. The function itself simply returns a query object; currently, this is handled in the presentation layer as HTML, but it could just as easily be invoked via Flash Remoting to populate a Flash UI. The same is true for much of the rest of the application.

- Usability: before we get to the point of building out rich UI, we also need to look at some simple improvements in usability. Example: right now, we have fixed options for activity types when creating a time sheet. It would make sense to have an 'other' category so that users don't have to bend categories to fit. This would also be a great way to gather information about what categories might be missing so we can add categories later. Another useful enhancement would be to highlight errors in form fields if validation fails on the server for any reason; this is pretty easy to do since we're using self-posting forms.

- Persistence: I've mentioned this in another memo, but right now I'm having to overload a lot of the storage functions because I'm not using **getMetaData()** to introspect the database field types. If I did it this way, I'd have much more generic and reusable code. I would have saved a lot of time if I'd implemented this the right way the first time around, but fixing it now will save time later.

- Forms builder: The forms builder is necessarily lacking in functionality, since it was a last-minute add-on. Its functionality and UI could be significantly improved. We should consider extending the forms builder so that it can actually create components as well as the relevant structures in the database for persistence. This shouldn't be too hard, especially if I improve the persistence layer as detailed above. Most common functions (storage, retrieval, listing) already exist in **persistedData.cfc**, so I should just be able to inherit those via a template CFC.

- Reporting: The reporting functionality is fairly basic. We should spend time talking to the various managers and administrators at Linley to see what else they need. Implementation shouldn't present too much of a challenge. This is really just a requirements-gathering and scheduling exercise. Further down the line, and depending on requirements, we should look at investing in an enterprise class reporting solution like Crystal Report or Actuate. Integration with either of these should be pretty simple using custom tags or object calls; plus, there are probably other internal applications that would benefit from this level of reporting power.

- Error handling: I cut a number of corners with error handling. In the next release, I need to beef this up. Better use of try/catch error handling and writing custom error messages to the log will make a big difference in how easy it is to manage the application and trace any errors.

- Improved code reuse: Although we've done a lot to promote reuse in the application, I still feel that more could be done. Example: in our self-posting forms, we repeatedly use **action="#cgi.path_info#?#cgi.query_String#"**. We made it easy to develop by building this into our template, but it's a pain if we need to change anything. It would make a lot of sense to wrap this up as a user-defined function in the function library and the access it via the request scope.

## Conclusion

**You can stay**

**Email**

**Date:** April 30

**To:** Laura

**From:** Stephen

**Subject:** You can stay

Laura,

I'm impressed with what you've achieved. Well done. Please make sure to congratulate the IT team. I know how much work they've put in to support you.

Not all of your systems are implemented yet, but I know you'll be keen to make progress moving forward.

Stephen

**Thanks**

**Email**

**Date:** April 30

**To:** Jane, Toshi

**From:** Laura

**Subject:** Thanks

Hi,

I just had email from Stephen, and it looks like we did it. I owe you both a big thank you, not only for getting this application up and running, but also for bringing me out of the dark ages.

Thanks. ;-)

TTFN. (See, I even know the acronyms now!)

L.

**The project is dead. . .Long live the project!**

**Email**

**Date:** April 30

**To:** Toshi

**From:** Jane

**Subject:** The project is dead....Long live the project!

Hey Toshi,

You saw the message from Laura earlier.... Thanks for all your work. Enjoy the next few days off.

When you get back, we need to talk. Engineering has a new project they need us to look into.... :)

Jane

# Part IV

# Product Requirements

Product Requirements is a project-planning application. It features systems to create and define projects and associated tasks, manage data, provide feedback, and more.

# Product Requirements

## The Problem

Every application starts with an idea. The idea may emerge as a sketch on the back of a Starbucks napkin—scribbled after a moment of blinding insight that follows a sip of latte on an otherwise lazy Sunday morning. Or it could come as the result of an expensive market-research project that identifies an audience and a need that no one has yet tapped.

Whatever the origin, an idea can often be stated succinctly and usually lacks details. Without fleshing out and organizing the details, however, the idea is likely to remain just that—an idea, never to see the light of day. The process of gathering those details is, in the software world, a matter of identifying the application's requirements. Whereas coming up with the original idea is often a solo operation, requirements gathering is very much a group endeavor. By definition, it needs to include those pesky end users.

Webworld Studios, a software consulting company, was recently called upon to develop an application for the Federal Agency of Bureaucratic Regulations (FABR), a U.S. agency of approximately 1,000 people with a single office in each of seven geographic areas in addition to its headquarters in Washington, D.C. Webworld was tipped off to the agency's need by the sales rep for a Webworld partner who was working a network integration contract with the agency. The partner's sales rep had been in a meeting at the agency in which they'd discussed the need for a Web-based content-management system and he knew such a project fell within Webworld's bailiwick. He called Webworld's sales manager, Tony, to brief him on the agency's need. Tony summarized the briefing and sent the information to Jesse, the head of the Webworld Studios service division:

## Re: FABR's long-term project

### Email

Date: September 2

To: Jesse (E-mail)

From: Tony Kitzmiller

Subject: Re: FABR's long-term project

Jesse,

I was briefed this morning from a friend of mine on the fact that the Federal Agency of Bureaucratic Regulations (FABR) wants to institute a Web-based content management system.

The agency is looking at moving to Macromedia ColdFusion MX for its Web site, as it's out of control right now. They're a relatively small agency with headquarters here in Washington, DC and 7 regional offices spread around the country. Just about every office is doing something different in terms of technologies, platforms, and levels of expertise. Headquarters really understands the importance of getting the management of each office's Web site under control. To have any hope of smoothly introducing a solution, however, they need to involve their regional offices in the planning.

---
**Re: FABR's long-term project**

---
**Email (continued)**

---

The FABR managers we'd be working with know it might take awhile to roll out a content-management solution across the agency, but they'd like to get started quickly and also feel it is important to show a "win" early on.

Here's the real issue, though: They've already been through a couple of contractors who didn't get the job done, and there's a lot of internal resistance to change. Key people are apparently skittish about the whole thing. So during the first phase, it's going to be very important to make the right impression and handle the internal politics.

They obviously need a content-management solution, but it seems that they don't know for sure what they need or how to go about getting it.

This whole problem is complicated by the fact that the remote managers get together only once a year, and the next meeting isn't for another six months.

I'd like to move on this from the sales side, but would like your input as to what process you see us using to actually deliver a new content-management system to them.

Tony

Webworld met individually with several of FABR's IT staff and some of their managers, which made it obvious that the agency wanted to improve what it was doing with its Web sites and get them under control. But it was equally obvious that internal disagreements and distrust could set up any development efforts for eventual failure.

## FABR

## Memo

**Date:** September 9

**To:** Webworld Sales Team

**From:** Jesse

**Subject:** FABR

We've spent a lot of time with FABR's IT staff and several of their key managers. They're good guys and want to get this done right, but quite honestly, even after spending several hours with them, we're still unclear about the details of what they really want to do.

More important, *they* are unclear about what they want, and they're worried that whatever they come up with will not involve the remote offices enough and end up being rejected. Every time they've tried to make changes to how they manage their Web sites, some internal issue has come up that's made it difficult, and the project has inevitably failed.

I'm not even sure those failures were technical, though lots of people seem to think they were.

Here are the challenges as I see them now:

- The FABR managers need to get input from their regional offices, as they want to make sure the needs of those offices are met. Fortunately, they realize they can't meet everyone's needs, and that at some point headquarters is just going to have to tell the remote offices how things will be done. In other words, the management seems willing to make the hard and possibly unpopular decisions when they need to be made.

- The FABR staff and managers are inclined to some infighting and finger-pointing over the failures of earlier projects.

---

**FABR**

**Memo (continued)**

- The FABR managers do want to get this started soon. They feel they'll need to show some progress in the next six months in order to keep attention focused on it and prove that it can be done. At the same time, they know they have to take the time to do the early stages right or they'll be setting themselves up for failure down the road.

The contractors who worked on earlier Web projects for FABR seemed technically competent, but they had no idea how to handle the agency's internal politics. When a project started to fall apart, they were scapegoated and, before they knew it, dismissed. Given the above, it's going to be very important for us to make a good impression early on. I'm not particularly worried about the technical issues for this client—the human factors are by far more important.

Normally, we'd sit down with the key people at the agency, gather requirements from them, and write them up in a Word document. That Word document would then be sent to the agency to review it, make comments, and then send back to Webworld for final edits.

That kind of process is going to be difficult in this case and doesn't provide the opportunity for individuals from each of the regional offices to contribute. What is needed is an online way for geographically distributed agency staff to contribute requirements and comment on others' requirements. The online version doesn't need to produce a beautiful requirements document, nor does it necessarily have to be the final one. But it would need to allow representatives from each regional office to participate by contributing and commenting on requirements. Once the basic requirements were gathered using the online application, we could then transfer them to Word and finalize them with the agency's management. So, here's my suggestion:

**FABR**

**Memo (continued)**

Instead of selling the agency on building the content-management system—since we really don't have any way of reliably pricing it because of their lack of clarity—let's push them in the direction of investing the time to do project-requirements and do it right. This will get people in the remote offices involved, it'll help the agency clarify for themselves what they really need to do, and it will provide the basis for general agreement within the agency on the details of the content-management application.

For us, of course, this approach provides some protection because we'll have a document to refer to when questions arise (and they will) about what it is we built for them.

Here's the catch: To do this right, we'll need to build the project-requirements application we've been talking about for the last year and a half. We don't have to build the entire thing, but we need to create something with basic functionality that we can use to involve agency employees in the process of gathering requirements no matter where they may be located geographically.

Tony approached the agency with the idea, which they loved, and a contract was issued to build the project-requirements application and then use it to gather requirements for the agency's content-management system. The next step was to design, build, test, and deploy the project-requirements application so the requirements gathering could be completed and the real work could begin.

# The Requirements

The Webworld team settled on using its standard application-development process for creating the requirements application (see Figure IV-1.1). Somewhere along the line the application was named ReqBuilder.

**Figure IV-1.1**
Webworld's standard application-development process was adopted for ReqBuilder.

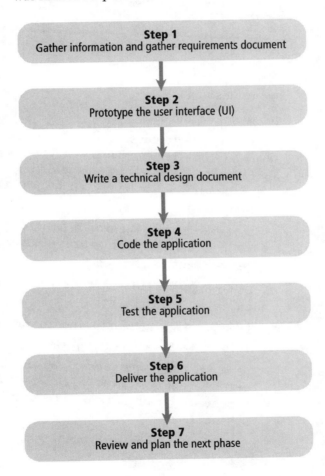

**Step 1**
Gather information and gather requirements document

**Step 2**
Prototype the user interface (UI)

**Step 3**
Write a technical design document

**Step 4**
Code the application

**Step 5**
Test the application

**Step 6**
Deliver the application

**Step 7**
Review and plan the next phase

One of the developers on the project, Teo, took a first shot at drafting the requirements document, which other developers on the team commented on. Based on these comments, Jesse put together a memo describing the high-level requirements for ReqBuilder and circulated this to the team.

---

**ReqBuilder requirements**

**Memo**

**Date:** September 16

**To:** ReqBuilder Team

**From:** Jesse

**Subject:** ReqBuilder requirements

Based on our discussions, the following is a high-level list of requirements for the project requirement application that we're now calling "ReqBuilder." The following is an overview of how the application will be used:

1. Several people (Webworld Studios staff or authorized customer representatives) enter requirements.

2. Others (Webworld staff or customers) comment on those requirements.

3. Someone from Webworld incorporates the comments into the individual requirements.

4. At any point, any user is able to view the full set of requirements which are automatically numbered and organized into sections and subsections.

The above is a simple process that requires the following functionality:

1. The ability for a user to log in to the application and be assigned a set of rights. (We are not certain at this point if management of user rights will need to be included in this application or if it will use an existing client security system.)

---

**ReqBuilder requirements**

---

**Memo (continued)**

---

2. The ability to create and name a new set of requirements. (Although ReqBuilder will initially be used just to manage the requirements for FABR's content-management system, we need to build it so it can manage more than one set of requirements.)

3. The ability for authorized users to enter a new requirement. This will consists of: a) deciding where the new requirement is placed in relationship to existing requirements and b) entering the requirement itself.

4. The ability for authorized users to select and edit an existing requirement.

5. The ability for authorized users to delete requirements.

6. The ability for authorized users to re-order existing requirements.

7. The ability for authorized users to comment on existing requirements. Although a relatively small number of people will be authorized to enter or edit requirements, anyone with access to the site will be able to comment on existing requirements. This invites participation from a wide set of users without encouraging chaos.

8. The ability to view a set of requirements. This view will dynamically renumber requirements so that as requirements are added or deleted, the numbering is adjusted.

---

Although the above list was pretty high-level, and details remained to be fleshed out, they provided enough information to get started with the prototype and technical design.

# Initial Thoughts

## Proposed Solutions

Armed with a basic grasp of what was needed to create ReqBuilder, Webworld Studios development team was ready to move forward with a prototype and a technical-design document. The purpose of the prototype is to show the screens that are needed for the new application and to provide a concrete visual representation of the site to help work through user-interface (UI) issues.

The purpose of the technical-design document is to provide instructions to the developers as to what Macromedia ColdFusion MX components need to be created, what the component methods are, and how the application is to function overall. Whereas the requirements document as presented in the previous chapter answers the question "What needs to be built?" the technical design document answers "How do I build it?"

Jesse and several members of the team discussed how they might proceed with designing the application. Andrew pointed out that two things were very clear about this particular application: it needed to have a simple, intuitive UI, and the end product was a requirements document. Although Webworld had used different kinds of requirements documents in the past, they all consisted of a document containing sections, sub-sections, and sub-sub-sections. Each lower section in the requirements document provided more precise detail about a particular feature or function. Because of the consistency of requirements documents, the team realized that almost no effort needed to be spent to describe what the requirements document should look like. The most important task, therefore, seemed to be to work out a good UI.

Rather than having the entire team start with a blank whiteboard, Teo was asked to throw together a visual prototype that included all the basic functions such as the ability to add, edit, and delete individual requirements and the ability to display a complete requirements document. He was given virtually no direction on what to do or how to approach it. The idea was to get something on a board that could serve as a place to start discussions. Teo went one step beyond the prototype and also wrote up some technical design notes to indicate how his prototype might be implemented in the back end. His prototype and design notes gave the team a starting point. The first issue Teo's prototype raised was an important usability problem because he had placed all the tools and buttons in the same space on the opening screen with no specific direction to users as to how they should proceed (see Figure IV-2.1).

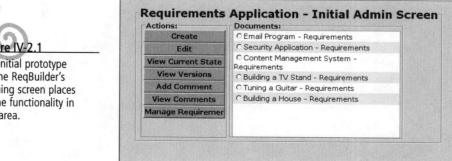

**Figure IV-2.1**

The initial prototype for the ReqBuilder's opening screen places all the functionality in one area.

Debbie pointed out that operations affecting an entire requirements document should be separated from operations affecting a single requirement. This would make the interface clearer for users because they could then associate areas of the screen with types of operations. For example, if all the single requirement operations were placed into the bottom right of the screen, the user would always know to go when he or she wanted to work on one requirement. Logically, it would make sense to put all the requirements document operations into a global navigation area such as the top of the screen.

A second prototype was done to address some of these issues. It demonstrated a general user experience that seemed intuitive and managed to visually separate out different types of functions. When the team met to discuss it, they immediately began to discuss how it might be implemented. Jesse took this as a good sign. Instead of the team debating general issues of usability, it had moved naturally into debating the details of the interface and how to implement it. Issues such as whether HTML frames should be used and what technology should be used for the drill-down interface were discussed (see Figure IV-2.2).

**Figure IV-2.2**

The second prototype improves the UI and provided the basis for discussing how the application would work.

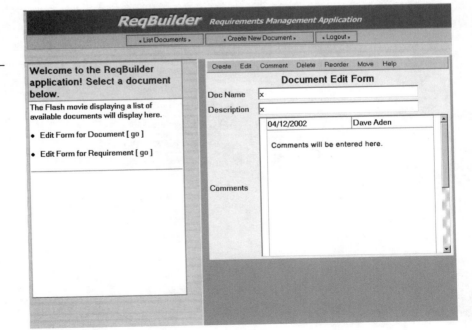

In fact, the meeting to discuss the second prototype resulted in most of the design details being fleshed out. Perhaps as important, the meeting also identified those nonessential items that could be deferred until the second phase of development. The project's short time frame and the specific needs of the client helped the team focus on keeping things simple.

The following meeting notes taken by Jesse summarized most of the issues that were discussed and the options that had been considered.

MEETING NOTES

**Date:** September 23
**TPresent:** Andrew, Debbie, Dmitry, Jesse, John and Teo
The meeting started with a review of the prototype. We discussed extensively how the interface would operate, starting with the user experience when they first come to the site. Jesse said he'd get this data into the technical-design doc. In particular, the following issues were raised and debated:

- Frames or no frames: The prototype uses three frames to keep functionalities separate. This makes the site more application-like because it decreases page refreshes, but it might increase complexity by having to manage interframe communication.

- We decided that it would be pretty easy to minimize the use of JavaScript and interframe communication because most of the UI refreshes were localized in the bottom right frame.

- We discussed compliance with the accessibility requirements of Section 508 (the federal law that mandates that all software purchased by federal agencies needs to be accessible to users with disabilities). The team decided to concentrate on functionality for the first phase and to defer Section 508 testing until after the basic coding was complete. Debbie noted that Macromedia Flash 6 makes it possible to build Flash interfaces that are Section 508-compliant, which makes it possible to put an all-Flash interface onto ReqBuilder.

- Because of this, we considered using an entirely Flash-based interface, but the team decided to use a mix of Flash and HTML for the first version with the option of going to an all Flash admin interface later. As the team is still coming up to speed on the Flash MX, it was decided that doing HTML with some Flash would be faster.

- John lobbied for separating content and presentation. He suggested that one way to do this would be to store all the data in Extensible Markup Language (XML) and transform it into the desired output using Extensible Stylesheet Language Transformations (XSLT). He pointed out that ColdFusion MX has new functions for interacting with XML and XSLT which would make the integration of XML/XSLT easier than it had been in earlier ColdFusion releases. However, the team decided to defer the use of XML/XSLT to a later phase as the customizability of the application's output was a second-level requirement. It was agreed, though, that this might be a useful approach when building the content-management system. In the meantime, the team decided to modularize data access by encapsulating the code in ColdFusion MX components. That way, should the team decide to move to XML/XSLT in the future, the changes would be localized to a handful of component methods.

- We talked about security. The team was aware of ColdFusion MX's new security model but didn't know much about it. Teo was asked to look into it and report back how it would fit with ReqBuilder.
- We also discussed versioning of individual requirements to track changes over time, but this also was deferred. For the current client, the team discussed controlling changes to individual requirements by minimizing the number of users granted requirement edit rights. Under this scheme, anyone would be able to comment on a requirement but only a few people would be able to add or edit a requirement, thereby reducing the risk of error (and the need for the ability to rollback to an earlier version). It was decided that if real-world use showed that versioning was needed, it could be added in the next phase.
- We explored a hierarchical representation of the data in the application, and a whiteboard helped to clarify the possible approaches (see Figure IV-2.3). We started to discuss possible ways to model requirements documents in a database but decided to ask Andrew and Teo to work this out after the meeting.

**Tasks:**

1. Teo will look into the new security features in ColdFusion MX and report back.
2. Dmitry will investigate the use of the Flash UI tree component to manage the hierarchy and what will it take to integrate it.
3. Andrew and Teo to settle on a database model to store requirements documents.

4. Jesse will write the technical-design document based on the discussions. One of the main things clarified at the meeting were the definitions the team settled on to describe parts of the application. These definitions were later included in the design document. Two key definitions emerged:

- Requirement: An individual requirement from a client. This is a single, identifiable item that describes some aspect of the functionality or performance required from a product or service.
- Requirements document: This is a set of related requirements that together describe the full set of functionality and performance needed from a product or service.

It was also decided that the application would not enforce any particular organization for a requirements document. Flexibility of requirements document organization was seen as a key design goal; ReqBuilder needed to allow each group of users to define the sections appropriate to their requirements document. This re-enforced the concept that the purpose of ReqBuilder was simply to provide a Web-based means for entering, commenting on, and approving individual requirements that together would make up a requirements document.

After the full team meeting, Teo and Andrew discussed the database model. They decided that the most straightforward approach would be to just model requirements documents as a hierarchical collection of individual requirements. When viewed this way, each requirement is a "node" within the hierarchy. Each requirement (except the top of the hierarchy) has a "parent." Some requirements also have "child" requirements. A decision needed to be made, though, as to whether all the requirements documents would fall under a single "super" node or whether each requirement document would be a unique hierarchy. Teo whiteboarded the two approaches (see Figure IV-2.3).

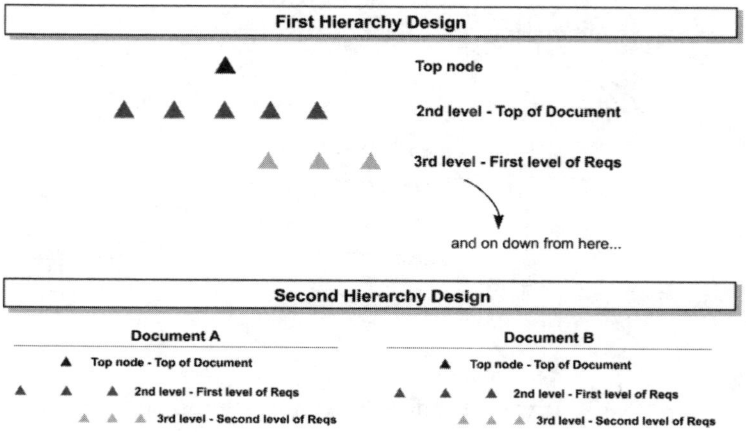

Figure IV-2.3
Whiteboards of possible hierarchical representations of the requirements documents helped clarify how to organize the hierarchies.

The first hierarchy design places all requirement documents under a single, top-level node. In this structure, all the second-level nodes of the hierarchy represent the top of a requirements document. To generate a list of requirement documents, the application would need to search only for the nodes whose "parent" was the top node.

The second hierarchy design uses a separate hierarchy for each requirement document. In this case, each hierarchy's top node contains the name and description of a requirement document as a whole, and each child node represents an individual requirement.

Although either approach could conceptually manage the data, the second one  was chosen because it would allow for more independence between requirement documents. The downside to using individual hierarchies is that it's more difficult to share or move requirements between requirement documents—a function that Teo and Andrew agreed was not critical.

Once Teo and Andrew settled on using a hierarchical representation of the core application (although the exact database structure was still to be finalized) the next question was how to implement the UI representation of the hierarchy. In the past Webworld had used various JavaScript solutions—many of which are available as free downloads from the Internet—for a drill-down interface, but these tended to suffer from cross-browser incompatibility problems and were often complicated or buggy. Using `<CFTREE>` was another option, but this requires a Java download which the agency did not want to allow. To get around these problems, the developers decided to use a Macromedia Flash tree component, which solved the browser-incompatibility problem. They also hoped they would be able to repurpose any work done with the Flash tree component when the interface was completely rebuilt in Flash.

Teo and Andrew presented their suggestion to Jesse who approved it and assigned Dmitry to work on the Flash tree, since he has skills with both Flash and ColdFusion. He was also assigned to build the back-end Cold-Fusion component that would serve up the hierarchical data.

A couple of days later, Teo reported to the group by email what he'd dug up about security under ColdFusion MX.

**Security update**

**Email**

**Date:** September 26

**To:** ReqBuilder Team (Email)

**From:** Teo

**Subject:** Security update

Everyone,

Just wanted to update you on what I found out about security under ColdFusion MX (CFMX). SiteMinder is no longer shipped with ColdFusion, and the architecture for managing security is simpler and much more open than it used to be. Thus we have a lot more latitude in how to approach security.

## Security update

### Email (continued)

Here's the nutshell version:

(1) CFMX uses the new **<cflogin>** and **<cfloginuser>** tags to set the group associations for a particular user.

(2) Within the **<cflogin>** tag, you can run any code you want to determine if the user is authenticated. You can also run whatever code you want to determine what roles (groups) the user is associated with.

This means we could write code that verifies the user against a simple Open Database Connectivity (ODBC) data source, a Lightweight Directory Access Protocol (LDAP) server, an NT domain, or whatever we want.

(3) Once you authenticate the user and you know the roles they belong to, you pass the data to the **<cfloginuser>** tag like this:

```
<cflogin>
    <!--- Do the code to authenticate the user
--->
    <cfif USER IS AUTHENTICATED>
        <cfloginuser
            name="USERNAME"
            roles="LIST OF ROLES THE USER
HAS">
    </cfif>
</cflogin>
```

(4) At this point CFMX knows the users and their roles, and you can use a CF function later in your code (**isUserInRole()**)to determine if the user has a specified role. Some of the security functions in earlier versions of ColdFusion have been deprecated, so it'll be important for us all to review the new security stuff to get familiar with how things are done in MX.

---

**Security update**

---

**Email (continued)**

(5) Security is integrated into components through the roles attribute of the **<cffunction>** tag that's used to define component methods. You can specify which roles have access to each method.

It seems to me that we should go with a really simplified security model for the first version of this app since we know the playing field exactly. For example, instead of controlling access to a requirement on a user-by-user basis, I think it will be sufficient to give a requirements editor the right to edit all requirements.

Non-editors can make contributions by adding comments to the Comments field, and then the requirements editor can incorporate those as he or she sees fit.

I think this approach is well suited to our client since it has some internal disorganization. Rather than sorting out that disorganization, they can just assign relatively few requirements editors but give many people access for commenting. This should keep the process under control while inviting wide participation.

In future revs, we'll have to deal with incorporating security for individual requirements.

Let me know if any of the above needs clarification.

Teo

In the meantime, Dmitry had made progress working with the Flash MX tools and integrating them with ColdFusion MX. The details of how the Flash drill-down and the back-end ColdFusion components were integrated is covered in the next chapter, "Development."

# Technical Design

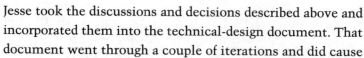

Jesse took the discussions and decisions described above and incorporated them into the technical-design document. That document went through a couple of iterations and did cause some changes in the prototype, such as suggesting some button-name changes and clarifying some parts of the functionality.

One of the basic premises Jesse wrote into the technical-design document was that all data would be represented using ColdFusion MX components. Those ColdFusion components would back-end into a set of database tables optimized for this application.

The decision to use ColdFusion MX components was pretty easy. They provide a set of related functionality, or methods, that resides in one package. By encapsulating the methods into a single unit, the application is architected to make it easier to update in the future. As business logic changes, or better ways to implement specific functionality are discovered, changes can be made by rewriting the highly localized code in a component method without changing overall application functionality.

For example, for the first phase the team decided to use a simple datasource for the security backend. All interaction with the security database would be encapsulated in component methods so that in the future, should it be necessary to interact with an LDAP server instead, only the code in the security methods would need to be adjusted. The rest of the application would continue to function without change.

Somewhere along the line, Jesse realized it was useful to distinguish between ColdFusion MX components, whose primary purpose was to manipulate data, and components whose primary purpose was to provide functionality. He proposed the team adopt *data component* and *functional component* as useful terms to distinguish between the two. So, we have two more key definitions:

- Data components were defined as components whose methods add, edit, delete, or retrieve information that is stored in a database or some other persistent data repository, such as an XML file or an LDAP server.

■ Functional components were defined as components whose methods provide some service or functionality that does not depend on a persistent data store.

## Database and Component Design

Although Andrew and Teo had decided the requirements documents should be represented as hierarchies of individual requirements and they had made some suggestions as to how to model this in the database, the exact schema still needed to be nailed down. Two possible designs were explored.

For storing the hierarchy data, Jesse suggested using a three-table representation that Webworld had used in other projects (see Figure IV-2.4).

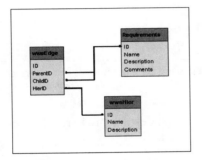

### Figure IV-2.4

In a three-table approach to representing hierarchical data, individual requirements are stored in the Requirements table. The relationships between requirements are stored in the wwsEdge table and the wwsHier table stores the names of an entire hierarchy.

Under this schema, the individual hierarchy nodes are contained in the Requirements table. The nodes connections (technically referred to as *edges*) live in the wwsEdge table, which is nothing more than a linking table that joins a parent node to a child node, using each one's primary key.

Each entry in the wwsEdge table also has a foreign-key relationship to the wwsHier table, which contains the name and description of the requirements document as a whole. A ColdFusion component would be used to manage the Requirements, wwsEdge, and wwsHier tables.

Using a three-table framework would allow a node to have more than one parent, since adding a parent for a node is accomplished by simply adding an entry into the wwsEdge table. The development team decided that this kind of functionality wasn't needed for this application because each requirement will only have one parent.

A simplified model was adopted for ReqBuilder using just the Requirements table to represent the hierarchy. The new design adds ParentID and DocumentID fields to the Requirements table (see Figure IV-2.5).

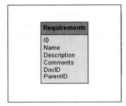

Figure IV-2.5
By including ParentID and DocumentID fields in the Requirements table, the hierarchical relationship of requirements can be managed in one table.

In the simplified database design, the ParentID for each requirement is a foreign key back to the Requirements table itself. It contains the ID of that particular requirement's parent. The DocumentID is also a foreign key to the Requirements table but it points to the top-level requirement that represents the top of the requirements document hierarchy.

This design made it clear that the type of information that needed to be displayed about the overall requirements document and about an individual requirement were largely the same. Both required only Name, Description, and Comments fields. Because of this, Jesse decided that a separate Document table was needed (which had been under discussion); instead, a document was just defined as the top-level node of a requirements document hierarchy. In the one-table design, you locate the top level of each hierarchy by searching for records whose ParentID is set to 0 since they have no parent.

Even though the back-end database was simplified so that the Requirements table alone would hold the key application data, Jesse specified that two ColdFusion components would manage the data in the table:

- Requirement component

- Document component

He architected it this way as a matter of convenience; the requirements component has methods that specialize in performing actions on individual requirements, whereas the document component has methods that specialize in performing actions on documents, or sets of requirements. (In fact, one component could have accommodated both methods, but dividing the functions would make the code easier to read and maintain, and also made it easier to assign two different developers to work on implementing the needed methods.)

## Component Inheritance

One of the big advantages of ColdFusion MX components over regular ColdFusion custom tags is that components support "inheritance." That is, a child component inherits the methods of its parent—and its grandparent, if it has one.

Although the database simplification results in storing the core ReqBuilder data in only one table, Jesse decided to make the requirements component a child of a more general wwsObject component. His reasoning for this is that generic methods could be placed into the wwsObject component that any child components, including the requirements component, would inherit. For example, Jesse specified a generic `Get()` method for the wwsObject component that could be used to retrieve data no matter what child component invoked the method. While this generic capability was not needed for the first phase of ReqBuilder, future phases might add data components that would benefit from the reusability of a generic `Get()` method.

## Security

The team decided to adopt Teo's suggestion for a simple security design, figuring that it's always easier to add functionality based on real-world, demonstrated needs, than it is to take it away.

Several roles were defined for ReqBuilder and included in the design document.

### ReqBuilder simplified user types

**Memo**

**Date:** September 30

**To:** ReqBuilder Team

**From:** Jesse

**Subject:** ReqBuilder simplified user types

OK, so we've decided to go with the simple security scheme. When a person is assigned to a particular role, he or she will have that role with regard to all the data in the system. In other words, we're not going to secure individual requirements or individual requirements documents.

We'll probably need to add that kind of granular control in a future phase, but for now this simple approach should be sufficient for us to get the FABR project done.

Here's a list of the roles we're going to have:

- Requirements viewer: Has the right to view (read only) requirements and requirements documents. This person also has the right to comment on requirements and requirements documents. (Pretty much anyone who can log in should have at least this right).

- Requirements author: Has the right to create and edit requirements. This person can add a requirement anywhere. They can also edit any requirement, not just ones they've created.

- Document owner: Has the right to create new requirements documents and can edit any requirements document. This person also has the right to add or edit requirements.

## Technical-Design Document

Jesse finished writing the technical-design document which included a description of each component and their methods. Although it was expected that changes would occur in that document as development proceeded, it provided a basis for the developers to move forward. At least one important issue surfaced late in the process but was not fully solved: specifically, how to manage locking the data when more than one person was adding requirements to a document at the same time. The issue was noted and assigned to Teo to draft a possible approach while coding began. The details of the components, their methods, and their implementation are covered in the next chapter.

# Development

With the technical-design document completed, the team is getting ready to code. A couple of design issues remain unresolved, such as the details of how to handle security, but the team decides to move forward while Jesse and Andrew work them out.

For source control, the Webworld team has been using the open source Concurrent Versioning System (CVS). (Information on CVS can be found at `http://www.cvshome.org`.) While setting up the development environment, Jesse and Seth, Webworlds internal network guru, meet to discuss which of two basic approaches to use. Most of the Webworld team operates remotely, so it's important to determine the better approach early in the process. Jesse and Seth meet to discuss how to manage the code for ReqBuilder. See Figure IV-3.1 for their whiteboard of two approaches that they discussed for managing code with source-control systems, especially for teams working remotely.

## Current Development Environment

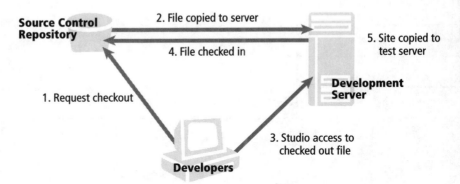

## MX Development Environment

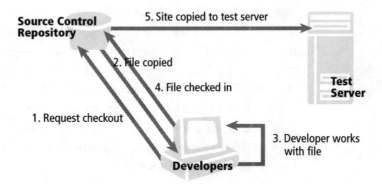

Seth sends a memo around to everyone describing where the development environment will be for ReqBuilder and how the code will be managed. He also gives them a heads up as to how ColdFusion MX development would be done for future projects.

## Source control

### Memo

**Date:** October 7

**To:** ReqBuilder Team

**From:** Seth

**Subject:** Source control

For the last year or so, we've been using shared working directories for our development environments, primarily because the development tools we've been working with have had so much overhead that it hasn't been feasible to install and maintain on each developer's workstation—especially since most everyone works remotely.

ColdFusion MX is going to change that: Setting up a development environment will be a lot simpler and a lot less expensive. So for future MX projects, you'll check out files to a working directory on your local machine instead of checking them out to a shared development server. An immediate benefit of this approach is that you'll be able to break things to your heart's content without worrying that you're messing someone else up. Not that Teo has ever done that. ☺

This will also save us a server: Right now we're developing on a shared server and then have to copy our app's to a test server. With MX, we won't need a central development server, just the test server.

In any case, now that I've given you the good news, here's the bad news: We're not going to implement this for the ReqBuilder application. This is mostly because we're all used to the shared working directory and we just need to get this thing out quickly. Fortunately, CVS supports both modes of operation—shared development server and local development—so there will be no change of tools when we move away from using shared servers.

ReqBuilder is on the shared dev server. Call me for the user names and passwords.

In the meantime, please install CFMX on your systems, as you'll need it for the next project. I'll send installation directions separately.

# Getting Started

## High-Level View

A team meeting is held to get any questions about the design answered and to give the developers the big picture of how the application would function. No one has any major questions about the design, so most of the meeting is spent whiteboarding the way the application will work from the user's perspective. This helps give everyone an overview of how all the pieces are intended to fit together. Andrew does most of the whiteboard sketching, beginning with what happens when a user successfully logs in (see Figure IV-3.2).

**Figure IV-3.2**

After a user logs in, the main, three-frame interface loads. A Flash movie in the left frame requests data from ColdFusion and then displays the list of available requirements documents.

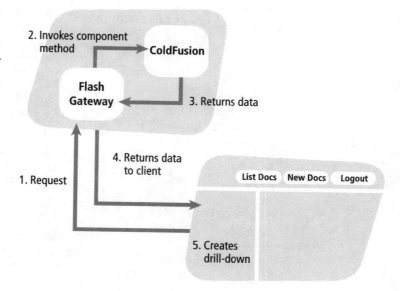

After successful log-in, the top frame displays buttons that control global functions such as displaying a list of available documents, creating a new document, or logging out. A Flash MX movie loads in the left frame and invokes a method on the document component that returns a list of existing documents. The Flash MX movie formats and displays that list.

When the user clicks on a document in the left frame, another Flash movie loads to display a drill-down representation of the requirements document. This movie also makes a request to ColdFusion to invoke a method on the document component that returns all the requirements in the selected document. The Flash movie then displays the requirements document as a drill-down hierarchy.

The requests from Flash to ColdFusion are made through the new Flash Gateway that ships with ColdFusion MX. The Flash Gateway brokers requests between client-side Flash movies and server-side ColdFusion services such as component methods. The Gateway passes requests to ColdFusion and returns data to the Flash movie where it can be processed using Flash's ActionScript scripting language.

When a user with edit permissions clicks a requirement in the left frame, an edit form is loaded in the right frame. If the user does not have edit permissions, the application loads a display-only version of the requirement (see Figure IV-3.3).

**Figure IV-3.3**
The bottom-right frame invokes component methods and displays the result.

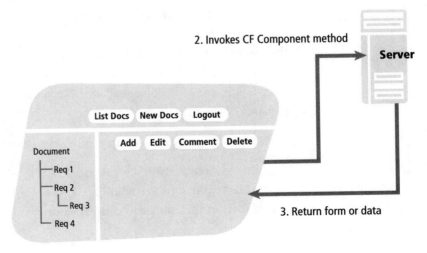

2. Invokes CF Component method

Server

List Docs  New Docs  Logout

Add  Edit  Comment  Delete

Document

— Req 1

— Req 2

  └ Req 3

— Req 4

3. Return form or data

1. User clicks Requirement to load button right frame

Buttons that display at the top of the bottom-right frame give access to other functions such as adding, editing, or deleting a requirement. The buttons are active only if the user has the necessary permissions. For example, requirement authors and document owners can add new requirements, but users in the "viewer" group can only display and comment on a requirement.

The top-level requirement contains the data about the document itself. Although it lives in the same table as the rest of the requirements, the team finds itself referring to the top-level requirement as "the document" when discussing the interface. They find this terminology potentially confusing and ask Teo to write a memo explaining the exact definitions (see Memo a little later in this chapter).

A discussion also ensues as to how often the application should go back to the server to repopulate the requirements drill-down. Although it would be possible to do most of the work on the client side and update back to the server only at the end of a session, the team decides it makes more sense to update the Flash movie whenever a requirement is added, edited, deleted, or re-ordered. The team thinks this approach will help them avoid data-integrity problems that might arise if multiple users submitted multiple, potentially conflicting additions or changes. The additional load caused by more frequent trips to the server should be minimal because the number of people using the application at any given time is expected to be fairly small. Jesse concluded the meeting by giving a high-level view of the sequence of actions needed to complete the application. In short, it consists of the following:

1. Assign areas of responsibility and tasks to each developer.

2. Build the application's basic framework. This includes writing the `Application.cfm` template, creating a mechanism for initializing application variables and coding security.

3. Build any needed generic methods which, according to the design, are localized in the wwsObject component.

4. Build the methods that manage individual requirements. These are localized in the Requirements component.

5. Build the methods that manage groups of requirements. These are localized in the Document component.

6. Integrate the Flash MX user interface (UI) with the back end.

---

**Terminology clarification**

**Memo**

**Date:** October 10

**To:** ReqBuilder Team

**From:** Teo

**Subject:** Terminology clarification

As we found out in the meeting the other day, the terminology we're using for this application can get pretty confusing, especially since we're using the word **document** to refer to more than one thing. Defining the terms clearly will ensure we're all talking about the same things.

1. A **requirement** is an individual item generated by a client or a Webworld staff member that describes a distinct piece of functionality or a feature related to a particular project. In the database it is represented by a single row in the Requirements table. Actions that operate on individual requirements are handled by the Requirements component.

2. A **requirements document** or **document** is a collection of individual requirements that together describe the features and functionality for a particular project. All the individual requirements that make up a requirements document are stored in the Requirements table. Actions that operate on groups of requirements are handled by the Document component.

## Terminology clarification

### Memo (continued)

The term **document** has a second definition, which applies when we discuss the UI. (Although it would be nice to come up with some other word to describe it, no one did in the meeting, so I guess we're stuck with it.) The top-level requirement in a requirements document is stored as a row in the Requirements table, just like any other requirement. However, instead of containing information on a single feature or functionality related to the project, it's a description of the project as a whole, including the name of the requirements document and a description of the document. It's natural, then, to refer to it as "the document" when talking about the UI. We'll just have to remember that **document** can mean either the top-level requirement used to describe the requirements document or the collection of all the requirements that make up a complete requirements document.

By the way, while we're on the subject of terminology, I just wanted to caution everyone that the word "component" is used for both server-side ColdFusion MX components and Flash MX UI "widgets" such as the Flash tree component we're using in ReqBuilder. When there is any chance of confusion between these two uses, make sure you specify whether you are talking about ColdFusion MX or Flash MX components.

If anyone comes up with better terminology for this, let me know!

## Assigning Tasks

Jesse later issues a memo parsing out responsibilities for different areas of the application so each developers would know what they have to do and exactly who will be working on what. When working with ColdFusion MX, specific components or groups of components can be assigned to individual developers. In some cases, especially when the application is relatively small, different developers can be assigned to build methods of a single component, although the preferred approach is to assign a developer to each component.

Using the technical-design document, Jesse assigns components and function areas to individual developers.

**Developer assignments**

**Memo**

**Date:** October 14

**To:** ReqBuilder Team

**From:** Jesse

**Subject:** Developer assignments

The following confirms in writing the assignments we've talked about informally, i.e. who's going to be responsible for what parts of ReqBuilder. Let me know if these assignments need to be rearranged or adjusted in any way.

Now that we've got the design pretty well fleshed out, let Andrew know if you have any questions about it or suggestions as to how it should be changed. Please don't change it without checking with Andrew first, because your change may not be compatible with what someone else is doing.

Here are the assignments:

1. Security: Integrate the log-in code with the **Application.cfm** template.
   Assigned to Debbie.

## Developer assignments

### Memo (continued)

2. Database: Build and populate the database manually so we have something to work with. Teo is going to be working on the basic methods such as **get()**, **save()** and **display()** and obviously needs to have tables to test against. It will help him to manually populate the tables so he can be testing his methods with real data right from the beginning.
   Assigned to Debbie.

3. Generic wwsObject component: Write the following methods for this component.

   a. A generic **Get()** method for retrieving information about a particular item.

   b. The generic **Save()** method.

   b. The generic **Display()** method.
      Assigned to Teo.

4. Requirements component: Write the methods specific to this component. See design doc for details.
   Assigned to Debbie.

5. Document component: Write all the document methods. This includes the code that queries the database to retrieve all the requirements in a particular requirements document and then transforms it into a query that is better suited for use by the Flash tree component. As we already have a ColdFusion Extension (CFX) custom tag to build queries that are "friendly" for creating drill-down interfaces, we might want to use that. However, since some changes may be necessary for the ReqBuilder application and it will be compiled to Java under CFMX anyway, it may be simpler to build it in CFML.
   Assigned to Dmitry.

---

**Developer assignments**

**Memo (continued)**

---

6. Flash tree: This is what we're using to display the list of documents and the full set of requirements for a particular document. To get the data it needs, the tree will use the Flash gateway to invoke a method of the document component. You can use "FTree", the free download, as the starting point. The code you write in ActionScript in the Flash movie obviously needs to integrate with the data returned by the Document methods.
Assigned to Dmitry.

7. The wwsToolBar component: This is the code that displays the buttons in the bottom right frame where work is done on an individual requirement. You can implement this as either a custom tag or a ColdFusion component (CFC). This code is responsible for displaying the buttons and following the security policies to grant access to only those functions a user has access to.
Assigned to Teo.

The application is defined and its basic operating environment established in the `Application.cfm` template. And since users must log in before they can gain access to any functionality, `Application.cfm` also needs to include code to catch users who haven't logged in and force them to do so. First, we check if the application has been initialized and, if necessary, initialize basic variables (see Listing IV-3.1).

Listing IV-3.1     ReqBuilder/Application.cfm (excerpt)

```
<CFAPPLICATION
  NAME="ReqBuilder"
  SESSIONMANAGEMENT="Yes"
  SESSIONTIMEOUT="#CreateTimeSpan(0,1,0,0)#"
  APPLICATIONTIMEOUT="#CreateTimeSpan(0,1,0,0)#">
```

Listing IV-3.1     (continued)

```
<!--- Check if the app is initialized. --->
<CFLOCK SCOPE="application" TYPE="READONLY" TIMEOUT="10">
  <CFIF StructKeyExists(APPLICATION,"stCommon")>
    <CFSET Initialized=TRUE>
  <CFELSE>
    <CFSET Initialized=FALSE>
  </CFIF>
</CFLOCK>
<!--- If Not initialized, set the application variables --->
<CFIF NOT Initialized>
  <CFLOCK TIMEOUT="10" THROWONTIMEOUT="No" TYPE="EXCLUSIVE"
          SCOPE="APPLICATION">
    <!--- The module sets application variables (an
          exception to
          our general rule that custom tags manage their own
          locking
          as we need to the tag as a whole from being run by
          more than
          one person at a time. We're also hardcoding the path
          here since the application variables we'd normally
          use to
          access the path is not initialized yet. --->
    <CFMODULE TEMPLATE="/Reqbuilder/custtags/
            rbInitAppVars.cfm">
  </CFLOCK>
</CFIF>

<!--- Move common app vars into the request scope --->
<CFLOCK SCOPE="application" TYPE="READONLY" TIMEOUT="10">
  <CFSCRIPT>
    REQUEST.stApp = StructNew();
    REQUEST.stApp = Duplicate(APPLICATION.stCommon);
  </CFSCRIPT>
</CFLOCK>
```

```
<!--- 3/23/03: jds: STYLE SHEET The CSS for this app is
included here. --->
<CFIF FindNoCase("frame_right_",CGI.script_name)
      OR FindNoCase("document", CGI.script_Name)>
  <CFOUTPUT>
    <LINK HREF="#REQUEST.stApp.cssdir#/RBstyle_workarea.css"
      TYPE="text/css"
      REL="stylesheet">
  </CFOUTPUT>
<CFELSE>
  <CFOUTPUT>
    <link HREF="#REQUEST.stApp.cssdir#/RBstyle.css"
      TYPE="text/css"
      REL="Stylesheet">
  </CFOUTPUT>
</CFIF>


<!---*************** BEGIN Security Section
*************************--->
<!--- Not running security if we're connecting to the Flash
      gateway.
      This bypasses security for that connection -- we'll
      probably
      want to add it in at some point. --->
<CFIF NOT FindNoCase("flashservices/gateway", CGI.ath_info)>
  <!--- Test the login. If the user hasn't logged in, then
        send them to the login page. --->
  <CFLOGIN>
    <CFLOCATION
      URL="#request.stapp.approot#/Security/login.cfm"
      ADDTOKEN="No">
  </CFLOGIN>
</CFIF>
```

**Listing IV-3.1**    (continued)

```
<!--- If the "logout" is passed into here or if
      session.UserProfile
      expired, then go to the security area and pass URL var
      to indicate we
      should log out.
      --->
<CFIF (IsDefined("logout") AND Logout) OR NOT
IsDefined("Session.UserProfile")>
  <CFLOCATION

URL="#request.stapp.approot#/Security/login.cfm?Logout=true"
    ADDTOKEN="No">
</CFIF>
<!---**************
/END Security Section ************************--->


<!---
      Copy the user profile into request scope. This needs to
      be done after
      the CFLOGIN because that is where session.UserProfile is
      set up. --->
<CFLOCK SCOPE="SESSION" TYPE="READONLY" TIMEOUT="10">
  <CFSET REQUEST.ses.UserProfile =
         Duplicate(Session.UserProfile)>
</CFLOCK>
```

Within this code, the `rbInitAppVars.cfm` custom tag consists of a series
of statements that set variables into the application scope. The variables
are set into the application scope only at application startup but are
copied into the request scope for every new request. This is done because
the variables in the application scope are shared amongst all application
users. In other words, application scope variables are available in code to
all users of the application. If one user carries out an operation that
changes an application variable while another user also tries to change
that variable, a problem could develop because both have access to the
same variable. To prevent this, any code that accesses an application variable should be surrounded with a `<CFLOCK>` tag.

However, another approach is to use one `<CFLOCK>` tag to copy the application variables into the request scope and then access the values in the request scope. This works because variables in the request scope are only available during the "life" of a single request from a single user. The request scope is therefore safe from the kind of conflict problems that the application scope can have. After reviewing the above, Andrew sends a note to the team about some items they might want to take up in a future phase.

---

**Initialization**

**Memo**

**Date:** October 17

**To:** ReqBuilder Team

**From:** Andrew

**Subject:** Initialization

Here are a few things we might want to refine for the next release (though they aren't worth hassling with right now):

1. The current initialization logic has a crack in it, as follows: If the application has not initialized, and two users request a page at the same time, they'll both check to see if **application.stcommon** exists, find that it doesn't, and both try to run the initialization code. The first one in will get the exclusive lock and will run the custom tag to initialize the app. Meanwhile, the other one waits until the first one is done initializing. When the first one completes, it releases the lock and the second one will start the initialization process all over again. This is not a big deal with the current app because of the anticipated light loads, but if we work on a site for which there's a lot of traffic and for which the initialization process takes a long time, we'd need to tighten this up so only one user would run the initialization code. Tell you what—I'll buy pizza for the first guy to come up with a simple solution (off hours, of course) that prevents duplicate running of the initialization procedure.

**Initialization**

**Memo (continued)**

2. It would be nice if we could avoid the obvious hard-coding of the path to the **rbInitAppVars.cfm** custom tag in **Application.cfm**. As it is, when the application is moved to another server with different paths, someone will have to go in and change the code to make the application work. In a future phase, it probably makes sense to put something like this into an .ini file that we can read with **GetProfileString()** or the new MX **GetProfileSections()** function. If that .ini file is in the root of the app, we would only need to hardcode the name of the file to get to it. Obviously, someone would need to change the .ini file, but at least they wouldn't be mucking around with code directly.

Another possibility is to create an XML file with all initialization data that needs to be hardcoded, then read and parse it at application startup using CFMX's new XML functions.

In either case we could either have an application administrator manually edit the .ini or XML file or we could build a component that manages the data in those files to avoid any direct file manipulation.

Debbie works on the security part of Application.cfm, using CFMX's new CFLOGIN to control security. But after reviewing it, she realizes her code doesn't take full advantage of some of the built-in features of CFLOGIN and decides to rewrite it. In the course of re-writing the code, she gathers some additional data about how to use CFLOGIN and writes it up as a memo for the whole team.

**CFLOGIN**

**Memo**

**Date:** October 21

**To:** ReqBuilder Team

**From:** Debbie

**Subject:** CFLOGIN

I found out some things about **<CFLOGIN>** that I've incorporated into the new security code. I thought the data would be of general interest:

1. The key thing to know about **<CFLOGIN>** is that its body, that is, the code that lies between the **<CFLOGIN>** and the **</CFLOGIN>**, only runs if the user is not logged in. Once the user is logged in, that code no longer runs.

2. **<CFLOGIN>** has to run on every page where you want to access security in order to establish a "context" for security—to make it active, in other words. Security-related functions such as **GetAuthUser()**, which returns the currently logged-in user, will not function unless **<CFLOGIN>** has already been run in the current request.

3. I found out the hard way that you can't branch out of a **<CFLOGIN>** before the **</CFLOGIN>** runs because the security context isn't fully established until the **</CFLOGIN>** runs. In other words, don't put any code inside a **<CFLOGIN>** that does a **<CFLOCATION>** or **<CFABORT>** or anything like that unless you don't care about the security context.

## CFLOGIN

### Memo (continued)

4. A specific example of making sure you run a **<CFLOGIN>** before doing other security activities is when you want to log out a user. The **<CFLOGIN>** has to run before the **<CFLOGOUT>** runs in order to actually log the person out. This is an easy trap to fall into because you kind of expect you can just run a **<CFLOGOUT>** wherever you want, but doing so doesn't log the person out unless **<CFLOGIN>** has run previously.

5. **<CFLOGIN>** provides a way to register an authenticated user to the CF server so you can access things like the user name (**GetAuthUser()**) and the roles they belong to (**IsUserInRole()**), but it does not provide a means to hold what we'd typically hold in a user profile—the user's full name, address, email address, and so on. I'm keeping that additional user data in the variable **Session.UserProfile**.
This is fine, but it means that the UserProfile could time out even though the **<CFLOGIN>** data has not. And since **Session.UserProfile** is only set during the **<CFLOGIN>** process, we need to catch this situation. There has been some talk by Macromedia about expanding the data that **<CFLOGIN>** can store, so perhaps that will be available in a future release.

## CFLOGIN

### Memo (continued)

6. If you use **j_username** and **j_password**, respectively, for the user name and password fields when you submit a log-in form, **<CFLOGIN>** automatically creates a **CFLOGIN** scope that exists within the **<CFLOGIN>**, **</CFLOGIN>** pair. This scope has the following keys: **CFLOGIN.name** and **CFLOGIN.password**. If you follow this convention everywhere, it makes your security code more generic because it will properly handle requests it receives as Web Services or from **FORM** or **URL** variables. This is because **CFLOGIN** looks for the names "j_username" and "j_password" in several places. According to Macromedia, the order of lookup goes like this:

   a. The authorization cookie created by CF.

   b. Flash Remoting (not sure about the details of how this is done, but it will be important as we start to work more with Flash MX).

   c. A log-in form that passes either **FORM** or **URL** variables—that is, **[FORM/URL].j_username** and **[FORM/URL].j_password**.

   d. The HTTP basic authorization header. This lets CF interact with Web server's basic authorization. It is important to specify **basic** authorization for the Web server (I made the mistake of trying this with the Web server set to use NT security; that does **not** work).

**CFLOGIN**

**Memo (continued)**

We also have a somewhat special circumstance in ReqBuilder because the main part of the app uses frames. When a form within a frame submits to the frameset template, the **FORM** vars do not automatically propagate down into the files in the individual frames. So, if we wanted to process log-in form submissions within a frame, we'd need to explicitly pass the **FORM** vars from the frameset down into the frame. I avoided this problem by moving the security code into its own directory with its own **Application.cfm** template and did not use frames. This results in some duplication of code in the two **Application.cfm** templates, but I decided this was acceptable.

The security code ended up in three different places: the `Application.cfm` template that controls access to the main pages of the application, the `login.cfm` template in the Security subdirectory (which has its own Application.cfm template with no security code in it), and the `rbSecurity.cfc` component whose `Authenticate()` method interacts with the back-end security data store. Listing IV-3.2 shows the code in the `Application.cfm` template.

Listing IV-3.2      `/ReqBuilder/Application.cfm` (excerpt)

```
<!---**************
BEGIN Security Section ************************--->
<!--- Not running security if we're connected to the Flash
      gateway.
      This bypasses security for that connection --
      we'll probably want to add it in at some point.
      --->
<CFIF NOT FindNoCase("flashservices/gateway",
                     CGI.ath_info)>
  <!--- Test the login. If the user hasn't logged in, then
        send them
```

```
      to the login page. --->
  <CFLOGIN>
    <CFLOCATION
      URL="#request.stapp.approot#/Security/login.cfm"
      ADDTOKEN="No">
  </CFLOGIN>
</CFIF>


<!--- If the "logout" is passed into here or if
      session.UserProfile
      expired, then go to the security area and pass URL
      var to indicate we
      should log out. --->
<CFIF (IsDefined("logout") AND Logout)
      OR NOT IsDefined("Session.UserProfile")>
  <CFLOCATION
    URL="#request.stapp.approot#/Security/login.cfm?
        Logout=true"
    ADDTOKEN="No">
</CFIF>
<!---**************
/END Security Section ************************--->
```

The security part of `Application.cfm` is straightforward: It runs the security code only when a browser requests a page, not when Flash requests data through the Flash gateway. This was done pretty much as a convenience; the Web team decided to defer creating the Flash security code until a later phase.

The `<CFLOGIN>` takes advantage of the fact that its body runs only if the current user has *not* yet logged in. So, if the user hasn't logged in, the code runs and the `<CFLOCATION>` sends the user to `login.cfm`, which lives in its own directory with its own `Application.cfm`. The subsequent `<CFIF>` checks if a `Logout=True` was passed to the current template or if the session has expired (by checking for the existence of `Session.UserProfile`). In either case, it does a `<CFLOCATION>` to `login.cfm` and passes a URL variable to indicate that a log-out has been requested.

Once the user has logged in, the `<CFLOGIN>` establishes the security context for all page requests. However, the code between `<CFLOGIN>` and `</CFLOGIN>` does not execute again. The `Application.cfm` template in the security directory is a stripped-down version of the main `Application.cfm` code; all the security code was removed to avoid any possibility of creating an infinite loop.

The next chunk of security work, part of which is shown in Listing IV-3.3, is done in the `login.cfm` template.

Listing IV-3.3    `/ReqBuilder/Security/login.cfm` (excerpt)

```
<CFLOGIN>
    <CFIF IsDefined("CFLOGIN")>

        <!--- Run the component that manages authentication--->
        <CFSCRIPT>
          // Convert the path into a dot-delimited
          CompDir=RemoveChars(REQUEST.stApp.ComponentDir,1,1);
          CompDir=ListChangeDelims(CompDir, ".", "/");

          // instantiate the component that manages security
          SecComp=CreateObject("component",CompDir &
                                   ".functional.rbSecurity");

          // Invoke the Authenticate method on it using the
             name and password
          //   contained in CFLOGIN
          stSec =SecComp.Authenticate(CFLOGIN.name,
                                   CFLOGIN.password);
        </CFSCRIPT>

        <!--- If it passes authentication, we'll have info in
              the
              returned structure and we can log the user in.
              --->
        <CFIF NOT StructIsEmpty(stSec)>
```

```
            <CFLOGINUSER NAME="#cflogin.name#"
              PASSWORD="#cflogin.password#"
              ROLES="#stSec.Groups#">

            <!--- Put profile into session scope which is also
                  returned
                  from the rbSecurity component --->
            <CFLOCK SCOPE="SESSION" TYPE="EXCLUSIVE"
            TIMEOUT="10">
              <CFSET SESSION.UserProfile = stSec.UserProfile>
            </CFLOCK>

          <!--- Otherwise, set a var to indicate that the login
            failed. --->
          <CFELSE>
            <CFSET LoginFailed = True>
          </CFIF>
        </CFIF>
</CFLOGIN>

<!--- If we passed a var to indicate we want to logout or
      if the session has expired, log the person out. This
      has to come after the CFLOGIN --->
<CFIF (IsDefined("Logout") AND Logout)
      OR NOT IsDefined("Session.UserProfile")>
  <!--- Do the logout --->
  <CFLOGOUT>

  <!--- Delete Session.UserProfile if we are logging out.--->
  <CFLOCK SCOPE="Session" TYPE="Exclusive"
          THROWONTIMEOUT="NO" TIMEOUT="10">
    <CFSET StructDelete(SESSION,"UserProfile")>
  </CFLOCK>
</CFIF>
```

Listing IV-3.3     (continued)

```
<!--- If we successfully logged in -- as evidenced by the
      existence of a
      valid user, then go to the home page --->
<CFIF Len( GetAuthUser()) GT 0>
  <CFLOCATION URL="#REQUEST.stApp.AppRoot#" ADDTOKEN="No">
</CFIF>
```

The block starts with a `<CFLOGIN>` of its own, the contents of which run only if the user has not logged in. The authentication code inside `<CFLOGIN>` is wrapped with a `<CFIF>` that checks for the existence of `CFLOGIN` which is a special scope that is created by `<CFLOGIN>` if it has access to the specially named `j_username` and `j_password` fields. The first time a user comes to this page before logging in, the contents of the `<CFIF>` are skipped, and processing picks up after the `</CFLOGIN>` tag.

The `<CFIF>` after the `</CFLOGIN>` tag checks if the variable `Logout` has been passed to this template or if Session.UserProfile does not exist (which would usually occur when the session times out). If either condition is met, it runs `<CFLOGOUT>` to log out the current user. Note that the `<CFLOGOUT>` must come after the `<CFLOGIN>`; otherwise the log-out won't actually log the user out. After the log-out, the code deletes the UserProfile from the session scope.

The next `<CFIF>` block checks if an authorized user does exist—that is, sees if someone has successfully logged in—and, if one does, returns the user to the main application page. Obviously this block doesn't run when the user first comes to this page, so the template continues by displaying the log-in form. See Listing IV-3.4 for an edited excerpt of this form.

Listing IV-3.4     /ReqBuilder/Security/login.cfm (excerpt)

```
<FORM ACTION="#CGI.Script_Name#"
      METHOD="post"
      NAME="rb_login">


<TABLE WIDTH="400" BORDER="0" CELLSPACING="0"
       CELLPADDING="0">
  <TR BGCOLOR="##cccc99">
```

```
    <TD COLSPAN="4" ALIGN="center" CLASS="subhead">
      Application Login
    </TD>
  </TR>
  <TR>
    <TD>Username:</TD>
    <TD COLSPAN="3">
      <INPUT TYPE="text" NAME="j_username" SIZE="25">
    </TD>
  </TR>
  <TR>
    <TD>Password:</TD>
    <TD COLSPAN="3">
      <INPUT TYPE="password" NAME="j_password" SIZE="25"
             VALUE="">
    </TD>
  </TR>
  <CFIF IsDefined("LoginFailed")>
  <TR>
    <TD COLSPAN="4">
      Invalid Username or Password. Please try again.
    </TD>
  </TR>
  </CFIF>
  <TR BGCOLOR="##cccc99">
    <TD COLSPAN="4" ALIGN="center" CLASS="subhead">
      <INPUT TYPE="submit" NAME="LoginSubmit"
             VALUE="&laquo; Log In &raquo;"
             CLASS="button_form">
         
      <INPUT TYPE="reset" VALUE="&laquo; Clear &raquo;"
             CLASS="button_form">
    </TD>
  </TR>
</TABLE>
</FORM>
```

Some parts of the full code have been removed to keep the listing shorter, but the key point is that it is a self-submitting form that uses the form field names j_username and j_password for the user name and password input elements.

These are "magic" names for <CFLOGIN> that cause the code to create the CFLOGIN scope. Look again at Listing IV-3.3 and the code within the <CFLOGIN> tag. When the log-in form is submitted, the <CFIF> checks for and finds the CFLOGIN scope if fields named j_username and j_password are available at the point when the <CFLOGIN> runs.

When CFLOGIN is found, the <CFSCRIPT> block instantiates and invokes the Authenticate() method on the rbSecurity.cfc component (it finds the path to the component using the Request variable that points to the component directory). This method returns an empty structure if the authentication fails, and a populated structure if the it succeeds. (In Cold-Fusion "structures" are a data type similar to an array but whose keys are strings rather than integers. In other languages a similar data type is some-times called an "associative array" or a "hash array.") If the authentica-tion succeeds, the code runs <CFLOGINUSER> to log in the user. It then copies the UserProfile, which is also returned by the Authenticate() method, into the Session scope.

To hook ReqBuilder to another back-end security system, such as an LDAP server or NT security, the developer would need to adjust the Authenticate() method so that it uses the new back end. See Listing IV-3.5 for the rbSecurity.cfc code.

Listing IV-3.5    /ReqBuilder/Components/Functional/rbSecurity.cfc (excerpt)

```
<!------------    BEGIN Authenticate method ---------------->
<CFFUNCTION NAME="Authenticate" HINT="This validates the
username and
password against the security DB and, if successful,
returns a
structure containing basic user information.">

   <!--- this is used to authenticate the user against the
backend
```

```
end security store, whatever that might be.  --->
  <CFARGUMENT NAME="username" REQUIRED="Yes">
  <CFARGUMENT NAME="password" REQUIRED="Yes">

  <!--- query database to validate user logging in --->
  <CFQUERY NAME="qGetUser" DATASOURCE="Reqbuilder">
    SELECT u.FirstName, u.LastName, u.ID, u.Username,
      u.password, g.GroupName
    FROM   Users u, Users_Groups x, Groups g
    WHERE  u.ID = x.UserID
    AND x.GroupID = g.ID
    AND u.username = '#trim(Arguments.username)#'
    AND u.password = '#trim(Arguments.password)#'
  </CFQUERY>

  <!--- Create the struct we'll return to the calling page
--->
  <CFSET stSec = StructNew()>

  <!--- If we returned struct is populated, then the
        user was authenticated, log the user in. --->
  <CFIF qGetUser.RecordCount EQ 1
        AND qGetUser.GroupName[1] NEQ "">

    <!--- create UserProfile to be used as session
          variable --->
    <CFSCRIPT>
      UserProfile = structnew();
      UserProfile.fNAME = qGetUser.FirstName;
      UserProfile.lNAME = qGetUser.LastName;
      UserProfile.ID = qGetUser.ID;

      stSec.UserProfile = UserProfile;
      stSec.Groups = ValueList(qGetUser.GroupName);
    </CFSCRIPT>
```

Listing IV-3.5    (continued)

```
        </CFIF>

        <CFRETURN stSec>

    </CFFUNCTION>
    <!------------    END Authenticate method ---------------->
```

The `Authenticate()` method is straightforward ColdFusion code. The `<CFARGUMENT>` tags identify the method's required arguments, and the database query validates the user name and password against the security tables. If the query returns a single record, the user profile and the user's groups are put into a structure that is returned to the calling template with `<CFRETURN>`.

As mentioned before, if a change of security back end needs to be made, it is done by changing the `rbSecurity.cfc Authenticate()` method. As long as the new security back end returns the same type of data as the current security back end, the rest of the application should work without any changes.

# wwsObject Component

The technical-design document specified that all data components would extend the wwsObject component, which implements basic, generic methods that can be used across a range of child components. Even though the first phase of Reqbuilder requires only two data components, this architecture was implemented to facilitate future additions.

Teo was assigned to build the generic methods in wwsObject, including `Get()`, `Save()`, and `Display()`. He started with the generic `Get()` method, which consists of a simple query to the table that holds the component's data. The `Get()` method determines which table to query based on the name of the component that invokes it (see Listing IV-3.6).

Listing IV-3.6    /ReqBuilder/Components/Data/wwsObject.cfc (Get() method excerpt)

```
<CFFUNCTION NAME="Get" HINT="Generic Get() method.">

    <!--- Get the name of the component that is calling
          this method as
          that will be the name of the table or view where
          the data is
          stored. --->
    <CFIF IsDefined("Arguments.TargetTable")
          AND Len("Arguments.TargetTable")>
      <CFSET CurrComp = ARGUMENTS.TargetTable>
    <CFELSE>
      <CFSET CurrComp =
             ListLast(GetMetaData(this).Name,".")>
    </CFIF>

    <!--- Do a general query on the component table to get
          the requested
          data --->
    <CFQUERY NAME="qGet" DATASOURCE="Reqbuilder">
      SELECT *
      FROM #CurrComp#
      WHERE 1 = 1
      <CFIF IsDefined("ARGUMENTS.ObjectID")
            AND Len(Trim(ARGUMENTS.ObjectID)) GT 0>
        AND ID = #ARGUMENTS.ObjectID#
      </CFIF>
      <CFIF IsDefined("ARGUMENTS.lObjectIDs")
            AND Len(Trim(ARGUMENTS.lObjectIDs)) GT 0>
            AND ID IN
(#ListQualify(ARGUMENTS.lObjectIDs,"'",",","CHAR")#)
      </CFIF>
      <CFIF IsDefined("ARGUMENTS.SortOrder")>
        <CFIF ARGUMENTS.SortOrder EQ 'ASC'>
            ORDER BY Name ASC
```

Listing IV-3.6     (continued)

```
                <CFELSEIF ARGUMENTS.SortOrder EQ 'DESC'>
                    ORDER BY Name DESC
                </CFIF>
            </CFIF>
            <CFIF IsDefined("ARGUMENTS.ActiveOnly")
                    AND ARGUMENTS.ActiveOnly>
                AND State = 1
            </CFIF>
        </CFQUERY>


        <!---Return the query containing the records we got--->
        <CFRETURN qGet>
    </CFFUNCTION>
```

Within ReqBuider, the generic get() method will be used to retrieve data from the Requirements table (see Figure IV-3.4). Using the GetMeta-Data() function, this method begins by determining which component invoked it because the code queries a table with the same name as the component. It constructs a query to get the requested objects based on the arguments passed into it and, optionally, sorting it on the Name field. Additional code could be added to this to make other aspects of it dynamic, but the existing query works for the ReqBuilder application. For those components whose data is stored in a table with a different name or for which there are more complex requirements for the Get() method, you would just write a component-specific Get() method to override this default method.

Figure IV-3.4

The fields in the Requirements table.

Next, Teo wrote the generic Save() method as shown in Listing IV-3.7.

Listing IV-3.7     /ReqBuilder/Components/Data/wwsObject.cfc (Save() method excerpt)

```
<CFFUNCTION NAME="Save" HINT="Generic Save() method.">

  <CFARGUMENT NAME="stObject" REQUIRED="True">

  <!--- Get the name of the component that invoked this
        which will be the
        name of the table it is stored in. --->
  <CFSET CurrComp = ListLast(getMetaData(this).Name,".")>

  <!--- Make a copy of the structure passed into the
        save() method that
        is local to this method so that we can change it
        without the risk
        of causing problems for the calling code. --->
  <CFSET stObj = StructNew()>
  <CFSET stObj = Duplicate(Arguments.stObject)>

  <!--- get the ObjectID into a local var --->
  <CFSET ID = stObj.ObjectID>

  <!--- Remove the fields that don't get updated --->
  <CFLOOP LIST="FieldNames,ObjectID" INDEX="CurrField">
    <CFSET Temp = StructDelete(stObj, CurrField)>
  </CFLOOP>

  <!--- Set a variable to hold the delimiter between
        clauses in the
        SET statement. --->
  <CFSET Delim = "">

  <!--- Do the update query --->
  <CFQUERY NAME="GenericSave"
  DATASOURCE="#REQUEST.stApp.DSN#">
    UPDATE #CurrComp#
```

Listing IV-3.7    (continued)

```
SET
  <!--- Loop through the data fields passed in --->
  <CFLOOP collection="#stObj#" item="CurrField">
    <!--- Check if the value is numeric to know how
          to do the SET clause --->
    <CFIF IsNumeric(stObj[CurrField])>
      #Delim##CurrField# = #stObj[CurrField]#
    <CFELSE>
      #Delim##CurrField# = '#stObj[CurrField]#'
    </CFIF>
    <!--- All SET clauses after the first have a
          comma before them --->
    <CFSET Delim = ",">
  </CFLOOP>
  ,Locked = 0
  ,LastUpdated = #CreateODBCDate(Now())#
WHERE ID = #ID#
</CFQUERY>
<CFOUTPUT>
  '#CurrComp#' Object Saved...<BR />
</CFOUTPUT>
</CFFUNCTION>
```

The Save() method has one required argument, stObject, which is a structure whose keys are the database fields to be updated and whose values are the values to use in the SQL UPDATE statement. This structure also needs to contain the ObjectID key, whose value is the ID of the record that needs to be updated. This would be the value of the primary key for the table, so it is not included in the SET clauses of the UPDATE statement. Normally, the structure passed in as stObject will come from an HTML <FORM> submission. ColdFusion MX makes the values of a <FORM> submission available in the FORM scope which is implemented as a structure.

As with the Get() method, the Save() method determines the name of the invoking component so it knows which table to update. Because ColdFusion passes structures by reference, the variable stObject points to the same data that is passed to it by the calling template. In order to avoid any possible odd side effects, the `Save()` method uses the `Duplicate()` function to make a local copy of the data in `stObject`. By doing so, the method can make changes to `stObject` without affecting the calling template. And, the `Save()` method does, in fact, change the structure by removing two fields that do not to be included in the SET clause: `Fieldnames` and `ObjectID`. ColdFusion MX adds `Fieldnames` to the `FORM` scope whenever a form is submitted. This field contains a list of all the fields in the `FORM`. As mentioned above, `ObjectID` contains the ID of the record that will be updated which is not included in the SET clause but is used in the `WHERE` clause.

The method constructs an `UPDATE SQL` statement based on the fields in the cleaned copy of `stObject`.

After Teo finishes with the code, Andrew reviews it and sends the following email to Teo:

**Generic Save() method**

**Email**

**Date:** October 23

**To:** Teo

**From:** Andrew

**Subject:** Generic Save() method

Teo,

The generic Save() method looks good. I noticed one thing we might want to consider changing if we use this in other apps. Right now, your code assumes that HTML fields passed to the Save() method all match up with fields in the database.

This is pretty safe for this application as we're building the forms and can make sure nothing rogue gets in there.

But there might be cases when a bunch of HTML fields get passed to this method—like if we're building something dynamically—and we need to figure out which HTML fields we should use to update the specific database table.

**Generic Save() method**

**Email (continued)**

One way to do this would be to query the target table with a SELECT statement guaranteed to return no rows:

```
<CFQUERY name="GetFields"
datasource="#request.stApp.DSN#">

SELECT *
FROM #CurrComp#
WHERE 1 = 2

</CFQUERY>
```

In CF, although this provides no data, it does give us access to a list of the database fields in GetFields.ColumnList.

We could then change the loop you're currently using in the save() method. Instead of looping over the fields passed in from the HTML form, we'd loop over GetFields.ColumnList and build the UPDATE query based on that.

Of course, this has the overhead of an additional database call, but it isn't expensive, and this approach ensures that we're only going to attempt to update database fields that actually exist. (Additionally, the code might have to take special measures to accommodate fields with spaces or other odd characters in their name, but we could worry about those cases when building it.)

No need to change this now, but wanted to note it.

Andrew

Next Teo tackles the generic Display() method. After studying different approaches to implement it, he opts for a slightly different approach than he used for the generic Get() and Save() methods. He drafts a memo to Jesse and Andrew to explain his decision.

## Making the Display() method generic

### Memo

**Date:** October 25

**To:** Jesse, Andrew

**From:** Teo

**Subject:** Making the Display() method generic

The **Get()** and **Save()** methods in wwsObject are generic—that is, they don't have any code in them that is specific to a particular component. Of course, to use them, the component has to conform to certain conventions, but if those conventions are followed (like naming the component's table the same as the component itself), then everything should work.

The **Display()** method works a bit differently. I could construct a general method that looks at the fields in a component and sort of randomly figure out how to display each of them, or I could construct an admin interface so that users can define how they want the display to look for each component. But I don't think either approach is good for this app.

The first approach is pretty much guaranteed to produce an ugly-as-sin display.

The second is far more complicated than we need for this.

However, there is another alternative. I think we want to make it fairly easy for someone to change the way a component displays within this system. But I'm not sure we want to have just anyone poking around in the CF component code. So here's what I'm proposing:

I'll write a generic **Display()** method in wwsObject. It will figure out what component invoked it and then **CFINCLUDE** customized code to actually render the display. So, the code in the wwsObject component is still generic, but it includes code that is specific to the type of component invoking it.

## Making the Display() method generic

**Memo**

The advantage of this is that we can give an entry-level CF developer access to the display code without giving them access to the component itself. That way, someone with minimal skills can make tweaks to the display interface without having to know about or poke around in the key components for the system.

Let me know if you object to this approach, but I'm going to proceed with it in the meanwhile.

Andrew and Jesse both thought the approach made sense and told Teo to continue. The generic `Display()` method is in Listing IV-3.8:

Listing IV-3.8    /ReqBuilder/Components/Data/wwsObject.cfc  (Display() method excerpt)

```
<CFFUNCTION NAME="Display" ACCESS="Remote"
            HINT="Generic Display() method.">

   <!--- Invoke the Get() method on whatever was passed in so
         we can display it. --->
   <CFSCRIPT>
      //Invoke the Get() method to get the data we need to
display.
      qRecords = this.Get(ObjectID=Arguments.ReqID);

      // Get the name of the calling component
      CurrComp = ListLast(getMetaData(this).Name,".");
   </CFSCRIPT>

   <!--- Try to include the file for the current type --->
   <CFTRY>

      <CFINCLUDE TEMPLATE="#REQUEST.stApp.IncDir#/
                          #currComp#.cfm">

      <!--- Catch any error with including the file. --->
```

```
<CFCATCH TYPE="Any">
  <!--- If a specific file isn't available, then include
         the
    default file. --->
  <CFTRY>
    <CFINCLUDE TEMPLATE="#REQUEST.stApp.IncDir#/
                           default.cfm">
    <CFCATCH TYPE="MissingInclude">
      <CFABORT SHOWERROR="Problems with the display.cfm
                           include files.">
    </CFCATCH>
  </CFTRY>
</CFCATCH>
</CFTRY>
</CFFUNCTION>
```

The Display() method invokes a Get() method on the current object, forwarding all the arguments that were passed to the Display() method to the Get() method. The method then uses the name of the calling component to construct a filename, which it tries to <CFINCLUDE>. If that fails, it tries to <CFINCLUDE> a default display template and finally displays an error message if that doesn't work.

The included display code must follow the convention of using qRecords, which is returned by Get(), to generate the display. In the case of a requirement, the included display code is trivial (see Listing IV-3.9).

Listing IV-3.9    /ReqBuilder/Components/Includes/Requirements.cfm

```
<CFOUTPUT QUERY="qRecords">
  <TABLE BORDER="0" ALIGN="center">
    <TR>
      <TD CLASS="subhead">Requirement Name:</TD>
    </TR>
    <TR>
      <TD>  #qRecords.NAME#</TD>
    </TR>
    <TR>
```

Listing IV-3.9    (continued)

```
          <TD CLASS="subhead">Description:</TD>
        </TR>
        <TR>
          <TD>  #qRecords.Description#</TD>
        </TR>
        <TR>
          <TD CLASS="subhead">Comment:</TD>
        </TR>
        <TR>
          <TD>  #qRecords.Comments#</TD>
        </TR>
      </TABLE>
</CFOUTPUT>
```

That completes the generic methods in the wwsObject component. Next is the Requirements component.

# Requirements Component

The Requirements component is the heart of the ReqBuilder application, so it's one of the first things to build after the wwsObject component. It's written as a child of the wwsObject component, extending it and taking advantage of the wwsObject's generic methods. The technical-design document specifies that the Requirements component uses the default Get(), Display(),, and Save() methods whereas it has its own Edit(), Comment(), Create(), and Delete() methods.

Before Debbie tackles creating the methods for the Requirements component, she has a question about the sequence to use when creating a new requirement—specifically, whether the requirement should be created at the beginning or the end of the creation process. She asks Andrew for some advise on how to approach this, and he emails his response to the team.

## Creating new objects

### Email

**Date:** October 28

**To:** ReqBuilder Team

**From:** Andrew

**Subject:** Creating new objects

Debbie asked how to create new requirements in ReqBuilder. We've approached this two ways in the past:

(1) Use a **Create()** method to create a new object, then invoke the **Edit()** method to edit the new item; or(2) Gather all the data needed to create a new item, then create it.

The first way has the advantage of allowing you to reuse the **Edit()** method code for creating objects. All you have to do is create a new instance of the object and then invoke the **Edit()** method on it. The disadvantage is that if the user starts to create a new object and then abandons the process, you're stuck with an orphaned object in the database.

The second method avoids those orphans, but can be more complex to write.

The technical design for ReqBuilder specifies the first approach, as it's the simplest to implement. When a new item is created, we mark it by putting "__New_Item__" in the Name field.

To manage the orphans, we could create a scheduled event to clean up the database periodically, but I think it would be much simpler to just include a SQL DELETE statement in the **Create()** method that deletes any requirements with the "__New_Item__" name that are older than a day. That will keep the database cleaned up with relatively little overhead for any one operation.

Andrew

Debbie incorporates the cleanup code into the **Create()** method she'd already written, with the results shown in Listing IV-3.10.

Listing IV-3.10        /ReqBuilder/Components/Data/Requirements.cfc

```
<CFFUNCTION NAME="Create" HINT="This is a requirement-
specific
create method that is needed because creating a requirement
involves the
requirement itself as well as its relationship to its
parent." >

  <CFARGUMENT NAME="ParentID" REQUIRED="True">
  <CFARGUMENT NAME="DocID" REQUIRED="True">
  <CFARGUMENT NAME="ReturnID" REQUIRED="True" DEFAULT="No">

  <!--- Clean up Old, unfinished Requirements that are more
    than a day old --->
  <CFQUERY NAME="CleanUp" DATASOURCE="#REQUEST.stApp.DSN#">
    DELETE
    FROM Requirements
    WHERE Name = '__New_Item__'
    AND CreateDateTime < (#now()# -
        #REQUEST.stApp.DBCleanUpInterval#)
  </CFQUERY>

  <!--- Need to have a transaction around the thing  --->
  <CFTRANSACTION>
    <!---  get last seq number and add 1 to it to create seq
           number for new reqt --->
    <CFQUERY DATASOURCE="#REQUEST.stApp.DSN#"
             NAME="getSeqNum">
      SELECT MAX(SeqNum) as SNum
      FROM   Requirements
      WHERE  ParentID = #ARGUMENTS.ParentID#
    </CFQUERY>
```

```
<!--- set seqNum --->
<CFIF LEN(getSeqNum.SNum) EQ O>
  <!--- if null value returned, starting new level,
        seqnum=1 --->
  <CFSET SeqNum = 1>
<CFELSE>
  <!---  if query returns a seqnum, add 1 to it --->
  <CFSET SeqNum = getSeqNum.SNum + 1>
</CFIF><!--- /END Set seqNum --->

<CFLOCK NAME="CreateReq" timeout="10" type="EXCLUSIVE">
  <!--- Create an Object (Record) --->
  <!--- insert data --->
  <CFQUERY NAME="CreateRequirement"
           DATASOURCE="#REQUEST.stApp.DSN#">
    INSERT INTO Requirements(
    OwnedBy,
    CreatedBy,
    Name,
    DocID,
    ParentID,
    SeqNum,
    State,
    CreateDateTime,
    LastUpdated
    )
    VALUES(
    '#REQUEST.Ses.UserProfile.ID#',
    '#REQUEST.Ses.UserProfile.ID#',
    '__New_Item__',
    #arguments.DocID#,
    #arguments.ParentID#,
    #SeqNum#,
    1,
```

Listing IV-3.10    (continued)

```
                    #now()#,
                    #now()#
                    )
                </CFQUERY>


                <!--- Get the Object ID. There are other database
                      specific ways
                    for getting the ID of the last inserted item,
                    but this will do
                    for now. --->
                <CFQUERY DATASOURCE="#REQUEST.stApp.DSN#"
                        NAME="GetRequirementID">
                    SELECT MAX(ID) as ObjectID
                    FROM Requirements
                    WHERE NAME ='__New_Item__'
                        AND ParentID = #arguments.ParentID#
                </CFQUERY>
            </CFLOCK>
        </CFTRANSACTION>


        <!--- If the user has requested the NewID be returned,
              then return it
            otherwise invoke the Edit() method on the new
            Requirement. --->
        <CFIF ARGUMENTS.ReturnID>
            <CFRETURN GetRequirementID.ObjectID>
        <CFELSE>
            <!--- Invoke the Edit method on the new item --->
            <CFSCRIPT>
                this.edit(ReqID="#GetRequirementID.ObjectID#",
                        Refresh="True");
            </CFSCRIPT>
        </CFIF>
    </CFFUNCTION>
```

The `Create()` method requires the `ParentID`—which identifies the parent for the new requirement—and the `DocID`, which identifies the document the new requirement belongs to. Next, it does the cleanup code to remove any incomplete requirements that are more than a day old. This assumes that only requirements that are mistakes will end up in the database, and they are simply removed with a `DELETE SQL` statement.

The next set of SQL queries is done within a `<CFTRANSACTION>` to ensure all the queries complete successfully. The first of these queries looks for the highest-sequence number (`SeqNum`) that already exists for any other requirements that have the same `ParentID` as the one that will be assigned to the new requirement. The sequence number is used to order all the requirements that have the same parent requirement. Next, the `SQL INSERT` statement creates the new requirement. Its `ParentID` is set to the `ParentID` that was passed to the `Create()` method. Finally, a SQL query is done to get back the ID of the newly created requirement. This assumes that the ID field is an autoincrement (or equivalent) field. Some databases, such as Microsoft SQL Server, provide a more elegant and reliable means of finding out the ID of a newly created requirement, but this more general means was used. The `INSERT` and subsequent `SELECT` to get back the ID of the new row is wrapped in a `<CFLOCK>` to prevent data consistency problems.

After the new requirement has been created, the method either returns the new ID or invokes the `Edit()` method on it. The `Edit()` method is where things start to get interesting. See the complete method in Listing IV-3.11.

Listing IV-3.11    /ReqBuilder/Components/Data/Requirements.cfc (Edit() method)

```
<CFFUNCTION NAME="Edit"
HINT="The method for editing the content of a
      requirement.">
  <CFARGUMENT NAME="ReqID" REQUIRED="True">

  <!--- CANCEL Action --->
  <CFIF isDefined("FORM.Cancel") >
    <CFOUTPUT>
      Edit has been Canceled.
```

Listing IV-3.11     (continued)

```
        </CFOUTPUT>

    <!--- SAVE Action --->
    <CFELSEIF isDefined("FORM.Save")>
     <CFSCRIPT>
        // Remove the key for the "Save" button
        StructDelete(FORM, "Save");

        // Init a var to hold the errors
        lErrors = '';

        // Required fields
        lRequiredFields = "Name,Description";

        // Loop through the required fields and make sure
           they are filled in.
        For (Counter=1;
             Counter LTE ListLen(lRequiredFields);
             Counter=Counter+1) {
          // Put the current fieldname into a convenient
             variable.
          CurrField = ListGetAt(lRequiredFields, Counter);
          // If the current field has no length in the info
             passed in from
          //  the form, then add it to the list of errors.
          if (NOT Len( Trim( FORM[CurrField] ) ) ) {
            lErrors = ListAppend(lErrors,
            "#CurrField# is required.");
          }
        }

        // If there are no errors, then save the object
           otherwise...
        If (NOT ListLen(Trim(lErrors)))
          This.Save(ObjectID="#ARGUMENTS.ReqID#",
          stObject="#FORM#");
          // Re-edit it and pass in the errors.
```

```
      Else
      This.Edit(ReqID="#ReqID#",stObject="#FORM#",
                 lErrors="#lErrors#");
   </CFSCRIPT>


   <CFOUTPUT>
      <!--- Refresh the hierarchy --->
      <SCRIPT LANGUAGE="JavaScript"
             TYPE="text/javascript">
      <!--
         // 5/8/02 dkrantsberg, changed the code to add
            reqID
         //   url parameter to the frame
         window.top.frames["frame_left"].document.
         location.href = 'frame_left.cfm?action=ListReqs
         &reqID=#ReqID#&docID=#url.DocID#';
      //-->
      </SCRIPT>


   </CFOUTPUT>

<!--- DISPLAY the Edit form (Default)  --->
<CFELSE>
   <!--- If arguments.lerrors exists, then output
         lErrors --->
   <CFIF isDefined("arguments.lErrors")>
     <CFOUTPUT>
       <TABLE CELLPADDING="0" CELLSPACING="0">
         <TR>
           <TD><SPAN CLASS="warning">THE FOLLOWING
                    ERROR(S) OCCURRED:</SPAN>
             <OL>
               <CFLOOP LIST="#arguments.lErrors#"
                    INDEX="err">
                 <LI>#err#</LI>
               </CFLOOP>
             </OL>
           </TD>
```

**Listing IV-3.11**    (continued)

```
            </TR>
          </TABLE>
        </CFOUTPUT>


        <!--- copy arguments.stObject into stObject
              structure as that
              is the object we're going to use.to output in
              edit form --->
        <CFSET stObject = StructNew()>
        <CFSET stObject = Duplicate(ARGUMENTS.stObject)>


      <!--- if no errors, then we're coming to the page
            newly and need
            to get the data for the selected object. --->
      <CFELSE>
        <!--- Run the Get method and turn its return into a
              structure --->
        <CFSCRIPT>
          qObject = this.Get(OBJECTID="#ReqID#");


          // Turn the query into a structure to match what
             we're
          //  using below.
          stObject = structNew();
          lCol = qObject.ColumnList;
          // Loop through the columns and create a key for
             each
          for (counter=1;
               counter LTE ListLen(lCol);
               counter=counter+1)
            stObject[ListGetAt(lCol,counter)] =
            qObject[ListGetAt(lCol,counter)];
        </CFSCRIPT>


      </CFIF>


      <CFOUTPUT>
```

```
<FORM ACTION="Frame_Right_EditReq.cfm?Action=
              Edit&ReqID=#ReqID#&DocID=#stObject.
              DocID#&ParentID=#stObject.ParentID#"
  METHOD="Post"
  NAME="EditReqt">

<!--- hidden fields --->
<INPUT TYPE="Hidden" NAME="ObjectID"
       VALUE="#ReqID#">
<INPUT TYPE="Hidden" NAME="State"
       VALUE="#stObject.State#">
<INPUT  TYPE="Hidden"
        NAME="Comments"
        VALUE="#HTMLEditFormat
        (stObject.Comments)#">
<INPUT TYPE="Hidden" NAME="DocID"
       VALUE="#stObject.DocID#">
<INPUT TYPE="Hidden" NAME="ParentID"
       VALUE="#stObject.ParentID#">
<INPUT TYPE="Hidden" NAME="SeqNum"
       VALUE="#stObject.SeqNum#">

<TABLE BORDER="0" ALIGN="center">
   <TR>
    <TD CLASS="subhead">Name:</TD>
   </TR>
   <TR>
  <!---  do not output name if = "__New_Item__" --->
    <TD>
       <INPUT TYPE="TEXT" NAME="NAME" SIZE="45"
              VALUE="<CFIF NOT
                     ListFindNoCase
                     (stObject.NAME, '__
                     New_Item__')>#stObject.
                     NAME#</CFIF>">
    </TD>
   </TR>
```

Listing IV-3.11    (continued)

```
                <TR>
                  <TD CLASS="Subhead">Description:</TD>
                </TR>
                <TR>
                  <TD>
                    <TEXTAREA COLS="45" ROWS="10"
                             NAME="Description">
                             #stObject.Description#</TEXTAREA>
                  </TD>
                </TR>
                <!---   Comments is a display field only --->
                <CFIF LEN(stObject.Comments)>
                  <TR>
                    <TD CLASS="subhead"><HR>Comments:</TD>
                  </TR>
                  <TR>
                    <TD>#HTMLEditFormat(stObject.Comments)#</TD>
                  </TR>
                </CFIF>
                <TR>
                  <TD>
                    <INPUT TYPE="submit" NAME="Save"
                           VALUE="Save"
                           CLASS="button_form">
                             
                    <INPUT TYPE="submit" NAME="Cancel"
                           VALUE="Cancel"
                           CLASS="button_form">
                  </TD>
                </TR>
              </TABLE>
            </FORM>
          </CFOUTPUT>
        </CFIF>
      <!--- /END of logic to process edit function--->
      </CFFUNCTION>
```

The Requirements `Edit()` method has several distinct sections and is set up as a self-posting form. `<CFARGUMENT>` identifies the requirement ID as a required argument for the method. The rest of the method consists of a `<CFIF>` with three sections:

- The code that runs when the user cancels the edit

- The code that runs when the user saves the data he has entered

- The default code that displays the edit form

Although the default code appears last in the method, it runs when the method is first invoked. However, it is easier to understand how the template works if we examine the code in the order given above. The first section runs when the user clicks Cancel from the edit form. It displays a message indicating that the edit has been cancelled.

The second section runs when the user clicks Save from the edit form (which is covered below). The form data is submitted back to `Requirements.cfc` in the FORM scope. (In ColdFusion MX, as in recent versions of ColdFusion, the FORM scope is implemented as a structure and can be manipulated programmatically using structure functions.) A `Struct-Delete()` removes the value of the Save button as that is not part of the requirement's data. The code then contains a list of the fields that are required and loops through that list to verify that each required field contains data. If it finds a field that does not contain data, an appropriate message is added to the list of errors in `lErrors`.

Finally, the code checks if `lErrors` contains any errors and, if not, invokes the save method. The Requirements component inherits the `wwsObject Save()` method which is invoked to do the database update. (See the description of the generic `Save()` method in the "wwsObject Component" section of this chapter.)

If `lErrors` does contain errors, the code re-invokes the edit method passing it the requirement ID, the submitted form data, and the list of errors.

The final section displays the edit form itself. It runs when the user clicks on a requirement in the left frame but also runs when the user submits a requirement without filling in a required field. If the edit form is being redisplayed as a result of a data-entry error, then `Arguments.lErrors` will exist, and the code loops through those errors and displays them. It then copies (using the `Duplicate()` function) the previously submitted form fields into the variable `stObject` and then displays the form.

If `Arguments.lErrors` doesn't exist, then we need to get the data for the requirement the user selected. To do this, we invoke the `Get()` method on the current instance of the component, which returns the requirement data into a variable, `qObject`. A short loop turns the query data into a structure for use by the edit form.

The edit form is straightforward HTML and CFML that submit back to the right-hand frame, which is where the form is displayed. The action attribute of the form includes the URL parameters necessary to reinvoke the same `Edit()` method. The form displays the requirement's name as a text box and the description as a text area. If comments exist, they are shown as read-only HTML. Comments are handled differently because they are generally entered by a distinct user type and adding a comment to a requirement is handled by another method.

The user can click Save or Cancel on the edit form; either button submits the form. If the user clicks Cancel, the edit method is reinvoked and the cancel section outputs the simple message covered above.

If the user clicks Save, the Save section of the `<CFIF>` runs, also as described above.

The Requirement component `Comments()` method is largely the same as the `Edit()` method, except that there are no errors that need to be caught, and the form shows display-only versions of the Name and Description fields, while the Comments field is displayed in a text area.

Debbie writes the Requirements component's `Delete()` method, which follows the same general pattern as the `Edit()` method; that is, it has a cancel section, a "delete" section that performs the deletion, and a default section that displays a form in which the user confirms the delete. (see Listing IV-3.12).

Listing IV-3.12    `/ReqBuilder/Components/Data/Requirements.cfc` (Delete() method excerpt)

```
<CFFUNCTION NAME="Delete"
          Hint="This method deletes the selected
          requirement and all its children.">
  <CFARGUMENT NAME="ReqID" REQUIRED="True">

  <!--- CANCEL Action --->
  <CFIF isDefined("FORM.Cancel") >
    <CFOUTPUT>
      Deletion has been Canceled.
    </CFOUTPUT>

  <!--- DELETE Action --->
  <CFELSEIF  isDefined("FORM.Delete")>
    <CFQUERY DATASOURCE="#REQUEST.stApp.DSN#">
      DELETE FROM Requirements
      WHERE ID IN (#FORM.lDeleteIDS#)
    </CFQUERY>
    <CFOUTPUT>
      Deletion Completed.

      <!--- Refresh the hierarchy --->
      <SCRIPT LANGUAGE="JavaScript" TYPE="text/javascript">
      <!--
        window.top.frames["frame_left"].document.
        location.reload();
      //-->
      </SCRIPT>
    </CFOUTPUT>

  <!--- DEFAULT: DISPLAY Warning message --->
  <CFELSE>

    <!--- Get info on the current item and its
          descendents. --->
    <CFSCRIPT>
```

Listing IV-3.12    (continued)

```
            // Get the data on the current object
            qReq = This.Get(ObjectID=ARGUMENTS.ReqID);


            // Instantiate a Document component
            Doc = CreateObject("component", "#REQUEST.stApp.
                                ComponentDir#.data.Document");


            // Instantiate a var to hold the array of children
            aDescendents = ArrayNew(1);


            // Invoke the method to get the descendents of the
               current
            //   Requirement.
            aDescendents = Doc.GetDescendents(ReqID=ARGUMENTS.
            ReqID,DocID=qReq.DocID);


            // initialize a variable to hold the list of children
and put
            //   the current requirement first in the list.
            lDeleteIDs = Arguments.ReqID;


            // If children, add children ID's to list
            If (NOT ArrayIsEmpty(aDescendents))
              For (Counter=1;
                   Counter LTE ArrayLen(aDescendents);
                   Counter=Counter+1)
                 lDeleteIDs = ListAppend(lDeleteIDs,
                             aDescendents[Counter].ID);
        </CFSCRIPT>


        <CFOUTPUT>
          <FORMACTION="frame_right_EditReq.cfm?Action=Delete&
                      ReqID=#Arguments.ReqID#&DocID=#qReq.
                      DocID#&ParentID=#qReq.ParentID#"
            METHOD="post" Name="Delete">
```

```
      <!--- hidden fields --->
      <INPUT TYPE="Hidden" NAME="ReqID"
             VALUE="#Arguments.ReqID#">
      <INPUT TYPE="Hidden" NAME="lDeleteIDs"
             VALUE="#lDeleteIDs#">


      <!---   added feature would be to add childrens names
              of reqt requested to be deleted --->
      <TABLE BORDER="0" ALIGN="center" CELLPADDING="3"
             CELLSPACING="3">
        <TR>
          <TD><SPAN CLASS="warning">WARNING:</SPAN>
            <BR />You are about to delete
                  "<strong>#qReq.Name#</strong>" and its
            #ListLen(lDeleteIDs)-1# descendents.
          </TD>
        </TR>
        <TR>
          <TD>
            <INPUT TYPE="Submit" NAME="Delete"
                   VALUE="Delete" CLASS="button_form">
                
            <INPUT TYPE="Submit" NAME="Cancel"
                   VALUE="Cancel" CLASS="button_form">
          </TD>
        </TR>
      </TABLE>
      </FORM>
    </CFOUTPUT>
  </CFIF>
</CFFUNCTION>
```

Before displaying the form, the code in the default section invokes a method of the Document component that returns a list of all the children of the current requirement as they also need to be deleted. This is done by instantiating an instance of the Document component and then invoking its GetDescendents() method which returns an array of structures. The structures contain the ID of each descendent. If the array is not empty, the code loops through each array element to get the descendent IDs which are added to the list contained in the variable lDeleteIDs.

When the user confirms the deletion, the list of IDs is passed to a SQL DELETE statement in the delete section which removes the requirement and its descendents from the database.

One Requirements component method remains to be built: the Reorder()method, which would allow a user to reorder requirements that share a common parent. However, in order to build this Debbie needs the Document component's GetSiblings() method as well as user-interface (UI) code for reordering items. She asks Dmitry to let her know when the GetSiblings() method is complete and asks Andrew to update code he developed for reordering items in a selection box. It takes Dmitry only a few minutes to write the GetSiblings() method, and Andrew finishes customizing his reorder UI code by the next day. With these things ready, Debbie finishes up the Reorder() method the next morning (see Listing IV-3.13).

Listing IV-3.13       /ReqBuilder/Components/Data/Requirements.cfc (Reorder() method)

```
<CFFUNCTION NAME="Reorder"
            HINT="This method allow a user to reorder
                  requirements that have the same parent.">
  <CFARGUMENT NAME="ReqID" REQUIRED="True">

  <!--- CANCEL Action --->
  <CFIF isDefined("FORM.Cancel") >
    <CFOUTPUT>Reorder has been Canceled.</CFOUTPUT>

  <!--- SAVE Action --->
  <CFELSEIF isDefined("FORM.Save")>

    <!--- Loop through the order list of Requirements and
          UPDATE
          their SeqNum field to put them into order. --->
    <CFSET Counter = 1>
```

```
<CFLOOP LIST="#FORM.OrderedReqs#" INDEX="CurrReq">
  <CFQUERY NAME="UpdateSeqNum"
            DATASOURCE="#REQUEST.stApp.DSN#">
    UPDATE Requirements
    SET SeqNum = #Counter#
    WHERE ID = #CurrReq#
  </CFQUERY>
  <CFSET Counter = Counter + 1>
</CFLOOP>

<CFOUTPUT>
  New Order Saved
  <!--- Refresh the hierarchy --->
  <SCRIPT LANGUAGE="JavaScript" TYPE="text/javascript">
    <!--
    // 5/8/02 dkrantsberg, changed the code to add
        reqID
    //  url parameter to the frame
    window.top.frames["frame_left"].document.
    location.href = 'frame_left.cfm?action=ListReqs&
    reqID=#ReqID#&docID=#url.DocID#';
    //-->
  </SCRIPT>
</CFOUTPUT>

<!--- DISPLAY Action (Default) --->
<CFELSE>
  <!--- Get the ParentID and DocID for the requirement
  --->
  <CFQUERY NAME="GetReqData"
            DATASOURCE="#REQUEST.stApp.DSN#">
    SELECT ParentID, DocID
    FROM Requirements
    WHERE ID = #ARGUMENTS.ReqID#
  </CFQUERY>
```

**Listing IV-3.13**    (continued)

```
<!---Get the siblings for the selected Requirement.--->
<CFINVOKE COMPONENT="ReqBuilder.Components.
                      Data.Document"
          METHOD="GetSiblings"
          REQID="#ReqID#"
          RETURNVARIABLE="qSiblings">


<!--- Set the action we're going to submit to --->
<CFSET ACTION="frame_right_editreq.cfm?action=
              reorder&reqid=#reqid#&ParentID=
              #GetReqData.ParentID#&DocID=
              #GetReqData.DocID#">


<!--- Show the HTML Form--->
  <CFOUTPUT>
    <FORM ACTION="#Action#" METHOD="Post"
          NAME="EditReqt">
  </CFOUTPUT>


<!--- Invoke the ReorderBox UI, pass it the query that
      contains
      the siblings. --->
  <CFMODULE TEMPLATE="#REQUEST.stApp.CustTags#/
                      ReorderBox.cfm"
            qOBJECTS="#qSiblings#"
            INSTANCENAME="Hier2"
            FORMNAME="EditReqt"
            WIDTH="400"
            SELECTED="#ARGUMENTS.ReqID#"
            r_IDS="OrderedReqs"
      />


<CFOUTPUT>
  <INPUT TYPE="Submit" NAME="Save" VALUE="Save"
```

```
            CLASS="Button_Form">
        
      <INPUT TYPE="Submit" NAME="Cancel" VALUE="Cancel"
            CLASS="Button_Form">
    </FORM>
  </CFOUTPUT>
 </CFIF>
</CFFUNCTION>
```

As with other Requirements methods, such as `Edit()`, the `Reorder()` method contains three sections: cancel, save, and the default section which displays the reorder form.

The cancel section displays a message that the re-ordering has been cancelled. The save section loops through the submitted form field, `OrderedReqs`, which contains a list of requirements in the order selected by the user. A SQL `UPDATE` statement runs within the loop to set each requirement's `SeqNum` (short for "sequence number") field to an incrementing number. (When requirements are retrieved from the database to display them on the site, the `SeqNum` field is used to order them.) After the loop completes, the code refreshes the requirements display in the left frame.

The default display section queries the Requirements table to get the `ParentID` and the `DocID` of the requirement that is passed into the method. This data is needed for the HTML form `ACTION` attribute.

The code then invokes the Document component's `GetSiblings()` method, which returns a query containing the requirement's siblings ordered by their `SeqNum` field. The `ReorderBox.cfm` custom tag does the heavy lifting of this section as it generates the HTML and JavaScript UI for reordering requirements (see Figure IV-3.5). This custom tag places the list of the sibling requirements, ordered by the user, into the variable specified by its `r_IDS` attribute. (The "r_" in `r_IDS` is a convention that Webworld uses to indicate that the attribute names a variable in which data is returned from the custom tag.)

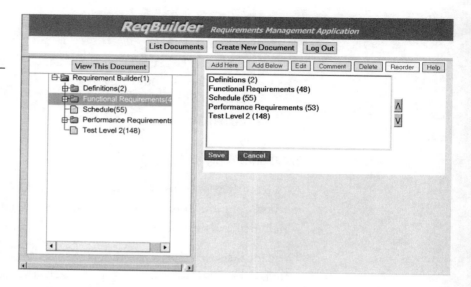

Figure IV-3.5

The Reorder function lets the user reorder requirements that have the same parent.

When the user finishes reordering and clicks Save, the list of ordered sibling requirements is submitted in the form field OrderedReqs. This is the variable through which the save section loops when performing the database updates.

# Document Component

The methods of the Document component operate on more than one requirement at once, whereas the methods of the Requirements component generally operate on one requirement at a time (although some Requirements methods, such as Delete(), can affect more than one requirement).

The Document component's set of methods, which is much larger than that of the Requirements component, includes Comment(), Create(), Delete(), Edit(), Get(), GetDescendents(), GetDocData(), GetDocList(), GetSiblings(), GetUIDoc(), MakeDisplayDoc(), and PopulateHier().

One of the points of the design document that seemed to generate some confusion was how the Document component would use the methods of the Requirements component. Andrew, as author of the design document, sent a memo clarifying the overall approach.

**Requirements vs. Document components**

**Memo**

**Date:** October 31

**To:** ReqBuilder Team

**From:** Andrew

**Subject:** Requirements vs. Document components

OK, there's seems to have been some confusion about whether Document methods should invoke Requirements methods from within Document component methods or whether all the code for the Document component should be self-contained.

Normally, we want to keep objects, functions, methods, and the like as loosely coupled as possible. In other words, we want components to stand on their own and have minimal dependencies on other components.

But that principle doesn't apply in this case. The Requirements and Document components work with the same data. What's more, the Document component, whose methods are by and large set oriented, does need to carry out some operations on single entries in the Requirements table. Since the Requirements component already contains methods that manage single-records in the Requirements table, we should use those methods. Why reinvent code we've already written?

So where appropriate, use Requirements methods to implement methods in the Document component. For example, we don't need to implement a totally unique Document **Edit()** method since that method just provides an interface for editing the top requirement in a requirements document. Instead, invoke the Requirement component's **edit()** method from within the Document **edit()** method. This is a great example of how the object-based approach allows us to easily re-use code.

Let me know if you have any questions on this.

With this approach, the Document component's `Get()`, `Create()`, `Edit()`, and `Comment()` methods can all be implemented by invoking the equivalent methods in the Requirements component. The only method that requires some special additional handling is `Create()`. Although creating a document is done by simply inserting a row in the Requirements table, that entry differs from regular requirements in two ways. One, its `ParentID` needs to be set to zero; and two, its `DocID` field must be set to point to itself. In other words, for a document entry in the Requirements table, the `DocID` field equals the ID field (see Listing IV-3.14).

Listing IV-3.14    `/ReqBuilder/Components/Data/Document.cfc` (`Create()` method)

```
<CFFUNCTION NAME="Create">
  <!--- Invoke the Requirement.Create() method to create
        the Document and get back the ID of the row
        created --->
  <CFINVOKE COMPONENT="ReqBuilder.Components.Data.
                       Requirements"
                       METHOD="Create"
                       PARENTID="0"
                       DOCID="0"
                       RETURNID="Yes"
                       RETURNVARIABLE="NewID">


  <!--- Update the DocID in the new Document to be the ID
        for the new Document itself. This is one of the
        things that marks the Document as being a
        Document and not just another Requirement. --->
  <CFQUERY DATASOURCE="#REQUEST.stApp.DSN#"
           NAME="SetHierID">
    UPDATE Requirements
    SET DocID = #NewID#
    WHERE ID = #NewID#
  </CFQUERY>


  <!--- Invoke the Edit method on the new item --->
  <CFSCRIPT>
    This.Edit(ReqID="#NewID#",Refresh="True");
  </CFSCRIPT>
</CFFUNCTION>
```

This method starts by invoking the Requirements component's `Create()` method. When used to create a requirement, this method inserts a new row into the Requirements table and then invokes the Requirements `Edit()` method to let the user enter data for the new requirement. However, in this case the `Create()` method is passed the attribute `RETURNVARIABLE` which tells the `create()` method it should insert the new row and then immediately return the ID for that new row. The returned ID is used in a SQL UPDATE statement to set the `DocID` field of the new requirement equal to its own ID; as mentioned before, rows in the Requirements table in which the `DocID` field equals the ID field represent the top of a requirements document. After the update, the Requirements `Edit()` method is then invoked to let the user enter the name and description for the new document.

The most important part of the Document component lies in the methods that manipulate sets of requirements. Some of these, such as `GetDocList()` and `GetDocData()`, consist of simple queries that return data to the calling template. For example, see the `GetDocList()` method in Listing IV-3.15:

Listing IV-3.15    /ReqBuilder/Components/Data/Document.cfc (GetDocList() method)

```
<CFFUNCTION NAME="GetDocList"
            RETURNTYPE="Query"
            ACCESS="Remote"
            HINT="This gets a list of all requirements
                  documents in the system by querying
                  for all rows in the Requirements
                  table whose ParentID equals zero.">
<!--- Run a query to get all of the Docs in the
      Requirements table --->
<CFQUERY NAME="qDocList" DATASOURCE="ReqBuilder">
    SELECT ID, Name
    FROM Requirements
    WHERE ParentID = 0
    ORDER BY Name
  </CFQUERY>
<CFRETURN qDocList>
</CFFUNCTION>
```

This method queries the Requirements table to find all the entries that are at the top of a hierarchy by retrieving those entries whose `ParentID` equals zero. These are, by definition, documents. (This query could have also found the documents by retrieving records where the `DocID` field equals the ID field.) The `<CFRETURN>` statement returns the query to the calling template.

Likewise, `GetDocData()` does a simple query to get all of the requirements associated with a particular requirements document (see Listing IV-3.16).

Listing IV-3.16    /ReqBuilder/Components/Data/Document.cfc (GetDocData() method)

```
<CFFUNCTION NAME="GetDocData"
            RETURNTYPE="query" OUTPUT="No"
            HINT="This does a simple query on the
                  Requirements table to get all the
                  requirements associated with the
                  DocID passed in to it.">

  <CFARGUMENT NAME="DocID" REQUIRED="Yes" TYPE="Numeric">
  <CFARGUMENT NAME="IncludeDescription" DEFAULT="No">

  <CFQUERY NAME="qDocData" DATASOURCE="ReqBuilder">
    SELECT
      ID,
      Name,
      ParentID,
      SeqNum,
      DocID
      <CFIF ARGUMENTS.IncludeDescription>
        ,Description
      </CFIF>
    FROM Requirements
    WHERE DocID = #DocID#
      AND State = 1
    ORDER BY SeqNum, Name
  </CFQUERY>
  <CFRETURN qDocData>
</CFFUNCTION>f
```

Within the first phase version of Reqbuilder, this method is not used by itself; instead the query it returns is passed to the `MakeDisplayDoc()` method, which creates a new query that is used to build the drill-down representation of the document. This two-step process for creating a query to use when building the drill-down representation is needed because SQL by itself doesn't provide a way to easily retrieve multi-level hierarchies (such as requirements documents in ReqBuilder) from a database in the order needed to build the drill-down representation. So, `GetDocData()` does a SQL query to retrieve the document data; `MakeDisplayDoc()` starts with that query's result set and massages it into another query that lends itself to producing a UI representation of the requirements document hierarchy.

`GetDocData()` is made into a separate method, rather than just including its code within `MakeDisplayDoc()` as the team anticipates that a future phase may have use for the query resultset it produces.

`MakeDisplayDoc()` is a more complicated method that calls the recursive `PopulateHier()` method to programmatically build a new query based on the query returned from `GetDocData()` (see Listing IV-3.17).

Listing IV-3.17    `/ReqBuilder/Components/Data/Document.cfc` (`MakeDisplayDoc()` method)

```
<CFFUNCTION NAME="MakeDisplayDoc"
            RETURNTYPE="Query" OUTPUT="No"
            HINT="This takes the output of GetDocData()
                  and builds a query that is usable by
                  the Flash drill-down UI. This was
                  written as a separate method in case
                  we came up with a need to use the
                  results of GetDocData() as-is.">
    <CFARGUMENT NAME="qReq" REQUIRED="Yes" TYPE="Query">

    <!--- If the passed in query doesn't have the
          Description field then add an empty one --->
    <CFSET aTemp = ArrayNew(1)>
    <CFIF NOT IsDefined("qReq.Description")>
      <CFSET QueryAddColumn(qReq, "Description", aTemp)>
```

Listing IV-3.17    (continued)

```
</CFIF>

<!--- Instantiate a structure that will be used to map
      the Requirement ID's to the row where the
      Requirement ID appears in qReq. --->
<CFSET stReqID2RowNum = StructNew()>

<!--- Instantiate a structure that maps each
      Requirements to an array of the Requirement's
      children (if any exist) --->
<CFSET stParent2Children = StructNew()>

<!--- Loop through the query containing all the
      Requirements for the current Document. --->
<CFLOOP QUERY="qReq">
  <!--- Populate the structure that maps ReqIDs (nodes)
        to the row number of the query that contains
        the Requirements daa (qReq) --->
  <CFSET stReqID2RowNum[ID] = qReq.CurrentRow>

  <CFIF ParentID EQ ID>
    <!--- Check if there are nodes which have themselves
          as their own parents and throw an error if
          there are such nodes otherwize it can cause an
          infinite loop in PopulateHier function --->
    <CFABORT SHOWERROR="Error: Wrong hierarchy data
                        (parentID = id) !">
  <!--- If the ParentID is 0, then this is the top node
        of the Document. --->
  <CFELSEIF ParentID EQ 0>
    <CFSET TopReqID = ID>
  <!--- Else add this ReqID to the array of it's
        parent's children. --->
  <CFELSE>
```

```
            <!--- If the array doesn't exist, create it and add
                  this as the first element --->
            <CFIF NOT StructKeyExists(stParent2Children,
                                      ParentID)>
              <CFSET stParent2Children[parentID] = ArrayNew(1)>
              <CFSET stParent2Children[parentID][1] = ID>
            <!--- Else append this to the array of children --->
            <CFELSE>
              <CFSET ArrayAppend(stParent2Children
                                 [ParentID], ID)>

            </CFIF>
          </CFIF>
      </CFLOOP>


      <!--- Create the page hierarchy query with "ID",
            "level", "Name"and "DocID" fields --->
            <CFSET qHier = QueryNew("ID,myLevel,Name,
            DocID,Description")>


<CFSET QueryAddRow(qHier)>


<!--- Add the top ReqID to the query --->
<CFSET QuerySetCell(qHier,"ID",TopReqID)>
<CFSET QuerySetCell(qHier,"myLevel",1)>
<!--- Get the row number in the query that holds the
      information on the TopNode --->
<CFSET RowID = stReqID2RowNum[TopReqID]>
<CFSET QuerySetCell(qHier,"Name", qReq.Name[RowID] )>
<CFSET QuerySetCell(qHier,"DocID", qReq.DocID[RowID] )>
<CFSET QuerySetCell(qHier,"Description",
                    qReq.Description[RowID] )>


<!--- Invoke a tag to recursively populate the query.
```

**Listing IV-3.17**   (continued)

```
          The arguments passed to it are:
          1) The stParent2Children structure.
          2) The "level" of the hierarchy we're on.
          3) The ID of the current Requirement.
          4) The query that this method creates.
          5) The original query that contains Requirements data.
          6) The stReqID2RowNum structure. --->
    <CFIF NOT StructIsEmpty(stParent2Children)>
    <CFSCRIPT>
      PopulateHier(stParent2Children,
                        1,
                        TopReqID,
                        qHier,
                        qReq,
                        stReq
                        ID2RowNum);
    </CFSCRIPT>
    </CFIF>

    <CFRETURN qHier>
</CFFUNCTION>
```

The method starts by requiring the argument **qReq** which contains the query generated by the **GetDocData()** method.

The method starts by instantiating two necessary structures: **stReq-ID2RowNum** and **stParent2Children**. StReqID2RowNum maps each requirement ID to the row number in the query **qReq** in which that Requirement appears. Essentially, StReqID2RowNum serves as an index into the **qReq** table, allowing the method to find a particular row using the requirement ID.

StParent2Children is a structure of arrays. The keys of the structure are the IDs for each requirement; the value associated with each key is an array of each requirement ID's children. The method uses this structure to determine if any particular requirement has children and, if so, loops through the array of children. To populate these structures, the method loops through qReq. While looping, it also looks for the top requirement (by looking for a requirement whose ParentID equals zero) and assigns it to the variable TopNodeID.

When the loop completes, the resulting structures look as shown in Figure IV-3.6.

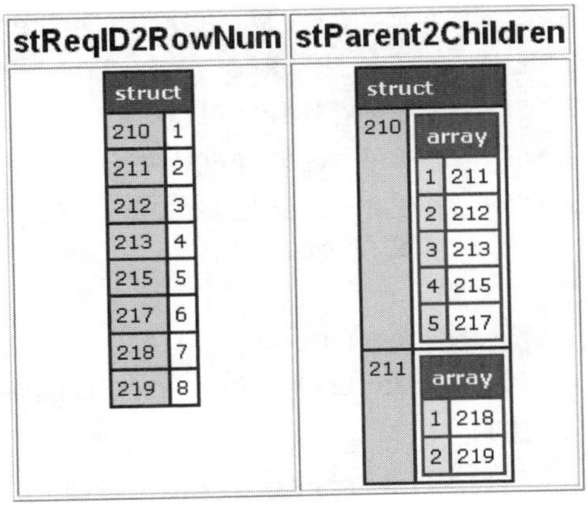

**Figure IV-3.6**
A dump of stReqID2RowNum results in these stParent2Children structures. After stReqID2RowNum and stParent2Children are populated, they contain information about the data contained in the qReq query.

Once these structures are populated, the method creates the new output query, qHier, and adds the first row to it. It does this by using stReq-ID2RowNum to translate the top requirement's ID to the row in the query that holds its data. It accesses the top requirement's data in the query using array notation.

To populate the rest of the qHier query, the method invokes the private method, PopulateHier(), passing it all the data it needs to build qHier. This data includes stParent2Children (the structure that relates a requirement ID to an array of its children), the current level of the hierarchy (for the top, the level is 1), the current Requirement (which is the top Requirement), the query we're building (qHier), the query that contains all the Requirements (qReq), and stReqID2RowNum (the structure that relates a requirement ID to a row number in the query aReq). See Listing IV-3-18.

Listing IV-3.18    /ReqBuilder/Components/Data/Document.cfc (PopulateHier() method)

```
<CFFUNCTION NAME="PopulateHier"
            ACCESS="Private" OUTPUT="No"
            HINT="An internal method that recursively
                  calls itself to help build the query
                  returned by the MakeDisplayDoc()
                  method.">
  <CFARGUMENT NAME="stParent2Children" REQUIRED="Yes"
              TYPE="Struct">
  <CFARGUMENT NAME="Level" REQUIRED="Yes" TYPE="Numeric">
  <CFARGUMENT NAME="ID" REQUIRED="Yes" TYPE="Numeric">
  <CFARGUMENT NAME="qHier" REQUIRED="Yes" TYPE="Query">
  <CFARGUMENT NAME="qReq" REQUIRED="Yes" TYPE="Query">
  <CFARGUMENT NAME="stReqID2RowNum" REQUIRED="Yes"
              TYPE="Struct">

  <CFLOOP INDEX="i" FROM="1"
          TO="#ArrayLen(stParent2Children[ID])#">
    <CFSCRIPT>
      currChildID = stParent2Children[ID][i];
      queryAddRow(qHier);
      querySetCell(qHier,"ID",currChildID);
      querySetCell(qHier,"MyLevel",Val(level + 1));
      querySetCell(qHier,"Name",
                   qReq.name[stReqID2RowNum[currChildID]]);
      querySetCell(qHier,"DocID",
                   qReq.DocID[stReqID2RowNum[ID]]);
      querySetCell(qHier,"Description",
                   qReq.Description[stReqID2RowNum
                   [currChildID]]);

      // If The current child itself has a structure of
         children, then
      //   invoke PopulateHier() on those children. This
         recurses through
      //   the list of children.
```

```
      if (StructKeyExists(stParent2Children,currChildID))
         PopulateHier(stParent2Children,val(level + 1),
                     currChildID,qHier,qReq,stReqID2RowNum);
   </CFSCRIPT>
  </CFLOOP>
</CFFUNCTION>
```

This method loops through the children of the requirement that was passed into it and builds a row in qHier for each child. It also checks each child to see if it has its own children and, if so, invokes PopulateHier() on those children. By looping through the children of each node it encounters, it fills out the entire hierarchy, thereby populating qHier, which is returned by MakeDisplayDoc() to the calling template.

Although the MakeDisplayDoc() method could be called from another component or a ColdFusion template, it is intended to be invoked by a Flash component that would use the data it returns to create the drill-down representation of a requirements document. The interaction between Flash and the Document component is covered in the upcoming section, "Flash MX Integration."

Dmitry realizes after building the above methods that it would be much easier to build the Flash UI drill-down if Flash were able to invoke a single method to create the query containing the full requirements document. So he adds a new method called GetUIDoc(), as shown in Listing IV-3.19.

Listing IV-3.19    /ReqBuilder/Components/Data/Document.cfc (GetUIDDoc() method)

```
<CFFUNCTION NAME="GetUIDoc"
            RETURNTYPE="Query"
            ACCESS="Remote" OUTPUT="No"
            HINT="This takes the output of the
                  GetDocData() method, passes it to the
                  MakeDisplayDoc() method and returns
                  the resulting query which is designed
                  to be used by the Flash drill-down UI
                  display.">
   <CFARGUMENT NAME="DocID" REQUIRED="Yes" TYPE="Numeric">
```

Listing IV-3.19    (continued)

```
<CFSET qHier = MakeDisplayDoc(
GetDocData(Arguments.DocID))>
<CFRETURN qHier>
</CFFUNCTION>
```

He gives the method remote-access rights because Flash needs to be able to invoke it remotely. It accepts only one argument, DocID, and then uses function notation to invoke GetDocData() and MakeDisplayDoc(), returning the query produced by MakeDisplayDoc() to the calling template.

Dmitry finishes up the Document component by creating two other methods, GetDescendents() and GetSiblings(). GetDescendents() calls the MakeDisplayDoc() method to create the query containing the hierarchy of requirements and then loops through that query to find all the descendents (children, grandchildren, and so on) of a selected requirement. The method puts all the descendents it finds into an array of structures that contains the requirement's ID and name, then returns it to the calling template. This work is needed for the Delete() method of the Requirements component to ensure that when a requirement is deleted, all of its descendents are also deleted.

The GetSiblings() method uses a simple query to get all the requirements at the same level of the hierarchy as that of a selected requirement and returns them to the caller. This is needed by the Requirements component's Reorder() method, which lets the user reorder a group of requirements that have the same parent.

## Flash MX Integration

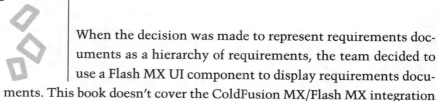

When the decision was made to represent requirements documents as a hierarchy of requirements, the team decided to use a Flash MX UI component to display requirements documents. This book doesn't cover the ColdFusion MX/Flash MX integration in detail, but the team's use of Flash for this part of the application demonstrates how Flash MX and ColdFusion MX can easily be combined to produce powerful interfaces.

After building the Document component, Dmitry downloads the Flash UI components from the Macromedia site. This is a set of prebuilt UI components that can be used in Flash MX that includes FTree, a component for building hierarchical drill-downs. (The Flash Extension Manager, which allows you to install new Flash extensions, and the Flash UI components, which contains the FTree component, are available from the Macromedia site at: `http://dynamic.macromedia.com/bin/MM/exchange/main.jsp?product=flash`)

To keep things simple, Dmitry decides to build two Flash movies, one to display a list of the available documents (DocList.fla), the other to display all the requirements in one document (HierMenu.fla). Although the code to make the connection from Flash to ColdFusion is written in Flash ActionScript language, it's easy to understand. An excerpt of the source code is in Listing IV-3.20.

Listing IV-3.20    `/ReqBuilder/Components/Flash/doclist.fla` (excerpt)

```
//Include the main NetServices Library.  This allows
connection to the server.
#include "NetServices.as"
// This second include is optional and allows the use of
   the NetConnect Debugger
// Useful in development, but would be omitted in
   production.
// #include "NetDebug.as"

// Check to see if the application has already loaded.
   We only want this
// code to execute once/
if (inited == null)
{
```

**Listing IV-3.20**    (continued)

```
// set the inited variable to prevent running this block
   of script again
inited = true;
 // set the default gateway URL (for use in authoring)
 // gatewayUrl parameter comes from the page which
 contains this component
 NetServices.setDefaultGatewayUrl(gatewayUrl);

 // connect to the gateway
 gatewayConnection =
NetServices.createGatewayConnection();

 // get a reference to the Component that will be used
 reqService = gatewayConnection.
                         getService("ReqBuilder.components.
                                      Data.Document", this);
 // call method to get the list of Documents
 reqService.GetDocList();
}
```

The script begins by including NetServices.as, an ActionScript file that defines objects and methods needed to establish a connection between Flash MX and ColdFusion MX. The movie then checks if it has already been initialized (inited == null) and, if not, uses the setDefaultGatewayURL() method of the NetServices object to identify the Flash Gateway it will use. The URL for the Flash Gateway is in the variable gatewayURL, which is passed to Flash from the calling Web page.

The next line runs createGatewayConnection() to establish the connection, and then runs getService() on that new connection to identify the component whose methods it will access—in this case, the Document component.

Finally, the code invokes the Document component method GetDoc-List(), which causes ColdFusion MX to run GetDocList()and return a recordset to Flash. When Flash receives the recordset from ColdFusion, another Flash function written by Dmitry loops through the recordset and builds the FTree object using methods provided by FTree.

FTree also includes a method that lets developers code actions to take when a user clicks one of the items in its drill-down. Dmitry codes this function `treeClickHandler()`, so it reloads the left frame, passing the document ID clicked by the user. The code that reloads the left frame is in Listing IV-3.21.

**Listing IV-3.21**    /ReqBuilder/Components/Flash/doclist.fla (excerpt)

```
url = "/ReqBuilder/frame_left.cfm?
        action=ListReqs&docID="+docID;
// go to the URL
getUrl(url);
```

The URL variables indicate to the ColdFusion template that it should run the second Flash movie (HierMenu.fla.). This movie is designed to display all the requirements in a particular document; the document to display is specified in the `DocID` URL variable.

The most significant difference between the two movies is that Hier-Menu.fla invokes `GetUIDoc()` instead of `GetDocList()` on the Document component. `GetUIDoc()` returns a query containing all the requirements for a particular document, and the Flash movie loops through that query to build the drill-down representation of the full requirements document.

Although the drill-down could be implemented using DHTML, Flash MX provides an easy way to integrate the front end with the ColdFusion MX back end.

With the basic elements of the application built, the team is ready to demonstrate the application for the Webworld staff who will be using it to build requirements for the Federal Agency of Bureaucratic Regulations (FABR) content-management system. The application's presentation is covered in the next chapter.

## The Solution

With the application largely complete, the team tests it, fixes the obvious bugs, then schedules a meeting with the client. Even though the ReqBuilder application was just created in order to facilitate the real work, the client does need to review the work and confirm that its users will be able to use it to create the requirements document for the content-management solution they ultimately want built.

The team discusses the possibility of skipping the briefing to the senior client staff and just scheduling a training session with the end users, but decides to meet first with a small group of select people. The intention of the meeting is to demonstrate the application, make any needed tweaks, and get buy-in from the people most likely to promote the introduction and use of the tool. Andrew, who is nominated to do the presentation, decides to give a simple walkthrough of the process for creating and editing a document. The meeting is scheduled and set up at the client's office. Andrew's simple agenda is circulated to the client staff ahead of time.

**ReqBuilder review agenda**

**Memo**

**Date:** November 4

**To:** Bureau Staff

**From:** Andrew, Webworld Studios

**Subject:** ReqBuilder review agenda

The purpose of this meeting is to walk through the ReqBuilder application and demonstrate how it will be used to build the requirements document for the new content-management application. Roughly, we'll walk through the following:

1. Logging into the system

2. Creating a new document

3. Creating an outline of the document

4. Filling in the details

5. Commenting on the document

6. Displaying a complete version of the document

## Product Demonstration

Andrew starts off by demonstrating the log-in screen (see Figure IV-4.1).

For convenience during the demonstration, the usernames and passwords for three types of users are displayed on the login page. When the user logs in successfully, he arrives at the main application screen, as shown in Figure IV-4.2.

The main application screen consists of a top frame, bottom-left frame, and bottom-right frame. The rest of the application operates from this basic framed interface. The top frame contains global functions: List Documents, Create New Document, and Log Out. Since Andrew logged in as a requirements owner—and not a document owner—the Create New

Document link is grayed out. The bottom-left frame loads a Macromedia Flash MX tree component that displays a list of existing documents. The bottom-right frame loads an empty document, although the client asks if general help text could be loaded into that frame to give the user tips on how to use the application. Andrew agrees this would be a nice addition, but asks them to have one of their trainers draft the help document after they've had the opportunity to work with the system; he suggests this because the client's trainers are more familiar with the style of documentation their staff is accustomed to using.

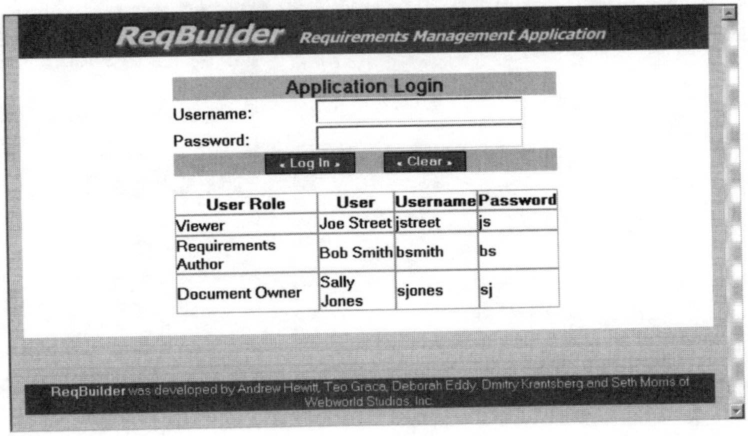

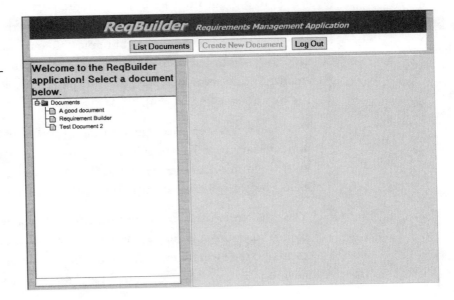

**Figure IV-4.1**
The user's roles are assigned at log-in.

**Figure IV-4.2**
The main application screen.

Andrew then clicks the Log Out button and logs back in as a document owner. The Create New Document button is now active. He clicks it to define a new document (see Figure IV-4.3).

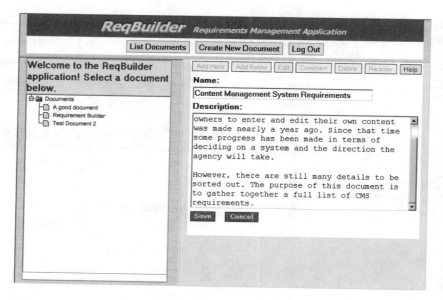

**Figure IV-4.3**

Clicking the Create New Document button displays a form for entering the document's name and description.

The form displays fields for adding information about a new document and greys out all the buttons at the top of the bottom-right frame (except Help) to prevent the user from adding requirements to a document that has not yet been created. When the user submits the form, a success message displays in the bottom-right frame ("'Requirements' object saved..."), and the bottom-left frame refreshes to show the new requirements document. At this point, however, the only part of the document that exists is its name (see Figure IV-4.4).

The user's next step is to begin creating an outline of the requirements document, starting with its high-level sections. Since the user is currently at the top level of the document, the Add Here button is grayed out, but the Add Below button is active, so the user can add a second level (see Figure IV-4.5).

The user enters the name and description of a second-level, or child, requirement and submits the form. (Note that the form for entering a document and the form for entering a requirement are the same.) This adds the new requirement to the document and sets the new requirement as the current requirement. To continue adding sections, the user clicks the Add Here button. This adds a new requirement at the same level as the current requirement; in other words, the new requirement will have the same parent as the current requirement. The user continues in this way to add second-level requirements to the document, eventually creating all the necessary sections (see Figure IV-4.6).

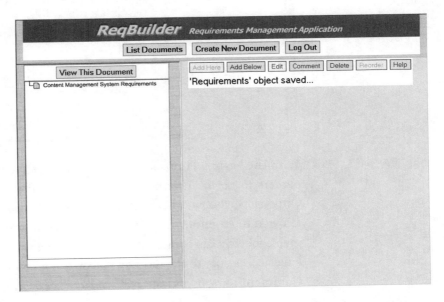

**Figure IV-4.4**

When a new document is created, only the name of the document exists.

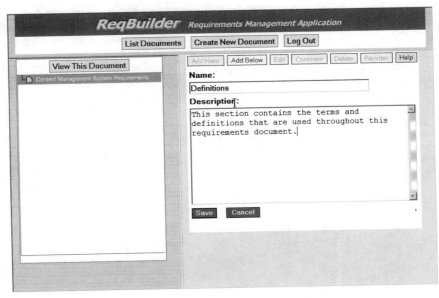

**Figure IV-4.5**

When the user clicks Add Below in a newly created document, a form opens for entering the name and description of a second-level requirement.

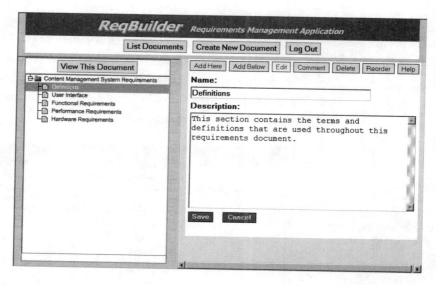

With the basic sections added, it is now possible for other requirements owners to begin entering their own requirements within each section. Only users who have been set up as requirements or document owners are allowed to enter new requirements. As requirements are added, requirements viewers can comment on those requirements. Requirements viewers have access only to the Display button (for viewing any requirement), the Comment button, and the Help button (see Figure IV-4.7).

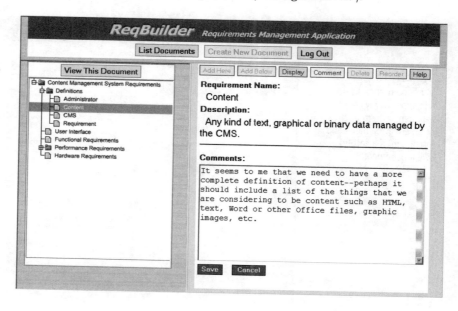

As requirements and comments are entered, it may become necessary to reorder requirements within a particular section. Requirements are automatically placed at the end of whatever section they are added to, but the user may prefer a different order. Andrew demonstrates the reorder tool that is available to requirements owners and document owners. To begin, he selects a requirement to reorder in the left frame, then clicks the Reorder button. This displays the reorder interface (see Figure IV-4.8).

**Figure IV-4.8**

The reorder tool lets requirements and document owners reorder a requirement within its own section.

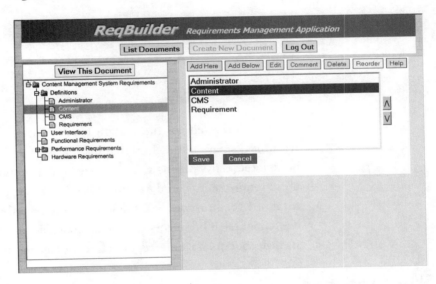

By clicking the up and down arrows, the user can reorder any of the requirements that share a parent. When the user clicks Save, the new order is stored into the database and the document in the bottom left frame is updated to reflect the change.

Andrew also demonstrates how to delete a requirement and a document. The process for deleting either is basically the same: To delete a requirement, he selects the requirement in the bottom-left frame, then clicks Delete in the bottom-right frame. To delete a document, he logs in as a document owner, selects the document to delete from the list of current documents, then selects the top level of the document in the bottom-left frame and clicks Delete (see Figure IV-4.9).

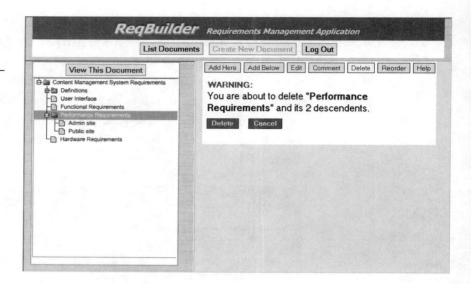

Figure IV-4.9

Figure IV-4.9
ReqBuilder displays a
warning when any
requirement is deleted
and tells the user how
many descendents will
be deleted along with it.

When Andrew clicks the Delete button in the bottom-right frame, a warning displays telling him that his selection and all its descendents will be deleted. This means that if he selects a requirement that has three child requirements, and each of those have four children of their own, a total of 13 requirements are deleted (the selected requirement and its 12 descendents). If he selects the top level of a document, its top level and all its descendents are deleted, effectively deleting the document.

## Client Feedback

When Andrew finishes the demonstration, the client is generally pleased and feels their users will be able to employ the tool to build a set of requirements for their content-management system. Of course, the client has some suggestions for improvements, which are discussed at some length. After the meeting, Andrew summarizes the suggestions in a memo to the rest of the team and asks for feedback on what it would take to implement each one.

**Client suggestions**

**Memo**

**Date:** November 7

**To:** ReqBuilder Team

**From:** Andrew

**Subject:** Client suggestions

We had the meeting with the client yesterday, and things generally went well. They feel their users will be able to use ReqBuilder to create the set of requirements for the content-management system we're going to build for them. They commented on some issues they'd like to see improved, but these items won't keep us from moving forward.

However, I'd like to get some idea from you of what it will take to implement these, so please go through each of the following and give me your feedback.

1. They'd like the ability to export the requirements document as an XML file. They feel this may be helpful as they are introducing some other applications that can process XML documents.

2. They need to be able to attach a binary document to individual requirements. For example, they might want to attach a Visio diagram to a requirement concerning the network architecture. They insisted they'd need to upload only a single document in association with each requirement. However, this is one those things that clients say early in a project and then, right before you deliver it, change their mind. In other words, I think we need to accommodate uploading multiple documents per requirement even if we don't build it initially.

### Client Suggestions

### Memo

3. They would like to be able to secure a specific requirement or set of requirements to an individual user. We're already storing the ID of the user who created the requirement but we didn't do anything with that data in the first phase. They'd like to limit it so only the creator (or "owner") of a requirement can edit it (of course, document owners would also be allowed to edit any requirement).

4. They'd like to be able to lock individual requirements as well as sections of the requirements document once those requirements have been approved. No users except the document owner would be able to edit locked items. This is actually a very good idea because it would allow us to finalize the document so that no more changes could be made.

5. They'd like to be able to add a versioning feature for individual requirements, although as we discussed this further, it became obvious this wasn't really a big deal for them.

These are the major items the client mentioned. Please get back to me and let me know what you think it will take to implement each.

Team members write back to Andrew, and he compiles the answers into a memo laying out the options. Fortunately, only the second item in the list—the ability to upload documents in association with individual requirements—is of short-term importance. However, everyone agrees to deploy ReqBuilder as is and start using the application right away, with the file-upload functionality scheduled for addition as soon as possible. Andrew takes on the task of writing the requirements and design document for the file-upload functionality and responds to the client's requests as follows:

**Requested functionality**

**Memo**

**Date:** November 13

**To:** Tom Jones, Federal Agency of Bureaucratic Regulations

**From:** Andrew, Webworld Studios

**Subject:** Requested functionality

The following contains our answers to your questions concerning additional functionality that was discussed during our recent meeting. Some of these requests are so large that they will not be part of this project but may be useful should Webworld continue to work with the agency on other projects.

1. XML version of the requirements document: This is straightforward. We already have the start of a generic method that uses ColdFusion MX's new XML functions to build an XML representation of a requirements document. So, it would be easy to deliver this feature but we'll wait on it until a specific use surfaces.

2. Uploading documents to associate with individual requirements: I am writing a technical-design document for this right now, and I'll firm up our estimate of how long it will take to add this functionality once I'm done with it. As agreed, we're going to launch without the file-upload feature, but we are shooting to add it to the existing functionality within a couple of weeks.

## Requested functionality

### Memo (continued)

3. Securing a requirement or set of requirements to a specific individual: As we thought, this involves a bit more work, but it's doable. We're laying the groundwork for this as part of the work we're doing on another project in which we're building a security component whose methods perform typical security actions such as determining what rights a specific user has to specific objects or types of objects. When that component is complete and we determine exactly what the business rules for ReqBuilder should be, we should be able to roll it into ReqBuilder.

4. Locking individual requirements so they can't be edited once they have been approved: This is an interesting one. Our team discussed it and concluded that a simple locking scheme would be inadequate. Instead, the entire process of developing the document should go through defined phases. That is, each document would be in a specific phase as follows:

   (a) Creation Phase. Any requirement owner may add a requirement. Any user may comment on existing requirements.

   (b) Comment Phase. Only document owners may add new requirements. Requirement owners can edit requirements based on comments received. Any user may comment on existing requirements.

   (c) Final Review. No new requirements are allowed. Only the document owner can edit existing requirements. Any user may comment on existing requirements.

   (d) Document Frozen. All comments have been incorporated, and the final requirements document is complete. No edits or additions are allowed.

## Requested functionality

### Memo (continued)

The document is frozen when all parties have signed off on it, at which point we'll need to take a snapshot of it to serve as a baseline. Naturally, there will be phases after the snapshot to accommodate the changes that occur as the project progresses, but the original, approved version of the document will need to be preserved.

Obviously, working out and implementing this plan will take some time, and we think it'd be best to do it after everyone has some experience working with the existing tool. With some experience under our belts, we'll be able to fashion a better, more realistic set of business rules, then design and code the phases appropriately.

5. Versioning: Although there may be some advantages to having this functionality now, our team agrees that versioning would be most needed when a phased process, such as what's described above, is implemented. Creating versions of individual requirements isn't difficult—we'd do it by creating a Version component that manages the storage, retrieval, and display of versions of individual requirements.

Hopefully, all this answers the questions you raised in our last meeting. The request we're moving forward with now is the ability to upload documents in association with individual requirements.

The client agrees with both the statement of the features to be added and on the time frame suggested for the implementation of each request. The following day Andrew finishes the requirements and design document for the uploads functionality and sends it to Teo to begin coding. While Teo works on adding the new code, the existing application is moved to the client servers as covered in the next chapter.

## File-upload requirements and design

### Memo

**Date:** November 14

**To:** Teo

**From:** Andrew

**Subject:** File-upload requirements and design

As you know, our next priority is to add file-upload functionality to ReqBuilder. Most of the work will center on adding code to the Requirements component's **Edit()**, **Display()**, and **Delete()** methods. But we'll also need to add something to the Document component—if nothing else, some graphical clue in the Document **Display()** method to show which requirements have associated files. The following describes an approach to adding file-upload capability.

1. **Terminology:** In some contexts it would be natural to call the uploaded files "documents," but if we do that, we're likely to introduce confusion as to whether we're referring to an uploaded file or a requirements document. To avoid this confusion, I will always use *"uploaded file"* to refer to a file that has been uploaded in association with a requirement. If you come up with a better name, let me know.

2. **Uploaded Files Functional Requirements:** The client has asked for the ability to upload a single file in association with each Requirement, but we want to design the file storage to accommodate multiple-file uploads, even if the user interface doesn't initially support it.

   We want to store the uploaded files under their original names. In other words we won't create a unique system name for uploaded files, so the design will need to allow for files to be stored under their original names while preventing name collisions.

## File-upload requirements and design

### Memo (continued)

We want to keep together all the uploaded files associated with each requirement document so they can be easily copied as a group.

When editing a requirement, we need to be able to see if it already has an uploaded file and, if so, what its name is. The user should be able to click on the uploaded file name in the **Edit()** form to view or download it.

Uploaded files need to be deleted when the requirement they are associated with is deleted.

When we display a full document, we need to show a graphical clue that indicates which requirements have uploaded files. This could be as simple displaying a graphical image of a file to indicate that a particular requirement has an associated uploaded file.

3. **Design:** Create an Uploads subdirectory off the main application directory. Add the path to this to the **rbInitVars.cfm** custom tag (the one that initializes global variables).

   Add code to the **Document Create()** method that creates a subdirectory of Uploads named **Doc_ID** where "ID" is the primary key of the requirements document.

   Add code to the **Requirements Edit()** method that uses **<CFFILE>** to choose and upload a file. When a file is uploaded, check in the Uploads/Doc_ID for a subdirectory named **Req_ID** where "ID" is the ID of the requirement for which we're uploading a file. If the directory doesn't exist, create it and copy the uploaded file into it.

## File-upload requirements and design

### Memo (continued)

If the Req_ID directory does exist, find the previously uploaded file using <CFDIRECTORY>, delete it, and copy the newly uploaded file into that directory.

Add code to the Requirements **Edit()** method that checks for the existence of the Req_ID subdirectory, gets the name of any file in it using **<CFDIRECTORY>**, and displays the filename as a link. Next to or under the link, put a check box that, when selected, indicates that the existing uploaded file should be deleted when the form is submitted. When the file is deleted, delete the directory as well.

Add JavaScript code to the **Requirements Edit()** method that runs when the user selects a file to upload but an uploaded file already exists for that requirement. This pops up a warning message that the user is about to overwrite an existing file and gives them the option of canceling the new upload.

Add code to the **Requirements Comment()** method to get the name of the uploaded file (if one exists) and to display a link to it. Do not provide a means for uploading a file.

For the **Document Display()** method, use **<CFDIRECTORY>** to get a list of all the requirements subdirectories under Uploads, and use that to display a graphical image of a file next to all requirements that have an uploaded file.

## File-upload requirements and design

### Memo (continued)

The previous covers the basics of associating one file with a requirement. Associating multiple documents is similar but with a couple of twists. Instead of waiting to upload the selected file until the entire requirements form is submitted, the user needs to upload files as they are selected. This raises the problem of what to do if a user uploads several files and then clicks Cancel to undo her actions. In that case, we need to get rid of the new files she uploaded without removing any existing uploaded files. Here are some general comments on how to address this architecturally (the interface details still need to be worked out):

In the Requirements **Edit()** method, provide an interface for selecting and uploading a file with **<CFFILE>**. This will have an Upload button that moves each file to the server, except that these will be uploaded into a temporary subdirectory of Req_ID. This allows the user to upload more than one file for each requirement without "committing" them. So, the exact sequence is: when the user uploads the first file associated with a requirement, check for the existence of the "temp" directory. If it exists, delete all its contents, then upload the file. As the user uploads additional files, put them into the "temp" subdirectory.

When the user clicks the Save button to save the requirement, move all the files from the temp subdirectory into the Req_ID directory. Some of these might overwrite prior versions of the same document.

## File-upload requirements and design

### Memo (continued)

If the user clicks the Cancel button, delete all the files in the temp subdirectory.

If the user leaves the interface without saving or canceling, then we'll have orphaned files in the temp directory but as covered above these will be deleted the next time a user tries to upload new files.

We also need to provide a way for the user to select one or more previously uploaded files to delete. All the files will be displayed in the **Requirements Edit()** form, so perhaps the simplest way would be to put a check box next to each file that, when checked, indicates it should be deleted. When the form is submitted, do the deletions first, then move any newly uploaded files from the temp subdirectory into the Req_ID directory.

We'll add the multifile-upload capability later if needed. I just wanted to make some notes on how it could be done for when we get there.

## Delivery

Now that the client has accepted ReqBuilder, it is time to install it to their server. Their data center staff want to do the installation themselves, so Seth sends them instructions on how to install Macromedia ColdFusion MX and the Flash Remoting UI Components available from the Macromedia site at http://dynamic.macromedia.com/bin/MM/exchange/extension_detail.jsp?product=flash&extOid=365880.

With the requisite server software installed, the next step is to deploy the ReqBuilder code which is done using ColdFusion MX's archive/deploy functionality. In the ColdFusion administrator archive wizard, Seth specifies the directory that contains ReqBuilder and the one datasource it uses (Reqbuilder). See Figure IV-5.1.

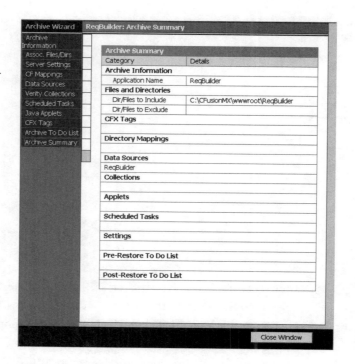

**Figure IV-5.1**

The ColdFusion MX administrator provides an interface for specifying directories to package as well as the datasource needed by the application.

When ColdFusion builds the archive, all the templates and the datasource definition are packaged into a *.car file that is FTP'd to the client. The client then uses the ColdFusion administrator deploy tool on their server to install ReqBuilder onto their server. The only changes to code that need to be made are in the custom tag `rbInitAppVars.cfm` which initializes the application level variables used by ReqBuilder for information such as the path to the components directory and the port to use (if something other than the default). (ColdFusion MX can run in association with either an existing Web server, such as Microsoft's Internet Information Server (IIS) or Apache, or with a built-in Web server. When it runs with the built-in Web server, by default it responds on port 8500.)

After testing the installation, the client deletes the test data that was entered by the Webworld team and schedules a training session for their staff who will be using ReqBuilder. They estimate the training will take no more than an hour or two and will consist of a simple walk-through of the application.

# Postmortem

With the application delivered, the Webworld team sets up its postmortem meeting to review the whole application development process, confirm what was done well, pinpoint the things they could have done better and discuss the functionality that should be added in the next phase.

The entire team had pretty much the same opinion about the project's technology:

1. Everyone liked working with Macromedia ColdFusion MX components (CFCs). Despite the complete change in the underlying ColdFusion engine no one ran into any incompatibility issues, so learning time wasn't wasted on figuring out problems but instead was directed towards learning how to use the new features, such as components. Everyone on the team was an experienced ColdFusion developer before starting ReqBuilder, but this was the first MX project any of them had done. Since everyone had prior extensive experience with ColdFusion custom tags and many of them had been developing in an object-based environment for several years, they found it easy to understand component basics, and everyone liked the modularity and re-usability of the component architecture.

   But, as Teo pointed out, that didn't mean they didn't have more to learn about components. The rest of the team agreed: the simplicity and elegance of the component architecture meant that it could be applied in many ways and so they all expected to continue to find new uses for components.

2. Everyone liked the decision to use Flash MX for the user interface (UI), but they all felt they needed more data about Flash, and ActionScript in particular. Although Dmitry had done the work on the Flash UI, the rest of the team had reviewed what he'd written. As the team was made up of back-end coders, not graphical designers, they had very particular questions about Flash and were having some trouble finding simple texts that defined basic Flash terms—that is, those terms that "everyone knows" who uses Flash regularly. Most of the documentation they found was

geared toward beginners or experienced Flash designers—not back-end developers who need to know how to interact programmatically with Flash. Dmitry volunteered to look for such a reference and pass it on to the rest of the team.

Although the discussion about the technology was important, most of the meeting was spent discussing the process they'd used to develop ReqBuilder from which several key successful actions emerged. The team agreed unanimously that the most important action was the fact that they had followed a process—they'd all had experience with internal projects that did not follow a process and those usually ended up with poor results.

Andrew summarized the highlights of the other successful actions after the meeting and distributed it to the team.

---

**Summary of ReqBuilder successful actions**

**Memo**

**Date:** November 18

**To:** ReqBuilder Team

**From:** Andrew

**Re:** Summary of ReqBuilder successful actions

The following summarizes the successful actions we talked about in the ReqBuilder postmortem meeting. I think we came up with some good observations that should be applied to other projects.

1. Rather than trying to figure out everything at once, we started with very general concepts and moved from there into greater specifics. This began with a high-level statement of what ReqBuilder needed to do, which Teo used to create the first prototype.

   That prototype formed the basis for further, more specific discussions, really giving us a place to start.

## Summary of ReqBuilder successful actions

### Memo (continued)

2. We kept both the client and the team focused on a real-world view of what ReqBuilder needed to do by focusing on the prototype and liberally using whiteboard diagrams. This was important because there were somewhat different purposes at play that needed to be reconciled. The client wanted ReqBuilder so they could involve their internal people in the process of requirements definition. We wanted ReqBuilder so we could get a clear-cut statement of requirements for their content-management system. Although those aren't exactly opposed purposes, neither are they the same. The prototype gave both the client and us a concrete way to make sure the final product would provide what was need by both.

3. With regards to the design phase, probably the most successful action was to work through the major design decisions with everyone in the room: the back-end database folks, the UI people, and the developers. Although this took a bit longer, it meant that the database people really heard what was needed from the user's perspective, the front-end designers got some understanding of why certain things couldn't be done in the available timeframe, and the coders got an overview of the entire application. Eventually, this led to a simple, flexible database back end that accommodated what the front-end designers wanted and that the coders could write within the schedule.

**Summary of ReqBuilder successful actions**

**Memo (continued)**

4. Another plus was the completeness of the design document. In the early days of ColdFusion—and of the Web for that matter—it was pretty common for a developer to sit down and just start coding. That worked fine as long as it was one developer and the application wasn't too complex. Of course, that also frequently produced some pretty lousy applications. Although ColdFusion is probably still the fastest way to build Web applications, the new features are at their best when well planned.

   Once the high-level design was established for ReqBuilder, it was important for it to be documented and reviewed by the team. I think we all agreed that probably the most important part of the design document was its definition of ReqBuilder's internal application programming interface (API). In other words, the design document's description of how all the pieces fit together. Because these interfaces were thought out and documented, it was possible for the developers to concentrate on the best way to implement the code, knowing that what they wrote would fit into the application as a whole.

5. Clearly delineating coding responsibility was also a successful action. We all agreed that assigning each developer to a specific part of the application (usually a specific component) was very helpful. By doing this, each person could become an expert in their area and they didn't have to worry about someone else changing what they were working on.

6. Using a source control system was also critical. Although this should be a "given," it doesn't hurt to repeat it. Too many Web projects don't use the important basic tools, even though once you've worked with a source control system, it's hard to imagine life without it.

The postmortem meeting also covers things that could have been done better or that were tried but didn't work. The team pretty much agrees that not including the file-upload functionality in the initial release was a mistake; it had been mentioned in one of the requirements meetings but didn't make it into the requirements document and wasn't caught when writing the design document. The good news is that despite the oversight, the basic system architecture was flexible enough so the file upload capability could be added easily as described in Andrew's memo included at the end of the previous chapter. Despite this glitch, the team doesn't feel they need to make changes to the basic process—rather than tweaking the process to try to achieve an unrealistic goal of never missing anything, the team feels it is more important to ensure that applications are always flexible and modular in construction so that as new or overlooked requirements surface, they can be accommodated.

One area the team feels should have been done much better was testing. With the short schedule, little time was allocated to test the application. Debbie suggests that a team member should be kept "on call" for the first week or two to ensure that someone is available should problems arise. She points out that, in effect, the client's use of the application is serving as the beta test that wasn't done. Teo volunteered to respond to any calls, and Jesse said he would contact the client to let them know who to contact.

# What's Next

At the end of the postmortem meeting, the team discusses the features that could be added to the next release of ReqBuilder. Some of these have already been covered in Andrew's "requested functionality" memo that addressed specific client requests. However, the team also raised some new ideas that are added to the list of possible additions for the next version.

Debbie started with an an issue that first surfaced during initial design— that users need a way to move a requirement and its descendents to another part of the document. Although the application includes a

Reorder function, it only lets the user move a requirement in relationship to its parents and siblings. What's needed is a way to pick up a requirement and move its location within the document—that is, give it a new parent.

Andrew points out that the back end for doing that is trivial: Just change the ParentID of the moving requirement to point to the new parent. All the moving requirement's children go along for the ride because their relationship to the moving requirement isn't changed.

Dmitry suggests that he might be able to extend FTree, the component he used to create the UI drill-down, to allow users to drag-and-drop requirements from one part of the document to another. The biggest issue with adding this feature would be how to manage simultaneous attempts to move requirements. Andrew suggests adding methods to both the Requirements and Document components that would lock a particular requirement or the document as a whole so that only one person at a time was able to make edits. This could be implemented by adding `lock()` and `unlock()` methods to the Requirements and the Document components and using those methods in the code to prevent two users from making contradictory changes at the same time.

While talking about the use of Flash MX, Teo suggests that the whole interface could be implemented in Flash MX. This would eliminate most page refreshes: Flash would simply invoke the ColdFusion MX methods needed to perform its actions and then update itself without making a trip back to the server for UI updates. This would also eliminate any potential cross-browser compatibility issues and would make the application more client-server–like.

One area the team discusses thoroughly is the handling of comments. No one is happy with the simple HTML <TEXTAREA> used to input comments, as it's impossible to tell who made which comment (unless users include their name), and it doesn't allow for a reliable history of comments. Andrew suggests a revised database schema on a whiteboard (see Figure IV-5.2).

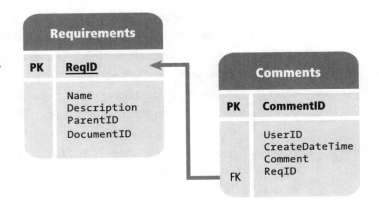

Figure IV-5.2
Splitting out comments
into their own table
allows ReqBuilder to
maintain a history of
comments and display
them in chronological
order.

The team agrees that the comments should be split out, and they discuss what changes need to be made to accommodate this. The changes seem to be localized to just a few methods:

- The `Comment()` method of the Requirements component will need a new SQL statement joining the Requirements table and the new Comments table in order to get and display all the comments associated with a particular requirement. Of course, the `Comment()` methods's UI also needs to be changed to display existing comments, with space for the user to enter a new comment.

- When a new comment is submitted, the handler code needs to *insert* it into the comments table instead of *updating* it in the Requirements table.

- The `Edit()` method of the Requirements component also needs to be changed to query the Comments table and then display the associated comments.

Debbie suggests that the UI for displaying comments within the `Comment()` and `Edit()` methods should allow the user to sort by date (ascending or descending) and by comment maker.

Teo points out that someone, probably the document owner, should have the ability to delete individual comments just in case something is entered by mistake. The team agrees that access to the delete comment functionality should be restricted to maintain an accurate record of what transpires.

Of all the new feature items discussed in the postmortem, security engages most of the team's time. Everyone agrees that granular security is an important prerequisite to being able to "phase" requirements documents, as they suggested to the client. Andrew notes that they spent a great deal of time and effort in previous object-based projects to come up with some grand, generic way to administer security across an application. Usually, those attempts resulted in overly complicated schemes that performed poorly in some areas or in other ways were inadequate. Trying to create a one-size-fits-all security model tended to fail, either by being overly complicated or because of the model's inability to accommodate the exceptions that inevitably arose.

Having talked with other developers who'd run into similar problems in other environments, Andrew comes to the conclusion that they should build a very simple security back end whose methods are customized to each application's specific security requirements. Andrew whiteboards his idea of how it should work. See Figure IV-5.3.

The `Authenticate()` method is obvious: It takes a submitted user name and password and validates the user against whatever back end the application uses. This could be a simple Open Database Connectivity (ODBC) datasource, a Lightweight Directory Access Protocol (LDAP) server, or an NT domain.

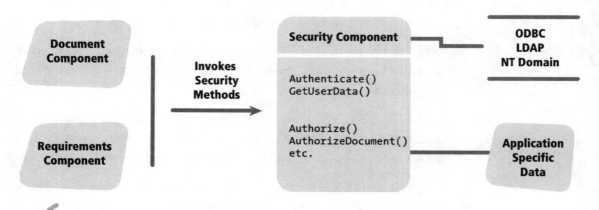

**Figure IV-5.3**

The Security component provides generic methods such as `Authenticate()`, which can be reused from one application to the next, as well as application-specific methods that access application-specific data.

Other methods such as `Authorize()` will vary substantially from application to application. In the case of ReqBuilder, the `Authorize()` method needs to determine whether a user is allowed to perform an action, say an edit, on a selected requirement. The team realizes that once some of the additional functionality discussed earlier is added to the application, determining whether a user should be granted access to a specific requirement could depend on one or more of the following:

- Whether the current user owns the requirement

- What role the current user is associated with

- Whether the requirement is currently locked

- What "phase" the requirements document is in—that is, whether any edits are allowed

The above represents quite a bit of work to simply find out whether the current user has access to a single requirement. This performance overhead is acceptable if the `Authorize()` method only runs when the user clicks on a specific requirement. However, such an interface could lead to user frustration because they won't know whether they have access to a particular requirement until they have clicked it.

Andrew explains that a better UI would provide visual clues in the left navigation to indicate which requirements the current user can access and what actions they can perform on each. To accomplish this, though, code would have to verify the user's access to each requirement as the left navigation is built. For a requirements document consisting of several hundred individual requirements, this could translate to several hundred calls to the `Authorize()` method every time the left navigation reloads. Performance would be terrible.

An alternative is to create an `AuthorizeDocument()` method that uses optimized queries on the security store, or internal caching of security data, to determine a user's access rights to each requirement within an entire requirements document. Such a method would be highly specific to ReqBuilder; it may or may not appear in any other application.

This discussion leads the team into a more general discussion of the Security component's architecture. The options already discussed assume that Security component methods are customized or created for each new application. In other words, the Security component has a somewhat different API for each application. An alternative that further generalizes security management is to use a "factory method," which is a method that creates or manufactures other objects (see Figure IV-5.4.)

Under this pattern, whenever part of the ReqBuilder application needs to perform a specific type of security action, it invokes the Security component's `CreateSecurityObj()` method, which returns a customized component whose methods provide the services needed by the context.

For example, when the application is building the left navigation, it would invoke `CreateSecurityObj("AuthorizeDocument")`, which returns a component whose methods would perform the actions of the `AuthorizeDocument()` method described above.

The advantage of constructing the system this way, which amounts to adding a layer of abstraction, is that all code interacts with the Security component in the same way. Everyone on the development team knows that whenever they need to get access to application-specific security functionality, they call the `CreateSecurityObj()` method and work with what it

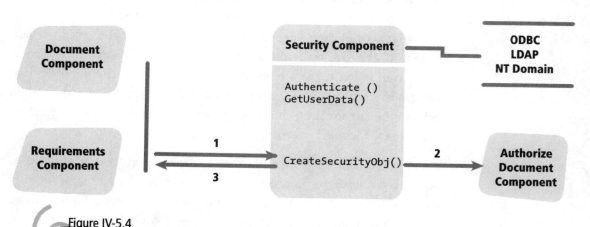

Figure IV-5.4

The factory method of the Security component (`CreateSecurityObj()`) instantiates and returns application-specific security components.

returns to carry out application-specific functions. This works because all the application-specific security methods are segregated into the components that `CreateSecurityObj()` creates. Of course, the Security component has other generic methods such as `Authenticate()` and `GetUserData()`, which are used across all applications.

Using this architecture, the task of creating a security system for any new application becomes a relatively straightforward matter—just code the specialized components needed for that application. This also makes it easier for application development to move forward without having to complete the security system first. While the developers assigned to security code the application-specific security components, the rest of the team can continue to code their parts of the application, knowing that their interaction with the Security component will always be the same. They invoke its CreateSecurityObj() method with the appropriate argument and it provides them with the component they need to carry out the security functionality particular to their area of the code.

After the postmortem meeting, Andrew writes up the design ideas that had been discussed and work begins on Phase 2 of ReqBuilder. In the meantime, the client continues to use ReqBuilder and makes progress on defining its content-management needs. When the requirements are completed and approved, the Webworld team moves on to designing and building the new content-management system.

# Part V

# User Interaction

User Interaction is a collection of related community applications. Included are a real-time chat engine, instant messaging, and threaded discussions.

Product Requirements

## Client Overview

*Fantasy Life* is a magazine for fans of the massively multi-player online game Ultimate Fantasy. *Fantasy Life*'s Web site has become hugely popular with players, thanks primarily to a discussion section where they communicate with each other, socialize, and arrange sales and trades of game items. The makers of Ultimate Fantasy have tried to halt the sale of game items outside the game, but *Fantasy Life* (which is not owned or controlled by the makers of Ultimate Fantasy) flatly refuses to censor the discussion boards on its Web site, citing free-speech rights. The publishers of Ultimate Fantasy have sued *Fantasy Life*, claiming infringement of intellectual property. Now, as a result of all the publicity surrounding the lawsuit, *Fantasy Life*'s Web site discussions are more popular than ever. In fact, they have become so popular that *Fantasy Life* has decided to stop publication of its printed magazine in order to focus all its resources on the Internet.

# Project Overview

*Fantasy Life*'s site is already about two years old. The editors don't want to take it down, but they do want to move the discussion section (which was originally added as an afterthought) and make it part of a whole new site. This section would be designed as an online community where Ultimate Fantasy players could socialize and interact with each other.

The site has not been revised yet because of a number of concerns—primarily, how changes would affect the experiences of loyal users, the potential for adding complexity to what is currently an incredibly simple (and thus highly usable) application, and an aversion to adding new technologies with new uncertainties.

Here's the email *Fantasy Life*'s editor-in-chief sends to the development folks, describing what he wants:

**New Fantasy Life community Web site**

**Email**

**Date:** March 2

**To:** Application Design Team

**From:** Corwin the Valiant (editor-in-chief)

**Subject:** New Fantasy Life community Web site

The Ultimate Fantasy lawyers are irritating me this week, but they're giving us so much free publicity, I can't really complain. Opening arguments in the trial will be in a month and a half, and I'd really love to launch our new Web site the same day so we can take advantage of the publicity.

I know that's short notice, but since the message board only has to be converted, not written from scratch, hopefully it won't take so long.

All Fantasy Life employees use their online names in their correspondence, never their real names.

## New Fantasy Life community Web site

### Email (continued)

Basically, I want a whole new site where users can interact with each other in lots of different ways, sort of like on America Online. In addition to the message board, I'd like real-time chat, instant messaging, and for users to be able to create accounts with profiles about themselves. Users should also be able to search for other users and read their profile information, as well as find out whether another user is logged in.

For the moment, this site will be paid for by banner ads, so accounts should be free to set up. You don't need to put in the ads themselves or any fancy graphics, since our own art department can easily add all that later. Just a simple functional site will be perfect.

One thing you should consider, though, is that we want to keep our options open to switch to a paid model later (in case advertising revenue isn't enough after the trial is over and the publicity dies down). So while you're creating the account setup, make sure you design it so it could easily be converted to a paid system later.

If you come up with any other ideas or features as you're working on the site, by all means include them. But always keep in mind that in this site the users *are* the content, and the purpose of the site is simply to facilitate players' communicating with one another—with as little interference as possible.

Thanks!

Corwin the Valiant
Editor-in-chief

Corwin also scribbles a brief note to himself:

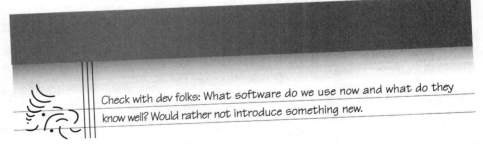

Check with dev folks: What software do we use now and what do they know well? Would rather not introduce something new.

A few days later, the application design team meets with the *Fantasy Life* editorial staff to get more details about exactly what features they want in the new site. The design team is relieved that the *Fantasy Life* staff doesn't come to the meeting in costume, and actually turns out to be very laid-back and easy to work with.

Here are the notes from that meeting:

MEETING NOTES

**Present:** Corwin the Valiant, editor-in-chief
Priscilla the Enchantress, writer/editor
Rooga the Dreadful, writer, application-design team
Application design team: Adam, Chad, Mina and Iran

**Facilitator:** Corwin

After everyone was introduced, the meeting focused on brainstorming a list of features the *Fantasy Life* staff wanted on the new Web site, and then organizing that list to determine which features could realistically be completed in time for the site launch in a month and a half, which features could be added after the launch, and which were too impractical to include at all.
Here are the features that were suggested during brainstorming:

- User Account Management/Log-in/User Profiles
- New users must set up an account, and returning users must log in before they can use any other features of the site (see Figure V-1.1).
- Account setup is free; each user may have multiple accounts.

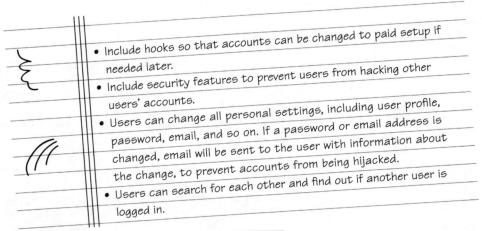

- Include hooks so that accounts can be changed to paid setup if needed later.
- Include security features to prevent users from hacking other users' accounts.
- Users can change all personal settings, including user profile, password, email, and so on. If a password or email address is changed, email will be sent to the user with information about the change, to prevent accounts from being hijacked.
- Users can search for each other and find out if another user is logged in.

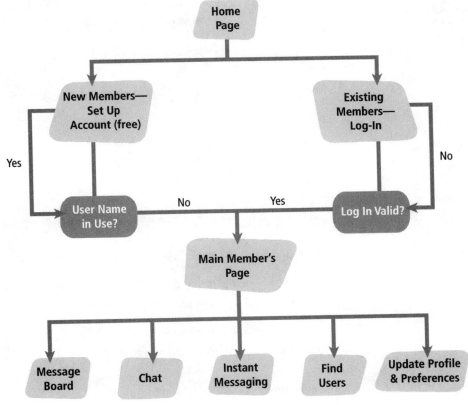

**Figure V-1.1**
Flowchart of login process and basic site layout.

## Message Board

Features from current board to retain:

- Browse by board, thread, or message (see Figure V-1.2).

- New messages (not replies) automatically create new threads.

- Users can edit or delete their own messages, as long as the message has not yet been replied to.

- Search feature lets users find messages by subject, date, author, and text.

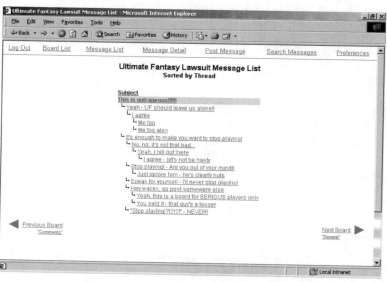

**Figure V-1.2**

The current message board, created in ColdFusion 4.5, shows a threaded discussion.

- Message list and detail layout can be customized to users' preferences.

- Users have the option to privately email one another, and can also specify if they do not wish to receive private emails.

- Administrators can create boards, edit or delete any message on any board, email any user, and assign administrator privileges.

### New Features to Add or Change

- Option for user to automatically receive an email or instant message when one of their messages is replied to.

- Combine message board preferences with other preferences and user profile, in one central location.

- Add option for "moderators," who can edit or delete messages on specified boards, but do not have other administrative abilities (these will typically be regular users the staff is familiar with, and will recruit to moderate specific boards, but are not to have full administrative rights).

## Chat

- List chat rooms—some that will always exist, and others that have been created by users and will exist only as long as users are in the room.

- Users can create public or private rooms that do not show up on the room list.

- Once in a room, users should have the option to chat, "whisper" to other users (send a private message, which only a single other user will receive), find other users, change rooms, list rooms, list users in a room, and log out.

- As much as possible, commands should be available both by mouse (clicking on links) and by keyboard (typing in chat text entry box).

- If possible, design the chat room so that once a user is in it, he or she can do everything with the keyboard, and do not have to use the mouse at all until leaving the room.

## Instant Messaging

- A user can send instant messages to another logged-in user, whose name will appear to the recipient in a pop-up box.

- If users wish to continue a discussion, they can automatically link to a private chat room, where the other user is invited.

- Users can enter information about their external instant-message account, so other users can send them an instant message even when they are not logged into the site.

- Ideally, the system should be able to communicate with the following IM networks: ICQ (I Seek You), America Online Instant Messenger (AIM), Microsoft Network (MSN Messenger), and the Yahoo Messenger.

### Administration (by *Fantasy Life* Staff)

- As much administration as possible will be done through the regular user interface, not a separate administrator interface. Administrators will be "super users" with additional privileges.

- Administrators can create and remove message boards, as well as edit or delete any message on any board.

- Administrators can create new accounts and edit any user's account, including the user's profile, preferences, and all other settings (administrators can change passwords but cannot read them).

- Administrators can kick users out of chat rooms, ban them temporarily from individual rooms or message boards, and ban them indefinitely from chatting or posting messages at all. (Note: What's to stop a banned user from just setting up a new account?) We hope to use these abilities rarely, if ever, but if we lose the lawsuit, they may become very important later.

After brainstorming, the application design folks agreed that most of these features were feasible. (They appeared surprised that we didn't have more outlandish requests.) They said they might postpone some of the new features for the message board and add them last. If they run out of time, those features will be added later, after the site goes live. The designers also said they would need to do some research to find out if all the instant-message features were possible. They agreed to get back to us with more information about that as soon as they had it, and to create a rough draft of the entire site in two weeks.

# Initial Thoughts

## Introduction

After returning from their meeting with *Fantasy Life*'s editorial staff, the design team members have a series of brainstorming sessions to come up with ideas for how to approach the applications. To keep things organized from the start, they break the project into four parts: message board, chat, instant messaging, and account management.

In addition, the team establishes a general set of objectives against which to measure possible solutions.

- **Rapid Development.** Since the project has a very firm deadline, it's important to find solutions that can be implemented quickly. Therefore, it's better to stick with familiar technologies, which have more predictable development times. After the site goes live, there might be some room to experiment with different enhancements or advanced features, but for the initial site, the team should use tried and true technologies as much as possible.

- **Cross-Platform.** Part of Ultimate Fantasy's popularity stems from the fact that it can be played on many different operating systems, including Windows, Macintosh, and Linux. Similarly, the *Ultimate Fantasy* Web site needs to be easily usable on all those platforms and by different Web browsers.

- **Modular Design.** In order to facilitate future growth, the site should be as modular as possible, to make it easy to change or upgrade individual components later on without having to rewrite entire sections of the site.

# Brainstorming

The team starts brainstorming with what appears to be the easiest section—the message board—which is already working and just needs to be upgraded to Macromedia ColdFusion MX. However, in order for the upgraded system to work with the existing data, it needs to conform to the existing data format. Also, the team wants to find an alternative for the custom tag currently used for threading messages.

**Message Board**

MEETING NOTES

**Present:** Adam, Chad, Mina, and Ivan (application design team)

**Facilitator:** Adam

First, the team comes up with three possible ways to tackle the overall project:

1. **Leave the application alone as much as possible.**
   We would still need to run the code through the new ColdFusion MX Code Compatibility Analyzer and remove or rewrite any outdated functions. Other than that, we would leave the code alone. This approach has the advantage of being the fastest solution (it might only take a couple of hours). Unfortunately, it does not take advantage of any of the new features of ColdFusion MX, and it would be more difficult to integrate the application with the other sections.

2. **Rewrite everything.**
   On the other end of the spectrum, we could revamp everything, including the code and the database. This would give us as much control over the completed application as if we wrote it from scratch (which would almost be the case). Unfortunately, this method would also take the longest and could easily lead to headaches when we import the old data into the new database structure.

3. **Rewrite the application, but leave the database alone.**
   Rewriting the code while leaving the database alone seems to be the best solution, since it would provide a huge amount of flexibility, yet minimize the headaches of importing the old data.

Mina is assigned the task of looking at the existing code and following up with a practical assessment.

A few days later, Mina sends this email back to the team:

---

**Message board update**

**Email**

**Date:** March 8

**To:** Application Design Team

**From:** Mina

**Subject:** Message board update

I've looked at the existing code and the database, and it's a little complex but pretty clean overall. Ironically, since it was written for ColdFusion 4.5 (and not 5), it doesn't use any of the now-obsolete CF 5 authentication tags, so it will be even easier to convert.

The current design uses the standard structure of starting each template with queries to access the database, then displays the retrieved data. The display is fine, and the existing users are already familiar with it, so I'm not planning to change that much.

However, I am planning to move all the queries from the templates into a single CF component (CFC). This will divide the application into layers, so the templates will call the CFC, which will then call the database. Changing to a layered design will have three advantages: First, it will be more efficient, because by using a CFC, we can do a better job reusing code. Second, it wil make the application easier to update in the future, since the code will be better organized, and all the queries stored in a central location. Third, we can leave the database alone for the moment, but if we ever decide to change it later, all we'll have to do is rewrite the one CFC instead of all the individual templates.

Mina

## Chat

Unlike with the message board upgrade, the team would be creating the chat application from scratch. This gives them a lot more options—and a lot less direction. Since everyone already has a basic idea of what a chat interface looks like, most of the discussion centers around which technology to use.

MEETING NOTES

**Present:** Adam, Chad, Mina, and Ivan

**Facilitator:** Adam

The group discusses several possible technologies for delivering an integrated chat interface. Though they eventually pick one, the group never reaches a unanimous agreement about which would be the best, since each method has its own advantages and disadvantages.

- **Java applet.** Many Web sites use Java applets for chat. Java works well on different platforms (unlike ActiveX controls, for example) and can provide an excellent interface. The only real disadvantage to this solution is that it would be hard to integrate the applet with the existing user database for authentication and identification.

- **Flash.** Flash is nearly as portable as Java, and it's even better for creating polished user interfaces. Also, since the new Flash MX is more tightly integrated with ColdFusion, it should be possible to make a Flash chat client that accesses the user database on the server. However, integrating Flash and ColdFusion in this way is a very new thing.

- **HTML and ColdFusion only.** Not using a client technology at all would result in the most portable application, though it would also result in fewer options for creating a UI.

Chad volunteers to create the chat application by using only HTML and ColdFusion. The other team members are skeptical, but Chad shows them an idea he has for how to create a UI using only HTML (see Figure V-2.1), and they agree to let him try it.

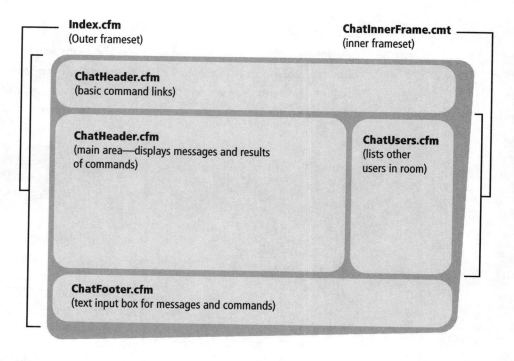

Figure V-2.1
A simple chat interface, as shown in this diagram, can be created by using HTML and ColdFusion alone.

A few days later, Chad returns with a prototype of the chat interface (see Figure V-2.2), and while it isn't fancy, it seems to work surprisingly well.

Figure V-2.2
The completed chat interface is plain but effective.

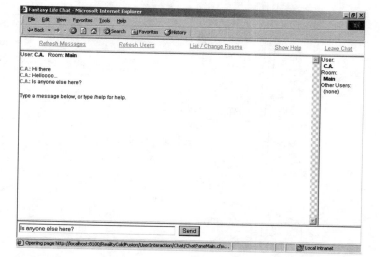

## Instant Messaging

Even though the team members are all familiar with instant-messaging (IM) clients like ICQ or Yahoo Messenger, they have different ideas about how to integrate instant messaging into a Web site.

MEETING NOTES

**Present:** Adam, Chad, Mina, and Ivan

**Facilitator:** Adam

First, the team discusses what external IM clients they want to support (if they can). They quickly agreed on four:

- ICQ
- American Online Instant Messenger (AIM)
- Yahoo Messenger
- Microsoft Network (MSN) Messenger

Then, the team discusses how a Web-based instant-messaging interface should work. Although they don't reach a consensus, they come up with several ideas:

- **Create a link for the recipient's IM service and ID.**
  By clicking on a link, the sender invokes her own locally installed IM client and opens a new message, addressed to the recipient. All four clients offer varying support for this type of link. This method also offers the big advantage of two-way conversing, and the recipient can easily reply to the sender. Unfortunately, this method requires the sender to have the necessary software installed (and an account created) for each of the four types of IM they want to send. Also, since client software isn't available for all four networks on all platforms, this method wouldn't be very portable; Linux or Mac users, for example, wouldn't be able to easily send messages on some networks.

- **Send messages from the Web site to remote IM clients through a form.** By filling out a Web form, a user sends another user a message, which the recipient receives through his IM client software. This interface requires the recipient to be running IM software, and only sends messages, since the sender might not be running the same IM software and cannot receive replies. If the sender wants to continue the conversation, he could always invite the recipient to join him in a chat room. But it's easy for the sender, who doesn't have to install any software, and doesn't even have to know what kind of client the recipient is using. Also, this approach makes it easy for users on any platform to send to recipients on other platforms. ICQ already has built-in support for this type of interface, though the other three clients would undoubtedly be more difficult to support.

- **Send "local" instant messages to other users currently logged into the site.** Similar to the previous method, this method accepts a message through a form. But instead of sending that message to an external client, the form causes the message to pop up in a small browser window on the recipient's computer. This would be created using JavaScript. This method has the big advantage of requiring neither the sender *nor* the receiver to install any software (or go through the hassle of signing up for any external IM accounts). Its disadvantage is that the recipient must be logged into the *Ultimate Fantasy* Web site in order to receive the message. (Users not logged in would not lose their messages; they just wouldn't receive them until the next time they logged into the site.) This disadvantage, however, might have the beneficial effect of encouraging users to log in often to see if they have any messages.

The development team members agree that even though links would be easy to program, they would be annoying to use, so they scrap that idea. They like both of the other ideas, though, and decide they would even work well together.

Finally, the team discusses how they could send messages from the Web server to remote IM clients. They have very little firm information about what will work and what won't, but they come up with some ideas worth investigating further:

- **Use <CFFORM> to post the message to a form on a remote server.** Since ICQ offers a simple form for sending messages, and the form posts to a central ICQ server, this method should work for ICQ. However, nobody knows if it works for any of the other IM services.

- **Use <CFMAIL> to send email.** Again, ICQ has an email-to-message gateway that should enable this method to work, but nobody knows if the other services offer similar gateways. Mina points out that because some recipients don't have IM clients at all, it might be useful to offer users the option to send regular email instead.

- **Find an existing ColdFusion custom tag.** Since Macromedia took over Allaire, the ColdFusion Tag Gallery has become significantly less user-friendly, but it may contain custom tags that would enable sending messages to some of the external services.

- **Write a new custom tag.** If a service has a complex API, and no custom tag to send messages to it, we could always write our own (probably in C++). Unfortunately, given the time frame, this option is probably not realistic.

- **Try Jabber?** A fairly new entry into the IM field, Jabber (www.jabber.org) is a completely open-source IM network that uses a thoroughly documented XML-based protocol to communicate. Also, the open-source Jabber server comes with built-in gateways for integrating it with the other four IM services. Since ColdFusion can communicate very well with XML, it might be possible to run a local Jabber server, use ColdFusion to communicate only with it, and let the Jabber server handle all the headaches of communicating with the other IM networks. Everyone agrees this solution shows the most promise for a long-term solution. Unfortunately, since none of the team members has ever used Jabber before, it might not be possible to get it running before the first deadline.

Ivan agrees to do further research on IM options and to follow up as soon as he knows more. He sends this email a few days later:

## IM options

### Email

**Date:** March 12

**To:** Application Design Team

**From:** Ivan

**Subject:** IM options

It looks like IM will be tougher than I thought. The short answer: It will be easy to work with ICQ, and nearly impossible to work with anyone else. The research I've done so far on Yahoo Messenger, AIM, and MSN Messenger (MSM) isn't promising, since they don't like to make it too easy for other programs to interact with their systems. But I'm still hopeful.

First, I struck out at the Tag Gallery. I found a few tags to send messages to ICQ, and one tag that would say if a user was online with Yahoo (but would not send messages). ICQ is the one service I already know how to interface with, so that didn't help me at all.

Then, I went looking for APIs for Yahoo, AIM, and MSM, with minimal success. MSM does publish an API, but it's so complicated that I think it would take a sophisticated C++ custom tag to work with it, and I don't think there's any way I could do that in the time we have. I couldn't find APIs for AIM or Yahoo, but I'm still looking.

Jabber still looks very attractive, but even it appears to have some problems interfacing with other networks. The Jabber FAQ describes how AIM has actively worked to block people from communicating with the AIM network through Jabber gateways. So much for working together. Anyway, despite the problems, I still think Jabber is our best long-term option.

---
**IM options**
---
**Email (continued)**

There are already Java-based Jabber clients, and even one Flash-based Jabber client (FLAIM) in early development. One of these clients might eventually enable us to offer full IM functionality (including receiving replies) right from the site, with no extra software to install. (Obviously, if a user wanted to receive IMs while not logged into the site, they'd still need to install additional software.) Very cool!

In the short run, however, I think we should start by offering support for ICQ and "local" instant messages. As long as we keep the design modular, we can easily add more services later.

Ivan

## Account Management

The discussion about account management is relatively short, since everyone has seen (and built) log-in systems before, and agrees that a plain Cold-Fusion and HTML interface will work just fine. Mina points out that the existing message board already includes an authentication mechanism, and asks if they should just continue using that. But Adam says he thinks they should use the new authentication framework in ColdFusion MX, since it should be easier to work with, and is definitely more secure. The team also briefly discusses how to detect if a user is "logged in" or not, and comes up with a few ideas:

- Set a "logged in" variable to "True" when a user logs in, and reset it to "False" when the user logs out again. (The obvious problem with this is that it is unrealistic to expect users to always log out.)

- Associate each user with their ColdFusion session variables (CFID and CFToken), and query the session variables on the server directly to see if the session is active. This solution might work but would be complex to implement.

- Set a "last accessed" variable each time a user loads a page and assume a user is logged in if that value is recent enough (within 10 minutes, for example). This solution isn't perfect, but it would be at least as good as the previous one, and should be a lot easier to create.

With little discussion, everyone agrees they like the third option best.

Finally, Adam volunteers to create the overall user-authentication and account-management structure. He says he will look at the existing system in the message board, and tells the team he will send them an update shortly.

---

**Project status**

**Email**

**Date:** March 14

**To:** Application Design Team

**From:** Adam

**Subject:** Project status

OK, looks like we've all got our jobs.

After looking at the authentication code in the original Fantasy Life message board, and also checking out the new ColdFusion MX authentication system, I'm even more sure we should go with completely new stuff here. In fact, I'm not going to use any of the old code at all. Instead, I'll create a new authentication system from scratch, using the new <CFLOGIN> tags.

Also, I contacted Corwin, and asked him about what information should be included in each user's profile. He wasn't sure, so he said to just add a large text field, so users can enter whatever they want. He also said to make the search interface as simple as possible, so users won't get confused.

I'll send you complete details on the log-in system as soon as I'm done.

Adam

# Development

## Introduction

In the last meeting before serious development is to start, Adam tells everyone on the application design team that once they finish the project, they will be turning it over to a full-time programmer whom *Fantasy Life* will hire to maintain and upgrade the site. He reminds them that in addition to commenting their code well, he wants them to make design notes, explaining any complex features in their applications. When everyone starts complaining about the extra work (because their applications include lots of complex features), Adam says, "Don't think of this as extra work; think of this as a way to show off your cool coding techniques." Adam also hands all the developers Ultimate Fantasy CDs, which Corwin the Valiant sent over so they could "get into the right mind-set" of the people who will be using the site. The developers agree to the task at hand and head home for a weekend of getting into the right mind-set before starting serious work on Monday.

# User Authentication

Adam realizes that all the sections within the Web site will need to share a single authentication method. Also, since their design will assume that all users are already logged in, the authentication method needs to be designed first. Adam comes into the office over the weekend to create the log-in system, so it will be ready when everyone else starts coding their applications on Monday.

After completing the log-in system, Adam sends the following memo the rest of the team, so they will know how to integrate it into their sections:

---

### Authentication, security, and app design

**Memo**

**Date:** March 24

**To:** Development Team

**From:** Adam

**Subject:** Authentication, security, and app design

OK, all, I've created a standardized authentication method for everyone to use. It's your standard "check-the-user-name-against-a-database" type log-in, but with a couple important changes.

First, I used the new Macromedia ColdFusion MX authentication mechanism. I want you each to create your applications in separate subdirectories. And to ensure all users are logged in, put the following code in your **Application.cfm** file (see Listing V-3.1).

**Listing V-3.1**   Application.cfm

```
<!--- Check if user is logged in --->
<CFLOGIN>
    <!--- If not, send user to login page --->
    <CFLOCATION URL="../loginform.cfm" ADDTOKEN="No">
</CFLOGIN>
```

## Authentication, security, and app design

### Memo (continued)

This guarantees that all users accessing your application are logged in (and sends them back to the log-in page if they're not). Then, since you already know all your users are logged in, whenever you need to know a user's name, just use the function **GetAuthUser()**.

For those of you who are interested, I'll send all the gory details of the login procedure in a follow up email. When a user logs in, since we want to use *Fantasy Life's* existing data as much as possible, I used the UserType field from the Users table in the current database to set the new Roles attribute. UserType is currently either User (the default) or Administrator. Since Mina may add moderators to the message board, we can add a third type, Moderator. You will all be able to check if a user belongs to any of these three roles by using IsUserInRole ("rolename"), in this way (see Listing V-3.2):

**Listing V-3.2   messagedetail.cfm** (and others)

```
<CFFUNCTION ... ROLES="Moderator,Administrator">
   <!--- Execute Administrator/Moderator code --->
</CFFUNCTION>
```

Since everyone is so enamored of the new ColdFusion MX components (CFCs—not that I blame you), when you create functions in your components, you can use the Roles attribute to make sure the user is authenticated when calling functions too, like so (see Listing V-3.3):

**Listing V-3.3   Code to use in .cfc components**

```
<CFFUNCTION ... ROLES="Moderator,Administrator">
   <!--- Execute Administrator/Moderator code --->
</CFFUNCTION>
```

## Authentication, security, and app design

### Memo (continued)

However, storing the data in this way means that a user will only be in one role at a time. So if you're creating something that can be accessed by everyone, either don't check roles at all or make sure to allow all three roles explicitly. If you allow only Users or Moderators, you will lock out Administrators. This can actually be useful, since you have the option to easily offer one interface to Users, or hide it, and offer a different one to Administrators. Here's how it works (see Listing V-3.4):

**Listing V-3.4**   Code to use in **.cfm** templates

```
<CFIF IsUserInRole("User")>
   <!--- Execute User only code --->
<CFELSEIF IsUserInRole("Moderator") OR
   IsUserInRole("Administrator")>
   <!--- Execute alternate Administrator /
Moderator only code --->
</CFIF>
```

That should be all you need to create your apps, but if you want more gory details, I've put some design notes in the file with a little more info about the new log-in mechanism.

Have fun, and let me know if you have any questions.

Thanks,

Adam

To give them an example of what he meant by "design notes" on useful topics, Adam wrote up the following samples:

## How the Log-in System Works

Since so many features of the new *Fantasy Life* site depend on being able to uniquely identify users, each user must have an account, which they use to log in each time they visit the site. All account information is stored in a Users table, in the *Fantasy Life* database.

So when a user first arrives at the site, she is immediately prompted to either create a new account (if she is new) or log in (if she is returning). Until a user has done one of these things, the links to the other sections of the site are not even active (see Figure V-3.1). (Also, I recognize the site is incredibly plain now—but the Fantasy Life graphic artists will take care of that later.)

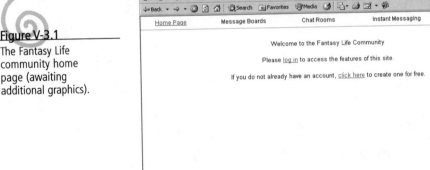

**Figure V-3.1**
The Fantasy Life community home page (awaiting additional graphics).

To create an account, new users must fill out a short form (`signupform.cfm`), which includes information about who they are and how to contact them (see Figure V-3.2). When the form is submitted, the next template (`signupcomplete.cfm`) checks to make sure the two passwords entered match, then (if they do) attempts to create the new account, and finally, verifies that the account was created successfully. If the template encounters an error, either because the passwords do not match, or because account creation failed (which will happen if the requested user name is already in use), the user is sent back to the log-in form and shown an appropriate error message (see Listing V-3.5).

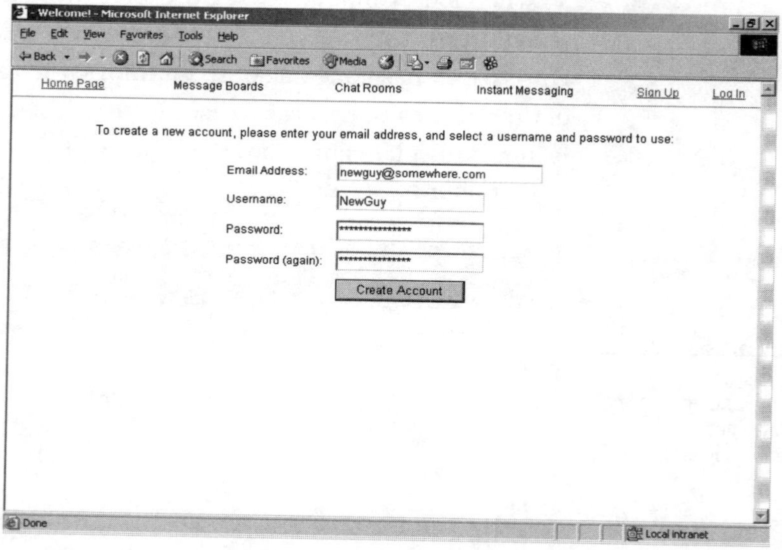

**Figure V-3.2**
The sign up form.

**Listing V-3.5**     Signupcomplete.cfm

```
<!--- Do two passwords entered match? --->
<CFIF FORM.UIPassword NEQ FORM.UIPasswordConfirm>
  <!--- If not, return to sign up form and display error --->
  <CFLOCATION URL="
     signupform.cfm?Message=Passwords%20do%20not%20match%20
     -%20please%20re-
enter&UserEmail=#URLEncodedFormat(FORM.UserEmail)#
  &UIUsername=#
             URLEncodedFormat(FORM.UIUsername)#"
             ADDTOKEN="No">
</CFIF>
```

```
<!--- Attempt to create account --->
<CFINVOKE COMPONENT="include/User"
          METHOD="CreateAccount"
          UIUSERNAME="#FORM.UIUsername#"
          UIPASSWORD="#FORM.UIPassword#"
          USEREMAIL="#FORM.UserEmail#"
          RETURNVARIABLE="CreateAccountSuccess">


<!--- Was account created successfully? --->
<CFIF CreateAccountSuccess>
  <!--- If not, return to sign up form and display error --->
  <CFLOCATION URL="
    signupform.cfm?Message=Username%20already%20in%20use%20-
    %20please%20select%20another&UserEmail=
    #URLEncodedFormat(FORM.UserEmail)#"
            ADDTOKEN="No">
</CFIF>
```

In order to keep all user authentication functions and database access separate, `signupcomplete.cfm` calls the component user.cfc in order to create the account. User.cfc does all the "heavy lifting," which has a nice side effect of keeping the other templates which reference it fairly simple, and easy to read.

The specific function in user.cfc called by `signupcomplete.cfm` is `CreateAccount()`. This fuction first checks the Users table in the database, to make sure the requested username is not already in use, then (if it's not) adds a record to that table, and finally, logs in the user, by calling the `Login` function (which will be explained shortly) (see Listing V-3.6). Depending on whether the account was created successfully, the function returns a 1 or 0.

Listing V-3.6   User.cfc (`CreateAccount()` function)

```
<!--- Create user account --->
<CFFUNCTION NAME="CreateAccount" RETURNTYPE="Boolean"
            OUTPUT="No">
  <CFARGUMENT NAME="UIUsername" REQUIRED="Yes">
  <CFARGUMENT NAME="UIPassword" REQUIRED="Yes">
  <CFARGUMENT NAME="UserEmail" REQUIRED="Yes">
```

**Listing V-3.6**    (continued)

```
<CFARGUMENT NAME="UserType" REQUIRED="No" DEFAULT="User">
  <!--- Search for existing account with the same
         user name --->
  <CFQUERY NAME="CheckForExistingAccount"
    DATASOURCE="#APPLICATION.UIDSN#"
    MAXROWS="1">
    SELECT *
    FROM Users
    WHERE UIUsername='#ARGUMENTS.UIUsername#'
  </CFQUERY>
  <CFIF CheckForExistingAccount.RecordCount>
    <CFRETURN 0>
  <CFELSE>
    <!--- Create new user account --->
    <CFQUERY NAME="AddUser"
              DATASOURCE="#APPLICATION.UIDSN#">
      INSERT INTO Users(Username,
        Password,
        UserEmail,
        UserType)
      VALUES ('#ARGUMENTS.UIUsername#',
        '#ARGUMENTS.UIPassword#',
        '#ARGUMENTS.UserEmail#',
        '#ARGUMENTS.UserType#')
    </CFQUERY>
    <CFSET Login(ARGUMENTS.UIUsername,
                 ARGUMENTS.UIPassword)>
    <CFRETURN 1>
  </CFIF>
</CFFUNCTION>
```

Finally, when the user has successfully created an account, `signupcom-plete.cfm` will welcome the user, and give them access to the other areas of the site (see Figure V-3.3). Notice that all the links on the top of the screen are now active—and that the Log In link in the top right corner has changed to Log Out.

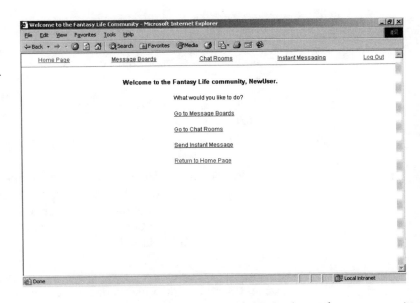

For returning users, the process is even simpler. When a returning user clicks on Log In he goes to an even shorter form (**loginform.cfm**) where he only has to enter a user name and password (see Figure V-3.4). When this form is submitted, the next template (**logincomplete.cfm**) simply attempts to log in, and returns the user to the previous page if the log-in fails (see Listing V-3.7). For security reasons, it is better not to give users too much information about why a log-in fails (descriptive error messages like "account does not exist" and "bad password" offer only a little extra assistance to legitimate users, but can be very helpful for hackers).

**Listing V-3.7**     Logincomplete.cfm

```
<!--- Attempt to log in --->
<CFINVOKE COMPONENT="include/User"
  METHOD="Login"
  UIUSERNAME="#FORM.UIUsername#"
```

Listing V-3.7    (continued)

```
          UIPASSWORD="#FORM.UIPassword#"
          RETURNVARIABLE="LogInSuccess">

<!--- Was login successful? --->
<CFIF NOT LogInSuccess>
  <!--- If not, return to log in page and display error -
-->
  <CFLOCATION URL="loginform.cfm?Message=
                  Unable%20to%20log%20in%20-%20Invalid
                  %20Login&UIUsername=#URLEncodedFormat
                  (FORM.UIUsername)#"
              ADDTOKEN="No">
</CFIF>
```

Again, all the real work, and database access, is accomplished through the user.cfc component, this time by calling the function Login() directly. Login() searches for the user's record in the Users table. If it finds the record, it then logs the user in, using the new CFLOGINUSER function, records the log-in time, and sets some session variables (for message board display, and a few other things). Finally, Login() returns a value to specify if the log-in was successful or not (see Listing V-3.8).

Listing V-3.8    User.cfc (Login() function)

```
<!--- Log in --->
<CFFUNCTION NAME="Login" RETURNTYPE="Boolean"
            OUTPUT="No">
  <CFARGUMENT NAME="UIUsername" REQUIRED="Yes">
  <CFARGUMENT NAME="UIPassword" REQUIRED="Yes">
  <!--- Get user information --->
  <CFQUERY NAME="GetUserInfo"
           DATASOURCE="#APPLICATION.UIDSN#"
           MAXROWS="1">
    SELECT *
    FROM Users
    WHERE UIUsername='#ARGUMENTS.UIUsername#'
      AND UIPassword='#ARGUMENTS.UIPassword#'
  </CFQUERY>
```

```
<!--- Is user authorized? --->
<CFIF GetUserInfo.RecordCount>
  <!--- Is user already loged in? --->
  <CFIF IsLogedIn()>
    <!--- If so, log out user --->
    <CFSET Logout()>
  </CFIF>
  <!--- Log in user --->
  <CFLOGIN>
    <CFLOGINUSER NAME="#ARGUMENTS.UIUsername#"
                 ROLES="#GetUserInfo.UserType#"
                 PASSWORD="#ARGUMENTS.UIPassword#">
  </CFLOGIN>
  <!--- Update user last log in time --->
  <CFQUERY NAME="UpdateLoginTimes"
           DATASOURCE="#APPLICATION.UIDSN#">
    UPDATE Users
    SET Users.UserCurrentLogin=
        #CreateODBCDateTime(Now())#,
      Users.UserLastLogin=Users.UserCurrentLogin
    WHERE UIUsername='#ARGUMENTS.UIUsername#'
      AND UIPassword='#ARGUMENTS.UIPassword#'
  </CFQUERY>
  <!--- Initalize user session variables --->
  <CFSET InitalizeUserVariables(ARGUMENTS.UIUsername)>
  <CFRETURN 1>
<CFELSE>
  <CFRETURN 0>
</CFIF>
</CFFUNCTION>
```

Notice how the CFLOGINUSER tag must be contained within CFLOGIN tags (even if nothing else is). Also notice how this one function is reused, called from both CreateAccount(), when signing up new users, and directly from the logincomplete.cfm template, when returning users log in. Having only a single log-in procedure makes updating the code in the future much simpler, since a single change to Login() will automatically affect both new and returning users, without having to update multiple templates.

## When to Use <CFLOGIN> Vs. When to Use <CFIF>

The new <CFLOGIN> tag is commonly used in Application.cfm templates to display log-in code only to unauthenticated users, and thereby secures all the templates in a directory. Also, since the function GetAuthUser() returns an empty string if the user is not logged in, you can use it in conjunction with a CFIF statement to check if the user is logged in. This makes the following code blocks nearly equivalent (see Listings V-3.9 and V-3.10):

Listing V-3.9    Login.cfc

```
<CFLOGIN>
<!--- Login Stuff --->
</CFLOGIN>
```

Listing V-3.10   Loginform.cfm

```
<CFIF NOT Len(GetAuthUser())>
<!--- Login Stuff --->
</CFIF>
```

The only time you *must* use <CFLOGIN> is when you also use <CFLOGINUSER>, which only works inside a <CFLOGIN> block, as we do in Login.cfc.

The Application.cfm files we use to secure our subdirectories also use <CFLOGIN>, but because they just redirect users to another page (and don't actually log in the users), they could use either method.

The log-in page users are sent to, Loginform.cfm, uses a <CFIF> block instead because it also doesn't use <CFLOGINUSER>, and it does use <CFELSE>, to which <CFLOGIN> has no equivalent.

# Chat Application

After spending the long weekend getting into the right mind-set, Chad attacks the chat application with gusto and has a working version done by the end of the week.

**Chat application**

**Email**

**Date:** March 25

**To:** Development Team

**From:** Chad

**Subject:** Chat application

OK all, I've redesigned this a couple times and I think I've finally got it nailed.

As we discussed before, all chat data is stored in temporary application variables on the server, as an array of structures. That way I can access the data faster, and don't have to worry about database bloat.

The chat section consists of two main parts:

1. All interaction with the structures will happen through a single CFC (**Chat.cfc**), which stays loaded in memory as an object. That component will accept commands sent to it as function calls.

   This modular design simplifies it and makes it easier to upgrade later. Someone could even change the entire data-storage mechanism later, if they had to, and would only have to rewrite a single component.

2. The UI handles all data input and display, and accesses the data by calling the Chat.cfc component.

**Chat application**

**Email (continued)**

The UI consists of two nested framesets, with four
frames. Common commands are listed on the top,
users on the right, and a text box for entering
messages and commands on the bottom. All messages
and other information are displayed by reloading
the main frame in the center.

Chad

Users can list other available chat commands with the /help command
(see Figure V-3.5).

**Figure V-3.5**

Chat interface, showing
available commands.

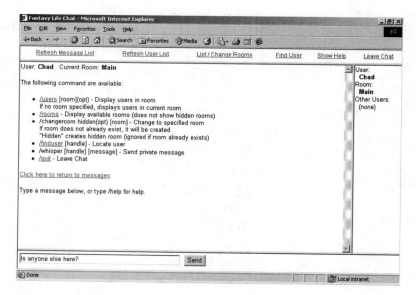

## Chat Component Initialization

Every template that calls the chat component, Chat.cfc, first calls the
template Verifychatlogin.cfm, which verifies the chat component is
loaded, and if it's not, loads it (see Listing V-3.11):

Listing V-3.11    `Verifychatlogin.cfm`

```
<!--- Load chat component --->
<CFOBJECT COMPONENT="Chat" NAME="Application.Chat">
```

The `<CFOBJECT>` tag instantiates the component and only does so once. Once the component is instantiated as an object, it works faster and can retain persistent data.

Originally Chad included the verification code in `Application.cfm`, but that caused it to run every time a page was loaded, whether or not it was needed (and due to the frameset, six pages are loaded, just on startup). So in the interest of speed, he copies it only to the templates that actually call the chat component.

## Chat Rooms

When the chat component is first called, Chat.cfc creates three single-dimension arrays—`Rooms`, `Users`, and `Messages`—and populates the `Rooms` array with a default type of Permanent (see Listing V-3.12).

Listing V-3.12    `Chat.cfc` (`Init()` function)

```
<!--- Define array for rooms --->
<CFSET THIS.Rooms=ArrayNew(1)>
<!--- Define array for users --->
<CFSET THIS.Users=ArrayNew(1)>
<!--- Define array for messaes --->
<CFSET THIS.Messages=ArrayNew(1)>
<!--- Initialize default permanent room --->
<CFSET THIS.Rooms[1]=StructNew()>
<CFSET THIS.Rooms[1].Name=ARGUMENTS.Room>
<CFSET THIS.Rooms[1].Type="Permanent">
```

Note how the new scope `THIS` refers to persistent variables within the chat application.

Later, when a user changes rooms (see Listing V-3.13), if the user moves to a room that does not exist, it is automatically created (see Listing V-3.14), either as Normal, or, if the user so specifies, as Hidden. When a user leaves a room, if that room is empty and not permanent, its element is automatically deleted from the array and it is thus removed (see Figure V-3.6).

Listing V-3.13    Chat.cfc (ChangeRooms() function)

```
<!--- Does new room already exist? --->
<CFIF NOT IsValidRoom(ARGUMENTS.Room)>
  <!--- If not, create new room --->
  <CFIF ARGUMENTS.Hidden>
    <CFSET CreateRoom(Room,"Hidden")>
  <CFELSE>
    <CFSET CreateRoom(Room,"Normal")>
  </CFIF>
</CFIF>
<!--- Get old room ID --->
<CFSET RoomElement=IsValidRoom(OldRoom)>
<!--- Get list of users in old room --->
<CFSET ListUsers=GetUsers(OldRoom)>
<!--- Move user to new room --->
<CFSET THIS.Users[UserElement].Room=Room>
<!--- Send enter room announcement --->
<CFSET AddMessage(4, ARGUMENTS.Handle)>
<!--- Is old room now empty and not permanent? --->
<CFIF ListUsers.RecordCount IS 1
      AND THIS.Rooms[RoomElement].Type NEQ "Permanent"
      AND RoomElement GT 0>
  <!--- If so, remove old room --->
  <CFSET ArrayDeleteAt(THIS.Rooms, RoomElement)>
</CFIF>
```

Listing V-3.14    Chat.cfc (CreateRoom() function)

```
<!--- Add room --->
<CFSET r=IncrementValue(ArrayLen(THIS.Rooms))>
<CFSET THIS.Rooms[r]=StructNew()>
<CFSET THIS.Rooms[r].Name=ARGUMENTS.Room>
<CFSET THIS.Rooms[r].Type=ARGUMENTS.Type>
```

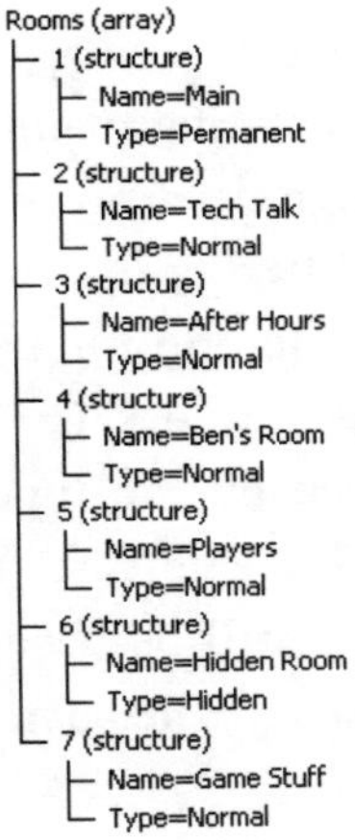

```
Rooms (array)
├─ 1 (structure)
│   ├─ Name=Main
│   └─ Type=Permanent
├─ 2 (structure)
│   ├─ Name=Tech Talk
│   └─ Type=Normal
├─ 3 (structure)
│   ├─ Name=After Hours
│   └─ Type=Normal
├─ 4 (structure)
│   ├─ Name=Ben's Room
│   └─ Type=Normal
├─ 5 (structure)
│   ├─ Name=Players
│   └─ Type=Normal
├─ 6 (structure)
│   ├─ Name=Hidden Room
│   └─ Type=Hidden
└─ 7 (structure)
    ├─ Name=Game Stuff
    └─ Type=Normal
```

Figure V-3.6

This diagram shows an array of structures for chat rooms.

Finally, rather than wandering around blindly, a user must be able to list the available rooms. This is accomplished by the function GetRooms(), which loops through all available rooms and returns a query listing all their names for the user (see Listing V-3.15).

Listing V-3.15    Chat.cfc (GetRooms() function)

```
<!--- Create query --->
<CFSET q=QueryNew("Name,Type")>
<!--- Loop through Rooms array --->
<CFLOOP INDEX="i" FROM="1" TO="#ArrayLen(THIS.Rooms)#">
  <CFIF THIS.Rooms[i].Type NEQ "Hidden"
        OR IsUserInRole("Administrator")>
```

**Listing V-3.15** (continued)

```
        <CFSET QueryAddRow(q)>
        <CFSET QuerySetCell(q, "Name", THIS.Rooms[i].Name)>
        <CFSET QuerySetCell(q, "Type", THIS.Rooms[i].Type)>
      </CFIF>
    </CFLOOP>
    <!--- Return query --->
    <CFRETURN q>
```

Notice how GetRooms() starts by creating an empty query, and then adds rows to the query as it loops through the array of rooms—essentially converting the array to a query and filtering it at the same time. The CFIF statement filters out hidden rooms for most users (except for administrators, who can list all rooms, hidden or not). The entire query containing the list of rooms is then returned by the function. Even though the method of creating this query is a little unusual (since there's no external database involved), the result can still be used exactly like any other query, which makes displaying the returned data very simple.

## Chat Users

After Verifychatlogin.cfm verifies that the chat component is running, it verifies that the user is logged into the chat application and, if not, it logs them in.

Note that logging into the chat application is different than logging into the overall application. Think of chat as an application within an application. To keep things simple, though, users are automatically logged into chat when they go to the chat page, and are automatically logged out of chat when they leave.

When a user is logged into chat, an element is automatically added to the Users array (see Figure V-3.7), with a structure containing the user's Handle (user name), Type (role), time Started, and current Room (see Listing V-3.16).

```
Users (array)
  ├── 1 (structure)
  │     ├── Handle=CA
  │     ├── Room=Main
  │     ├── Started=1:00 pm
  │     └── Type=Administrator
  ├── 2 (structure)
  │     ├── Handle=MA
  │     ├── Room=Players
  │     ├── Started=1:05 pm
  │     └── Type=User
  ├── 3 (structure)
  │     ├── Handle=MB
  │     ├── Room=Hidden Room
  │     ├── Started=1:07 pm
  │     └── Type=User
  ├── 4 (structure)
  │     ├── Handle=IM
  │     ├── Room=Game Room
  │     ├── Started=1:10 pm
  │     └── Type=User
  └── 5 (structure)
        ├── Handle=Corwin
        ├── Room=Main
        ├── Started=1:15 pm
        └── Type=User
```

**Figure V-3.7**

This diagram displays the structures in the Users array.

Listing V-3.16    Chat.cfc (Login() function)

```
<!--- Add to user list --->
<CFSET NextUser=ArrayLen(THIS.Users)+1>
<CFSET THIS.Users[NextUser]=StructNew()>
<CFSET THIS.Users[NextUser].Handle=Handle>
<CFSET THIS.Users[NextUser].Type=Type>
<CFSET THIS.Users[NextUser].Started=Now()>
<CFSET THIS.Users[NextUser].Room=THIS.Rooms[1].Name>
<CFSET THIS.Users[NextUser].LastMessage=
IncrementValue(ArrayLen(THIS.Messages))>
```

As seen earlier, when a user changes rooms, the Users.Room variable is reset to the new room, and when a user logs out of chat, the user's entire array element is deleted (see Listing V-3.17).

Listing V-3.17    Chat.cfc (Logout() function)

```
<!--- Is room now empty and not permanent? --->
<CFIF ListUsers.RecordCount IS 1
AND THIS.Rooms[RoomElement].Type NEQ "Permanent"
AND RoomElement GT 0>
```

Listing V-3.17     (continued)

```
    <!--- If so, remove room --->
    <CFSET ArrayDeleteAt(THIS.Rooms, RoomElement)>
</CFIF>
<!--- Remove user --->
<CFSET ArrayDeleteAt(THIS.Users, UserElement)>
```

When a user searches for another user, the function `FindUser()` checks if the user being sought is logged in, and if so, returns the room that user is in (see Listing V-3.18).

Listing V-3.18     Chat.cfc (FindUser() function)

```
<!--- Get user ID --->
<CFSET UserElement=IsLoggedIn(ARGUMENTS.Handle)>
<!--- Is user logged in? --->
<CFIF UserElement GTE 1>
  <!--- If so, return user's room --->
  <CFRETURN THIS.Users[UserElement].Room>
<CFELSE>
  <!--- If not, return error message --->
  <CFRETURN "Not Logged In">
</CFIF>
```

One interesting thing about `FindUser()` is the way it uses `IsLoggedIn()` (see Listing V-3.19). The function `IsLoggedIn()` actually serves two distinct purposes. The first, as suggested by its name, is to determine if a user is logged in to chat. `IsLoggedIn()` does this by returning zero if the user does not exist in the array of users, and a non-zero value if the user does exist. This means the function can be used as a Boolean condition, to verify that a user is logged in (as the CFIF statement in the `FindUser()` function does). The second purpose of `IsLoggedIn()` is that for users who are logged in, the function returns that user's location in the array of users. This is very useful for finding out additional information about the user (as the first CFRETURN statement in `FindUser()` does).

**Listing V-3.19**    `Chat.cfc` (`IsLoggedIn()` function)

```
<!--- Set default to not logged in --->
<CFSET LoggedIn=0>
<!--- Loop through Users array --->
<CFLOOP INDEX="i" FROM="1" TO="#ArrayLen(THIS.Users)#">
  <CFIF THIS.Users[i].Handle IS ARGUMENTS.Handle>
    <!--- Set ID of user in array --->
    <CFSET LoggedIn=i>
    <CFBREAK>
  </CFIF>
</CFLOOP>
<CFRETURN LoggedIn>
```

## Posting Chat Messages

When a user posts a normal message, the template `postmessagecom-plete.cfm` calls the function `SendMessage()` and passes it parameters for message `Type`, `Sender` (user name), `Room`, time `Sent`, and the `Message` itself. (See Table V-3.1 for a list of legal message types.) `SendMessage()` also accepts a parameter for `To`, but in the case of a normal message, it is an empty string (see Listing V-3.20):

**Listing V-3.20**    `Chat.cfc` (`SendMessage()` function)

```
<CFARGUMENT NAME="To" REQUIRED="No" DEFAULT="">
...
<!--- Is recipient specified? --->
<CFIF Len(Trim(ARGUMENTS.To))>
  <!--- If so, send private message (whisper) --->
  <CFSET AddMessage(6, Handle, To, Message)>
<CFELSE>
  <!--- If not, send public message --->
  <CFSET AddMessage(5, Handle, To, Message)>
</CFIF>
```

| Table V-3.1 | Legal Messages |
| --- | --- |
| Message Type | Description |
| Log-in system notice | Announces when a user logs in to chat. |
| Log-out system notice | Announces when a user logs out of chat. |
| Leave Room system notice | Announces when a user enters a room. |
| Enter Room system notice | Announces when a user leaves a room. |
| Public message | A message which is visible to everyone in a room. |
| Private message (whisper) | A message which is visible only to sender and recipient. |

SendMessage() then calls AddMessage(), which adds an element to the Messages array, with a structure containing the all the parameters previously passed to SendMessage() (see Listing V-3.21):

Listing V-3.21    Chat.cfc (AddMessage() function)

```
<!--- Get user element --->
<CFSET UserElement=IsLoggedIn(Handle)>
<!--- Add message --->
<CFSET NextMsg=ArrayLen(THIS.Messages)+1>
<CFSET THIS.Messages[NextMsg]=StructNew()>
<CFSET THIS.Messages[NextMsg].Type=ARGUMENTS.Type>
<CFSET THIS.Messages[NextMsg].Sender=ARGUMENTS.Handle>
<CFSET THIS.Messages[NextMsg].To=ARGUMENTS.To>
<CFSET THIS.Messages[NextMsg].Room=
THIS.Users[UserElement].Room>
<CFSET THIS.Messages[NextMsg].Sent=Now()>
<CFSET THIS.Messages[NextMsg].Message=ARGUMENTS.Message>
```

Again, the function IsLoggedIn() retrieves the number of the user's element in the Users array. That number is then used when setting the Room variable to set it to the user's current room.

In addition to sending regular messages, which everyone in a particular room can read, users also need the ability to send private messages, which can only be read by a single other user. This is done using "whispers," which are sent to another individual user, rather than the entire room. Also, as a side effect of sending the message user-to-user, rather than user-to-room, users can send and receive whispers, even if they are not in the same room.

When a user "whispers" to another user, the exact same method is used as when sending a regular message, with one small difference: The To user is specified. So in terms of storage, whispers are almost identical to normal messages (see Figure V-3.8). The real difference is in how they are displayed (see Figure V-3.9).

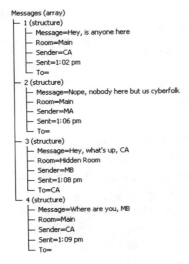

**Figure V-3.8**
Here's a diagram of the structures in a Messages array.

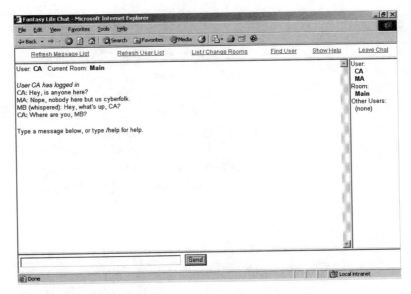

**Figure V-3.9**
The chat interface shows the conversation from Figure V-3.8.

## Reading Chat Messages

By default, when a user is in a chat room, all the current messages in that room are repeatedly refreshed, automatically displaying new messages as they are posted. The function GetMessage() does this, by looping through the Messages array and creating a query containing all public messages in the current room as well as private messages to or from the current user (see Listing V-3.22).

Listing V-3.22    Chat.cfc (GetMessages() function)

```
<!--- Create query --->
<CFSET q=QueryNew("Type,From,To,Time,Message,Whisper")>
...
<!--- Loop through Messages array --->
<CFLOOP INDEX="i" FROM="#StartFrom#"
        TO="#ArrayLen(THIS.Messages)#">
  <CFIF (THIS.Messages[i].Room IS
          THIS.Users[UserElement].Room
    AND (THIS.Messages[i].Sender IS Handle
      OR THIS.Messages[i].Type IS "5"))
     OR THIS.Messages[i].To IS Handle>
    <CFSET QueryAddRow(q)>
    <CFSET QuerySetCell(q, "Type",
            THIS.Messages[i].Type)>
    <CFSET QuerySetCell(q, "From",
            THIS.Messages[i].Sender)>
    <CFSET QuerySetCell(q, "To", THIS.Messages[i].To)>
    <CFSET QuerySetCell(q, "Time",
            THIS.Messages[i].Sent)>
    <CFSET QuerySetCell(q, "Message",
            THIS.Messages[i].Message)>
  </CFIF>
</CFLOOP>
```

Notice how again, GetMessages() creates an empty query, then populates it as it loops through the array of messages, this time with much more complex filtering criteria. Specifically, the CFIF statement means (in English) that the query should list all messages in the user's current room which were sent by the user, or are public, and in addition should list all private messages for that user, regardless of where they were sent from. This is the same basic structure used before in GetRooms(), just with additional fields and additional filter criteria.

Also, it is here, in the message retrieval function, where we start to appreciate the power of storing all the data in arrays of structures, instead of a regular database. Since speed is so critical in chat, this storage method enables ColdFusion to keep all the data in memory and access it any time, without the intermediate step of having to read write to an external database.

## The User Interface (UI)

Since so much work is done by the chat engine, creating the UI is actually fairly simple. A frameset divides the screen into four panes, displaying command links, users, a simple message input form, a large pane to display the results of commands, and the chat messages themselves. When a message is entered, or a command is selected, the results are sent to the main pane (chatpanemain.cfm) to display. If the main pane needs to do something other than display messages, a parameter Command is sent, telling it what to do.

When the main pane is displaying messages, it automatically refreshes itself every 8 seconds, so as to automatically display any new messages, and also adds a bit of JavaScript to the BODY tag, to automatically scroll down to the bottom of the page (see Listing V-3.23). When not displaying messages, the pane does not refresh, so as not to put unnecessary load on the server, and eliminates the JavaScript.

Listing V-3.23    Chatpanemain.cfm

```
<CFPARAM NAME="Command" DEFAULT="Display Messages">
...
<!--- Check if displaying messages --->
<CFIF Command IS "Display Messages">
  <!--- If so, repeatedly refresh page --->
  <META HTTP-EQUIV="Refresh" CONTENT="8">
</CFIF>

...
<CFIF Command IS "Display Messages">
```

**Listing V-3.23**   (continued)

```
<!--- If displaying messages, use JavaScript to scroll
      page to bottom --->
<BODY BGCOLOR="#FFFFFF" TEXT="#000000" LINK="#0000FF"
      VLINK="#CC0000"
      ALINK="#CC0000" LEFTMARGIN="2" TOPMARGIN="2"
      MARGINHEIGHT="2"
      MARGINWIDTH="2" onLoad="scrollTo(4000,4000)">
<CFELSE>
  <!--- If displaying command, don't use JavaScript --->
  <BODY BGCOLOR="#FFFFFF" TEXT="#000000" LINK="#0000FF"
        VLINK="#CC0000"
        ALINK="#CC0000" LEFTMARGIN="2" TOPMARGIN="2"
        MARGINHEIGHT="2"
        MARGINWIDTH="2">
</CFIF>
```

Chatpanemain.cfm also handles formatting and display, to make sure
chats are easy to read. Just as chat.cfc contains all commands to control
and retrieve chat data, **chatpanemain.cfm** contains all formatting information for chats and commands, which helps make the application easier to maintain. It does this with a **CFSWITCH** structure, which displays
the apropriate output, based on the value of the **Command** variable, and
takes up most of the template. In the default case, when **Command** is
"Display Messages," the template invokes **GetMessages()** from the chat
component, then uses a **CFOUTPUT** to display the results of the returned
query, and a second **CFSWITCH** structure to correctly display each message, based on its type (see Listing V-3.24).

**Listing V-3.24**   Chatpanemain.cfm (Command="Display Messages")

```
<!--- Get messages --->
<CFINVOKE COMPONENT="#APPLICATION.Chat#"
          METHOD="GetMessages"
          Handle="#GetAuthUser()#"
          RETURNVARIABLE="ListMessages">
<!--- Display messages --->
<CFOUTPUT QUERY="ListMessages">
  <CFSET FontColor=Iif(From IS GetAuthUser(),
```

```
                                "'####FF0000'","'####000000'")>
    <CFSWITCH EXPRESSION="#Type#">
      ...
      <CFCASE VALUE="5">
        <STRONG>
        <FONT COLOR="#FontColor#">#From#:</FONT>
        </STRONG>
        #Message#<BR>
      </CFCASE>
      <CFCASE VALUE="6">
        <STRONG><FONT COLOR="#FontColor#">#From#
        (whispered<CFIF To NEQ GetAuthUser()> to
         #To#</CFIF>):
        </FONT></STRONG> #Message#<BR>
      </CFCASE>
    </CFSWITCH>
  </CFOUTPUT><P>
```

When messages or commands are entered, they are posted to chatac-
tion.cfm, which invokes the chat component to perform the necessary
action (if any) and then uses a CFLOCATION tag to refresh chatpane-
main.cfm, which again invokes the chat component, to display the
results (see Listing V-3.25).

Listing V-3.25    Chatpanemain.cfm (Command="ListRooms")

```
<CFCASE VALUE="ListRooms">
  <!--- Get room list --->
  <CFINVOKE COMPONENT="#APPLICATION.Chat#"
            METHOD="GetRooms"
            RETURNVARIABLE="Rooms">
  <!--- Display rooms --->
  The following rooms are available:<BR>
  (Click on a name to switch to that room)
  <UL>
  <CFOUTPUT QUERY="Rooms">
    <LI><A HREF="ChatAction.cfm?Message=#URLEncodedFormat
                ("/changeroom "&Name)#&RefreshPage=
                ChatInnerFrame.cfm"
```

Listing V-3.25    (continued)

```
        TARGET="ChatInnerFrame">#Name#</A>
    </CFOUTPUT>
    </UL><P>
    <A HREF="ChatPaneMain.cfm">Click here to return to
        messages</A><P>
    </CFCASE>
```

Notice how when `chatpanemain.cfm` lists the available rooms, it automatically creates links, which the user can click on to automatically invoke the `/changeroom` command for that room (see Figure V-3.10).

**Figure V-3.10**
The results of the
`/rooms` command.

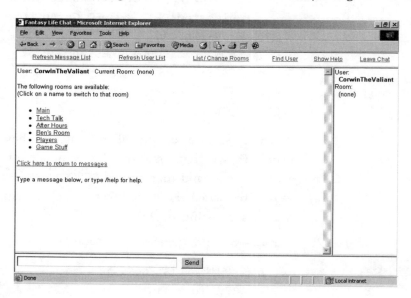

# Message Boards

## Basic Design

Message board applications are deceptively simple. The most basic form of a message board is the old-fashioned guest book, in which users post messages, which are stored in a database, and users read a list of messages posted by other users. More complicated message boards use almost exactly the same basic posting and reading structure; the only significant difference is in how the messages are organized so the board can handle a large number of messages while making it relatively easy for users to find the messages they're interested in.

*Fantasy Life's* existing message board has been working well for about two years. However, since the application was originally written for Cold-Fusion 4.5, Mina improves its organization and programming in several ways, taking advantage of the new abilities of ColdFusion MX. The original site consisted of 25 different templates, which handled both UI and all commands for accessing the database.

Inspired partially by Chad's approach to the chat room, Mina decides to move all commands and access to the database into a single component, Messageboard.cfc. Utilizing a component enables her to consolidate all database commands into one place, which saves development time and will make porting the existing data much easier. In addition, Mina also combines similar queries into single functions, which she then can then call from different templates, with different parameters. This makes the individual templates much more readable, and by reusing code whenever possible, also makes the entire application more efficient, and smaller.

Finally, Mina uses the new Code Compatibility Analyzer (CCA) to find obsolete tags and any other compatibility issues.

### Data Storage

Unlike the unique storage method used by chat, data storage for the message board is much more traditional, consisting of a database, attached as an external datasource. This method makes the most sense here, both because messages need to be kept for a longer period of time, and because the database will undoubtedly grow fairly large, with much of the older data accessed very rarely. Even the newer data will be written to and read from much less frequently than in chat.

For such a complex application, the table structure is remarkably simple though, consisting of only three tables: Boards, Messages, and Users (see Figure V-3.11). Note that this is the same Users table used during log-in and for instant messaging, so not all the fields are used by the message board.

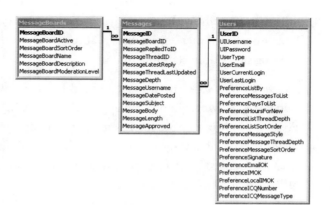

## Organizing Messages by Board

First, the message boards organize messages by subject matter. In this message board, each subject is a different "board" and is listed on the first page users see when they enter Message Boards, `Boardlist.cfm` (see Figure V-3.12). Individual boards can be created or removed only by administrators.

### Message Boards

| Board Name | Messages | Latest | New? |
|---|---|---|---|
| General | 1 | 4-24-02 | 2:54 PM |
| Comments | 6 | 4-25-02 | 2:06 PM |
| Ultimate Fantasy Lawsuit | 1 | 3-13-02 | 3:25 PM |

## Threading Related Messages

Within each board, messages are further organized into threads, which keep track of which messages reply to earlier messages. Unlike boards, though, all thread information is stored with individual messages. This makes it much easier to use or ignore thread information, either within a board or within a single thread.

Threads aren't message containers, the way boards are, but are more of a special way to sort messages. Users automatically create new threads every time they post a new message. When users reply to messages, the replies are automatically added to the existing thread. Sorting a message list by thread organizes it into a tree structure (similar to a directory tree), with replies and replies-to-replies listed under their parent messages (see Figure V-3.13).

Figure V-3.13
Messagelist.cfm
shows a threaded
discussion.

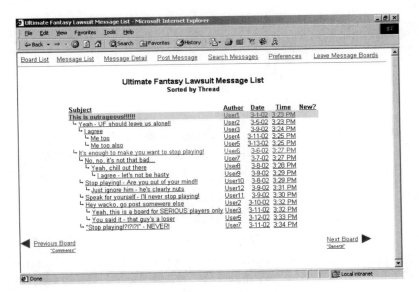

Sorting messages this way requires creating a tree structure with unlimited nesting, sometimes referred to as a "tree sort." This is done by using two fields, one of which contains the ID of the item itself, and another that contains the ID of the parent item (if there is one). A simple example of this type of sort is shown in Figure V-3.14.

Figure V-3.14
A simple example of a
tree sort, which provides
unlimited nesting.

```
Original List

ItemID  ParentID  Location
101     0         Earth
102     101       North America
103     102       United States
104     101       Europe
105     102       Canada
106     103       California
107     104       Germany
108     104       France
109     107       Berlin
110     109       Paris
111     106       Berkley
112     103       North Carolina
113     106       Los Angeles
114     112       Chapel Hill
```

```
Sorted List

ItemID  ParentID  Location
101     0         Earth
102     101       North America
103     102       United States
106     103       California
111     106       Berkley
113     106       Los Angeles
112     103       North Carolina
114     112       Chapel Hill
105     102       Canada
104     101       Europe
107     104       Germany
109     107       Berlin
108     104       France
110     109       Paris
```

```
Tree

Earth
├─North America
│ └─United States
│   ├─California
│   │ ├─Berkley
│   │ └─Los Angeles
│   └─North Carolina
│     └─Chapel Hill
├─Canada
└─Europe
  ├─Germany
  │ └─Berlin
  └─France
    └─Paris
```

In the case of the message board, the fields `MessageID` and `MessageRepliedToID` serve the roles of `ItemID` and `ParentItemID`. The sort itself is done by a custom tag called `CFX_Make_Tree` (see Listing V-3.26).

Listing V-3.26        `Messageboard.cfc` (`ListMessages()` function)

```
<CFQUERY NAME="ListMessages"
         DATASOURCE="UserInteraction">
...
</CFQUERY>
...
<CFIF SortOrder IS "Thread"
  AND ListMessages.RecordCount GT 1
  AND ThreadDepth NEQ "Original Only">
  <CFX_MAKE_TREE QUERY="ListMessages">
</CFIF>
<CFRETURN ListMessages>
```

Notice how the ListMessages query is executed first, and then `CFX_Make_Tree` is executed second, to reorder the records within the existing query. As long as the first query filters the records correctly, `CFX_Make_Tree` does all the complicated work of recursively traversing the tree and organizing the records into the correct order. (A side effect of doing a tree sort this way is that the sort order of the original query is irrelevant, since it will be changed anyway.) Finally, the entire correctly ordered ListMessages query is returned as the result of the `ListMessages()` function.

Users are not restricted to listing messages by thread though, and can also list them by subject, author, or date.

### Listing Messages

After the user selects a message board, `Messagelist.cfm` lists all recent messages posted to that board. It does this by calling the function `ListMessages()` from the message board component to query the database, and by using session variables to keep track of the user's preferences for which messages to display, and how to display them.

The most important function in the entire message board application is `ListMessages()`, which is very simple in principle—all it does is list messages by returning a query—but much more complex in practice. `ListMessages()` accepts eight possible arguments, but they are all optional and never used all at once (see Table V-3.2).

| Table V-3.2 | ListMessages() Arguments |
|---|---|
| **Argument Name** | **Explanation** |
| `BoardID` | ID of single board to return (use 0 for all boards) |
| `ThreadID` | ID of single thread to return |
| `MessageID` | ID of single message to return (can be used by itself) |
| `ThreadDepth` | How much of a thread to return |
| `SortOrder` | How to sort returned messages |
| `DateFrom` | Return messages after this date |
| `MaxMessages` | Maximum number of messages to return |
| `IncludeBody` | Specifies if message body fields should be returned with the query (Boolean) |

To view recent messages on a board, `Messagelist.cfm` invokes `ListMessages()`, passing it the user's preferences, which are stored in session variables (see Listing V-3.27):

Listing V-3.27    `Messagelist.cfm`

```
<!--- List recent messages, by date --->
<CFINVOKE COMPONENT="include/MessageBoard"
          METHOD="ListMessages"
          BOARDID="#SESSION.UserPrefs.CurrentBoard#"
          THREADDEPTH="#SESSION.UserPrefs.
          ListThreadDepth#"
          SORTORDER="#CurrentSortOrder#"
          DATEFROM="#CreateODBCDate(SESSION.
          UserPrefs.StartDate)#"
          RETURNVARIABLE="ListMessages">
```

Notice that if the display needs to be threaded, "Thread" is passed just like any other sort order, and `ListMessages()` takes care of the rest.

`Messagelist.cfm` also displays the messages in a table, which is fairly straightforward when the list is non-threaded. When displaying a threaded list, however, `Messagelist.cfm` must adjust the display of each row, to bold the first message of each thread and indent each reply appropriately. It does this by calculating the necessary depth as a variable, `CurrentLevel`, and then using that variable to stretch a clear single-pixel .gif to create a spacer which will indent the message the appropriate amount (see Listing V-3.28).

Listing V-3.28        `Messagelist.cfm`

```
<TD ALIGN="left" BGCOLOR="#BGColor#">
<CFIF CurrentLevel IS 1>
   <STRONG><A HREF="messagedetail.cfm?MessageID=
                    #MessageIDLink#">
     #MessageSubject#</A></STRONG>
<CFELSE>
   <IMG SRC="../images/pixel.gif"
       WIDTH="#Evaluate((CurrentLevel-2)*13)#"
     HEIGHT="1" BORDER="0">
   <IMG SRC="../images/ReplyArrow.gif" WIDTH="11"
       HEIGHT="13" BORDER="0">
   <A HREF="messagedetail.cfm?MessageID=#MessageIDLink#">
          #MessageSubject#</A>
</CFIF>
</TD>
```

### Expiring Old Messages

Allowing messages to expire after a certain period of time is a critical feature for making a message board usable, since it's the only way to let users continue posting new messages without quickly overwhelming the board with a plethora of messages that users must wade through. This message board hides expired messages instead of deleting them. This gives users much more control, because they can set their own duration for how long messages stay on the boards before expiring. (A user on a fast connection, for example, might set a longer expiration time so he can see a longer list of messages; while a user on a slower connection would set a shorter time so as to get a shorter list, with just the most recent messages). Also, saving old messages lets users search for specific messages, regardless of how old they are.

One of the disadvantages of threads is that as they get longer—as replies are added over a period of time—they can get harder to manage and can even break apart into separate threads when parent messages get old and expire. And, unfortunately, a side effect of expiring old messages from a thread is that each of the replies whose parents have expired becomes the root of its own new thread, which can be confusing (see Figure V-3.15).

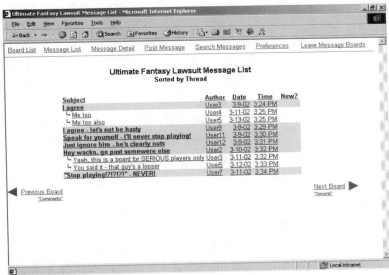

**Figure V-3.15**
The Recent Only message list in `Messagelist.cfm` has fragmented threads as a result of expired parents.

Mina deals with this problem by giving users a Thread Depth preference setting, which users can set through the message board preference page (see Figure V-3.16), which lets them set how threads are kept together, or not, on either the Message List page or the Message Detail page. The three basic settings for Thread Depth are Entire Thread, Recent Only, and Original and Recent. A fourth setting, Original Only, is available only on the Message List page.

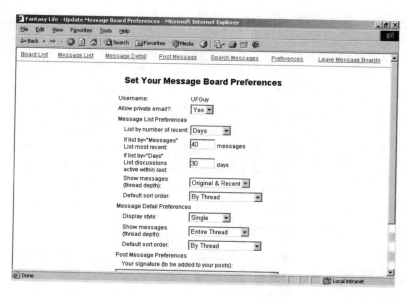

**Figure V-3.16**

The Message Board
Preference page
(`updatepreferences
.cfm`), where users can
customize the message
board display.

The Entire Thread setting shows every message from a thread (even messages that are older than the user's expiration date), as long as there is at least one reply that hasn't yet expired, as in Figure V-3.13. This method has two problems, though. First, threads can get quite long, listing lots of old messages that a user has already read or doesn't care about. Also, when the last message in a thread expires, the entire thread disappears all at once. If someone posts a new reply after a thread has expired, that entire thread reappears, which some users find confusing.

The Recent Only setting allows only old messages to expire from a thread, while still showing new messages. This is less jolting for users, since old messages never reappear. But single threads can break apart, as in Figure V-3.15, causing a different type of confusion.

The Original and Recent setting attempts to compromise between the first two methods by enabling reply messages to expire, while keeping the original message that started the thread (see Figure V-3.17). This still makes the list of messages shorter but keeps all replies together by reconnecting any message whose parent has expired to the original parent message. This is the default for the Message List.

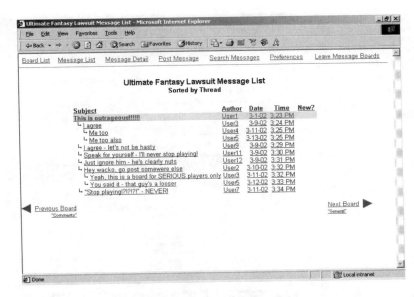

The Original Only setting creates the most compact list, since it hides the entire thread and shows just the subject of the original message. This isn't very interesting by itself but is useful on the Message List page when combined with another method on the Message Detail page.

### Reading Messages

When a user selects a message to read, they can choose to read a single message at a time (see Figure V-3.18) or read a guest book–style list of messages from the same thread (see Figure V-3.19). Users can change this any time they like, by updating the "display style" in their preferences (see Figure V-3.16).

When the user selects to view a single message, Messagedetail.cfm sets the ID of that message as a session variable and invokes ListMessages() twice, first to display the entire message, then again to list the other messages in the same thread (see Listing V-3.29).

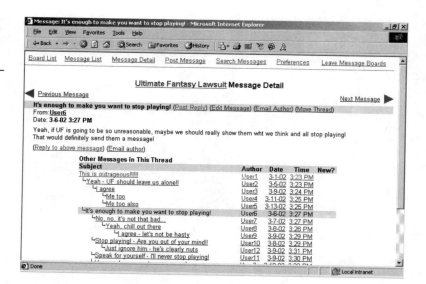

**Figure V-3.18**

`Messagedetail.cfm`
shows how users can
read a single message
at a time.

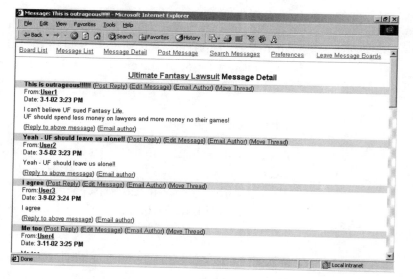

**Figure V-3.19**

Here,
`Messagedetail.cfm`
shows a guest book–style
message list from one
thread.

Listing V-3.29    `Messagedetail.cfm`

```
<CFIF CurrentMessageStyle IS "Single">
<!--- Get message --->
<CFINVOKE COMPONENT="include/MessageBoard"
        METHOD="ListMessages"
```

```
                    MESSAGEID="#SESSION.UserPrefs.CurrentMessage#"
                    INCLUDEBODY="1"
                    RETURNVARIABLE="ListMessages">
<!--- List thread --->
<CFINVOKE COMPONENT="include/MessageBoard"
          METHOD="ListMessages"
          THREADID="#ListMessages.MessageThreadID#"
          THREADDEPTH="#SESSION.UserPrefs.
          MessageThreadDepth#"
          RETURNVARIABLE="ListThread">
```

Note how the first invocation of ListMessages() uses the argument
INCLUDEBODY="1" to tell the function to return the entire message body.
Also, the first function references the MessageID from the session variable, and the second function references the ThreadID returned from the
first function.

Alternately, if the user sets preferences to viewing messages in guest book
style, Messagedetail.cfm uses ListMessages() to get the ThreadID,
and then again to list every message in the thread (see Listing V-3.30).

Listing V-3.30    Messagedetail.cfm

```
<CFELSEIF CurrentMessageStyle IS "Guestbook">
<!--- Get thread ID --->
<CFINVOKE COMPONENT="include/MessageBoard"
          METHOD="ListMessages"
          MESSAGEID="#SESSION.UserPrefs.CurrentMessage#"
          RETURNVARIABLE="GetThreadID">
<!--- List messages --->
<CFINVOKE COMPONENT="include/MessageBoard"
          METHOD="ListMessages"
          THREADID="#GetThreadID.MessageThreadID#"
          THREADDEPTH="#SESSION.UserPrefs.
          MessageThreadDepth#"
          INCLUDEBODY="1"
          RETURNVARIABLE="ListMessages">

</CFIF>
```

The structure is very similar to that for listing a single message, but here the RETURNVARIABLE name of the second function is ListMessages and uses INCLUDEBODY="1". By returning the same query name, one set of code can later format and display the messages, regardless of what the user's preferences are.

By combining different settings for thread depth, sort order, and display style on the list and detail pages, it is possible to make the message board act drastically differently for different users.

In practice, many users won't understand (or care) what thread depth is, and most new users will just accept the default. But offering users the option to change these settings is very helpful for those who have used other Web-based message boards and may complain if this board doesn't act like the other boards they have used. Since other boards act in many other ways, it's impossible to make one set of default preferences that everyone likes, but by offering enough preferences, it's possible to let most users change the boards to their liking.

Two configurations are very popular on other boards:

1. List topic names on one page; topic names link to the full text of all messages in that topic. This is the equivalent of setting the Message List to Original Only and the Message Detail to Entire Thread and Guestbook.

2. List all recent messages (threaded or not) on one page; messages link to individual message bodies. This is the equivalent of setting the Message List to Recent Only (or Original and Recent, to keep threads together) and setting the Message Detail to the same, and as Single.

### Posting Messages

When a user posts a message, if she is replying to a previous message, her new message is automatically added to the current thread by setting the new message's MessageRepliedToID to the MessageID of the previous message, and by setting the message's ThreadID to the same as the previous message.

Also, several redundant fields are created or updated, including MessageThreadID, MessageLatestReply, MessageThreadLastUpdated,

MessageDepth, and MessageLength. These fields all contain information that could be calculated for each query, but storing it increases the database size only slightly and seriously reduces the calculations needed to list and read messages.

### Administrative Functions

In a perfect world (the kind computer programmers often like to think they live in), no one would make mistakes, post anything inappropriate, or need to take back anything they posted. But in the real world these things happen, so having functions to deal with them are very important to keeping a message board running smoothly. Messageboard.cfc includes two functions for administration, UpdateMessage() and DeleteMessage(). Neither function is restricted by role in the CFC, so that users can administer their own messages if no one has replied to them yet. Administrators can use either of these functions anytime.

# Instant Messaging

After much investigating, Ivan decides that the only instant messaging (IM) features he can complete by the deadline are sending instant messages to ICQ and sending/receiving local instant messages. He puts everything else on a future-upgrade wish list and crosses his fingers that the big IM players—America Online, ICQ, Microsoft, and Yahoo—will agree on a common IM standard soon, though he doesn't hold his breath.

To organize his code, he creates a separate component for each type of message, and a single interface, to access all the components. That way, it should be easy to add support for additional IM networks in the future.

### Sending Instant Messages to ICQ

Unlike the other three major IM clients, which make sending to their networks as difficult as possible, ICQ offers not one, but two simple ways to send messages to anyone with an ICQ number. To determine which to use, Ivan tests both.

The first method is to send WWWPage messages, which is usually used for adding a simple "Send me an ICQ message!" form on a user's home page. The form just uses specifically named fields, which are then posted to a server at icq.com, which then sends the message. Within ColdFusion, it's very easy to bypass the form and just contact the icq.com server directly using a CFHTTP tag (see Listing V-3.31).

Listing V-3.31    Sendicq.cfc

```
<!--- Send WWWPage Message --->
<CFHTTP URL="http://wwp.icq.com/scripts/WWPMsg.dll"
        METHOD="POST" RESOLVEURL="false">
  <CFHTTPPARAM TYPE="FORMFIELD" NAME="from"
               VALUE="#FromName#">
  <CFHTTPPARAM TYPE="FORMFIELD" NAME="fromemail"
               VALUE="#FromEmail#">
  <CFHTTPPARAM TYPE="FORMFIELD" NAME="subject"
               VALUE="#MessageSubject#">
  <CFHTTPPARAM TYPE="FORMFIELD" NAME="body"
               VALUE="#MessageBody#">
  <CFHTTPPARAM TYPE="FORMFIELD" NAME="to"
               VALUE="#ToICQNumber#">
</CFHTTP>
```

Alternately, ICQ accepts Email Express messages, which are just email messages sent to a special email address (again, at icq.com) that are redirected and sent to the ICQ user. Again, ColdFusion can send these messages using a CFMAIL tag (see Listing V-3.32).

Listing V-3.32    Sendicq.cfc

```
<!--- Send Email Express Message --->
<CFMAIL FROM="#FromEmail#"
        TO="#ToICQNumber#@pager.icq.com"
        SUBJECT="#MessageSubject#">
#MessageBody#
</CFMAIL>
```

After evaluating both methods, Ivan finds that they both work reasonably well. He also finds that ICQ lets users selectively disable services like EmailExpress and WWWPage. Indeed, many users do this in order to reduce the amount of ICQ spam they receive. Ivan is a bit annoyed that he can't easily send a regular ICQ message, but he also understands the benefit of helping users protect themselves from spam. (Ironically, the openness of WWWPage and Email Express contributes quite a bit to the additional spam ICQ users receive.) Since an ICQ user might have either method disabled, Ivan decides to implement both methods and allow the users to choose one when they enter their ICQ number.

### Sending and Receiving Local Instant Messages

The whole idea of "local" instant messages is a bit odd, and at first the rest of the team can't picture exactly what Ivan has in mind. He builds a prototype to show them what he means.

Like chat messages, local instant messages are stored in an array of structures in an instantiated component on the server, Instantmessage.cfc. So sending a local IM is handled very much like sending a chat message (see Listing V-3.33). The biggest difference is in the UI (see Figure V-3.20).

Listing V-3.33    `Instantmessage.cfc` (SendMessage() function)

```
<CFSWITCH EXPRESSION="#IMService#">
<!--- Send local IM --->
<CFCASE VALUE="Local">
  <!--- Check if local IM message storage initialized --->
  <CFIF NOT IsDefined("THIS.InstantMessages")>
    <!--- If not, define IM message array --->
    <CFSET THIS.InstantMessages=ArrayNew(1)>
  </CFIF>
  <!--- Add message --->
```

Listing V-3.33    (continued)

```
<CFSET NextMsg=ArrayLen(THIS.InstantMessages)+1>
<CFSET THIS.InstantMessages[NextMsg]=StructNew()>
<CFSET THIS.InstantMessages[NextMsg].
        From=SendFromUsername>
<CFSET THIS.InstantMessages[NextMsg].To=SendToUsername>
<CFSET THIS.InstantMessages[NextMsg].Time=Now()>
<CFSET THIS.InstantMessages[NextMsg].
        Message=MessageBody>
</CFCASE>
```

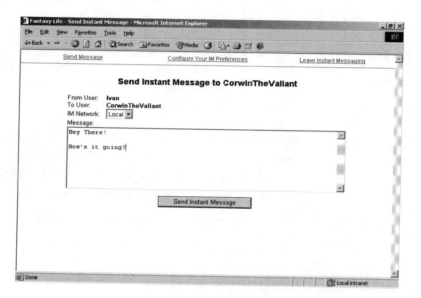

**Figure V-3.20**
The form for sending
an instant message,
**sendim.cfm**.

This is how a user receives a local IM: Every time a user loads a new page
on the site, a component (**Displayinstantmessages.cfm**) is called from
**Application.cfm** and checks to see if the user has any new messages. If
not (which will be most of the time), the component does nothing. When
the user does have a message, the component inserts JavaScript code into
the page the user is viewing, to pop up a small window with the message
(see Figure V-3.21).

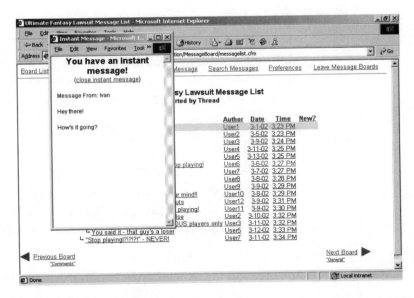

This method has a few small problems, primarily with pop-up–blocking tools. But since many pop-up blockers let users specify sites from which it is OK to accept pop-ups, Ivan doesn't consider this a serious problem. However, it does mean he will need to add a reminder to the sign-up form to tell people to set their pop-up blockers to accept pop-ups from the *Fantasy Life* site. Also, some people *hate* pop-up windows—which is the reason pop-up blockers exist in the first place. But Ivan figures most people won't mind pop-ups with personal messages for them (as opposed to ads, which are nearly always unwanted). For those who don't want any pop-ups, or for those who have all pop-ups blocked and can't selectively unblock certain domains, Ivan adds an option for users to specify if they don't want to receive local IMs.

The code for displaying the messages is very simple; the JavaScript is only one line long. But there is one small catch: the JavaScript is in a component (Displayinstantmessages.cfc), but the path to the page displayed by the JavaScript must be specified relative to the page *calling* the component, not the component itself. And since calling pages are in several different locations, the path must be dynamic. Ivan considers calculating the relative path each time the component is called, but decides that's too slow, and not necessary. Instead, he specifies the relative path as a parameter in each template which invokes the component. And since the value is fixed within each calling template, he just hard-codes the parameter, like so (see Listing V-3.34):

Listing V-3.34    Application.cfm

```
<!--- Check for and display instant messages --->
<CFMODULE TEMPLATE="InstantMessaging/include/
                    displayinstantmessages.cfm"
          RELATIVEPATH="InstantMessaging/">
```

To keep things straight, each directory in the site requires a separate Application.cfm with its own relative path, but by just copying the first Application.cfm to each directory and then modifying the path, it's no big deal to set up.

Here's the code with the JavaScript that actually displays the message (see Listing V-3.35):

Listing V-3.35    Displayinstantmessages.cfm

```
<!--- Check for Local Instant Messages --->
<CFINVOKE COMPONENT="#APPLICATION.InstantMessage#"
          METHOD="CheckLocalMessages"
          RETURNVARIABLE="ListMessages"
          UsernameToCheck="#GetAuthUser()#">
<!--- If Local Instant Messages found, display them --->
<!--- Note: The JavaScript path is called from the
      client, and is relative to the location of the
      PARENT template (the template which includes this
      one) --->
<CFOUTPUT QUERY="ListMessages">
  <SCRIPT language=JavaScript>
  <!--
  window.open('#Attributes.RelativePath
  #instantmessagepopup.cfm?From=
```

```
#URLEncodedFormat(From)#&Message=
#URLEncodedFormat(Message)#',
'_blank','menubar=1,scrollbars=1,
resizable=1,width=250,height=350');
 -->
</SCRIPT>
</CFOUTPUT>
```

And finally, the function CheckLocalMessages() in the IM component, which actually retrieves the data (see listing V-3.36).

Listing V-3.36    Instantmessage.cfc (CheckLocalMessages() function)

```
<!--- Create query --->
<CFSET Q=QueryNew("From,To,Time,Message")>
<!--- Check if any Instant Messages exist --->
<CFIF IsDefined("THIS.InstantMessages")>
  <!--- If so, loop through array --->
  <CFLOOP INDEX="i" FROM="#ArrayLen
         (THIS.InstantMessages)#"
           TO="1"
           STEP="-1">
    <!--- Check if message was sent to User --->
    <CFIF THIS.InstantMessages[i].To IS UsernameToCheck>
      <!--- If so, add message to query --->
      <CFSET QueryAddRow(Q)>
      <CFSET QuerySetCell(Q, "From",
             THIS.InstantMessages[i].From)>
      <CFSET QuerySetCell(Q, "To", UsernameToCheck)>
      <CFSET QuerySetCell(Q, "Time",
             THIS.InstantMessages[i].Time)>
      <CFSET QuerySetCell(Q, "Message",
             THIS.InstantMessages[i].Message)>
      <!--- Delete message from server --->
      <CFSET ArrayDeleteAt(THIS.InstantMessages, i)>
    </CFIF>
  </CFLOOP>
</CFIF>
```

**Listing V-3.36**   (continued)

```
<!--- Return query --->
<CFRETURN Q>
```

Note that one big difference between receiving a chat message and a local IM is that a local IM can only ever be received once, since as soon as it is retrieved, it is deleted.

When Ivan tests it, local IM works pretty well. Chad asks why a user wouldn't just go into a chat room if he wanted to talk to another user. Ivan points out that users go into chat rooms only if they're seeking conversation. If a user is browsing the message boards or another part of the site, for example, he might be receptive to hearing from other users but wouldn't want to keep a chat window open all the time just in case someone contacted them. Local IMs are perfect for short messages, and if the two users want to continue their conversation in more depth, they could go into a chat room.

Also, even though Ivan originally intended the local IM system for users who are both online at the same time, he discovers that if one user sends a local IM to another user who is not online at the time, the recipient gets the message the next time they log on—a very nice feature (and another advantage over chat). Of course, since local IMs are not saved permanently, all undelivered messages are erased every time the server is rebooted. Fortunately, since most users don't expect IM to be 100-percent reliable, and most servers aren't rebooted too often, this shouldn't really be a big issue.

Finally, after a few weeks of feverish coding, the development team members are ready to present the final product to the *Fantasy Life* editorial staff. They didn't succeeded in implementing every requested feature, but what they have works well, and they are eager to show it off to their clients.

## Prologue: Political Problems

A few days before the meeting a potentially serious problem arises when the Ultimate Fantasy (UF) lawyers present a serious offer to settle the lawsuit. If it goes through, the offer will completely scuttle *Fantasy Life's* marketing plans. Fortunately, Corwin the Valiant comes up with an idea at the last minute, as he explains in an email message.

## Close call

### Email

**Date:** April 3

**To:** Development Team

**From:** Corwin the Valiant (editor-in-chief)

**Subject:** Close call

The Ultimate Fantasy lawyers gave me a good scare recently when they offered to leave us alone as long as we included a disclaimer on our site that we do not officially endorse the selling of UF items (though we could still allow it), and that we recognize those items as UF intellectual property. I guess the UF executives finally realized what we knew all along, that they are probably going to lose the lawsuit, and even if they don't, it will make them look really bad.

The offer was so good, it would have been hard to turn down without making it obvious that we're just looking for the publicity (which we are). Of course we couldn't easily accept it, either, since we could never afford to buy the amount of press the lawsuit will generate for us. And without that marketing boost, the release of the site you guys have been working on so hard might flop. I decided drastic action was called for.

I told the Ultimate Fantasy executives we loved their idea and invited them and their lawyers down for a conference to work out the details. It was the first time many of us had met in person. I had instructed all our staff to come to work that day in full costumes, and we put on a show.

## Close call

### Email (continued)

In the meeting I referred to the game creators as "gods," and ourselves as "humble servants." I agreed to all their terms, but politely insisted on a few of my own, including that UF needed to do a better job communicating to the "unbelievers" that theirs was "the one true world." I also said I wanted to work with them to organize a campaign along the lines of the Crusades to speed up the process of converting more people to see the truth.

The executives were speechless, but the lawyers (who have no sense of humor) told us that while they basically liked my idea, they doubted they could defend such an action in court. So I stood up, pulled out my sword, and pointed it at the chief executive. I loudly chastised him for allowing his insolent lackeys to speak on his behalf, and called him out to a duel. He was flustered, but managed to politely decline (sort of), before gathering everyone up and hurrying out of the building, saying he'd see us in court in a couple weeks. As they left, I overheard him telling one of the lawyers, "There's no way to do business with these kooks!"

I wish you could have seen the expressions on their faces. Man, I haven't had that much fun since I participated in the sword fights at the last Renaissance Fair.

When they were gone, we all ditched our costumes and went out for a victory beer.

So the marketing plan is going well. Now it's your turn. We look forward to seeing what you have.

Corwin the Valiant
Editor-in-chief

# The Presentation

A few days later, the application design team returns to the *Fantasy Life* offices to present their application. Unlike the meeting Corwin described in his email, this one turns out to be very low-key, with everyone dressed in their street clothes.

For the demonstration, the development team sets up two laptops connected over the same network, one running the server and both acting as clients, so the *Fantasy Life* staff can see exactly how the applications work.

### Administration

Adam starts the meeting by showing the new log-in and sign up procedure (see Figure V-4.1), and how once a user logs in (or signs up), she can access all the features of the site (see Figure V-4.2).

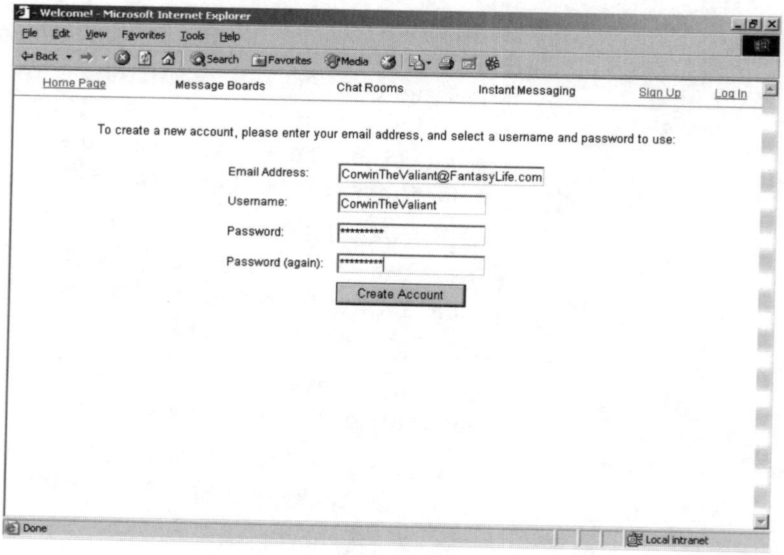

**Figure V-4.1**
The sign-up screen is simple, but effective.

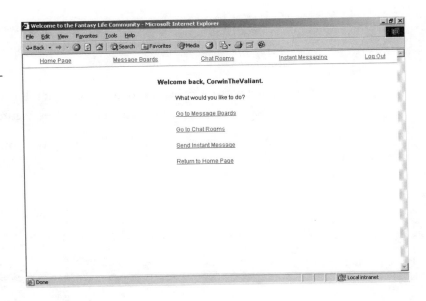

Figure V-4.2
Once a user logs in, all
the features of the site
become available.

## Message Board

Mina then shows off the message board. The *Fantasy Life* staff is already
familiar with the old message board, but they let her go through all the
important features anyway, the team checking to make sure their favorite
features weren't removed:

- Browse, read, post, and search messages.

- Messages are organized first by board, then by thread, and finally by
  message (see Figure V-4.3).

- The message list for a board can be customized by message age, sort
  order, and how threads are kept together (see Figure V-4.4).

- The message detail can also be customized to show either a single message, or a guest book style list of messages in a thread (see Figure V-4.4).

- When posting a message, if the message is a reply, it is added to the existing thread, if the message is not a reply, it automatically creates a new thread (see Figure V-4.5).

- Users can also privately email one another, but will not see the email address of the person they are emailing (see Figure V-4.6).

- Users can search for messages by date, board, author, or text (see Figure V-4.7).

**Figure V-4.3**

An example of how users move from board list to message list to message detail.

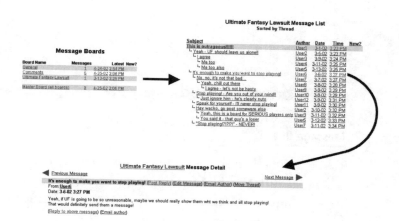

**Figure V-4.4**

The preference screen, where users can customize the message board display.

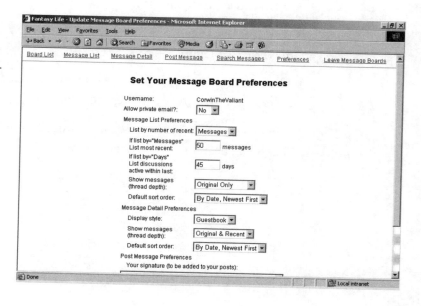

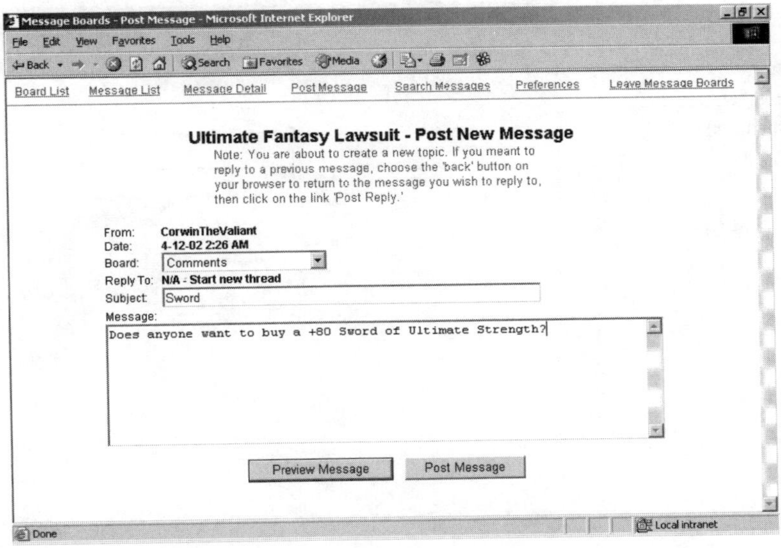

**Figure V-4.5**
Corwin posts a new message. Since he is not replying to another message, a new thread is automatically created.

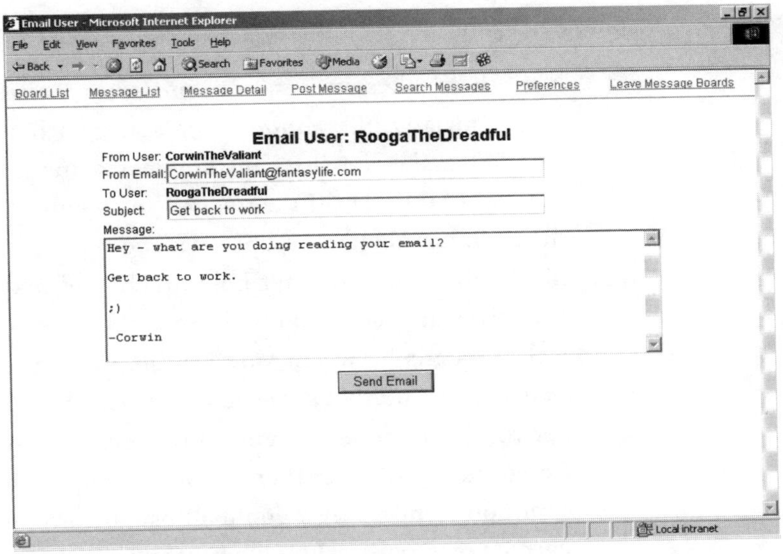

**Figure V-4.6**
On the email page, notice how Corwin can send Rooga a message, but cannot actually see his email address.

Mina then tries to explain all the work she has done to convert the message board to use Macromedia ColdFusion components (CFCs) so it would be more flexible, but her explanation appears to go over the heads of the *Fantasy Life* staff. Rooga the Dreadful does ask how difficult it will be to migrate the existing data to the new site and is very happy when Mina explains that it will be easy because the underlying data structure has changed very little.

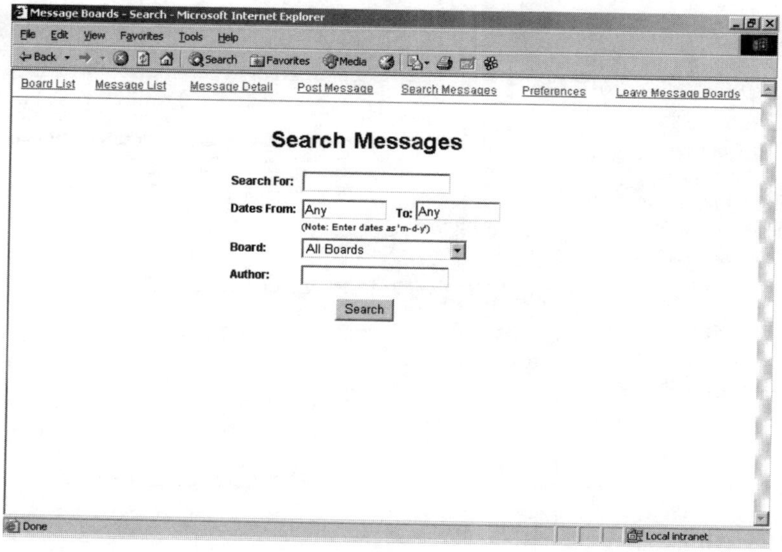

**Figure V-4.7**
The search page.

## Instant Messaging

Next, Ivan takes over and demonstrates the instant messaging (IM) features. Initially, the *Fantasy Life* staff is a little disappointed that Ivan couldn't make the site's instant messaging interoperate with a greater number of different IM networks (see Figure V-4.8). Ivan tries to explain the technical challenges, but since the *Fantasy Life* staff can't follow technical details, that doesn't help much (and may make things worse). So Ivan gives up on describing the technology. Instead he explains the political problems between America Online and Microsoft, including their struggle over market share, and how each has tried to tap into the other's network while trying to prevent the reverse—and how even an order from Congress failed to get them to play nicely with each other or agree on a common standard they could all use to communicate. Having just dealt with its own political problems, the *Fantasy Life* staff grasps that immediately, and afterward seems much more understanding about the lack of IM networks supported.

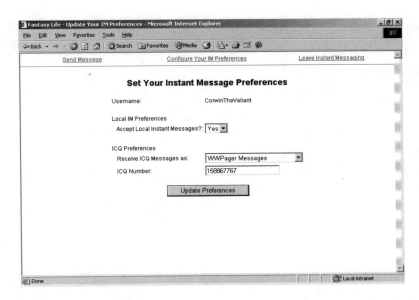

Figure V-4.8
The Instant Message
Preference page only
includes settings for
local instant messages
and ICQ.

Then Ivan tells the *Fantasy Life* staff about possible options for the future, including Jabber—the open-source IM network—and the Macromedia Flash and Java clients for it. Everyone seems very interested in the technology, especially because of the tight integration between Flash and ColdFusion. Corwin says that once the Flash client matures (and the IM political fight settles down a bit), they would definitely look into that.

Finally, Ivan explains the local IM function. When explaining just seems to confuse the *Fantasy Life* folks, Ivan seats Corwin the Valiant in front of one laptop and Priscilla the Enchantress in front of the other and walks them through a demonstration of how to send a message to each other (see Figure V-4.9). Corwin and Priscilla are a little puzzled by the delay (since they don't receive a message until they click to view another page) (see Figure V-4.10) but seem happy with it overall.

When Priscilla comments that IMs aren't very convenient for carrying on conversations, Ivan takes his cue and sits down, while Chad gets up to demonstrate the chat interface.

**Figure V-4.9**
**Figure V-4.9**
Corwin sends an instant message to Priscilla.

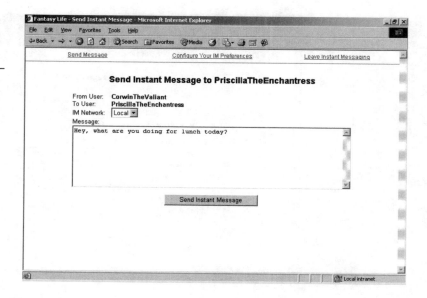

**Figure V-4.10**
Corwin's message, as it appears on Priscilla's screen.

## Chat

Chad wastes no time with explanations, and instead directs Corwin and Priscilla how to go into a chat room. Even with no instruction, they quickly start chatting back and forth and seem very happy with the interface. Then Rooga the Dreadful asks to take a turn, but neither Corwin nor Priscilla wants to give up a seat. The development team appropriates another nearby computer and plugs it into the network so all three can chat at the same time.

Rooga checks the help feature to figure out how to send private messages, and sends disparaging comments about Corwin to Priscilla. Corwin responds by creating a hidden room, then sends a private message to Priscilla and invites her into the room. Unfortunately, Rooga uses the /finduser command to figure out where they are and follows them (see Figure V-4.11).

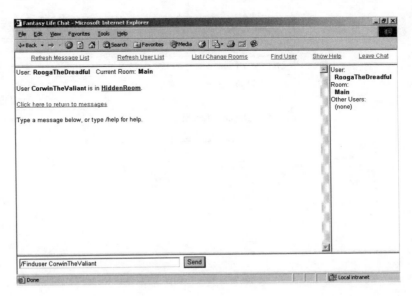

**Figure V-4.11**
Rooga uses the /finduser command to find Corwin, even tough he is in a hidden room (oops).

Overall, everyone has a good time, and even though the development team doesn't say much (or perhaps because of that), the *Fantasy Life* staff appear to like the chat feature best of all.

## Conclusions

Corwin requests that when someone in a chat room uses /finduser to look for another user in a hidden room, the interface not reveal the name of that room. Instead, it should confirm the user is online, but list the room as *hidden*.

The *Fantasy Life* staff also make a list of possible features to add to the instant messaging interface, but agree to put off most of them until later (see Table V-4-1). Overall, the *Fantasy Life* staff is very happy with the application and is eager to have its graphics department add artwork so they can make it live as soon as possible.

| Table V-4.1 | To-Do List |
|---|---|
| **Item** | **Time Frame** |
| Change `/finduser` to not display hidden rooms | Immediately |
| Add Jabber support to IM | Later—after Jabber Flash client is available |
| Add Flash client for IM | Later—after Jabber Flash client is available |

## Going Live

Over the following week, the *Fantasy Life* staff creates graphics, while Chad fixes the `/finduser` feature to keep hidden chat rooms private. Then, on the Sunday before opening arguments in the lawsuit, Chad and Mina go over to the *Fantasy Life* offices to make the new site live.

It takes them about two hours from the time they shut down the old site to the time they migrate the message board data and get the new site up and running. Overall, it goes very smoothly. Everyone goes home and waits to see what will happen the next day.

# Live: Day One

Site traffic on the first day remains average, and consists mostly of regulars. Returning users are briefly disconcerted by the drastic change in the design of the site, because *Fantasy Life* neglected to announce on the site that they would be updating it. Fortunately, the users adapt quickly, find the new message boards, and soon continue posting messages back and forth (mostly about the trial). Unfortunately, for the most part, the users ignore the new features of the site. The few who do try the chat feature quickly get bored and leave because no one else is in the chat rooms to talk to.

In the early afternoon, a *Fantasy Life* staffer—who has been observing the court proceedings all morning—posts an update about the trial in the message boards (see Figure V-5.1):

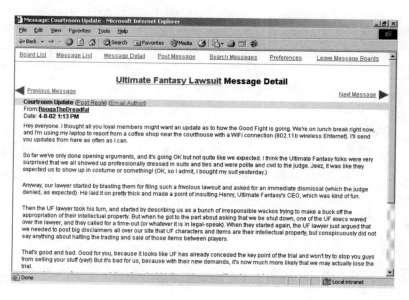

**Figure V-5.1**
Rooga's message, as it appears on the message board.

## Courtroom update

## Message Board

**Time:** 1:13 PM

**From:** RoogaTheDreadful

**Board:** Ultimate Fantasy Lawsuit

**Subject:** Courtroom update

Hey everyone. I thought all you loyal members might want an update as to how the Good Fight is going. We're on lunch break right now, and I'm using my laptop to report from a coffee shop near the courthouse with a WiFi connection (802.11b wireless Ethernet). I'll send you updates from here as often as I can.

So far we've only done opening arguments, and it's going OK but not quite like we expected. I think the Ultimate Fantasy folks were very surprised that we all showed up professionally dressed in suits and ties and were polite and civil to the judge. Jeez, it was like they expected us to show up in costume or something! (OK, so I admit, I bought my suit yesterday.)

Anyway, our lawyer started by blasting them for filing such a frivolous lawsuit and asked for an immediate dismissal (which the judge denied, as expected). He laid it on pretty thick and made a point of insulting Henry, Ultimate Fantasy's CEO, which was kind of fun.

Then the UF lawyer took his turn, and started by describing us as a bunch of irresponsible wackos trying to make a buck off the appropriation of their intellectual property. But when he got to the part about asking that we be shut down, one of the UF execs waved over the lawyer, and they called for a time-out (or whatever it is in legal-speak). When they started again, the UF lawyer just argued that we needed to post big disclaimers all over our site that UF characters and items are their intellectual property, but conspicuously did *not* say anything about halting the trading and sale of those items between players.

## Courtroom update

## Message Board (continued)

That's good and bad. Good for you, because it looks like UF has already conceded the key point of the trial and won't try to stop you guys from selling your stuff (yay!). But it's bad for us, because with their new demands, it's now much more likely that we may actually lose the trial.

Anyway, keep your fingers crossed. I've gotta go back into the courtroom now. I'll post more later.

Oh, and to encourage everyone to use the chat room, Corwin the Valiant (editor-in-chief) will be in the room LawsuitUpdate this evening at 8 p.m. EST to answer questions.

Hope you enjoy the new site!

Rooga

After court that afternoon, *Fantasy Life* sends out a press release describing the day's events and invites journalists to join the "virtual press conference" in the chat room that evening. They even send a copy to Ultimate Fantasy, though they doubt anyone from UF will actually show up. Here is the transcript from that chat.

Administrator: **CorwinTheValiant**

Current Room: LawsuitUpdate

*User CorwinTheValiant has entered this room.*

**CorwinTheValiant:** Anyone here?

FLFanBoy: i am!

DragonKiller: Hey Corwin, glad you could make it

DeadlyDamsel: So, did we win yet?

**CorwinTheValiant:** Not quite . . .

*User UFGuy has entered this room.*

**CorwinTheValiant:** The UF folks appear to have changed their minds, and so far aren't trying to get us to stop trades anymore.

DeadlyDamsel: So we did win!

**CorwinTheValiant:** Well, in one sense, yes, assuming they don't have anything else up their sleeves.

**CorwinTheValiant:** But we were hoping to crush them for having a frivolous lawsuit, then countersue them for lawyers fees.

**CorwinTheValiant:** But their revised complaint is now much more reasonable, so even if we win (which we may not), it's now almost impossible for us to countersue.

FanBoy: So what?

**CorwinTheValiant:** Well, lawsuits are pretty expensive, and since we just spent quite a bit on this new site, we need to be careful how we spend our money.

FanBoy: but that won't effect us

**CorwinTheValiant:** Well, as long as we don't overextend and go out of business, no, it won't

DragonKiller: If there's anything we can do to help, please let us know

FanBoy: hoo cares. tell us how you kicked their asses!

'DragonKiller: Shut up, FanBoy

FanBoy: yu shutup

*User FanBoy has left this room.*

DeadlyDamsel: What a dweeb

**CorwinTheValiant:** Go easy on him. If you want to kill him in UF, go ahead, but try to play nice in RL (real life).

**CorwinTheValiant:** We do need to decide what to do with this court case. It looks like UF is in for the long haul, and ultimately they have more money that we do. So just by dragging out the case until we run out of money, they can beat us.

**UFGuy** *(whispered):* So, are you ready to negotiate yet?

**CorwinTheValiant** *(whispered to UFGuy)*: Who are you?

**UFGuy** *(whispered):* Well, you threatened me at sword point recently, so I'm not sure if I should reveal too much.

**CorwinTheValiant** *(whispered to UFGuy)*: Oh, uh, yeah— heh, wasn't that funny?

**UFGuy** *(whispered):* Not at the time. I actually thought you were serious until this morning. But if you're ready to be serious for real now, I think we might be able to work something out.

**CorwinTheValiant** *(whispered to UFGuy)*: Um, right. Hang on a sec.

**CorwinTheValiant:** Sorry, guys, something important has come up. I'm afraid I've got to go for the evening.

**CorwinTheValiant:** I'll be back tomorrow, hopefully with more news.

DragonKiller: See you later, Corwin!

**CorwinTheValiant** *(whispered to UFGuy)*: I'm going to switch to the private room UFNegotiations. Join me there, and we can talk.

DeadlyDamsel: C'mon, let's go find FanBoy on UF and kill him!

*User CorwinTheValiant has left this room.*

*User UFGuy has left this room.*

Administrator: **CorwinTheValiant**

Current Room: UFNegotiations

*User CorwinTheValiant has entered this room.*

*User UFGuy has entered this room.*

**CorwinTheValiant:** So, uh, sorry about that whole sword thing.

**UFGuy:** I'll get over it. I've actually received worse threats. Someday, maybe it will even seem funny.

**CorwinTheValiant:** Um, yeah, I hope so.

**CorwinTheValiant:** So what did you have in mind?

**UFGuy:** I suspect our objectives are more compatible than you think.

**UFGuy:** It's clear you just want the free advertising from the trial.

**CorwinTheValiant:** I'm insulted by your suggestion that I would abuse our noble legal system in such a way.

**UFGuy:** Yeah, right. Fortunately, I don't care (and no, I'm not recording this transcript).

**UFGuy:** I just want to avoid the embarrassment and expense of a trial. If you agree to settle quickly, I'll help you get the advertising you want.

**CorwinTheValiant:** I'm listening.

**UFGuy:** I want you to come to court in costume tomorrow. You and I will stage a big argument, and both get thrown out. Then our lawyers will call for a recess and come back to announce they have reached a deal.

**UFGuy:** Afterward we'll each hold a press conference, timed so they don't conflict with one another.

UFGuy: We'll each rant about how unreasonable the other is and launch the beginning of a long-running feud, which we can milk for free press for years to come.

UFGuy: Remember, press conferences are a LOT cheaper than trials.

**CorwinTheValiant:** Man, you ARE devious. I like that.

UFGuy: Just look how well it's worked for Coke and Pepsi.

**CorwinTheValiant:** Or you could be trying to trick me into making a fool of myself tomorrow.

**CorwinTheValiant:** If you just stand there and look puzzled instead of yelling back when I yell at you, I'll look like a total fool, and you'll be guaranteed to win the case.

UFGuy: True. But I give you my word I won't do that. I guess you'll just have to trust me.

## Live: Day Two

Fortunately, Henry, Ultimate Fantasy's CEO, was telling the truth. The ensuing courtroom scene actually got both Henry and Corwin cited for contempt of court and thrown in jail for a couple hours. Fortunately, the judge could not have been more relieved when the lawyers returned and announced that a settlement had been reached, and agreed to release them early. Later, the news of the fight and the name calling at the press conferences generated lots of publicity.

As a result, traffic on the site started seriously picking up.

The chat rooms soon got so full, they started slowing down. Overall, though, the site held up well. Corwin posted another rant about Henry on the message boards, then sent Henry a local IM before heading back into the chat room to talk to his excited fans.

Figure V-5.2
Corwin's Instant
Message to Henry.

Figure V-5.3
Henry's Instant
Message reply to
Corwin.

# Epilogue

A few months later, the design team looked back on their project, to see what worked, what didn't, and what they would have done differently, if they could.

The *Fantasy Life* site is a big success. The feud strategy works well for both sides, and continues to periodically return both the game and the magazine to the headlines, with minimal expense.

In terms of site design, the message boards continue to be the most popular feature of the site, though chat and IM each attract a niche group of users.

Some users love the chat rooms, and a few advanced users even log in to chat while simultaneously playing Ultimate Fantasy so they can communicate privately with other players outside the game. The *Fantasy Life* staff continues to hold scheduled chats with staff members, and Henry makes a point to show up from time to time and say what kooks they are, visits that always keep the chats lively. Unfortunately, the chat rooms don't hold up well to huge numbers of users, and every time they start to become too popular they slow down and, as a result, never become as popular as the message boards.

The problem with the chat interface is simply that HTML is not well suited for such an application. In other chat applications (IRC, for example), the server usually only sends a single line of text at a time to the client, as messages are posted by other users. In the HTML chat interface though, the client must request an entire Web page, instead of a single line of text, for every refresh. Further, since the server has no way to notify the client when new messages are available, unless the client first initiates the request, the client must request the message Web page be constantly refreshed over and over. This increases the load (on both the client and server) by a factor of several hundred over a regular chat application, and leads to problems both for users on dial-up connections, and for the server as more and more users try to use the system at once.

Despite those issues though, Chad was happy with what he built. If he had had more time, he knew a Macromedia Flash or Java interface would have worked better, but given his constraints, he was glad the application worked as well as it did.

One of the few complaints the site receives is that IM supports only ICQ, not America Online Instant Messenger, Yahoo, or Microsoft Network Messenger. Users agree that a single interface that can send messages to any of the four would be useful but supporting just one is dumb. Those who use ICQ can just use their ICQ clients to contact other users and don't need the Web interface. And those who don't use ICQ are frustrated that the site doesn't support their IM clients. Ivan admitted that if he had it to do over, he wouldn't have bothered with the ICQ support.

The *Fantasy Life* team decides to remove ICQ support, so as not to frustrate users, and leaves support only for local IMs, which a few users still like. Those users include Corwin and Henry, who continued to use local IMs to privately coordinate their insults and schedule occasional bar breaks—at which they eventually become good friends.

Proper IM support is still on hold—waiting for either the Macromedia Flash Jabber client to improve or for the big four IM networks to agree on a common standard (don't hold your breath).

In the mean time, *Fantasy Life* is drafting plans for version 3 of their site. The following features are currently on the drawing board:

- Move the "email user" feature out of the message boards and put it in the IM section. This will involve removing the code from the message board and creating a new "send to email" CFC in the IM section.

- Add support for sending other types of instant messages, like SMS messages, or pages. This will involve adding more CFCs to the IM section.

- Detect when the recipient of a local IM is in a chat room, and automatically send the message as a whispered chat message, instead of a local IM. This will involve modifying the local instant message CFC, to make it communicate with the chat CFC.

- Add an auction section. Corwin and Henry are working out the details of a deal where *Fantasy Life* would act as an officially sponsored marketplace for the selling of Ultimate Fantasy items, and in exchange, Ultimate Fantasy would get a percentage of the profits. This will involve creating an eBay-style auction interface, which will have some of the features of the message board, but will need many new features as well.

# Index